Leftism in India,
1917–1947

Leftism in India, 1917–1947

Satyabrata Rai Chowdhuri

⑤SAGE | TEXTS

Los Angeles | London | New Delhi
Singapore | Washington DC | Melbourne

First published in 2007 by
PALGRAVE MACMILLAN, UK
[Palgrave Macmillan in the UK is an imprint of Macmillan Publishers Limited, registered in England, company number 785998, of Houndmills, Basingstoke, Hampshire RG21 6XS]

This Second Edition published in 2017 by

⑤SAGE | TEXTS

SAGE Publications India Pvt Ltd
B1/I-1 Mohan Cooperative Industrial Area
Mathura Road, New Delhi 110 044, India
www.sagepub.in

SAGE Publications Inc
2455 Teller Road
Thousand Oaks, California 91320, USA

SAGE Publications Ltd
1 Oliver's Yard, 55 City Road
London EC1Y 1SP, United Kingdom

SAGE Publications Asia-Pacific Pte Ltd
3 Church Street
#10-04 Samsung Hub
Singapore 049483

Published by Vivek Mehra for SAGE Publications India Pvt Ltd, typeset in 10/12 pts Berkeley by JMV Design Solutions, Chandigarh, and printed at Sai Print-o-Pack, New Delhi.

Library of Congress Cataloging-in-Publication Data
Name: Rai Chowdhuri, Satyabrata, 1935–2016 author.
Title: Leftism in India, 1917–1947 / Satyabrata Rai Chowdhuri.
Other titles: Leftism in India, nineteen seventeen–nineteen fourty seven
Description: Second edition. | New Delhi, India ; Thousand Oaks, California, USA : SAGE Publications Inc., [2017] | Includes bibliographical references and index.
Identifiers: LCCN 2017012286 | ISBN 9789386446183 ((pb) : alk. paper)
Subjects: LCSH: Communism—India—History. | Nationalism and communism—India—History. | India—Politics and government—1919-1947. | Right and left (Political science) | Social movements—India—History.
Classification: LCC HX393 .R35 2017 | DDC 320.53/2095409041—dc23
LC record available at https://lccn.loc.gov/2017012286

ISBN: 978-93-864-4618-3 (PB)

SAGE Team: Amit Kumar, Indrani Dutta, Priya Arora, Madhurima Thapa and Ritu Chopra

In revered memory of my grandfather the late Janaki Nath Sarkar,
my mentor and ne plus ultra

Bulk Sales

SAGE India offers special discounts
for bulk institutional purchases.

*For queries/orders/inspection copy requests
write to* **textbooksales@sagepub.in**

Publishing

Would you like to publish a textbook with SAGE?

Please send your proposal to **publishtextbook@sagepub.in**

Get to know more about SAGE

Be invited to SAGE events, get on our mailing list.

Write today to **marketing@sagepub.in**

TABLE OF CONTENTS

PRAISE FOR THE FIRST EDITION

'We are in debt to Professor Satyabrata Rai Chowdhuri for writing this excellent overview of the Indian Left. This will be a very useful book for experts and for people who want an overview of the Left. His book is especially welcome because of its wide scope. Let us hope that he is planning a successor volume that will bring this remarkable story of communism in India up to the present day.'

—**Stephen P. Cohen, The Brookings Institution**

'Professor Rai Chowdhuri has to be congratulated on such a comprehensive coverage of not only the Communist Party history but also the Left movements in general in India. I also like his interweaving of the history of the mainstream nationalist movement with a history of the Left. There are not many books which cover the same ground and this one, I am sure, will stay a standard reference work for a long time.'

—**Meghnad Desai, London School of Economics and Political Science**

'[This book is] one of the most lucid, nuanced and comprehensive accounts of the role of the political Left in Indian nationalism I have ever read. While many other scholarly accounts have commented on the heterogeneity of Leftist movements in India, few have attempted to delineate in such detail and with such clarity every hue, every highlight and every shade in the entire spectrum of Left politics in the era of high nationalism from 1917 to 1947. It is a task of commendable magnitude accomplished by a distinguished scholar. It will serve as an invaluable resource for both undergraduate and postgraduate students of Indian political history.'

—**Debjani Ganguly, Australian National University**

'*Leftism in India, 1917–1947*, is an excellent account of the political manoeuvres and theoretical ruminations of Indian radicals during the last thirty years of the liberation movement ... [The] book is an attempt to interweave a study of the mainstream nationalist movement with not only the trajectory of the Communist Party of India, but that of the Left wing of the Indian National Congress.'

—**New Politics, USA**

'It is a welcome addition to the existing literature, both for its comprehensiveness and the discussion its critical conclusions could generate.'

—**The Hindu**

'The volume is definitely a significant contribution to the history of the Left movement in India. One would expect Rai Chowdhuri to come out with a successor volume that will cover the history of the communists in India and their transformation, if any at all, up to the present day, especially in the backdrop of Deng Xiaoping's famous dictum: "To be rich is glorious, that is the Marxism of today."'

—**The Statesman**

'It is necessary to know the early history of the Left in order to make sense of its politics today…this book brings it alive with detailed and objective accounts. The author captures remarkably well the complex milieu in which the communists and other Leftists struggled to find an identity for themselves.'

—**The Telegraph**

'The book is a history of the nationalist struggle for decolonisation told from the standpoint of the Left in India, as well as an evaluation of the role of Leftism in this struggle. The result is a useful study of the impact that the communists and the Left wing of the Congress had on each other…. Rai Chowdhuri covers in great detail M.N. Roy's role in introducing ideas of Marxism in India, Jawaharlal Nehru's encounter with Fabian socialism, the emergence of working-class parties in urban centres and the Congress socialists' resolve to stay within the Congress but fight for radical socio-economic changes. The very fact that this is a history that looks at different aspects of Leftism in India together must be welcomed.'

—*Economic and Political Weekly*

'This is a useful reference book that highlights a rather neglected but a significant aspect of Indian politics in the early 20th century. Indeed, by tracing the origin of the Left movement in the era of the national Independence struggle, the author demonstrates how and why the Left movement came to acquire the shape it had in an Independent India.'

—*Journal of Asian and African Studies* (SAGE Publications)

'This may well be the ultimate work on Indian Leftists covering a tumultuous period—from when Lenin seized power in Russia in 1917 to when India gained freedom in 1947.'

—**Indo-Asian News Service**

FOREWORD TO THE FIRST EDITION

We are in debt to Professor Satyabrata Rai Chowdhuri for writing this excellent overview of the Indian Left. Despite the wide acceptance and demonstrable success of market economy principles in India, the Left persists in India, holds power in several Indian states and has been a member of several central government coalitions. One reason why there still is a Left in India is that some of its elements have moved to adapt their practice, if not their ideology, to the realities of the world, and are part of the process by which the Indian economy has found a niche in the global economic order, to everyone's overall benefit.

It was not always so. As Professor Rai Chowdhuri notes, the Indian Left is diverse and complex. Based on 'foreign' ideologies, and sometimes dependent upon foreign financial support and even arms, India's Left splintered early on, and while there was always a component that looked outside India for its inspiration (notably the communists), there was also a powerful Left, or socialist movement within the Indian National Congress, and eventually a number of Left and communist parties arose from breakaway factions. Thus, while the orthodox communists opposed Gandhi, the Congress Left wing and socialists worked alongside him. An important lesson that I draw from his narrative is that if there is a wide spectrum of ideologies, then violent extremists are eventually tamed by the political process; this is also apparent in the way in which Islamic extremism has been softened by an Indian political system that allows for the ventilation of grievances.

Professor Rai Chowdhuri's book is especially welcome because of its wide scope. Thirty years ago, when it appeared that pro-Soviet (and pro-Chinese) communist movements had taken deep root in India, there were numerous studies, many of them by American scholars, of the Indian communists. This volume is broader in scope and narrates the interplay between the always powerful Left and socialist elements in Congress, the communist parties themselves and the smaller socialist parties that have sprung up, mostly in northern and eastern India. There is an excellent discussion of the major turning points in the evolution of the Left, from the formation of the Communist Party of India by M.N. Roy (who only took this name when he became a student at Stanford University in the United States) to the Second World War, which saw the rise of mass political movements in India, the attempted manipulation of the communists by the Soviet Union (and support for them from the Germans) and the great importance of the 'victory' of communism after the Soviet Revolution.

Of special value are the discussions of the ideologies and theories propounded by various branches of the Indian Left and communist movements—this was a movement that thrived on ideas and theories; some of them were hopelessly irrelevant to Indian conditions, while many of them were the products of foreign parties and movements.

The Left remains alive in India despite the downfall of the Soviet Union and China's transformation. Indeed, it is perhaps because international communism has disappeared that the Indian Left and communist movements are freer to adapt to real Indian circumstances and real Indian grievances. This would be the supreme irony of the Left that a movement born abroad, and inspired by Western thinking, now comes into its own to the degree that it learns how to harness the power of a market economy and how to function within a governmental system that is based on liberal democratic principles.

Let us hope that Professor Rai Chowdhuri is planning a successor volume that will bring this remarkable story of communism in India up to the present day. As he notes, the communists themselves find it difficult to write their own history, so we must rely upon others to set the record straight, a vital task in any democracy, especially in India, with its profusion of theories about the governance, economic progress and social justice of over a billion people.

Stephen P. Cohen[1]
Washington, DC, 2006

---

[1]Stephen P. Cohen is an American expert on South Asia. He is at present a Senior Fellow in the India Project at The Brookings Institution and an Emeritus Professor of History and Political Science at the University of Illinois-Urbana Champaign.

PREFACE TO THE SECOND EDITION

It is heartening to learn that the second edition of *Leftism in India, 1917–1947* is getting published. The book was first published by Minerva Associates, Calcutta, in 1977 as *Leftist Movements in India, 1917–1947*. The publisher went into liquidation after a few years. As a result, the book also had to go out of print. But it always remained in demand just as the demand for a robust Left, which would stand for its core objectives while adapting itself to newer socio-economic and geopolitical realities, never waned in the system of the Indian parliamentary democracy.

Palgrave Macmillan had done a wonderful job publishing a new edition of the book in the United Kingdom and India in 2007 and 2011, respectively, renaming it as *Leftism in India, 1917–1947*. This ensured the book's availability to teachers and students of history and political science in colleges and universities. It is deeply satisfying that even decades after the book was written, it continues to find acceptance among scholars and general readers. Many universities have adopted *Leftism in India, 1917–1947* as a text for their undergraduate and postgraduate programmes in both history and political science.

SAGE's attempt to publish the book anew is equally appreciable and encouraging. The vivid description of political currents and cross-currents in the heady years of Indian national movement, I believe, would cater immensely to the academic needs of social science students.

In seven chapters, the book traces the early twentieth century socio-political awakening of the bourgeois-democratic class of Indian society, the rise of Left-wing nationalists following the Swadeshi Movement, the activities of the intrepid early revolutionaries and the formation of the Communist Party of India (CPI) abroad, the growth of communism in India, the growth of the Left wing within the Indian National Congress (INC; aka Congress socialists), various labour and peasant movements and the formation of various Leftist parties. It will help students understand not only India's colonial past and the shaping of its Left-wing ideologies but also provide them with multi-sided accounts of the interaction of the Congress with the Leftists both outside and inside the party that often gave rise to dramatic developments in India's quest for freedom, making this period one of the most interesting and complicated phases in the country's political history.

Last but not least, as some reviewers have also pointed out, the book may be of help to general readers as well. The issues discussed in the book may interest anyone who wants an overview of the initial phase of Left politics in the country in order to make better sense of its political standing and practices today.

In so far as the adaptability of the Indian Left to changing circumstances is concerned, this book will perhaps remain in demand even in the days to come as it can be a ready reckoner for looking at events of the past, taking lessons from them and adopting a pragmatic approach to present-day political problems. From that perspective, the book may be a helpful companion to the study of pragmatics in the annals of communism and socialism in India. Because, though much time has passed since India's Independence, many of the problems and confusions faced by the Left have essentially remained the same in nature. That is why their history can be useful in both assessing where they stand now and strategizing their future course of action.

I am thankful to Amit Kumar, Sunanda Ghosh, Indrani Dutta and Priya Arora of SAGE and all members of its production team for taking a kind interest in this work. The second edition could not have been possible without their support. Lastly, I owe an immense debt of gratitude to academics across the country who treasure this book as a useful text.

Satyabrata Rai Chowdhuri
Kolkata, 2016

PREFACE TO THE FIRST EDITION

In this study, an attempt has been made to present a comprehensive account of the Leftist movements in India during the most decisive phase of the country's struggle for freedom and to describe the manner in which they interacted with the mainstream of the Indian national movement. The purpose of this study is to discover the elements that contributed to the emergence of these movements, the factors that moulded them, the ideologies that gave strength and guidance to them, and the part they played in India's freedom movement, their characteristics, temper and outlook.

A study which sets out to present an integrated account of different forces and elements of the Leftist movements in India since their inception imposes limitations of which I am only too conscious. It may be pertinent, however, to state that it is not proposed here to dissect every aspect of the movements but to trace their developments in the broader context of India's struggle for freedom. Obviously, this cannot be done without trespassing upon works of scholars who have already explored different corners of the field. It is not intended here to rival any of these works. For my part, I only claim that extent of familiarity with the subject which is required to make an objective assessment of a so complex historical phenomenon.

The bibliography appended to this study clearly shows that there are several existing scholarly works on particular aspects of Leftist movements in India since their inception. This study does not overlap but supplements these works because of the following reasons. First, it offers not only a comprehensive account of the Leftist movements in India since the early 1920s but also traces their development showing how they were historically linked with the extremist school of nationalism that emerged in India during the first decade of the last century. Second, it discusses the ideologies and orientations of these movements and describes how they interacted with the mainstream of the national movement. Finally, it presents the Leftist movements in their proper setting and attempts to evaluate their role in India's freedom struggle. I hope that this study will contribute in some measure to a fuller understanding of the Leftist movements in India.

In gathering materials for this study, it was necessary to draw on a wide range of works dealing with various aspects of the British rule and the Indian national movement scattered in India and abroad.

Taken together, all these materials present a detailed account of the evolution of Indian nationalism and Indian national movement. Although they neither trace the development of Leftism in India nor indicate its role in the freedom movement, these works have contributed both facts and perspective to this study. However, they often suffer from the weakness inherent in the very nature of such works, that is, they reflect the subjective and individual viewpoints of the authors.

Obviously then, this approach does not fully explain the true role of Leftism in Indian politics. What were the actual factors responsible for the emergence of Leftism in India? What were the sources of its strength and weakness? How did it help or hinder India's struggle for freedom? How did the Leftist movements interact with the mainstream of Indian nationalism? These questions are rarely answered in an objective way by those who took leading part in the movements because their versions are too frequently biased. Moreover, in these works there are many factual omissions—often deliberate. In the present study, care has been taken to describe and analyse every event with scholarly objectivity and to present different points of views where informed opinion is divided. I have not hesitated to indicate my own point of view when facts and judgement so warranted.

It has been my privilege to obtain a closer knowledge of many aspects of the Leftist movements and Indian nationalist movement through personal discussions and correspondence with many personalities concerned with this particular area of study. I owe a debt of gratitude to the late Pritthwish Chandra Chakravarti, a former professor of international relations at Jadavpur University, who introduced me to this field. In Oxford, the late Nirad Chandra Chaudhuri told me about endless anecdotes and events of the twentieth-century political movements of British India. The late Susobhan Sarkar in Calcutta and the late Rajani Palme Dutt and his brother the late Clemens Dutt in London also furnished me with many facts which were then unknown to me, and are perhaps still unknown to many. To all of them, I am grateful for the contributions they have made, sometimes unknowingly, to this work.

I am hugely indebted to Professor Stephen P. Cohen of The Brookings Institution, Professor Meghnad Desai of London School of Economics and Professor Debjani Ganguly of Australian National University for painstakingly going through the manuscript and showering kind words.

I have no adequate words to express my gratitude to my parents. My cousin Prafulla Kumar Chakravarti and student Tridib Chakraborti were of much help and encouragement at various stages of the research. My nephew and indispensable companion Tathagata Ray Chowdhury spent months working on this project with the dedication of a perfectionist. It would not have been possible to republish this book without his invaluable participation.

Professor Timothy Shaw and Professor Richard Crook have been of particular support at the Institute of Commonwealth Studies, London. Palgrave Macmillan has done a wonderful job republishing this work. I am thankful to Michael Strang, Ruth Ireland, Sue Hunt and Molly Beck of Palgrave and Barbara Slater of Steam Mill.

Satyabrata Rai Chowdhuri
Kolkata, 2006

ABOUT THE AUTHOR

Satyabrata Rai Chowdhuri, PhD, DLitt (1935–2016), was a renowned political scientist of his times, specializing in South Asian politics and international relations. He taught at various government colleges in West Bengal early in his career before joining Rabindra Bharati University in Kolkata where he held a long stint as a Professor and the Head of the Department of Political Science. In 2000, the University Grants Commission conferred on him the Emeritus Fellowship.

Professor Rai Chowdhuri also lectured on Indian politics at the University of Oxford and was a Senior Fellow in International Relations at the Institute of Commonwealth Studies, University of London. In 2006, he was elected a Fellow of the Royal Asiatic Society of Great Britain and Ireland. A prolific writer, he was a commentator and columnist on South Asian politics with several esteemed publications across the globe. His other recent book is *Nuclear Politics: Towards a Safer World*.

LIST OF ABBREVIATIONS

AICC	All India Congress Committee
AIKC	All India Kisan Congress
AIKS	All India Kisan Sabha
AIRF	All India Railwaymen's Federation
AISF	All India Students' Federation
AITUC	All India Trade Union Congress
BLP	Bengal Labour Party
BPI	Bolshevik Party of India
BTUC	British Trade Union Congress
CC	Central Club [also known as Central Club Clique]
CPGB	Communist Party of Great Britain
CPI	Communist Party of India
CPSU	Communist Party of the Soviet Union
CSP	Congress Socialist Party
CWC	Congress Working Committee
ECCI	Executive Committee of the Communist International
IFTU	International Federation of Trade Unions
ILO	International Labour Organization
INA	Indian National Army
INC	Indian National Congress
INTUC	Indian National Trade Union Congress
LCC	Left Consolidation Committee
NTUC	National Trade Union Congress
NTUF	National Trade Union Federation
PPTUS	Pan-Pacific Trade Union Secretariat
RILU	Red International of Labour Unions
RCPI	Revolutionary Communist Party of India
RSP	Revolutionary Socialist Party
RTUC	Red Trade Union Congress
USSR	Union of Socialist Soviet Republics
WPP	Workers' and Peasants' Party

1 Historical Background

EARLY CONGRESS, *SWADESHI*, MODERATES AND EXTREMISTS

Prior to the dawn of the twentieth century, the prospect of a revolution in India figured in nationalist thinking primarily as an event that would ensure a greater degree of Indian representation within the British system of rule. In 1878, an editorial in the *Hindu Patriot* observed:

> Our rulers may rest assured that the symptoms of dissatisfaction which they notice among the princes and people of India are no symptoms of a wish for a political revolution. Far from it. Both the princes and people of India fully appreciate the order which the English have introduced, the protection and security which they have given, and the principles of progress which they have instilled into life.[1]

Romesh Chunder Dutt, the president of the Indian National Congress (INC) in 1890, declared that the people of India were not fond of sudden changes and revolutions. They wished to strengthen the British rule and to bring it more in touch with the people. Their most cherished desire, he said, was to see some Indian members in the Secretary of State's Council and in the Viceroy's Executive Council so that they could represent the interests of the Indian people 'in the discussion of every important administrative question'.[2] Ananda Mohan Bose, who was made the president of the INC in its 1898 Madras session, looked hopefully for the cooperation of the British rulers in the fight against the evils of economic backwardness, obscurantism, ignorance and administrative shortcomings of the 'bureaucratic system' and declared that 'the educated classes' were the friends and not the foes of England—its 'natural and necessary allies'.[3] Even Surendranath Banerjee pleaded for the permanence of British rule in India[4] and proclaimed that the object of the Indian people was 'not the suppression of British rule in India' but 'to work with unwavering loyalty to the British connection', for 'the broadening of its basis, the liberalising of its spirit, the ennobling of its character and placing it on the unchangeable foundation of a nation's affection'.[5]

For two decades after its formation in 1885, the INC developed along the path laid down by its founders and remained essentially a moderate political body looking upon British rule almost as a dispensation of providence.[6] During these 20 years, the Congressmen did not fight for self-government in any form but only wanted to assert their right to greater participation in the administration. They were by no means against the British rule. They merely desired, as Michael Edwardes pointed out, the status that their education had fitted them for and that Britain had said would one day be their reward.[7] Their political ideas were not revolutionary. They did not agitate for India's freedom, but only for a few crumbs of the cake.[8] And as they wanted to get their grievances—grievances not of the people of India, but of a 'minority of the minority'—redressed through prayers and petitions or mendicancy, as it was called, they came to be known as the moderates.

However, according to Will Durant, it was in 1905 that the Indian revolution began.[9] It began as a local movement against the partition of Bengal, but like a tiny brook, it 'gradually widened itself by receiving affluents and tributaries and became a mighty torrent of nationalism before it merged itself into the broad stream of India's national struggle for freedom'.[10]

The national upheaval following the partition of Bengal not only aroused the dormant political consciousness of the people but also gave new orientation and a definite shape to the spirit of nationalism. It brought into prominence a new means to fight the British, which was remote from all the previous methods of political agitation and bore an essentially modern and economic character—the weapons of boycott and *swadeshi*, that is, refusal to buy foreign goods and the promotion of indigenous industry.[11] Indeed, as pointed out by Surendranath Banerjee in 1906, *swadeshism* was not merely an economic or political movement but a comprehensive movement coextensive with the whole of national life—'the shibboleth of our unity and industrial and political salvation'.[12] Describing the Swadeshi Movement as a landmark in the history of India's struggle for freedom, Gopal Krishna Gokhale also said that for the first time since the British rule began, all sections of the Indian people, without any distinction of caste and creed, had been moved by a common impulse and that at its touch, old barriers had been thrown down, personal jealousies had vanished and all controversies were hushed.[13]

The revolutionary forces which now gathered for a new phase of struggle derived inspiration from the cult of nationalism preached by Bankim Chandra Chatterjee, Swami Vivekananda and others during the last quarter of the nineteenth century. In his immortal novel *Ananda Math* or *Abode of Bliss*, published in 1882, Chatterjee put the soul-stirring cry of *Bande Mataram* or *Hail to the Mother* into the mouths of the rebel *sanyasins* (monks) in their revolt against the tyranny of the Muslim rulers. This cry of *Bande Mataram* as conceived in the *Ananda Math* became the hymn of nationalism in India's struggle for freedom.[14] It was sung by countless voices in the historic Town Hall meeting in Calcutta when the resolution on boycott and *swadeshi* was promulgated on 7 August 1905.[15]

The greatest influence of the spirit of *Bande Mataram* was on the new school of Left-wing nationalism, known as the extremists in opposition to the moderates, which emerged on the Indian political scene as a repercussion of the Swadeshi Movement.[16] However, it should be noted that while this new school, associated especially with the leadership of Aurobindo Ghosh and Bal Gangadhar Tilak, emerged in the last decade of the nineteenth century, it could not play a decisive role until the situation became ripe after 1905.[17] Even as early as 1893–94, Ghosh described the INC as an 'unnational body' because its policy was divorced from the realities of Indian political life. The aims of the INC, he said, were mistaken, and the spirit in which it proceeded towards their accomplishment was not the spirit of sincerity and the methods it had chosen were not the right methods and the leaders in whom it trusted were not the right sort of men to be leaders.[18]

In the 1890s, a new political force had also emerged in Maharashtra under the leadership of Tilak who lost faith in the mendicant policy of the INC leaders and sought to 'nationalize the unnational movement' by infusing in it a militant spirit and bringing political questions to the masses. In fact, while Ghosh put nationalism on the high pedestal of religion, Tilak brought it to the masses, thus making it a formidable force in India's struggle for freedom.[19] They dealt a death blow to the old INC ideal of compromise and conciliation and entered on a path of militant and uncompromising struggle against British imperialism.

Thus, the seed of nationalism which had been sown in the last quarter of the nineteenth century and drew its sustenance from the spirit of sacrifice preached by Vivekananda on the basis of the philosophical teachings of *Vedanta* and *Gita* and the religious devotion to motherland expounded by Chatterjee in *Bande Mataram* burst forth in 1905 and began to shoot and sprout with astounding vitality.

The extremist party which thus came into being under the leadership of Ghosh and Tilak differed in fundamental points from that which had hitherto been followed by the moderate leaders of the INC. And as the Swadeshi Movement outstripped its original limitations and as eminent nationalists, such as Bipin Chandra Pal, Lala Lajpat Rai and G.S. Khaparde, joined its ranks, the extremist party soon became an all-India revolutionary organization. It may be noted here that during the last decade of the nineteenth century, Pal did not share the extremist views of Ghosh and Tilak. He held that the Indians were loyal to the British because they believed that the God himself had led the British to India to help it in working out its salvation. Their loyalty, he declared, was so natural, unconscious and automatic that no effort was needed on the part of the government to train the Indians in the virtue of allegiance. But when the British government, in total disregard of the popular will, decided to partition Bengal, his 'illusions' were destroyed and he fell in line with Ghosh and Tilak. R.C. Majumdar observed, 'The political changes and transformations through which Bipin Chandra Pal himself passed were typical of what was taking place all over India, and brought into sharp relief the two political parties labelled as moderates and extremists.'[20]

The main difference between the moderates and the extremists lies in the concept of an Indian political goal and the method to be adopted for achieving it. The 'old guards' of the INC, who 'had built their habitation away on the horizon', were extremely moderate in their demands. They were imbued with the spirit, principles and the methods of mid-Victorian liberalism and bent on winning not complete self-government but only piecemeal reforms. They were careful not to pitch their demands too high. Some of them might have cherished in their heart of hearts the goal of self-government, but almost all of them wanted to work with least resistance and therefore framed their demands for reforms on such moderate and cautious lines as not to arouse any serious opposition. They were confirmed believers in the British sense of justice and fair play and followed the method of prayers, petitions and representations in order to get their grievances redressed.[21]

The extremists, on the other hand, looked upon the British rule as an unmitigated evil and believed that *swaraj* (independence) was the birthright of every Indian, not a sort of gift to be doled out by the British government. They were convinced that the method of political mendicancy would never bring India near *swaraj*. What India needed was to create its own strength so that Britain could be compelled to part with power. They approached the question of violence and non-violence purely from the standpoint of political pragmatism and expediency. Ghosh, for example, never mixed up ordinary ethics with politics which, he believed, had its own ethics—the ethics of the *Kshatriya*, not of the *Brahmin*. He pointed out that to impose the brahminical virtue of 'saintly sufferance' in politics was to preach *Varnasankara* or confusion of duties which was not conducive to political advancement. Non-violence, he declared, was not a speciality of Indian genius.[22]

EXTREMISTS ABROAD: IN THE UNITED KINGDOM, THE UNITED STATES AND GERMANY

The most significant development of the militant nationalist movement was the activities of the revolutionaries who set out for different parts of the world with the aims of establishing international contacts, spreading anti-British propaganda, explaining India's aspirations and securing foreign help for the overthrow of British rule in India. That even the orthodox nationalist leaders felt the necessity of such activities abroad was evident from the fact that Dadabhai Naoroji, the veteran INC leader who once appealed to the British rulers not to drive the educated Indians into opposition instead of drawing them to their side,[23] placed the case of India before the International Socialist Congress in 1904 in Amsterdam.

One of the earliest Indians to achieve concrete results in organizing fellow revolutionaries abroad was Shyamji Krishna Varma[24] who founded the Indian Home Rule Society in London in 1905 and brought out a journal called *The Indian Sociologist*. Other prominent Indian revolutionaries who collected around Varma were Vinayak Damodar Savarkar, Lala Har Dayal, Madan Lal Dhingra, Sardarsinh Rawabhai Rana and Bhikhaiji Rustom Cama.

Cama left India in 1902 and dedicated her life to the achievement of India's freedom by means of revolutionary propaganda in Europe and America. She represented India at the International Socialist Congress in Stuttgart in August 1907, and delivered a brilliant speech highlighting the evils of British rule in India. Describing the continuance of British rule as 'positively disastrous and extremely injurious to the best interests of India', she appealed to all lovers of freedom all over the world to cooperate in freeing India from the bondage of slavery. She concluded her address by unfurling the national flag, a tricolour in green, yellow and red, and earned the undying reputation as the 'Mother of Indian Revolution'.[25]

While Varma and Cama were busy in Europe, their activities inspired the Indians in America who had migrated to that country after being unable to earn the bare minimum of livelihood in India, to start the Ghadr Movement. They formed the Ghadr Party (later known as Ghadar Party) in San Francisco in 1913 and brought out a weekly newspaper, *The Ghadr* in Urdu, Marathi and Gurumukhi languages. The key members of the party were Lala Har Dayal, Vishnu Ganesh Pingle, Sohan Singh Bhakna, Abdul Hafiz Mohamed Barkatullah, Kartar Singh Sarabha, Tarak Nath Das, Seth Husain Rahim, Baba Jawala Singh, Wasakha Singh Dadehar, Santokh Singh, Keshar Singh, Kanshi Ram and Rash Behari Bose.[26] The aims of the party, as proclaimed by its founders, were the overthrow of British imperialism in India and the establishment of a national republic based on freedom and equality. These aims, it was further proclaimed, could be achieved only by an armed revolution.[27]

When the war broke out between England and Germany in 1914, the Indian revolutionaries abroad seized the opportunity to enlist the sympathy and support of the Germans for India's freedom. The Germans were equally anxious to exploit the Indian unrest and anti-British activities of the Indian revolutionaries abroad. Assured of German sympathy and support, the Indian revolutionaries set up an organization in Berlin known as the Indian Independence Committee. The committee lost no time in inviting all revolutionaries in India and abroad to formulate a common plan of action and to send men and money to India to prepare the ground for the overthrow of British rule in India.[28]

Thus, with the outbreak of the First World War, the Indian revolutionary movement merged itself with the march of events all over the world and entered into an era of great and far-reaching changes. According to R. Palme Dutt, 'It was the shock of the First World War, with the lasting blow to the whole structure of imperialism, and the opening of the world revolutionary wave that followed in 1917 and after, which released the first mass movement of revolt in India.'[29]

BOLSHEVIK WAVE, AFTERMATH OF THE FIRST WORLD WAR, MARX AND LENIN ON INDIA

As the war came to a close and as mankind awaited the new years of peace, a shadow lay across the Peace Conference at Versailles—the shadow of revolution. In a memorandum to the Peace Conference, Lloyd George pointed out that there was a deep sense not only of discontent but also of anger and revolt amongst workers against pre-war conditions. The whole existing order—in its political, social and economic aspects—was being questioned by the masses of the population from one end of Europe to the other, and the continent was filled with a spirit of revolution. Bolshevik imperialism, he averred, did not merely menace the states on Russia's borders but also threatened the whole of Asia and was as near to America as it was to France. He warned that there could be no peace and security as long as the scourge of Bolshevism threatened the world.[30]

A similar foreboding about the coming shadows of Bolshevism also troubled the mind of President Woodrow Wilson during his journey to France on board the *George Washington*. Bolshevism, he realized, was reaction against the way in which the world had worked and it was to be the victorious powers' business at the Peace Conference to fight for a new order.[31]

Indeed, after the victory of the Bolshevik Revolution in Russia in 1917, when the revolutionary wave began to extend in varying forms and degrees to the countries of Asia and Europe, the entire programme of Wilsonian principles to make the world safe for democracy seemed to recede into the background. A choice of greater magnitude now confronted mankind, the choice between Wilson and V.I. Lenin.

> Wilson represented the path of bourgeois-democratic reform while maintaining the essence of imperialism and the class ownership of the means of production .... The path of Lenin was the path of the mass revolution against imperialism, of the dictatorship of the proletariat in the imperialist countries and of the democratic dictatorship of the workers and of peasantry in the colonial and backward countries, of the liberation of the colonial peoples, of the collective organization of societies .... The issue of these paths was the issue of the post-war epoch.[32]

It was the beginning of the epoch marked by the awakening of the overwhelming majority of the human race to revolution and an advancement of national revolutionary movement all over the world—in Central and South America, in the Near and Middle East, in Africa, in China and in India.

In India, the aftermath of the war had not only brought into being new forces which were to transform the struggle for freedom from the concern of a 'minority group' into a mighty national upheaval but had also drawn it into the general maelstrom of the world revolutionary movement. And this was a phenomenon of profound significance not to India alone but to the colonial world as a whole. Writing on the significance of an Indian revolution, Soviet commentator P. Kerzhentsev observed that the liberation of India from British domination would be a signal for all the Asian countries to take up the struggle against imperialism. It would ignite revolutions throughout the entire colonial world—Mesopotamia, Syria, Arabia, South Africa, Egypt, China, Tibet, Persia—all these countries, he said, would follow the Indian example.[33]

But the prospect of a revolution in India had been the subject of discussion long before the outbreak of the First World War. As early as 1853, Karl Marx and Friedrich Engels began to evince such keen interest in India that between 1853 and 1857 as many as 23 articles by Marx and 8 by Engels were devoted to the exposure of the British imperialist misrule which, Marx said, was laying the foundations of a socio-economic revolution in India. According to Marx, in causing this social revolution in India, England was actuated by the vilest interests and foolish in its manner of enforcing them. But, he said, that was not the real question. The fundamental question was: Could mankind fulfil its destiny without a revolution 'in the social state of Asia'? If not, whatever might have been the crime of England, it was the unconscious tool of history in bringing about that revolution.[34] Again, in a letter to Karl Kautsky in 1882, Marx expressed the opinion that while the countries occupied by European population—Canada, the Cape, Australia—would all become independent, the countries inhabited by native population and subjugated by Europeans—India, Africa, the Dutch, Portuguese and Spanish possessions—must be taken over by the proletariat and led as rapidly as possible towards independence. Although Marx could not predict how this process would develop, he had no doubt that India would make a revolution. He further held that as the proletariat in the process of emancipation could not conduct any colonial wars, the revolution would have to be allowed to run its course bringing in its train all sorts of destruction. But that sort of thing, Marx averred, was inescapable from all revolutions.[35]

Lenin's interest in the Indian nationalist movement dates from the dawn of the twentieth century when in an article titled 'Inflammable Material in World Politics', he declared that in India the proletariat had already developed a conscious political mass struggle and that being the case, 'the Russian style

British regime' in India was doomed. The class-conscious European workers, he said, had comrades in Asia and their number would grow with every passing day and hour.[36] Five years later, in 1913, Lenin reiterated that everywhere in Asia, a mighty democratic movement was growing, spreading and gaining in strength. There the bourgeoisie was siding with the people against forces of reaction. Hundreds of millions of people in these countries, who had reliable allies in all 'civilized countries', were awakening to life, light and liberty and no force on earth could prevent their victory.[37]

When the war broke out, Lenin was convinced that its most important effect would be the immediate emancipation of the colonial countries, including India, which would ultimately bring about a world-wide proletarian revolution. The war, he hoped, would sever the last chain that bound the workers to their masters, their slavish submission to the imperialist state. And the last limitation of the proletariats' philosophy, their 'cringing to the narrowness of the national state', would be overcome.

From the Marxian angle, therefore, the post-war situation in India presented all the conditions in which a proletarian revolution seemed just around the corner. But although this was a highly exaggerated view of the actual state of affairs, there is some truth in the fact that the war had not only drawn India into the world revolutionary movement and projected it into the company of other colonial countries, but had also given the national movement a unique mass dimension and a revolutionary context, however diminutive. At the close of the war, while the world 'was sitting on an anxious seat',[38] India had been the scene of a great liberation movement and a national awakening. To this movement, in combination with the emergence of Mohandas Karamchand Gandhi on the one hand and with the new ethos produced by the Bolshevik Revolution on the other, Indian politics of the post-war years owed its most distinctive character. After the war, nationalism in India emerged with a new character, giving rise to new leaders who were to conduct the fight both against the British in India and the legislators in Westminster. The struggle for freedom was no longer to be fought 'in the obscurity with which the nineteenth century and Britain's international prestige had cloaked India. It was now to take place under the bright lights of a growing world interest'.[39]

POST-WAR DISCONTENT, GANDHI AND MASS AWAKENING

By the time the war came to a close, Indian blood, said Annie Besant, had soaked the soils of Flanders, Gallipoli, Egypt and Mesopotamia. The England that had welcomed Giuseppe Garibaldi, the England that had sheltered Giuseppe Mazzini, could not but give the same welcome to Indians who had fought for the same cause.[40]

The war had brought about a truce in the nationalist movement and India placed all its resources at the disposal of Britain in its hour of need. The Indian soldiers' bravery in various theatres of war in Europe, Africa and West Asia won them the gratitude of Britain and the admiration of the world. In fact, India incurred such an enormous cost in men and material that it was now in an economic crisis of the most serious magnitude.[41] India had to incur this enormous economic burden largely because of the fact that Indian policies at the time were determined by the British. Moreover, Indians were tricked into believing that self-determination for all people was the battle cry and the war was being fought to make the world safe for democracy. They naively believed that helping the Allies might lead to a victory which would ultimately bring some tangible reward for India. It was with this fond hope that Annie Besant, presiding over the Calcutta session of the INC in 1917, secured the adoption of a resolution expressing 'deep loyalty and profound attachment to the Throne' and 'firm resolve to stand by the British empire at all hazards and at all costs'.[42] Such expression of loyalty found another occasion when an INC delegation to London with Lala Lajpat Rai, Muhammad Ali Jinnah, Lord Satyendra Prasad Sinha and others as its members sent a letter to the secretary of state reiterating their conviction that Indians would readily and willingly cooperate with the British and place all resources of their country 'at His Majesty's disposal' for a victory in the war against Germany.[43] Thus, the INC moderates, who were then in control of the party machine, proclaimed their loyalty to the British and support to the Allies in resolutions at each of the INC sessions during the war. And when the war came to a close in 1918, they congratulated the British government on the successful termination. Little did they realize that protestations of self-government and democracy were not meant to be applied to the Indians, that the Allies never intended self-government to anyone outside Europe, where the splitting up of the Austro-Hungarian empire demanded some high-flown justification.[44]

At the Lucknow session of the INC in 1916, Surendranath Banerjee declared that the object of the war was to vindicate the sanctity of treaty obligations—to uphold the sacredness of 'scraps and bits of paper'. The moral law, he said, did not work by latitudes and longitudes.[45] In 1922, in a speech at his trial, Gandhi also admitted that in all their efforts at service to the Allied victory, the INC leaders were actuated by the belief that it would be possibly by such service to gain the status of full equality for their country. But subsequent events were to make a mockery of such optimism.

In the face of the German peril, the British government, in order to make sure of Indian cooperation, had held out specious promises of constitutional reform and self-government for the Indians. It was clear, as Charles Roberts admitted, that India was no longer a mere dependent of but a partner in the British empire and as such the problems of the Government of India Act had to be looked at from an altogether different angle.[46]

But with the termination of the war, such professions of partnership in spirit began to wear thin. Official British opinion now professed thanks that by helping the Allies, India had only expressed its heartfelt gratitude to the King for the blessings of British rule in India.

Disillusionment was followed by discontent and unrest. The Indian soldiers' brilliant performance in the battlefield not only gave the people an unprecedented sense of national honour but the near collapse of the Allies in the face of German challenge also exploded the myth of invincibility of British arms. The Indian soldiers, who had been hastily demilitarized lest they turned their weapons against their British masters, now came back to their villages carrying with them new grievances and new ideas which they had picked up from foreign lands. Their experience abroad taught them to shake off their traditional submissiveness. As a result, the placidity of the countryside was disturbed and discontented peasantry began to rise in revolt against the intolerable conditions of life.[47]

The termination of the war had also brought back the old administrators and with them came back the worst features of British rule in India. These administrators, who treated the war as an unhappy 'interlude in the happy superiority of British life in India', once again decided to carry on the administration by means of terror, internment and repression. But despite the Sedition Acts, which followed the Rowlatt Report, terrorism and revolt began to spread like wildfire.[48]

To roll back the tide of unrest among almost all sections of Indian people, the government adopted extremely repressive measures resulting in a virtual reign of terror all over the country and culminating in the Jallianwala Bagh massacre and the barbarous enforcement of martial law in Punjab. The Defence of India Act, which was passed on 18 March 1915, to meet the new situation arising out of the war, was now being abused to terrorize the people and crush their normal political activities. To replace the Defence of India Act which was to cease to be operative at the end of the war, two more bills were prepared by the government on the basis of the report of the Rowlatt Committee, which was appointed to investigate the growing spate of revolutionary movement and to recommend appropriate legislative measures to quell it. Of these bills, only one was actually passed into law, namely the Anarchical and Revolutionary Crimes Act, 1919, which provided for summary trial of political offences by a special court empowered to meet in camera and take into consideration evidence not admissible under the

Indian Evidence Act, 1872. There could be no appeal against the decisions of this court. The Act also empowered the provincial governments to order any person, on mere suspicion, to furnish any security or to notify his residence or to reside in a particular area or to abstain from any specified act or finally to report himself to the police. Provincial governments were also given wide powers to search any place and to arrest any person without warrant and to keep detainees confined in whatever place and under whatever conditions as it may specify. In addition to these 'lawless laws', numerous other restrictive measures were taken by the government to suppress the civil and political liberties of the people. The extent of such repressive measures can be gauged from the fact that by the end of 1919 as many as 350 printing presses had been seized, 300 newspapers closed down, 500 books proscribed and thousands of persons interned under the Defence of India Act, 1915.[49] But despite such ruthless repression, which in the words of British politician Henry Mayers Hyndman, stood almost 'on a level with the outrages committed by Germany in Belgium, France and Poland',[50] popular unrest began to assume menacing proportions and underground revolutionary groups began to spring up all over the country. Moreover, as already noted above, many revolutionaries left India to organize revolutionary groups in various parts of the world—in Berlin, New York, London, Kabul, Japan and Mexico.[51]

On 20 August 1917, Edwin Samuel Montagu announced in the House of Commons that the policy of the British government was that of increasing the association of Indians in every branch of the administration and the gradual development of self-governing institutions in India. The progress of this policy, he added, could only be achieved by successive stages and the British government in India would determine the time and the measure of each advance.[52]

Although this declaration indicated a radical change in the government's policy towards India, neither this declaration nor the Report on Indian Constitutional Reforms, on the basis of which the Government of India Act, 1919, was passed, could stem the tide of simmering discontent. Whatever good effect this declaration might have had was more than offset by the repressive policy of the government in crushing what it called 'criminal conspiracies'. Thus, while the British at Westminster were envisaging some delegation of powers and gradual development of self-governing institutions in India, the British in Delhi were strengthening their authority with all the apparatus of oppression—trial without jury and summary internment. Edwardes said that Indians naturally saw this 'as giving with one hand and slapping down with the other'.[53]

And it was at this time that Gandhi came. Commenting on his impact on the millions of Indians, Jawaharlal Nehru said:

> He was like powerful current of fresh air, that made us stretch ourselves and take deep breaths; like beam of light that pierced the darkness and removed the scales from our eyes; like a whirlwind that upset many things, but most of all the working of people's minds. He did not descend from the top; his seemed to emerge from the millions of India speaking their language and incessantly drawing attention to their appalling conditions. 'Get off the backs of these peasants and workers', he told us, 'all you who live by exploitation; get rid of the system that produces this poverty and misery.' Political freedom took new shape then and acquired a new content.[54]

The quintessence of Gandhi's philosophy was *satyagraha*, a vow to hold to the truth and *ahimsa*, the abjuration of malice and hatred. His weapons were non-violent non-cooperation, passive resistance and civil disobedience—the most drastic remedy in the pharmacopoeia of *satyagraha*. Out of these ethico-moral principles stepped forth a virile fighter for freedom who used these weapons for political ends and this was Gandhi's prime contribution to the technique of revolution. With Gandhi's emergence, therefore, Indian politics became a strange mixture of nationalism and religion and ethics and mysticism and fanaticism.[55]

KHILAFAT AND NON-COOPERATION MOVEMENTS

The first opportunity to experiment with this unique technique as a weapon of mass action was provided by the *khilafat* agitation and the subsequent Non-Cooperation Movement. *Khilafat* was basically a part of the romantic pan-Islamic movement born of religious fanaticism, but it also involved a cross-current of rivalries—political, economic and strategic—between the Turks, the Arabs and the Allied powers. In fact, the *khilafat* was a moribund institution in which even the Turks had little interest. The Indian Muslims, obviously ignorant of the fact that the pan-Islamic movement was politically motivated, were moved by the religious fanaticism and angrily protested against the dismemberment of Turkey and the consequent destruction of the *khilafat*—the traditional symbol of Islamic unity. But in spite of the fact that the Sultan of Turkey's claim as the supreme religious authority of the Islamic world had little practical significance outside the Ottoman empire[56] and that the pan-Islamic movement 'based on the extraterritorial allegiance of the Indian Muslims cut at the very root of nascent Indian nationalism',[57] Gandhi sought to create out of this movement a united front against the British.[58] Under his leadership, the INC also lent its power, prestige and organization to the *khilafat* and sent a deputation to the viceroy to impress him upon the consequences if the 'just demands' of the Muslims were not accepted. But the viceroy, while expressing his sympathy for the Muslim sentiment, made it clear that the contention that Turkey should be allowed to preserve in full the integrity, sovereignty and the dominions which it possessed before the war could not be recognized by the Allied powers. Turkey could not expect, he said, any more than any other power which drew the sword in the cause of Germany.[59]

Gandhi then decided to launch the Non-Cooperation Movement against the government. He had become 'convinced' that non-cooperation was the only effective remedy both for avoiding violence and healing the wounds inflicted on the Indian Muslims. He also returned all the decorations awarded to him by the British government for his war services. He could not wear them, he wrote to the viceroy, with an easy conscience so long as the Indian Muslims had to labour under the wrong done to their religious sentiment.[60] The movement, however, took a mass character when to the original issue of the *khilafat* were added other questions of wider national importance. According to Pattabhi Sitaramayya:

> The *triveni* [the confluence of the three streams of a river] of the *khilafat* and the Punjab wrongs and the invisible flow of inadequate reforms became full to the brim and by their confluence enriched both in volume and content of the stream of non-cooperation.[61]

At a special session of the INC held in Calcutta on 5 September 1920, Gandhi moved a resolution expressing the opinion that there could be no contentment in India without redress of the wrong done to the Indian Muslims and those of Punjab and that the only effectual means to vindicate national honour and to prevent repetition of similar wrongs in future was the establishment of *swaraj*. The resolution then declared that there was no course left open for the Indian people but to adopt the policy of non-violent non-cooperation until the said wrongs were righted and *swaraj* established.[62] As to the programme of the movement, the resolution advised: (a) surrender of titles and honorary offices and resignation from nominated seats in local bodies, (b) refusal to attend government functions, (c) gradual withdrawal of children from schools and colleges owned, aided and controlled by government and establishment of national schools and colleges in the country, (d) gradual boycott of British courts by lawyers and litigants and establishment of arbitration courts for the settlement of private disputes, (e) refusal on the part of the military, clerical and labouring classes to offer themselves as recruits for service in Mesopotamia, (f) withdrawal by candidates of the candidature for election to the Reforms Councils and refusal on the part of the voters to vote for any candidate who may, despite the advice of INC, offer himself for election and (g) boycott of foreign goods. The concluding part of the resolution was of great importance in as much as it suggested measures by which the economic ills of the country and hardships of the people were to be removed. It advised the people to adopt *swadeshi* in piece goods and their manufacture on a large scale by means of reviving hand spinning and hand weaving throughout the country.

After an animated debate that lasted for three days, the resolution was adopted on 9 September 1920 and 'demoralized, backward and broken-up people suddenly straightened their backs and lifted their heads and took part in disciplined, joint action on a countrywide scale'.[63] The special session of the INC in Calcutta in 1920 marked not only a turning point in Indian history but also a personal victory for Gandhi; he not only captured the INC but also became the undisputed leader of India's struggle for freedom.[64]

In making common cause with the *khilafat* agitation, Gandhi was actuated by his intense desire to bring about Hindu–Muslim unity, the absence of which had always been a terrible scourge of Indian political life. Besides, by stressing the non-violent character of the movement he wanted to make the most spectacular political conquest in history,[65] through a means hitherto unknown to any conqueror. But in the achievement of these two goals, the Non-Cooperation Movement was not a great success. 'The country was all agog to witness the final triumph of the soul force over physical might. But the Gods had willed it otherwise.'[66] Gandhi's dream of Hindu–Muslim unity was shattered when the Moplahs, a band of fanatic Muslims settled on the Malabar Coast, rose in revolt against the British but in their fanatical zeal perpetrated bestial savagery upon the Hindus. According to contemporary reports, massacre, forcible conversion, desecration of temples, foul outrages upon women, pillage, arson and destruction—all the accompaniments of unrestricted barbarism were committed freely until troops could be hurried to restore order.[67]

But the final collapse of the Non-Cooperation Movement followed an outbreak of violence in a village named Chauri Chaura in Uttar Pradesh. Gandhi decided to suspend the movement and the decision was endorsed by the All India Congress Committee (AICC) on 25 February 1921.

GRIM ECONOMIC SCENARIO, LABOUR AND PEASANT UNREST

Although the Non-Cooperation Movement failed to achieve *swaraj* within a year as was promised to the people by Gandhi, its most remarkable result was the shift of political emphasis from the elite to the newly awakened masses. The tremendous enthusiasm that Gandhi was able to evoke among the masses with his slogan of *swaraj* and *swadeshi* showed the extent of unrest, discontent and anti-British feeling that had been aroused by the conditions of grinding penury created by the war. The crippling financial burdens of the war, the soaring prices of essential commodities and reckless profiteering had created conditions of unprecedented mass misery and impoverishment. To make things worse, an influenza epidemic broke out at the end of the war, which took the unparalleled toll of nearly 14 million people.[68] But despite such poverty and suffering, the post-war years witnessed an unprecedented awakening of the masses of the population to a new purpose of life.

This spirit of awakening did not die out with the collapse of the Non-Cooperation Movement. On the contrary, the spirit of revolt and defiance generated by the movement continued unabated and the feeling of fear, oppression and frustration completely disappeared.[69]

On the economic front, this all-pervading atmosphere of defiance and restlessness stimulated labour and peasant movements all over the country. But as a background to this new ferment among the workers and peasants, some attention should first be given to the general economic condition of the people during and after the war.

During the first two years following the outbreak of the war, India benefitted from the generally good harvest but the next two years recorded crop failures almost all over the country, resulting in widespread famine. To meet the situation, the government regulated export of food grains and introduced a rigid system of internal control.[70] But these measures could not alleviate the distress of the rural population, most of whom were landless labourers. The growth of the population of these landless labourers from decade to decade resulted in agrarian unrest which expressed itself in such social maladies as petty thefts, rioting and looting.[71] The pitiable condition of the people was revealed in a report of the Directorate of Public Health in Bengal, which said that the diet of the peasantry was such that even rats could not live on it for more than five weeks.[72]

But, as Nehru observed, while the problem of the peasantry was the supreme problem of India, it was ignored by political leaders and government alike. Nehru said:

All the unending talk of constitutional reform and Indianization of services was a mockery and an insult when the manhood of our country was being crushed and the inexorable and continuous process of exploitation was deepening our poverty and sapping our vitality. We had become a derelict nation.[73]

The condition of the industrial proletariat was also no better. Although during the war, Indian industries, particularly the jute mills in Bengal and cotton mills in Ahmedabad, produced enormous dividends—100 to 200 per cent—the workers who had created these dividends lived at an incredible low level of existence.[74]

The war had strikingly exposed India's industrial backwardness and made the government realize that industrialization was important not only from the economic point of view but also for political and military considerations. From the political point of view, as R. Palme Dutt pointed out, it was essential for the government to secure the cooperation of the Indian bourgeoisie and for this purpose, it was necessary to make certain concessions to them in the economic field.[75] From the military point of view, it was also realized that without some sort of industrial base in India, there would always be the danger of exclusive dependence for vital military needs on long-distance overseas supplies.

These compelling reasons led the government to proclaim a new policy of industrialization in India. Soon after the announcement of this policy, a crash followed resulting in a feverish boom and all round acceleration of industrial activity throughout the country. The number of organized factories increased from 2,936 in 1914 to 3,436 in 1918. An industrial census taken in 1921 showed that the number of workers in organized factories employing 20 or more workers increased from 2.1 million in 1911 to 2.6 million in 1921.[76] Moreover, encouraged by the government's liberal policy, British capital began to flow in and colossal profits were made by almost all industrial establishments in the country. The phenomenal extent of profits made by Indian industries can be realized from the fact that during the war while the average earnings of industries in the United Kingdom and the United States were 10.5 per cent and 10.6 per cent, respectively, in India it was as high as 17.1 per cent.[77]

A delegation of the Dundee Jute Trade Union to India reported in 1925 that in the jute industry the total profit to the shareholders during 1915–24 amounted to £300 million, that is, 90 per cent per annum of the capital, whereas the average wage of the workers in the industry was only £12 per annum.[78] According to another survey, the average dividend paid by the jute mills was more than 140 per cent— the highest being 420 per cent. A leading jute mill, which paid 250 per cent dividend in 1918, paid 420 per cent in 1919.[79]

In the cotton industry, an enquiry committee of the Indian Tariff Board reported that in 1920, 35 companies comprising 42 mills declared dividends of 40 per cent and over, of which 10 companies comprising 14 mills paid 100 per cent and two mills paid over 200 per cent. According to P.A. Wadia and K.T. Merchant, the average dividend paid by the cotton mills in 1920 was 120 per cent, the highest figure being 365 per cent. In some mills, the shareholders were not satisfied with 400 per cent dividends and demanded 500 per cent.[80]

Against the background of such fantastic profit making by industrial enterprises, the condition of the common people presented a wretched spectacle. According to the Simon Commission, the average per capita income of the Indians during the post-war years was only £8 per annum. This, however, was only the average gross income, not the actual income of the teeming millions because, as pointed out by economists K.T. Shah and K.J. Khambata, 1 per cent of the population got one-third of the national income while 60 per cent of the population received only 30 per cent of that income. In fact, the average Indian income was just enough either to feed two out of three members of the population or to give them all two instead of three meals a day provided they all consented to go naked, live out of doors all the year round, had no recreation and wanted nothing else but food—the lowest, the coarsest and the least nutritious.[81]

Dissatisfaction with these subhuman conditions of life had already produced ferment among the agricultural and industrial proletariat and with the outbreak of the war came a wave of peasant and labour movements in various parts of the country. In the industrial field, the unrest assumed such serious proportions that very few industrial enterprises were left unaffected by labour disputes or strikes.[82] But these movements had an entirely different character from those taking place before the war. Until the war, these movements had been locally inspired and organized and were completely devoid of any ideology or leadership. For this reason, as B. Shiva Rao pointed out, they aroused no great interest among the political leaders who looked upon industrial disputes with almost complete unconcern.[83] Speaking about the growing consciousness of the industrial proletariat, Nehru also observed that no strike could succeed in those days because the workers were unorganized and helpless. Moreover, there were millions of unemployed who could be easily drawn upon by the employers. Before the war, the numbers of industrial proletariat were not sufficient to affect the Indian political scene. But after the war, the voice of the Indian labour began to be heard. It might have been ignored, Nehru pointed out, but for the fact that the Russian Revolution had forced the working people to attach some importance to the industrial proletariat.[84]

The Royal Commission on Labour (also known as Whitley Commission) expressed a similar opinion when it stated that prior to the war a strike was a rare occurrence in India because the vast majority of workers not only lacked leadership and organization but were also imbued with a passive outlook on life. It was the war that brought about a radical change in the attitude of the industrial proletariat. They began to realize the potentialities of strike 'and this was assisted by the emergence of the trade union organizers, by the education which the war had given to the masses'.[85]

Apart from the dissatisfaction with the existing conditions of life, there were other factors that served to bring about a new outlook, a new consciousness and militancy among the Indian peasants and workers.

In the first place, as already noted, the Indian soldiers returning home from the war brought with them new ideas and convictions that completely dispelled their sense of inferiority and passivity. As these soldiers were drawn mostly from the ranks of the peasantry, their experience had a profound effect upon all villagers. The war almost completely destroyed the notion that the superiority of the white men was unquestionable. This was indeed a thrilling experience for the docile workers and peasants who used to bear all kinds of insult without protest. It was also the most significant change brought about by the war.[86]

In the second place, when Gandhi appeared on the Indian political scene and launched the Non-Cooperation Movement, the country was overtaken by a tremendous awakening of the masses and the voices of the workers and peasants began to be heard for the first time in India's struggle for freedom.

Many philanthropists, intellectuals and political leaders also began to take an interest in the problems of workers and peasants. Indeed, it was at this time that India witnessed the inauguration of the organized-and-ideologically-inspired labour and peasant movements. The significance of this new development, as L.P. Sinha rightly observed, was that it created an intellectual and emotional atmosphere of fearlessness, defiance and revolt which became an indirect factor in the origin of Left-wing movements in India.[87]

The workers and peasants were drawn to the mainstream of political movement by Gandhi's slogan for *swaraj* and *swadeshi*. But to sustain the spirit of mass support, it was necessary for the INC to come up with a concrete programme vindicating the grievances of the workers and peasants. With this end in view, the INC, at its Nagpur session in 1920, adopted resolutions soliciting the participation of workers, peasants and students in the national movement. The resolution on labour upheld the cause of the workers, expressed support for their trade union activities and denounced the policy of exploitation and persecution of the workers. The resolution on peasants welcomed the *kisan's* (peasant's) struggle against exploitation and expressed satisfaction at their role in the boycott movement.

But although the INC expressed sympathy and support for the demands of the workers and peasants, it was less enthusiastic about identifying their class interests with its own. As pointed out by Narendra Deva, the INC sought the cooperation of the *kisans* in its own struggle, but it was unwilling to fight for their economic demands.[88] According to Edwardes, the INC was opposed to any reform in tenants' rights because much of its financial support came from large-landed proprietors. Similarly, the INC attitude to industrial reform also showed that its members were no friends of the workers.[89]

In the third place, the ideals of the British labour movement had a profound influence upon intellectual and political leaders, such as Lala Lajpat Rai, N.M. Joshi, R.R. Bakhale and others, who championed the cause of the workers and peasants in India. They were impressed by the principles of the British Labour Party and began to educate the people on its lines and formulate measures which would secure real freedom for them. Rai said, 'India will not be a party to any scheme, which shall add to the powers of the capitalists and the landlord and will introduce and accentuate the evils of the expiring industrial civilization into our beloved country.'[90]

In this connection, it may be noted that the British and Indian working classes were unconscious allies in at least one respect—both were struggling against privileges and exploitation. As long as loyal and quiescent India remained a source of wealth and as long as enough surplus capital was available in Britain for export to the colonial countries, the British working people accepted the empire as a symbol of national glory. But after the war when the empire lost its glamour and colonies were looked upon as a brake upon their own progress, a section of the British working class became indifferent to the empire's mystique and sympathized with the Indian labour movement, disguising their self-interest under the cloak of democratic slogans. As rightly pointed out by Edwardes, the British working class, which had acquired some political importance after the extension of the franchise and formed a powerful anti-colonial lobby, now began to ask why there should be poverty and unemployment in Britain when millions were being spent in the administration of faraway colonies.[91] The more radical elements of the British labour movement thought that the empire had a class connotation—a symbol of privilege, discrimination and exploitation. They found in Britain's dependence on its colonial possessions a convenient stick by which to beat successive Tory governments. But although they argued that Britain would be better off without the colonies, they did not advocate outright surrender of power. They wanted gradual transformation of the colonies into self-governing dominions. But even then, their logic provided a timely stimulus to the labour movement in India.

Another factor that contributed to the mass awakening in India was the enlargement of people's conception of democracy brought about by a changed outlook towards social ideas and institutions characterized by division of race, religion, caste and language. At one end of the social scale were the servile industrial and agricultural proletariat and at the other end stood the frustrated middle class and the intelligentsia, many of whom were anxious to associate themselves with the administration of the country and ordering its affairs. Moreover, as M.R. Masani put it, 'The Indian Maharaja, the big feudal landlord and the rising industrialist and bureaucrat stood like mountain peaks above the plain of poverty.'[92]

The condition of the peasantry and the industrial workers was marked by poverty, illiteracy and degradation of all kinds. But between these two classes, there were further inequalities, so much so that a peasant would look upon the urban population, including the industrial workers, as a privileged class. This was largely on account of the fact that while the peasantry used to contribute the lion's share to the state coffers, government expenditure would seldom go beyond the urban areas. This economic disparity between the urban and rural population provoked Gandhi to comment that the people in the towns and cities had been riding, like the Old Man of the Sea, on the back of the rural Sinbad and they would do everything but get off his back. Apart from poverty, the rural population had a burdensome heritage in the caste system, the essential elements of which were endogamy, a hierarchy from top to bottom headed by the *Brahmins*, rigid restrictions on every sphere of social life, occupational discrimination and even inequality before the law. But after the war and under the forces of industrialism, the people began to question the very *raison d'etre* of these social institutions.[93]

The condition of the déclassé middle classes, who received some measure of English education and joined the army of unemployed malcontents, was perhaps worse. As Nehru rightly pointed out, they were frustrated and had nowhere to turn. Neither the old nor the new could offer them any hope.

> There was no adjustment to social purpose, no satisfaction in doing something worthwhile, even though suffering came in the train. Custom ridden, they were born old, yet they were without the old culture. Modern thought attracted them, but they lacked its inner content, the modern social and scientific consciousness.[94]

Unable to find their rightful place in society, these frustrated elements turned not only against the alien rulers but also against the well-to-do upper-class social elites who monopolized the country's leadership and dominated the INC. Their discontent was therefore against both the British imperialists and the bourgeois leaders whom they considered as nothing but lackeys of British imperialism. Thus, feeling themselves betrayed by the moderate policy of the 'bourgeois leadership', they were drawn to the cult of revolutionary violence. And it was from these discontented elements that a new type of movement emerged, more militant and defiant and representing the broad spectrum of the lower-middle classes, workers, peasants as well as students and unemployed youth.

The upper class, the social and political ideas of which provided dynamism to the freedom movement before the advent of Gandhi, was composed of the *noblesse de la robe*, professional prodigies, landed aristocracy, captains of industry, leaders of thought and intellectuals who drank deep of British liberalism.[95] Many members of this class were honoured by the government with offices, titles and dignities because it became scared by the growing extremism of the middle-class leaders who had little faith in the efficacy of constitutional agitation against British rule in India. But the upper-class intellectuals were imbued with the ideas of English nineteenth century liberalism—freedom of the individual, parliamentary democracy, evolutionary change of society, moral suasion as an instrument of political action and constitutionalism. Their concept of democracy was that of an aristocracy of intellect and wealth. This attitude was well expressed by Sir Romesh Chandra Mitter in an address to the INC in 1896:

> The educated community represented the brain and conscience of the country and were the legitimate spokesmen of the illiterate masses, the natural custodian of their interests. To hold otherwise would be to

presuppose that a foreign administration in the service knows more about the wants of the masses than their educated countrymen. It is true in all ages that those who think must govern those who toil, and could it be that the natural order of things was reversed in this country?[96]

But although these upper-class leaders were fervently patriotic and anxious for the political emancipation and socio-economic advancement of India, they suffered from a number of difficulties which rendered them incapable of identifying themselves with the masses. They were so deeply influenced by the aristocratic liberalism of Edmund Burke that they found it difficult to adjust themselves to the doctrine of mass action which Gandhi advocated and the poor man's paradise which he wished to see established in India. They were no doubt anxious to see the conditions of the workers and peasants improved, but they could not reconcile themselves to the idea of political rights for the oppressed classes. They were, in fact, isolated from the rest of the community—strangers in their own land. Essentially urban, they were indifferent to the problems of the rural community. Cut off from the masses whom they claimed to represent, they lived in a world of their own. In short, as K.M. Panikkar put it, 'They were aliens in India, strangers to their own people, and their ideas and beliefs were not shared by any but a small class of educated people.'[97]

It is, therefore, no wonder that the ideas of these upper-class leaders did not reach the hearts of the discontented lower-middle-class literates whose condition was becoming increasingly desperate in the absence of any avenue of fulfilment for them and who had little patience with the comfortable doctrines of gradual advance propagated by the moderate leaders of the INC. Unable to find their role in the national movement, they found satisfaction either in anarchist individualistic terrorism or in exalted doctrines of revolutionary idealism.

Of great significance in the eyes of the intellectuals of this class but of little influence on the illiterate and politically inarticulate masses was the Bolshevik Revolution in Russia.[98] In the words of M.N. Roy, the downfall of 'Tsarism in Russia had electrified the democratic and liberal world [and] galvanized the waning faith in the possibility of capturing power through armed insurrection organized and led by a determined minority.'[99] To a section of the Indian intelligentsia, the Russian Revolution, with its slogan of proletarian internationalism, liberation of all dependent peoples, racial equality and self-determination of all nationalities, heralded the triumph of liberty over despotism, oppression and exploitation. To them, Lenin's declaration that the revolutionary movement of the people of the East could develop effectively only in direct association with the revolutionary struggle of the Soviet Republic against international imperialism[100] was an explosive statement, and all the nations of Asia struggling for liberation heard it with a new hope.[101]

But despite the romantic appeal of the Russian Revolution, most of those who were attracted by it in India had no clear conception of the forces that provided momentum to the Russian revolutionary movement, the ideals and ideologies that stimulated it, the price that had to be paid for the fulfilment of those ideals and above all its relevance to the Indian situation. In fact, it was only after the overthrow of the Tsarist regime that Russia began to interest Indian nationalists, and the Marxist literature 'was finding its way to the bookshelves of the educated few'.[102] Besides, news about the Soviet Union was so exiguous, distorted or full of legends that it was almost impossible for the Indian people to examine and appreciate the revolution in its true perspective.[103]

The initial reaction of the Indian press, marked more by caution than by optimism, clearly indicated that the voice of those who thought that the Russian Revolution had ushered in a new era of hope for mankind was indeed feeble. But there is no doubt that the overthrow of Tsarist tyranny in Russia raised the *amour propre* of the Indian people smarting under the repressive British rule. As a result, as the political, economic and social ideas of the revolution were beginning to be better understood by the Indian intellectuals, their conviction in radical ideas also began to gain strength and a new voice, strident and zealous, was added to India's cry for freedom. More important still, the ideological monopoly so far exercised by the worshippers of conservative liberalism was broken and a rival ideology emerged instilling new socio-economic forces into the content of Indian nationalism. And it was from among the followers of this new ideological current that the Leftist movement in India was born.

NOTES AND REFERENCES (CHAPTER 1)

1   J.K. Majumdar, ed., *Indian Speeches and Documents on British Rule: 1821–1918* (Calcutta: Longmans, Green and Company, 1937), 186.
2   R. Palme Dutt, *India Today and Tomorrow* (Delhi: People's Publishing House, 1955), 121.
3   Ibid., 122.
4   Haridas Mukherjee and Uma Mukherjee, *Sri Aurobindo and the New Thought in Indian Politics* (Calcutta: Firma K.L. Mukhopadhyay, 1964), xviii.
5   Dutt, *India Today and Tomorrow*, 121.
6   Ibid., 114–15 and 117.
7   Michael Edwardes, *The Last Years of British India* (London: Cassell and Company, 1963), 8.
8   R.C. Majumdar, *History of the Freedom Movement in India*, Vol. II (Calcutta: Firma K.L. Mukhopadhyay, 1963), 180.
9   Ibid., xvi.
10 Ibid., xv–xvi.
11 For a detailed account of the Swadeshi Movement, see Majumdar, *History of the Freedom Movement in India*, Vol. II, 1–16.
12 Ibid., 129.
13 Ibid., 136.
14 Mukherjee and Mukherjee, *Sri Aurobindo and the New Thought in Indian Politics*, xvi.
15 B.K. Sarkar, *Naya Banglar Godapattan* (Bengali), Vol. I (Calcutta: Chuckervertty, Chatterjee and Company, 1932), 190–91. Also see *The Englishman* (8 August 1905); *The Bengalee* (9 August 1905) and *Sanjivani* (10 August 1905).
16 Apart from the partition of Bengal, other factors that helped the growth of the extremist movement were: (a) apathy of the government to the demands of the INC for greater Indian participation in the councils; (b) Hindu revivalism brought about by Swami Vivekananda, Aurobindo Ghosh, Bal Gangadhar Tilak and others; (c) discontent created by the famine of 1897; (d) Repressive policy of Lord Curzon; (e) Ill treatment of Indians abroad and (f) end of the myth of European supremacy after Japan's victory over Russia in 1904–05.
17 Dutt, *India Today and Tomorrow*, 49.
18 For the articles written by Aurobindo Ghosh during 1893–94, see Haridas Mukherjee and Uma Mukherjee, *Sri Aurobindo's Political Thought, 1893–1908* (Calcutta: Firma K.L. Mukhopadhyay, 1958).
19 Aurobindo Ghosh, *Bankim–Tilak–Dayananda* (Calcutta: Arya Publishing House, 1947), 12–20.
20 Majumdar, *History of the Freedom Movement in India*, Vol. II, 155.
21 R.G. Pradhan, *India's Struggle for Swaraj* (Madras: G.A. Natesan and Company, 1930), 24.
22 Mukherjee and Mukherjee, *Sri Aurobindo and the New Thought in Indian Politics*, xxxi, and the authors' article 'The Alleged Uniqueness of India's Freedom Movement' in *Modern Review* (Calcutta, 1962, August). Also see article 'The Realism of India's Nationalist Policy' *Bande Mataram* (Bengali; 24 April 1908).
23 Dutt, *India Today and Tomorrow*, 122.
24 Majumdar, *History of the Freedom Movement in India*, Vol. II, 318–19.
25 Ibid., 321–22.
26 Those who started the Ghadr Movement made good money in America, but everywhere they were treated as slaves. 'Everywhere they were insulted and despised. In hotels and trains, parks and theatres, they were

discriminated against. Everywhere hung noticeboards: "Hindus, i.e. Indians, and Dogs Not Allowed." This sort of inhuman treatment brought a political consciousness and yearning for liberty'. See Randhir Singh, *The Ghadr Heroes* (Bombay: People's Publishing House, 1945), 4–7. Also see Majumdar, *History of the Freedom Movement in India*, Vol. II, 389–97.

27 Randhir Singh, *The Ghadr Heroes*, 8–9.

28 For the history of the formation and activities of the Indian Independence Committee in Berlin, see Majumdar, *History of the Freedom Movement in India*, Vol. II, 402–13. Also see Lala Har Dayal, *Forty-four Months in Germany and Turkey, February 1915 to October 1918: A Record of Personal Impressions* (London: P.S. King and Son, 1920).

29 Dutt, *India Today and Tomorrow*, 130. Dutt further remarked here:

> This unity of the development of the struggle in India with the world struggle is of especial importance to realize in view of the subjective and isolationist tendencies frequently prevalent in some of the conventional schools of Indian political thought to interpret profound movements simply in terms of the personalities or particular groups which in varying degree sought or failed to give them leadership.

30 R. Palme Dutt, *Problems of Contemporary History* (London: Lawrence and Wishart, 1963), 16. Lloyd George's memorandum is quoted by Dutt in his book *World Politics, 1918–1936* (Patna: Adhar Prakashan, 1961), 54.

31 Dutt, *World Politics, 1918–1936*, 55.

32 Ibid., 51–52.

33 P. Kerzhentsev, *Angliiskii Imperializm* (Russian; Moscow: Izdatel'stvo Vsersossiiskogo Tsentral'nogo Ispolnitel'nogo Komiteta Sovetov R.K., K.I.K. Deputatov, 1919), 32. Quoted by Gene D. Overstreet and Marshall Windmiller, *Communism in India* (Bombay: Perennial Press, 1960), 8.

34 Karl Marx, 'The British Rule in India' in *New York Daily Tribune* (25 June 1953). According to Jayantanuja Bandyopadhyaya:

> Marx, presumably on account of his conviction that socialism could not be achieved by any country until and unless capitalism had grown and matured in it, was giving an exposition of the imperialist case which no imperialist could possibly excel and it is against each step in this argument that the assault of nationalism in India and elsewhere came.

See Jayantanuja Bandyopadhyaya, *Indian Nationalism Versus International Communism* (Calcutta: Firma K.L. Mukhopadhyay, 1966), 96–97.

35 Karl Marx and Friedrich Engels, *On Colonialism* (Moscow: Progress Publishers, 1968), 306–07. R. Palme Dutt ascribes the authorship of this letter to Engels. Also see Dutt, *Problems of Contemporary History*, 87.

36 This article was originally published in Bolshevik journal *Proletary* on 5 August 1908. It has been reproduced in V.I. Lenin's *The National Liberation Movement in the East* (Moscow: Foreign Languages Publishing House, 1957), 14–15.

37 V.I. Lenin, *Selected Works*, Vol. I (Moscow: Foreign Languages Publishing House, 1947), 66.

38 *Manchester Guardian* (8 January 1923).

39 Edwardes, *The Last Years of British India*, 30.

40 B.R. Nanda, *The Nehrus: Motilal and Jawaharlal* (London: George Allen and Unwin, 1962), 140.

41 For details of India's contribution to the First World War, see R.C. Majumdar, H.C. Ray Chaudhuri and K.K. Datta, *An Advanced History of India* (London: Macmillan, 1950), 930. Also see Majumdar, *History of the Freedom Movement in India*, Vol. II, 344–49.

42 Dutt, *India Today and Tomorrow*, 134.

43 Ibid., 131.

44 Edwardes, *The Last Years of British India*, 42.

45 Surendranath Banerjee's speech is quoted by Nanda in *The Nehrus: Motilal and Jawaharlal*, 125.

46 Ibid., 124–25.

47 M.N. Roy, *Memoirs* (Bombay: Allied Publishers, 1964), 543–44.

48 Edwardes, *The Last Years of British India*, 41. Also see E.S. Montagu, *An Indian Diary* (London: William Heinemann, 1930), 156.

49 Prabhat Kumar Mukhopadhyay, *Bharate Jatiya Andolan* (Bengali; Calcutta: Granthan, 1960), 134–35.

50 R.C. Majumdar, *History of the Freedom Movement in India*, Vol. III (Calcutta: Firma K.L. Mukhopadhyay, 1963), 41–42.

51 Overstreet and Windmiller, *Communism in India*, 8–9.

52 R.N. Aggarwala, *National Movement and Constitutional Development of India* (Delhi: Metropolitan Book, 1956), 78–79.

53 Edwardes, *The Last Years of British India*, 41.

54 Jawaharlal Nehru, *The Discovery of India* (London: Meridian Books, 1956), 361.

55 *Chicago Tribune* (1 March 1922).

56 I.H. Qureshi, *The Muslim Community of the Indo-Pakistan Subcontinent: 610–1947* (The Hague: Mouton and Company, 1962), 770.

57 Majumdar, *History of the Freedom Movement in India*, Vol. III, 65.

58 It is interesting to note that in the wake of the Muslim agitation against the humiliating terms of the peace treaty, Enver Pasha 'approached the Russians with the offer to cooperate in the plan of inciting the Muslim peoples of the Middle East to revolt against British imperialism...'. The Bolshevik leaders were naïve enough to believe that the *khilafat* agitation had tremendous revolutionary possibilities. See Roy, *Memoirs*, 398, 417.

59 *Indian Annual Register* (Calcutta, 1921), 156.

60 Ibid., 206.

61 The term 'triveni' refers to the sacred confluence of the three Indian rivers—the Ganges, the Yamuna and the Saraswati. See Pattabhi Sitaramayya, *The History of the Indian National Congress*, Vol. I (Bombay: Padma Publications, 1946), 335.

62 D. Chakravarty and C. Bhattacharya, *Congress in Evolution: A Collection of Congress Resolutions from 1885 to 1934 and Other Important Documents* (Calcutta: The Book Company, 1935), 33.

63 Jawaharlal Nehru, *An Autobiography* (Bombay: Allied Publishers, 1962), 76.

64 In his autobiography, M.K. Gandhi himself admitted that in the face of opposition by a phalanx of veteran leaders, such as Madan Mohan Malaviya, Chittaranjan Das and Lala Lajpat Rai, his 'plight' was 'pitiable' at the Calcutta session of the INC in 1920. See M.K. Gandhi. *An Autobiography or The Story of My Experiment With Truth* (Ahmedabad: Navajivan Publishing House, 1945), 266.

65 Nanda, *The Nehrus: Motilal and Jawaharlal*, 151.

66 Majumdar, *History of the Freedom Movement in India*, Vol. III, 156.

67 *Indian Annual Register* (Calcutta, 1921), 41.

68 Dutt, *India Today and Tomorrow*, 132.

69 D.G. Tendulkar, *Mahatma: Life of Mohandas Karamchand Gandhi*, Vol. II (Bombay: Vithalbhai K. Jhaveri, 1951), 46.

70 N.T. Abraham, R.S. Sabnis, A.N. Desai and K.U. Mada, *A Text Book of Economic History* (Bombay: A.R. Sheth and Company, 1964), 27.

71 P.A. Wadia and K.T. Merchant, *Our Economic Problem* (Bombay: New Book Company, 1950), 263.

72 Nehru, *The Discovery of India*, 360.

73 Ibid., 356, 360.

74 Ibid., 359.

75 Dutt, *India Today and Tomorrow*, 59. In another book, *Problems of Contemporary History*, Dutt remarked that the creation of a financial oligarchy revealed the disastrous effects of imperialism in as much as it 'pursues a policy of co-operation with the capitalists to paralyse the political will of the working class and prevent the advance of socialism'. See Dutt, *Problems of Contemporary History*, 96.

76 Wadia and Merchant, *Our Economic Problem*, 339.

77 Ibid., 380.

78 Ibid.

79 Ibid., 388.

80 Ibid., 380. Also see the *Report of the Indian Tariff Board, Cotton Textile Industry Enquiry Committee*, Vol. I (Calcutta: Government of India Central Publication Branch, 1927), 83.

81   Dutt, *India Today and Tomorrow*, 8–10.

82   For a detailed account of the strikes that took place during and after the First World War, see R.K. Das, *Labour Movement in India* (Berlin: Walter de Gruyter and Company), 1923.

83   B. Shiva Rao, *The Industrial Worker in India* (London: George Allen and Unwin, 1939), 13.

84   Nehru, *The Discovery of India*, 356.

85   Bandyopadhyaya, *Indian Nationalism Versus International Communism*, 243.

86   Rao, *The Industrial Worker in India*, 18–19.

87   L.P. Sinha, *Left Wing in India* (Muzaffarpur: New Publishers, 1965), 41.

88   Yusuf Meherally, ed., *Acharya Narendra Deva, Socialism and the National Revolution* (Bombay: Padma Publications, 1946), 60.

89   Edwardes, *The Last Years of British India*, 23.

90   Lala Lajpat Rai, *The Political Future of India* (New York, NY: B.W. Huebsch, 1919), 201.

91   Edwardes, *The Last Years of British India*, 12.

92   M.R. Masani, *The Communist Party of India—A Short History* (London: Derek Verschoyle, 1954), 15.

93   Dutt, *India Today and Tomorrow*, 105.

94   Nehru, *The Discovery of India*, 361.

95   Dutt, *India Today and Tomorrow*, 108.

96   K.M. Panikkar, *The Foundations of New India* (London: George Allen and Unwin, 1963), 86.

97   Ibid., 93–94.

98   For a detailed account of the impact of the Russian Revolution on the Indian people, the nationalist press and the Indian leaders, see Bandyopadhyaya, *Indian Nationalism Versus International Communism*, 116–48.

99   Roy, *Memoirs*, 233.

100   Lenin, *The National Liberation Movement in the East*, 223.

101   K.M. Panikkar, *Asia and Western Dominance* (London: George Allen and Unwin, 1953), p. 250.

102   Overstreet and Windmiller, *Communism in India*, 37–38.

103   Sinha, *Left Wing in India*, 59. Here, L.P. Sinha commented:

> An idea of how hazy and inadequate pictures of Russian Revolution and Bolshevism percolated through the press can be had on a perusal of Ram's [Ram Prasad Bismil] *Bolsheviks ki Kartut* [The Deeds of the Bolsheviks], a novel in Hindi published in October, 1920 …. Another book of this period to be noted is *Socialism—Its Embryonic Development in India*, by D. Pant, published from Lahore in 1919. The book is written in a confused way; one of its theses is that socialism has always been a part of Indian culture.

Ideologies and Orientations

NATURE AND GENESIS OF INDIAN LEFT

Leftism in India emerged out of the matrix of the Indian national movement. The starting point, therefore, for any attempt to elucidate its ideologies and orientations must be the fact that it was both a nationalist and a revolutionary movement. The Leftist movement was historically linked with India's struggle for freedom under the INC and the ideologue leadership that sprang within it was naturally shaped by the ideas and modulations of the early nationalist leaders. The Left-wing leadership within the INC concentrated its entire attention on national liberation and propagated radical socio-economic changes only as a means of strengthening the nation. They believed that national independence could be restored and the nation could flourish only through a radical socio-economic transformation. They were disillusioned with the conservative socio-economic ideas of the early nationalist leaders as well as with the 'anti-modern' philosophy of M.K. Gandhi who was not only opposed to any drastic change in the traditional social hierarchy, but also set his face against modern science, technology and industrialism. The growing number of intellectuals within the INC was intent upon radical socio-economic transformation of the country, but they did not want to cast off the intrinsic values of Indian life and society. Their response to the Marxian doctrine of class struggle was, therefore, lukewarm. They were attracted to the socialist ideology because it offered not only a programme of rapid socio-economic advancement but also provided an alternative to conservatism and capitalism. With the emergence of these intellectuals, therefore, Indian nationalism promised a more dynamic content, a more purposeful orientation and a more positive role in the liberation movement.

The communist variant of the Left wing, on the other hand, gave its attention more to propagating class struggle and proletarian internationalism than national liberation, thus neglecting a cause which would have been far more likely to fire the imagination of the mass of Indians. The First World War, it was believed, created the objective conditions for the overthrow of imperialism as a step towards the ultimate goal of world proletarian revolution, a goal more revolutionary and uncompromising than that of the radical nationalists. During the early years of the communist movement, their overriding concern was to form a revolutionary party—a vanguard of the proletariat—and to bring about a revolution under its leadership. But under the existing circumstances, this could hardly be done without identifying themselves with the nationalist cause and forging a common platform of struggle with the national bourgeoisie. Thus, the most crucial question that confronted them since the formation of the communist groups in the early 1920s was how to fit the precepts of proletarian internationalism into the ethos of Indian nationalism.

In short, although Leftism in India, in all its ramifications, whether inside the INC or as a projection of the international communist movement, had shared roots in the conditions of imperialism and as a reaction against the ideologies of the orthodox leadership of the INC, the various Left-wing groups differed from one another with respect to their tactics and ideological orientations towards India's struggle for freedom.

LEFT INSIDE CONGRESS

The Left wing inside the INC was, however, an amorphous body with leaders who were more attracted to socialist ideas than to the orthodox liberalism of the INC itself. Having found themselves in such a position, they did not consider themselves disloyal to the party. On the contrary, they believed that their departure from the orthodox INC ideology was an indication of the proud fact that the INC represented not only a broad cross section of the people but also different shades of political opinion. If they drew sustenance from socialist ideology, they believed that they did not betray the INC but endeavoured to redeem its objective of a fuller life for the people. To them, the INC symbolized the nation's aspirations for a fuller life and they owed themselves a duty to strengthen it for the fulfilment of this aspiration. Thus, the Left wing of the INC tended to express itself in two ways, one which might be termed an orthodox strain, and the other a radical strain, the former tending to uphold and preserve the existing ideals of the party and the latter tending to fit it with a revolutionary ideal which was to develop out of the prevailing order. But as Nehru confessed, the Left elements did not quite know how or when this new order would come to India. He, however, thought that every country would fashion it after its own way and fit it with its own genius keeping the essential basis of that order that would emerge out of the existing chaos.[1] This doubt and hesitation notwithstanding, there was a growing awareness among the radical elements of the inadequacy of the INC ideology in the context of the far-reaching revolutionary ideas all over the world. As pointed out by Nehru, the whole world was face-to-face with a vast question mark and every country and every people were in the melting pot. The age of faith was past and old certainties were under pressure. Everywhere there was doubt and restlessness and the foundations of the state and society were in a process of transformation. Old established ideas of liberty, justice, property and even the family were being attacked and the future hung in the balance. He said: 'We appear to be in a dissolving period of history, when the world is in labour and out of her [its] travail will give birth to a new order.'[2]

Thus, Leftism inside the INC was a complex phenomenon, an osmosis, which tended to develop along the mainstream of Indian nationalism and expressed itself through such ideas as socialism, anti-imperialism, internationalism, democracy and constitutionalism. National independence had been intended to serve as the basis for the realization of far-reaching socio-economic changes, which were not to be merely moderate reforms but to be so radical as to entail a revolution. In other words, Congress Leftism was bound up with a national ideal which required a broad-based socialistic environment for its fulfilment. Although the Congress socialists were walled in by the traditions and organization of the party, their radical ideas had grown organically in the prevailing political climate of the country. This was, indeed, one of the most significant developments in India's struggle for freedom.

The programme of socio-economic transformation contemplated by Left-wing Congressmen was to be based not on Gandhian socialism, which synthesized the philosophies of John Ruskin and Leo Tolstoy with the *vaishnava* ethics of non-possession and human equality, but on socialism in the Marxian sense of the term. According to Nehru, the theory of trusteeship advocated by Gandhi was 'barren' because it meant that the power for good or evil remained with the self-appointed trustee who could exercise it as he desired. The sole trusteeship, he pointed out, that could be fair was the trusteeship of the nation and not of one individual or a group. Many Englishmen honestly considered themselves the trustees for India and yet to what condition had they reduced the country! Therefore, the INC must decide for whose benefit industry must be run and land produce food. He lamented that in India the abundance that the land produced was not for the peasant or the labourer who worked on it and that industry's chief function was to produce millionaires. However golden the harvest and heavy the dividends, the mud huts and hovels and nakedness of the people testified to the glory of the British empire and the Indian social system. The economic programme of the INC must, therefore, be based on a human outlook and must not sacrifice man to money. If an industry, Nehru declared, could not be run without starving its workers, then the industry must close down and if the peasants had not enough to eat, then the intermediaries who deprived them of their full share must go.[3]

The Left-wing elements in the INC, most of whom belonged to the urban intelligentsia, were sceptical about Gandhian socialism which discarded the methods of industrialization and advocated the establishment of self-governing village *panchayats* (administrations) as the basis of an ideal society. And as they believed that only industrialization could improve the economic condition of the masses, they were deeply impressed by the Russian example of revolutionary socio-economic transformation brought about by a determined political leadership committed to the ideology of socialism.

The Congress socialists were attracted by Marxism, because it provided them with a philosophy, a dogma, a scientific method of studying the socio-economic problems and above all a concrete programme of action all of which contrasted with the traditional religious–metaphysical way of looking at things. Marxism taught them that all political phenomena were the reflection of economic forces and imperialism was the inevitable product of the economic system in which it originated, that is, capitalism. They were now convinced that the long course of history showed a succession of different forms of government and changing economic forms of production and organization. The two shaped and influenced each other and when economic change went ahead too fast and the forms of government remained more or less static, a hiatus occurred, which was bridged over by a sudden change called revolution.[4] In conformity with the Marxian analysis of history, the Congress socialists diagnosed the political subjection and economic degradation of India as the direct result of the capitalistic system of production and distribution. As Nehru pointed out, the question now was whether the capitalist system had outlived its day and must give place to a better and saner ordering of human affairs which was more in keeping with the progress of science and human knowledge. And it was clear enough, he said, that the capitalist system, whatever its services in the past might have been, was no longer suited to the present methods of production. Technical advance had outrun the existing social structure and this lag was responsible for most of the existing disorders. Until the lag was made up and a new system in keeping with the new technical advance was adopted, disorders were bound to continue. But this change to a new system was opposed by those who had vested interests in the old system and although this old system was dying before their eyes, they preferred to 'hold on to their little rather share a lot with others'.[5] The Left-wing intellectuals also came to realize that the capitalistic system of production and imperialist expansion had inevitably brought in their train a serious challenge from the growing forces of labour all over the world. This challenge, Nehru opined, had induced the possessing classes to sink their petty differences and band themselves together to fight for their survival. This had led to fascism and, in its milder form, to the formation of so-called national governments. In fact, these were the last-ditch efforts of the possessing classes to hold on to what they had. The struggle was becoming more and more intense and the forms of nineteenth-century democracy were being discarded. But fascism or national governments offered no solution to the fundamental economic inconsistencies of the capitalist system and so long as they did not remove the inequalities of wealth, they were doomed to fail.[6]

Unlike some early nationalists who believed that the continuation of the British connection in a progressively liberalized and mutually cooperative form was of great advantage to India,[7] the radical intellectuals refused to have any truck with Britain and for that matter with any other imperialist power.

While the former sought evolution of the British Raj into a mutually advantageous political order—a commonwealth[8]—the latter believed that there could be no true commonwealth so long as imperialism was its basis and the exploitation of other races were its chief means of sustenance. India could never be an equal partner of the commonwealth, Nehru argued, unless imperialism and all that it implied was discarded. So long as this was not done, India's position in the empire was bound to be one of subservience. The embrace of the British empire, he said, was a dangerous thing since it was not a life-giving embrace of affection freely given and returned, but an embrace of death. So long as there was the domination of one country over another or the exploitation of one class by another, no stable equilibrium could be achieved. Out of capitalism and imperialism, he declared, peace could never come. And it was because the British empire was based on the exploitation of the colonial people that India could find no peace in it. No gain that might come to India was worth anything unless it helped in removing the grievous burdens of the masses. Nehru concluded: 'The weight of a great empire is heavy to carry and long our people have endured it. Their backs are bent and down and their spirit has almost broken. How will they share in the commonwealth partnership if the burden of exploitation continues?'[9]

Taking lessons from the Marxian analysis of colonialism, the Congress socialists now came to realize that political freedom without economic emancipation of the masses was meaningless and that the national movement should be directed towards the liquidation of all vested interests, whether indigenous or foreign. Leaders and individuals might come and go, said Nehru, they might compromise or betray, but the exploited masses would carry on the struggle, for their drill sergeant was hunger. *Swaraj* for them was not a paper constitution or a problem of the hereafter. It was a question of here and now, of immediate relief. According to Nehru:

> Roast lamb and mint sauce, may be a tasty dish for those who eat it, but the poor lamb is not likely to appreciate the force of the best of arguments which point out the beauty of sacrifice for the good of the elect and joys of close communion, even though dead, with mint sauce.[10]

India's immediate goal, therefore, could only be considered in terms of the ending of the exploitation of its people. Politically, this meant complete independence and severance of the British connection, and economically and socially it meant the liquidation of all class privileges and vested interests. The whole world was struggling to that end and India could do no less. And it was in that way that India's struggle for freedom linked up with the world struggle. Nehru asked:

> Is our aim human welfare or the preservation of class privileges and the vested interests of pampered groups? The question must be answered clearly and unequivocally by each one of us. There is no room for quibbling when the fate of nations and millions of human beings is at stake.[11]

The one and only way of emancipating India from capitalist–imperialist exploitation and of creating a healthy political, economic and social order was to build a new India on the foundations of democracy and socialism. It was only through democratic socialism that the three principal maladies of the Indian body politic—political subjection, economic exploitation and social maladjustment—could be cured. As Nehru pointed out, the only key to the solution of the world's problems, including India's problems, lay in socialism, which was not only an economic doctrine but also a philosophy of life. There was no other way of ending the poverty, the vast unemployment, the degradation and subjection of the Indian people except through socialism, which involved revolutionary changes in the sociopolitical structure and the ending of vested interests in land and industry. It also meant the ending of private property, the replacement of the profit system by the higher ideal of cooperative service and a change in the human instincts, habits and desires. In short, it meant a new civilization, radically different from the existing capitalist order.[12]

In their anti-capitalist, anti-imperialist and revolutionary stance, the Congress socialists were clearly influenced by Marx; but their adherence to Marxism was only to a degree for, if the inspiration for a socialistic society came from Marx, intrinsically their ideology was rooted in the humanist and liberal tradition of India's past. And here we have a prime example of how an alien ideology was sought to be modified, remoulded and absorbed by the genius of Indian non-conformism.

The Congress socialists were anxious to remove inequality and exploitation, but their idea of social-ism was mainly based on the liberal experience of the nineteenth century. In contrast to Marxism, as interpreted by Lenin, which rejected the idea of gradualism and reform, they believed in the evolutionary transformation of society into a socialistic pattern. Their faith in gradualism and piecemeal social engi-neering was influenced by the study of British constitutional history, the achievements of the socialist movement in Britain and above all, the lessons of Fabianism.[13] They did not, therefore, blindly admire everything that happened in the Soviet Union. They believed in the basic economic theory which under-lay the social change in Russia but did not approve of everything that had taken place in that country—the ruthless suppression of all contrary opinion, the wholesale regimentation and unnecessary violence in carrying out socialist programme.[14] Thus, so far as civil rights and liberties were concerned, they were more attracted by Western liberalism than by the Marxian doctrine of proletarian dictatorship.[15] Socialism held out a new hope of an idyllic socio-economic order, a rationalist, secularist and scientific outlook as against the ethical, conservative and revivalist approach of the orthodox nationalist leaders. They accepted socialism as a goal but rejected the Marxian precept that there could be no socialism without violent revolution.[16]

Congress socialism, in fact, represented a complex assortment of ideologies including Marxism, Leninism, Fabian socialism and even some aspects of Gandhism and humanism. What distinguished the Congress socialists from the orthodox nationalists was that they sought to yoke socialism to the chariot of Indian nationalism.[17] This socialist orientation of Indian nationalism inevitably demanded a concrete programme which was to be 'socialist in action and objective'.[18] And as the Congress socialists felt that the INC could accept a socialist programme only in 'mutilated form', the responsibility for carrying on the struggle was bound to devolve upon the masses.[19]

The most strident criticism of a section of the Congress socialists came from the communists who described Congress socialism as a 'Left manoeuvre of the Indian bourgeoisie' and an example of 'social fascism'. But this was too brusque a judgement of the Congress socialists' predilection for the ideal of democracy. In fact, when one discards irrelevant hypotheses and misleading historical analogies and looks dispassionately at the underlying spirit of the Indian freedom movement, the ideological orientation of the Congress socialists ceases to be a Left manoeuvre of the Indian bourgeoisie. Drawing its inspiration mainly from Western liberalism and Fabian socialism and to a lesser extent from Marxism, Congress socialism had emerged by responding to the problems and requirements of the peculiar Indian situation. As pointed out by Thomas A. Rusch, the Congress Left wing was 'divided by three amorphous and overlapping tendencies—Marxism, social democracy of the British Labour Party type and a democratic socialism tempered by Gandhian concepts and the use of non-violent civil disobedience techniques of nationalist and class struggle'.[20] Although Congress socialism was receptive to such tenets of Gandhism as moderation and non-violence, it rejected his asceticism, traditionalism and the concept of village-based democracy. Like the communists, the Congress socialists recognized the class antagonism in the Indian society, the need for the liquidation of inequality and exploitation, rapid industrialization and the paramount role of the state in bringing this about. They, however, discarded the communist methods of coercion, insurrection, violent overthrow of the existing order and the dictatorship of the proletariat.[21] They stood for a revolution by consent, a revolution without fear.

LEFT'S DISILLUSION WITH GANDHIAN POLITICS

In striking contrast to Congress socialism, communism in India had not grown organically in the country's own political and spiritual climate. It came to India when a section of radical nationalists, utterly diss-atisfied with the leadership of Gandhi, started grouping for a more militant ideology and found in the Marxist–Leninist revolutionary doctrine an answer to Gandhism. When the Non-Cooperation Movement was suspended by Gandhi, consequent on the outbreak of violence at Chauri Chaura, these extremist elements felt themselves betrayed and blamed Gandhi for 'pandering to the government'.[22] Since that day, many of them permanently lost faith in Gandhi and his technique of non-violent struggle. M.N. Roy observed: 'If India will not have freedom conquered by violent means, she [it] will have to go without it.'[23] Castigating the Gandhian principle of non-violence, Evelyn Roy also wrote:

> That three hundred million Indians will cheerfully endure all kicks and insults, all hunger and nakedness, all poverty and wretchedness at the hands of their exploiters, until these, touched and overcome by such a demonstration of man's innate divinity, will respond to it by throwing away their machineguns and fleshpots, their treasure hoards and princely power, and will welcome their three hundred million brethren to a new fraternity of man where liberty and equality will rule the human race under the aegis of perfect love…. Non-violence, resignation, perfect love and release from the pain of living—this is the substance of Indian philosophy handed down through the ages by a powerful caste of kings, priests and philosophers who found it good to keep the people in subjection. Mr Gandhi is nothing but the heir to this long line of ghostly ancestors; he is the perfect product of heredity and environment. His philosophy of *satyagraha* is the inevitable fruit of its spiritual forebears. What is unfortunate is that Mr Gandhi's revived philosophy of the other worldliness coincides with the most unprecedented growth…of a spirit of revolt against material privation, on the part of the Indian masses.[24]

Imbued with the teachings of Marx, these radical nationalists had not only broken with Gandhi's cult of non-violence but also found that their newly acquired ideas were absolutely incompatible with the whole range of Gandhian theories and attitudes. M.N. Roy, perhaps the first communist writer to present a Marxist appraisal of Gandhi, identified him with the feudal class interests of India. He found in Gandhi and his principles an 'unerring instinct for safeguarding class-interests' and averred:

> This strong instinct of preserving property rights above all betrays the class affiliation of Gandhi, in spite of his pious outbursts against the sordid materialism of modern civilization. His hostility to capitalist society is manifestly not revolutionary but reactionary. He believes in the sanctity of private property, but seeks to prevent its inevitable evolution to capitalism.[25]

R. Palme Dutt also identified the INC leadership of Gandhi with the petty-bourgeois elements which 'wished on the one hand to stand forward as leaders of the masses, but also feared to break with the propertied interests of the bourgeoisie'.[26] The leaders of the international communist movement also held identical views on Gandhi and Gandhism. In an article entitled 'The Constitution for the Enslavement of the Indian People and the Policy of the Indian Bourgeoisie' in the *Communist International*, Valia observed that Gandhian teachings represented 'the cowardly antirevolutionary bourgeoisie, linked up with the landlord system and in deadly fear of a national revolution'.[27] P.C. Joshi, another communist intellectual, summed up Gandhism as the 'outlook of negation, the policy of passivity and the practice of subservience'.[28]

MARXIAN INTERPRETATION OF INDIAN SITUATION

Communism originally came to India as a body of ideas intended to provide an ideological leaven to India's liberation movement. But before long, Indian communism became deeply involved in the international communist movement controlled at that time by the Communist International. Consequently, its ideology and orientation developed around the Marxian doctrines of class struggle, dictatorship of the proletariat, liberation of the dependent peoples and proletarian internationalism on the basis of an alliance of the working class and the peasantry. And it was with these ideologies that Gandhism was to be combated and a socialist revolution in India was to be achieved.[29]

Applying the dicta of Marx that the history of all hitherto existing societies was the history of class struggle,[30] that the existence of classes was bound up with particular phases in the development of production, that the class struggle would inevitably lead to the dictatorship of the proletariat and that the dictatorship constituted the transition to the abolition of all classes and ultimately to a classless society,[31] to contemporary history, the communists found an inherent class contradiction in Indian society and felt that the Indian national movement arose from the social and economic forces generated within Indian society under the conditions of this contradiction. They came to believe that the bourgeoisie had once functioned as the national class that is the class which represented the interest of the whole of society as against its retrograde members.

> For the proletariat to aim at political power meant that it must prove its ability to take over the bourgeoisie's role as the socially-progressive class, and to this end it must take the lead in reorganizing society. Failure to rise to this level would count as evidence that the working class was not yet ready to play the part for which history had cast it.[32]

In his first book, entitled *India in Transition*,[33] M.N. Roy attempted to interpret the contemporary Indian situation by using the laws of historical development of society set forth by Marx. He pointed out that India had passed through different stages of social evolution analogous to those in the West, although as a result of variable physical and climatic conditions, slavery, feudalism and even capitalism, has assumed somewhat modified forms.[34] Rejecting the theory, then widely prevalent among a section of Marxists, that India's socio-economic structure was feudal in character, Roy observed that the prevailing Indian condition was characterized by the rising bourgeoisie, which allowed only a little participation in the economic opportunities opened up by the growing industrialization of the country, had started political agitation against British rule in India. Corresponding to this growth of bourgeois nationalism had been the awakening of the masses to an unprecedented political consciousness. The development of the bourgeoisie, he pointed out, stiffened the national struggle as well as intensified the class cleavage by creating a proletariat class. Thus, according to Roy, the bourgeois-nationalist movement in India had its origin in the desire of the nascent bourgeoisie to augment its own class interest and as such it had grown as an appendage of British imperialism.[35] But the bourgeoisie was well aware of the fact that its bargaining strength vis-à-vis the imperialists ultimately depended on its ability to make a common cause with the revolutionary mass movement. This posed a dilemma to the bourgeoisie for it was also haunted by the fear that the emergence of the working class as a formidable revolutionary force might eventually destroy its own existence. On the other hand, the imperialists, afraid of the possibility of coalescence between the bourgeoisie and the masses which might drive them out of their imperial domain, made all sorts of concessions to the bourgeoisie in order to wean it away from the truculent masses. This made the bourgeoisie to capitulate and compromise. It could not, therefore, be expected to play any revolutionary role in India's struggle against imperialism. Roy, however, recognized the revolutionary significance of the conflict between imperialism and bourgeois nationalism and wrote:

> Unless the bourgeoisie came into existence and became leaders of the society, the national struggle cannot take place with all its revolutionary possibilities. So in all these countries in proportion as the bourgeoisie is developing, the national struggle has become intensified. From this point of view, although we know there is danger of the colonial bourgeoisie always compromising with the imperial bourgeoisie, we must

on principle stand for them … a bourgeois-national movement in the colonial countries is objectively revolutionary, therefore it should be given support; but we should not overlook the fact that this objective force cannot be accepted as unconditional, and that particular historical reasons should be taken into consideration. The bourgeoisie becomes a revolutionary factor when it raises the standard of revolt against backward, antiquated forms of society, that is, when the struggle is fundamentally against the feudal order, the bourgeoisie leading the people. Then the bourgeoisie is the vanguard of the revolution.[36]

Roy also maintained that the most serious defect of bourgeois nationalism in India championed by the INC was that it had neither an ideology nor a revolutionary programme. It was deeply rooted in obscurantist, religious and revivalist ideas which found their culmination in the philosophy of Gandhi, 'the acutest and most desperate manifestation of the forces of reaction'.[37] He, therefore, averred that the 'impending wane of Gandhism' following the collapse of the Non-Cooperation Movement signified the collapse of the reactionary forces and their total elimination from the political movement. The INC under Gandhi's leadership was a reactionary organization which could not lead a revolutionary struggle against imperialism. A political party, Roy argued, was of no importance without a programme because in that case it could not count upon the conscious support of any social element. Therefore, if the INC was to be a political party, it had to base itself on one or another of the three principal classes into which Indian society was divided. It must either be the party of the landlords or of the propertied upper and middle classes or of the exploited workers and peasants. And its programme would show which class it represented.[38] Roy then suggested that the revolutionary elements believing in revolutionary mass action should form an opposition bloc within the INC which would eventually grow into a revolutionary party of the people 'destined to be the leader of the final struggle'. It would be necessary for this party to put forth a programme calculated to give fresh impetus to the waning enthusiasm of the masses and to draw them into the political struggle.[39]

Roy's thesis on the class character of bourgeois nationalism in India and the role of social forces in the liberation movement was further elaborated in his book *The Future of Indian Politics*. Here, he contended that the bourgeois bloc sought to make a united front with the imperialist forces to safeguard their interests against any possible revolution. And as the middle class, which made a show of constitutional fight was in hopeless political bankruptcy, the future of Indian politics would be determined by the social forces which would always remain antagonistic to imperialism 'even in the new era dominated by the higher ideals of *swaraj* within the empire'. These social forces were composed of the workers, peasants, students and the petty bourgeoisie, that is, small traders, employees, petty intellectuals and so on. In the existing condition of the Indian society, he said, all these belonged to the exploited class and the national liberation movement would take place on the basis of the struggle between these exploited classes and their exploiters.[40] Roy then added that this fight against exploitation must be led by a party of the people which would be broad enough for all the forces of national revolution. The proletariat would be in it though it would not be a proletarian party. In this party, the proletariat would stand side by side with the petty bourgeois and peasant masses as the most advanced democratic class.[41]

This revolutionary struggle of the oppressed people against the exploiters, both native and imperial, would be fought on an international scale irrespective of national boundaries because, as Marx pointed out, the working people had no country.[42] The communists, Marx declared, must bear in mind that in the national struggle of the proletarians of different countries, their duty was to bring to the front the common interests of the entire proletariat, independent of all nationality; and 'in the various stages of the development which the struggle of the working class against the bourgeoisie has to pass through', they always and everywhere represented the interests of the movement as a whole.[43] This struggle of the exploited people, under the leadership of the communist party, would be aimed at organizing the forces of the proletariat for the revolutionary onslaught on the forces of exploitation and for the final victory of socialism.[44] But the victory of socialism could not be complete until and unless it was achieved in every part of the globe. Therefore, the success of the socialist revolution in one country was to be regarded not as an isolated event but as a step towards the victory of the proletariat in all countries. Lenin declared: 'When the Bolshevik Party tackled the job alone, took it entirely into its own hands, we were convinced that the revolution was maturing in all countries and that in the end ... the international socialist revolution would come.'[45] This international perspective of the Russian Revolution was further elucidated by Joseph Stalin when he said that the revolution which had been successful in one country must be regarded not as a self-sufficient entity but as an aid; a means for hastening the victory of the proletariat in all countries. For, the victory of the revolution in one country was not only the product of the uneven development and progressive decay of imperialism but also the beginning and the groundwork for world revolution. The significance of the Bolshevik Revolution, he declared, lay in the fact that it constituted the first stage of world revolution. The Bolshevik Revolution had laid the powerful base for the world revolutionary movement and created the open centre around which the oppressed people of all countries would organize a united revolutionary front against imperialism.[46]

This supreme objective of proletarian internationalism was also embodied in the statute of the Communist International which declared that the international association of workers was established to organize joint action by the proletariat of the different countries to overthrow capitalism and to establish an international Soviet Republic which would completely abolish all classes and realize socialism, the first stage of communist society.[47] The statute declared:

> The task of the Communist International is to liberate the working people of the entire world .... [It] supports to the full the conquests of the great proletarian revolution in Russia, the first victorious socialist revolution in the world history, and calls on the proletariat of the entire world to take the same path ... [it] undertakes to support every Soviet Republic, wherever it may be formed ... [it] must, in fact and deed, be a single communist party of the entire world. The parties working in the different countries are but its separate sections.[48]

The first congress of the Communist International, held in March 1919, issued a manifesto to the proletariat of the whole world and proclaimed its programme for the emancipation of the colonial countries. It declared that the emancipation of the colonies was possible only in conjunction with the emancipation of the metropolitan working class. The workers and peasants not only in Amman, Algiers and Bengal but also in Persia and Armenia would gain their opportunity of independent existence only when the workers of England and France had overthrown Lloyd George and Georges Clemenceau and captured state power into their own hands. The manifesto further added that the 'small peoples' could be assured the opportunity of free existence only by the proletarian revolution which would liberate the productive forces of all countries from the constraint of the nation–state and unite the peoples in closest economic collaboration on the basis of a common economic plan. It warned that if capitalist Europe forcibly dragged the backward sections of the world into the capitalist whirlpool, then socialist Europe would come to the aid of liberated colonies with its technology, organization and spiritual forces to facilitate their transition to a planned socialist economy.[49]

In his 'Draft Theses on National and Colonial Questions', Lenin pointed out that the cornerstone of the whole policy of the Communist International must be closer union of the proletarian and working classes of all countries for a united struggle for the overthrow of the landlords and the bourgeoisie; and that the colonial countries could achieve national liberation only in alliance with the Soviet Union.[50] Explaining the point, Stalin observed that a coalition between the proletarian revolution in Europe and the colonial revolution in the East in a worldwide united front against imperialism was inevitable. It was formerly the accepted idea, he said, that the only method of liberating the oppressed nations was the method of bourgeois nationalism. But one of the important results of the Bolshevik Revolution was that it dealt that myth a mortal blow, having demonstrated in practice the possibility and expedience of the proletarian method of liberating the oppressed nations as the only correct method.[51]

The principal method of the revolutionary struggle of the working class all over the world could not be peaceful. Marx declared in the *Communist Manifesto*: 'The communists disdain to conceal their views and aims. They openly declare that their ends can be attained only by the forcible overthrow of all existing social conditions.'[52] All revolutionary people, therefore, must learn to wage people's war against imperialism and the bourgeoisie; they must learn to take up arms, to fight battles and become skilled in civil war and insurrection. An oppressed class which did not strive to learn the use of arms, to acquire arms, deserved to be treated like slaves.[53] Explaining the nature and technique of insurrectionary war, Lenin said:

> To be successful, insurrection must rely not upon a part, but upon the advanced class. That is the second point. Insurrection must rely upon the critical moment in the history of the growing revolution, when the activity of the advanced ranks of the people is at its height, when the vacillations in the ranks of the enemies and in the ranks of the weak, half-hearted and the irresolute friends of the revolution are strongest. That is the third point. All these three conditions in the attitude towards insurrection distinguished Marxism from Blanquism.[54]

Not a single revolution in history, Lenin further added, had ever been carried out without a civil war and no serious Marxist would believe it possible to make the transition from capitalism to socialism without a civil war.[55]

The violent overthrow of capitalism, said Marx, would inevitably lead to the dictatorship of the proletariat.[56] In his letter to the workers and peasants in connection with the victory over Kolchak, Lenin declared:

> Either the dictatorship [that is the iron rule] of the landowners and capitalists or the dictatorship of the working class. There is no middle course. The scions of the aristocracy, the intellectualist, and other doubtful characters, badly educated on bad books, dream of a middle course. There is no middle course anywhere in the world, nor can there be. Either the dictatorship of the bourgeoisie [masked by ornate socialist-revolutionary and Menshevik phraseology, about a people's government, a Constituent Assembly, liberties and the like] or the dictatorship of the proletariat. He who has not learned this from the whole history of the nineteenth century is a hopeless idiot.[57]

Thus, according to Lenin, only he was a true Marxist who extended the acceptance of the class struggle to the acceptance of the dictatorship of the proletariat.[58] The dictatorship of the proletariat, explained Stalin, was the rule 'unrestricted by law and based on force, of the proletariat over the bourgeoisie'.[59]

Thus, Marxism represented a movement and a body of doctrine—the doctrine of violent revolution. At the Meerut Conspiracy trial Philip Spratt declared:

> It seems to me that we who are communists need not apologize, we need not be careful to disguise the brutal blood-thirsty side of our proposals. We say these things are inevitable. Modern society is based upon fierce brutality, and if we want to get rid of it we have to use fierce brutality .... We shall not disguise the fact that in the course of attainment of our aims and the establishment of communism, we shall have to indulge in brutal dictatorial methods. We shall have to indulge in civil war in most countries.[60]

Thus, the new world of revolutionary ideas opened to the extreme nationalists by Marxian doctrines led them to believe that freedom must develop dimensions other than the nationalist if it were to be meaningful to the millions of exploited Indians. The subsequent chapters would show, however, that this belief was yet to come out of the thin layer of the middle-class intelligentsia and find an echo in the teeming millions walled in by traditional conceptions of life and society and firm in their adherence to the pre-existing ideas and values of Indian nationalism. The overthrow of the Tsarist tyranny, especially the radical socio-economic changes brought about by the Bolsheviks, no doubt struck the imagination of the Indian people. But the Leftist awakening in even the educated few was at such a nascent stage that they were yet to be in a position to properly interpret on their own the core ideological postulates of communism in the Indian context. And it was for this reason that communism remained alien to the commoners in India at that time and its foundation was laid on a narrow base—like an overturned pyramid.

NOTES AND REFERENCES (CHAPTER 2)

1   Jawaharlal Nehru's presidential address to the INC in Lucknow session, April 1936. *India's Freedom* (London: George Allen and Unwin, 1965), 36.
2   Jawaharlal Nehru's presidential address to the INC in Lahore session, December 1929. *India's Freedom*, 8.
3   Jawaharlal Nehru, *India's Freedom*, 15–16. When M.K. Gandhi declared: 'If there is a genuine real clash [of interests], I have no hesitation in saying, on behalf of the Congress [INC], that the Congress [INC] will sacrifice everything for the sake of the interests of these dumb millions', the radical elements inside the Congress [INC] pointed out that the expression 'if' clearly showed Gandhi's hesitation to recognize a class conflict between labour and capital, tenants and landlords. While replying to this criticism, Gandhi remarked: 'I know that I am not keeping pace with the march of events. There is, therefore, a hiatus between the rising generation and me'. See Pattabhi Sitaramayya, *The History of the Indian National Congress*, Vol. I (Bombay: Padma Publications, 1946), 735. *Indian Annual Register*, Vol. II (Calcutta, 1929), 14.
4   Nehru, 'Whither India?' in *India's Freedom* (London: George Allen and Unwin, 1965), 23.
5   Ibid., 26.
6   Ibid., 28.
7   Ray T. Smith, 'The Indian Liberals and Constitutionalism in India', in *Studies in Indian Democracy*, ed. S.P. Aiyar and R. Srinivasan (Bombay: Allied Publishers, 1965), 30.
8   Amvika Charan Mazumdar, *Indian National Evolution—A Brief Survey of the Origin and Progress of the Indian National Congress and the Growth of Indian Nationalism* (Madras: G.A. Natesan and Company, 1917), 431–33.
9   Nehru, *India's Freedom*, 12.
10   Ibid., 32.
11   Ibid.
12   Jawaharlal Nehru's presidential address to the INC in Lucknow session, April 1936. *India's Freedom* (London: George Allen and Unwin, 1965), 35. Here it is interesting to note the following observation of Nehru:

> … while I accepted the fundamentals of the socialist theory, I did not trouble myself about its numerous inner controversies. I had little patience with Leftist groups in India, spending much of their energy in mutual conflict and recrimination over fine points of doctrine which did not interest me at all. Life is too complicated, too illogical for it to be confined within the four corners of a fixed doctrine.

Also see Jawaharlal Nehru, *The Discovery of India* (London: Meridian Books, 1956), 17.
13   Sibnarayan Ray, 'Socialism in India', in *Studies in Indian Democracy*, ed. S.P. Aiyar and R. Srinivasan (Bombay: Allied Publishers, 1965), 47–48.
14   Jawaharlal Nehru, *Eighteen Months in India: 1936–1937* (Allahabad: Kitabistan, 1938), 13; and *An Autobiography* (Bombay: Allied Publishers, 1962), 361.
15   K.M. Panikkar, 'Marx—The Two Faces: Socialist and Communist', in *The Foundations of New India* (London: George Allen and Unwin, 1963), 189–90.
16   It should be noted here that although the Indian socialists disliked some of the happenings in the Soviet Union, they, on the whole, admired the achievements brought about by the new regime. As pointed out by Jayaprakash Narayan:

> When with test tubes mistakes cannot be avoided, much less can they be avoided when you are experimenting with millions of men and one-sixth of the globe …. Let not the Russians' mistakes blind us to their great

achievements .... Let wise parlour philosophers grin over them and shake their sceptic little heads. For us who are to do things, who have a task before us, it is the practising that alone is of value.

See Jayaprakash Narayan, *Why Socialism?* (Benaras: CSP, 1936), 57.

17 L.P. Sinha, *Left Wing in India* (Muzaffarpur: New Publishers, 1965), 329.

18 *Indian Annual Register* (Calcutta, 1934), 341. Also see, Nehru, *Eighteen Months in India: 1936–1937*, 36.

19 Yusuf Meherally, ed., *Acharya Narendra Deva, Socialism and the National Revolution* (Bombay: Padma Publications, 1946), 3.

20 Thomas A. Rusch, 'Dynamics of Socialist Leadership in India', in *Leadership and Political Institutions in India*, ed. Richard L. Park and Irene Tinker (Madras: Oxford University Press, 1960), 189.

21 Ray, 'Socialism in India', 48.

22 Jawaharlal Nehru, *Nehru on Gandhi* (New York, NY: John Day Company, 1948), 38–39.

23 M.N. Roy, *The Aftermath of Non-Cooperation: Indian Nationalism and Labour Politics* (London: CPGB, 1926), 118.

24 M.N. Roy and Evelyn Roy, *One Year of Non-Cooperation: From Ahmedabad to Gaya* (Calcutta: CPI, 1923), 48–50.

25 M.N. Roy, *India in Transition* (Geneva: J.B. Target, 1922), 236.

26 R. Palme Dutt, *Modern India* (London: CPGB, 1927), 81.

27 Valia, 'The Constitution for the Enslavement of the Indian People and the Policy of the Indian Bourgeoisie', *Communist International*, Vol. X, (15 June 1933), 390. It may be noted here that the communists intensely disliked such resolutions of the INC as: 'The Working Committee [CWC] assures the *zamindars* [landlords] that the Congress [INC] movement is in no way intended to attack their legal rights and that even where *ryots* have grievances, the committee [CWC] desires that redress be sought by mutual consultation and arbitration'. See Sitaramayya, *The History of the Indian National Congress*, Vol. I, 392.

28 P.C. Joshi, *The Indian Communist Party: Its Policy and Work in the War of Liberation* (London: CPGB, 1942), 267.

29 It is interesting to note here that in 1927, Harold Laski, the most distinguished British Labour Party theoretician and political scientist of his time, remarked: '...the effort to read the problem of India in the set terms of Marxism is rather an exercise in ingenuity than a serious intellectual contribution to socialist advance'. See R. Palme Dutt, *India Today and Tomorrow* (Delhi: People's Publishing House, 1955), 31.

30 Karl Marx and Friedrich Engels, *Selected Works*, Vol. I (Moscow: Foreign Languages Publishing House, 1955), 34.

31 Karl Marx and Friedrich Engels, *Selected Correspondence* (Moscow: Foreign Languages Publishing House, 1965), 69. In their famous 'circular letter' to A. Babel, W. Liebknecht, W. Bracke and others, Marx and Engels wrote:

> As for ourselves, in view of our whole past there is only one road open to us. For almost forty years we have stressed the class struggle as the immediate driving force of history, and in particular the class struggle between bourgeoisie and proletariat as the great lever of the modern social revolution.

Ibid., 327.

32 George Lichtheim, *Marxism: An Historical and Critical Study* (London: Routledge and Kegan Paul, 1961), 87. Lichtheim further added:

> ... Marxism always implied that the rise to power of the working class would bring about a total reorganization of society. This conclusion followed because the labour movement represented a higher form of social organization rendered possible by the development of the productive forces beyond the point compatible with capitalism.

Ibid., 87–88.

33 This book, written in collaboration with Abani Mukherjee, was published in 1922. It was printed in Berlin but published from Geneva in the name of a fictitious publisher. About the impact of the book in India and abroad, Roy observed in his *Memoirs*:

> In spite of all difficulties the book was widely read by many serious students of contemporary history. All were much impressed. The pioneers of the Communist Party of India [CPI] had all their first lessons in applied Marxism, and indeed in revolutionary politics, from this book. Subsequently, they denounced me as a renegade. But that is the ethics of communism, which was one of the main reasons for me to part company

with the immoral cult …. A professor of history in Finland and another in Argentina expressed the identical opinion that the book was the first realistic picture of modern India available to critical and discerning readers.

See M.N. Roy, *Memoirs* (Bombay: Allied Publishers, 1964), 555.

34 Roy, *India in Transition*, 96. For Marx's theory of social development, see Marx and Engels, *Selected Correspondence*, 96.

35 In line with this analysis of Roy, Eugene Varga, in the famous article entitled 'Economics and Economic Policy in the Fourth Quarter of 1927', argued that the Indian bourgeoisie had launched an attack on the British regime only to improve its own 'position within the empire' and its struggle was not a 'revolutionary fight against British imperialism'. See *International Press Correspondence* (14 March 1928), 294.

36 *Advance Guard* (Zurich, 15 January 1923), 3.

37 Roy, *India in Transition*, 205.

38 *Advance Guard* (Zurich, 1 November 1922), 3.

39 *Advance Guard* (Zurich, 1 December 1922), 2.

40 M.N. Roy, *The Future of Indian Politics* (London: R. Bishop, 1926), 90–95.

41 Ibid., 114.

42 Marx and Engels, *Selected Works*, Vol. I, 51. It may be mentioned here that in reply to the contention of Maulana Hasrat Mohani and Malaypuram Singaravelu Chettiar that the struggle of the Indian working people was purely Indian in character, M.N. Roy replied:

> Nothing can be more non-communistic than to say that the Indian working class will play its historic role in the struggle for national freedom and work out its salvation independently of the international proletarian movement. Those who maintain and propagate this point of view are far from being communists—they are the veritable enemies of the Indian working class.

See *Masses of India*, March 1926, 6.

43 Marx and Engels, *Selected Works*, Vol. I, 46.

44 V.I. Lenin, *Collected Works*, Vol. XVIII (Moscow: Progress Publishers, 1968), 89.

45 V.I. Lenin, *Selected Works*, Vol. II (Moscow: Foreign Languages Publishing House, 1947), 297.

46 Joseph Stalin, *Problems of Leninism* (Moscow: Foreign Languages Publishing House, 1947), 120–23, 202.

47 Gunther Nollau, *International Communism and World Revolution: History and Methods* (London: Hollis and Carter, 1961), 336.

48 Ibid., 335–36.

49 Jane Degras, *The Communist International Documents, 1919–1943*, Vol. I (London: Oxford University Press, 1956), 42–43.

50 Lenin, *Selected Works*, Vol. II, 655.

51 Stalin, *Problems of Leninism*, 30, 201.

52 Marx and Engels, *Selected Works*, Vol. I, 65. Emphasizing the violent nature of the communist revolution, Mao Tse-Tung also said: 'We are the advocates of the omnipotence of the revolutionary war …. With the help of guns the Russian communists brought about socialism … the whole world can be remoulded only with the gun'. See Mao Tse-Tung, *Selected Works*, Vol. II (Peking: Foreign Languages Press, 1965), 225.

53 Lenin, *Selected Works*, Vol. I, 728.

54 Ibid., Vol. II, 120.

55 Lenin, *Collected Works*, Vol. XXVIII, 457.

56 Marx and Engels, *Selected Correspondence*, 15.

57 V.I. Lenin, *Alliance of the Working Class and the Peasantry* (Moscow: Progress Publishers, 1965), 293.

58 Lenin, *Selected Works*, Vol. II, 163.

59 Stalin, *Problems of Leninism*, 43.

60 Meerut Sessions Court, Judgement delivered by R.L. Yorke, Esq., I.C.S., Additional Sessions Judge, Meerut, on 16th January 1933, in the Meerut Communist Conspiracy Case. Sessions Trial No. 2 of 1930. *King Emperor Versus P. Spratt and Others*, Vols. I–II (Simla: Government of India Press, 1932–33), 225.

About the relevance of violent revolution and dictatorship of the proletariat to India's struggle for freedom, Jayantanuja Bandyopadhyaya observed:

> … for a long time the level of political articulation was rather low in India, and large sections of Indian opinion were swayed by the superficial resemblances between some of the ideals of Indian nationalism and of international communism. They were especially impressed by the policies of anti-imperialism, anti-racialism and proletarian internationalism …. But on some fundamental questions, especially those of dictatorship and the use of force, Indian nationalism stood uncompromisingly firm and eventually brought about the frustration of international communism in India.

See Jayantanuja Bandyopadhyaya, *Indian Nationalism Versus International Communism* (Calcutta: Firma K.L. Mukhopadhyay, 1966), 92.

3   Communism in India

A. EARLY YEARS OF THE COMMUNIST MOVEMENT: FORMATION OF CPI

THE FIRST WORLD WAR, HINDU–GERMAN CONSPIRACY AND RISE OF M.N. ROY

The history of Indian contacts with the international communist movement and the formation of the CPI abroad is a long and fascinating story. A good starting point is in the heady days of the First World War when a section of militant nationalists realized the naivety and futility of sporadic terrorism and felt that it was only with external assistance that an organized national revolutionary movement could be brought about and the country's independence won. This tempting vision called a generation of brave young men to revolutionary adventures. A large number of them left India as emissaries of revolutionary nationalism and set out in quest of arms and money for liberating their country from alien rule.

But the quest for financial and material support for a war of independence had started some years before war broke out in Europe. After the Alipore Bomb Case in 1908, a group of revolutionaries left India and found shelter in Germany and the United States. Chief among these emissaries who travelled through the Western world in search of support from foreign governments were Lala Har Dayal, Virendranath Chattopadhyaya, Abdul Hafiz Mohamed Barkatullah, Abani Mukherjee, Surendranath Kar, Bhupendranath Datta and many others. But apart from organizing revolutionary groups in various parts of the world, their mission remained unfulfilled because these handful of young men, intrepid and devoted though they were, could convince no government that they could really overthrow an empire.[1]

When the war broke out in 1914, a rare opportunity for the fulfilment of their mission presented itself to these revolutionaries. The time had come, they thought, to get the Germans on their side and to deliver a mortal blow to British rule in India. The gathering darkness in Europe justified their expectation of a coming storm in India.

Believing that the favourable conditions created by the war had brought them to the very threshold of success, the revolutionaries in Berlin promptly came out with a pamphlet soliciting German cooperation in the final onslaught against the common enemy. Their appeal did not fall on deaf ears, for the revolutionaries were immediately invited for consultation. Meanwhile, Har Dayal, the most prominent member of the Ghadr Party in California, travelled from Switzerland to Berlin and was asked to take charge of the organization known as the Indian Independence Committee in Berlin.[2] After discussions with the revolutionaries, the German government finally decided to patronize an armed uprising in India. It was agreed that the money given to the Indians would be regarded as a national loan to be repaid after India becomes free, that the German government would supply arms through its diplomatic missions abroad and that Turkey would be urged to join hands with Germany so that the Indian Muslims could be enthused to take up arms against the British.[3]

The German assurance had stimulated revolutionary activities in India and abroad to a new fever of intensity. At the call of the Indian Independence Committee, hundreds of student revolutionaries abroad began to return home to help smuggle German arms and money into India. On their way home through Persia, Kedarnath Sealuddin, Basanta Singh and a few others fell prey to British agents and lost their lives. Heramba Lal Gupta and Chandra Chakraberty were entrusted with the task of procuring arms from the United States where in September 1914, 8,080 Springfield rifles, 2,400 carbines, 4,000,000 rounds of ammunition and assorted other weapons were purchased.[4] Barkatullah met the Indian soldiers who were taken prisoner by Germany and incited them to take up arms against Britain. After the Battle of the Marne when the German plan of inflicting a crushing blow to France was foiled by General Ferdinand Foch, the Germans became more and more intent on helping the Indian revolutionaries in their attempt to overthrow British rule in India. On 10 April 1915, Raja Mahendra Pratap,[5] along with Barkatullah and General Von der Goltz, went to Afghanistan on a 'mission of conquering India'. There, the Provisional Government of India was formed on 1 December 1915, with Mahendra Pratap as president, Barkatullah as prime minister and Ubaidullah Sindhi as home minister. While in Kabul, they gained the release of the arrested Indians who had come to Afghanistan from India. Chief among them was Mohammad Ali who became the secretary of the provisional government and later took an active part in the Indian communist movement.

The nerve centre of Hindu-German conspiracy (also known as Indo-German conspiracy) in the East was Java, the nearest neutral country to India. As transporting arms and money all the way from Germany to India was out of the question, it was decided that the Germans should deliver the arms to the Indian revolutionaries in Java. Accordingly, an elaborate plan was worked out in the United States in collaboration with the Ghadr Party leaders for the shipment of a large consignment of arms in the SS *Maverick*. Five Indians escorting the precious cargo left San Diego in the *Annie Larsen*, which was to rendezvous with the *Maverick* off the coast of lower California. But *Annie Larsen's* tryst with the *Maverick* did never take place because when the former failed to turn up in time, the latter, afraid to stay too long, sailed on.[6]

Meanwhile in India, the news of German promise of arms and money 'spread like wildfire' and many believed that revolution was 'round the corner'. The imminence of the attainment of national independence induced several secret revolutionary organizations to abandon their traditional feuds and clandestine conferences led to the formation of a general staff of the coming revolution, with Jatin Mukherjee as the commander-in-chief. The job of finding money for the initial expenditure was entrusted to M.N. Roy who left for Java before the end of 1914. He returned within two months 'with some money, not much; but as regards arms, the coveted cargo of the *Golden Fleece*—it was a wild goose chase. They failed to arrive, because, as it was discovered later, the whole plan was a hoax, a veritable swindle.'[7]

But 'youthful enthusiasm, thoughtless optimism and above all, faith in the liberating mission of Germany' were not so easily daunted. They resolved to try again, a new plan was made and Roy left India for the second time early in 1915 in search of the precious cargo, which he fondly believed, was floating somewhere in the Pacific Ocean. But as it happened, he did not return until 16 years had passed.[8] And when he returned, he brought with him arms of a different kind. G.D. Parikh said:

He had come back, with a vision and with ideas, with a devotion to freedom and justice which while mobilising the Indian people against British imperialism would also arouse them against their native exploiters. He had outgrown the naive inspiration of colonial nationalism. The new world of ideas and values opened to him by Marxism led him to insist that freedom must develop dimensions other than the nationalist if it were to be meaningful to millions of his countrymen.[9]

The original name of Manabendra Nath Roy (M.N. Roy) was Narendranath Bhattacharya. He was born on 6 February 1889, in a priestly family in Arbelia, a village in 24 Parganas, Bengal.[10] His father, in Roy's own words, 'spent his life in teaching Sanskrit to would be clerks or prospective lawyers'.[11] As a schoolboy in his teens, he joined the terrorist movement in Bengal and soon earned distinction for his dedication and daring. He received his early education in the village school and later joined the Bengal National College founded by Aurobindo Ghosh. But Roy had little attraction for academic studies. While in school, the revolutionary activities of Vinayak Damodar Savarkar captured his imagination and like many other restless and intrepid young men he joined the Yugantar group, one of the two revolutionary organizations of Bengal. Those were the days of the partition of Bengal when the nationalist leaders adopted the methods of *swadeshi* and boycott to right that grievous wrong. But Roy had little penchant for the politics of petition and representation. It was the politics of armed struggle that appealed to his romantic mind.[12]

It was Roy's dour determination and courage that made him an automatic choice for the errand to Batavia in 1914. He arrived there under the pseudonym of C. Martin. On his arrival in Batavia, Martin was introduced by the German consul to Theodor Helfferich who stated that a cargo of arms and ammunition was on its way to Karachi to assist the Indians in a revolution. Martin urged that the ships should be sent to Bengal and not to Karachi. This was eventually agreed after reference to the German consul general in Shanghai. Martin then returned to make arrangements to receive the cargo of SS *Maverick*, as the ship was called, at Rai Mangal in Bengal's Sundarbans. It was informed to him that the cargo would consist of 30,000 rifles with 400 rounds of ammunition each and 200,000 rupees. Meanwhile, Martin had telegraphed to Harry and Sons in Calcutta, a bogus firm kept by a revolutionary, that 'business was helpful'. In a series of remittances from Helfferich in Batavia to Harry and Sons in Calcutta between June and August, funds were sent which aggregated to 43,000 rupees of which the revolutionaries received 33,000 rupees before the authorities discovered what was going on. Martin returned to India in the middle of June and the conspirators—Jatin Mukherjee, Jadu Gopal Mukherjee, M.N. Roy (Martin), Bholanath Chatterjee and Atul Ghosh—made plans to receive arms and ammunition from the *Maverick* and employ it to their best advantage. They decided to divide the arms into three parts and planned to send it to: (a) a place in Bengal called Hatia for the East Bengal districts to be worked by the members of the Barisal Party, (b) Calcutta, the then capital of India and (c) Balasore, near the Bay of Bengal in the Indian state of Orissa.[13]

But a few days afterwards, the police successfully uncovered the conspiracy and apprehended a number of revolutionaries. Moreover, *Maverick* failed to arrive. Therefore, fresh attempts had to be made to get arms and it was on this mission that Roy left India for a second time, in 1915. According to Roy, the whole plan of transferring arms and ammunition to the Indian revolutionaries failed because he underestimated the duplicity of the Germans.[14] 'In disgust, but still full of hope',[15] Roy decided not to return home empty-handed but to continue his search for arms. From Java, he travelled through Malay, Indonesia, Indo-China, the Philippines, Japan, Korea and China until he landed in San Francisco in the summer of 1916. Throughout this dangerous errand, he was disguised as an Indian student of theology named Father Martin. Roy wrote: 'The Pacific had been crossed by a novice from Pondicherry going to study theology in Paris—duly armed with a copy of the Bible and a golden cross dangling from the watch-chain.'[16]

A few days after his arrival in San Francisco, an American newspaper carried a banner headline: 'Mysterious Alien Reaches America—Famous *Brahmin* Revolutionary or Dangerous German Spy?' Roy immediately took the warning, decamped from his hotel and made for the nearby town of Palo Alto, the seat of Stanford University. There he was received by Dhan Gopal Mukherjee, younger brother of his friend Jadu Gopal Mukherjee, who advised him 'to wipe out the past and begin as a new man'. The same evening, Father Martin was reborn on the campus of Stanford University as M.N. Roy.[17]

At Stanford, Roy met a young graduate, Evelyn, and fell in love with her. When, after a couple of months on the west coast, Roy crossed the continent to celebrate 'his rebirth spiritually as well as politically, in the city of New York',[18] Evelyn went with him. In New York, he came in contact with some prominent Indian nationalists, most notably Lala Lajpat Rai, and began to make preparations to go to Germany in order to join the Indian Independence Committee in Berlin. Roy also made acquaintance with eminent American socialists and anarcho-syndicalists who were sympathetic to the cause of Indian independence. It was at this time that Roy began to frequent the New York Public Library to read the works of Marx and 'discovered the new meaning in them'.[19]

While Roy was drinking deep of the Marxian literature, preparations were being made for his journey to Germany. According to Chandra Chakraberty one of the leading Indian revolutionaries in New York, while negotiations with the captain of the German cargo submarine *Deutschland* were in progress to take Roy to Germany, Roy was arrested on a complaint to New York police by Evelyn's father. But Evelyn defied her father, married Roy in jail and the couple was released.[20]

In the meantime, with the sinking of the *Lusitania*, the war had entered a crucial phase and the United States could no longer maintain its neutrality. This put the Indian revolutionaries in America in a quandary. As long as the United States remained neutral in the First World War, the Indians who had gone there to enlist sympathy and support for their cause, could carry on anti-British propaganda with a good deal of encouragement from various circles among the American public. But most of these exiles did not discriminate in seeking support and alliance and, as a result, their anti-British propaganda got mixed up with German propaganda which came to be regarded as violation of American neutrality. When the United States abandoned its neutrality, anti-German hysteria reached fever heat and anti-British propaganda of Indian nationalists was condemned as pro-Germanism. Thus, they not only forfeited American sympathy but were also arrested and tried as German agents.[21] Roy, however, escaped arrest by fleeing to Mexico.

Although Roy knew no one in Mexico, he felt neither alone nor helpless. Rather he was buoyed up by the atmosphere.[22] In Roy's own words:

> The Bolsheviks had just captured power in Russia, and a faint echo of the revolution reached across the Atlantic. All Left-wing socialists were in an exuberant mood, and lived in an atmosphere surcharged with great expectations. They were all would-be communists. I was sucked up in that electrified atmosphere. In my case, it was not a few degrees rise of the revolutionary temperature. It was a mutation in my political evolution, a sudden jump from die-hard nationalism to communism. With the fanaticism of a new convert, reformism was an anathema.[23]

In Mexico, Roy came in contact with a number of American radicals many of whom had crossed over to that country to evade conscription during the war. Notable among them were Linn A.E. Gale, 'a class by himself, an evangelist of the New Thought',[24] Charles Francis Philips, who had attained notoriety by organizing pacifist demonstrations on Columbia University campus,[25] Irwin Granwich, a novelist who was subsequently known as Michael Gold, painter and cartoonist Henry Glintenkamp, poet and cartoonist Maurice Barker and journalist Carl Beals. With these 'slackers', as they were derogatorily called, Roy began to contribute to Mexican publications supporting Mexico's grievances against the United States. Not surprisingly, he was encouraged in these activities by the Mexican government.

During this period, Roy had almost lost contact with India. Ever since he had left China, he was practically cut off from all relations with India. Although while in the United States he was associated mostly with Indians, it was, he felt, neither a fruitful nor a pleasant association. After reaching Mexico, he was completely out of touch with India and became entirely ignorant of what was happening at home. But he did not care very much since he was beginning to realize the narrowness of the vision of his earlier life. Now he chose a wider field of activity in pursuance of a new ideal of revolution and the experience was gratifying to him.[26] Roy thus felt that the failure of his last attempt to carry out the mission with which he had left India two and a half years ago definitely closed a chapter of his political career. Convinced that he could do nothing for the liberation of India in the near future, he resolved to apply himself wholeheartedly to the new fields of revolutionary activities, which 'promised satisfaction, if not success'.[27]

It was also during this period that Roy delivered a series of lectures on India in the Theosophical Society. These lectures were subsequently printed in a book in Spanish entitled *La India: su Pasado, su Presente y su Porvenir* (India's Past, Present and Future). It was Roy's first attempt to apply Marxism to the study of Indian history, an attempt 'of a new, not yet fully convinced convert'.[28] In this book, while admitting that the religious mode of thought predominated in the culture of ancient India, he laid stress on the fact that India was also inhabited by mortal human beings, who were necessarily and primarily concerned with the requirements of their physical existence. From that premise, Roy argued that the social structure and cultural pattern of ancient India could not be essentially different from those of any other country of an ancient civilization. He also discounted the Aryan legends and maintained that there was greater evidence to trace the descent from Dravidian stock. He expressed the view that ancient Indian culture was pre-Aryan, several years before the discovery of the ruins of the Indus Valley Civilization. But whether the Indus Valley Civilization was Dravidian or Sumerian, Roy maintained, it was pre-Aryan and that before the nomadic Aryans of Central Asia came to the north-west of India, the rest of the country was not a wilderness.[29] About literacy and education in ancient India, Roy maintained that under the Hindu monarchs, illiteracy was almost an unknown phenomenon among the Indian people.[30]

During the closing months of 1918, exciting news kept on coming from across the Atlantic and the ripples of the receding flood of European revolution reached the Mexican backwaters. Encouraged by the success of socialist revolution in Russia, the Left-wing intellectuals of Mexico started a movement for the formation of a national socialist party and Roy became one of its most active participants. He not only patronized the socialist paper, *El Socialista*, but with his wife presided over a number of conferences of the Mexican Socialist Party.

In September 1919, the month of a socialist conference in Mexico, Roy met Mikhail Borodin, also known as Michael Borodin, who came to the new world as the first emissary of the newly founded Communist International.[31] And thus began Roy's association not only with the man 'who subsequently attained a good deal of notoriety for his activities in China',[32] but also with the international communist movement. From the time that they met until Roy left Russia in 1929, Borodin was one of Roy's closest friends, although politically they often disagreed very strongly, as ultimately happened in China. According to Roy, it was a human relationship with no illusion on either side and they learned from each other. And as Borodin initiated him in the intricacies of Hegelian dialectics and taught him the history of European culture, Roy's lingering faith in the special genius of India began to fade.[33]

The object of Borodin's visit to Mexico was exploratory. He went there to announce the foundation of the Communist International and to help the Mexican socialists to form the first communist party outside Russia.[34] But this mission could not be successful without the approval of Venustiano Carranza, the president of Mexico. Accordingly, Roy introduced Borodin to Carranza who was so impressed with the Bolshevik that he not only requested Borodin to transmit his good wishes to the head of the new regime in Russia but also made Mexican diplomatic facilities available to him for communication with Moscow.[35] A few days later, Borodin decided to return to Europe and asked Roy to follow him because, he told Roy, Lenin wanted him to come to Russia.[36] Roy accepted the offer and early in November 1919, he, and Evelyn boarded the Spanish transatlantic liner *Alfonso XIII* at Vera Cruz. They carried a Mexican diplomatic passport under the names of Mr and Mrs Roberto Alleny Villa Garcia and left Mexico for Berlin on their way to Moscow.[37] Roy left the land of his rebirth as an intellectually free man, though with a new faith.

He no longer believed in political freedom without economic liberation and social justice. He had also realized that intellectual freedom, freedom from the bondage of all tradition and authority, was the condition for effective struggle for social emancipation. He had lost faith in the original mission with which he had left India. Although he still believed in the necessity of armed insurrection, he had learned to attach greater importance to an intelligent understanding of the idea of revolution. With the new conviction that propagation of the idea of revolution was more important than arms, he started on his way back to India, around the world.[38] According to his new faith, although Roy believed that revolution would take place of necessity, he maintained that no individual was indispensable in bringing about revolution. Revolution would be brought about by the operation of new social forces and as such the maturity and consciousness of the latter were the objective conditions for a revolution to take place. And until that basic condition was created, no armed insurrection should be undertaken. Therefore, social forces antagonistic to the established order must be politically mobilized and recruited in the army of revolution. Only then would the question of arming of the soldiers ready to fight for liberation arise. Roy felt:

> Our old idea of revolution put the cart before the horse. It attached the decisive importance to arms and [once] the opportunity of getting them appeared to present itself, we believed that revolution was round the corner. We did not stop to consider the problem of recruiting men to carry arms. The number of members of an underground party was too small to compose an army of revolution.[39]

Roy's new idea of revolution and the mental picture of how it should take place made him feel that there was no sense in his going back to India in a hurry. From the scanty news available, he gathered that under the economic and psychological impact of the war, social discontent was growing under the surface of a purely political anti-British nationalist movement. Surveying the Indian scene from a long distance in the light of the Marxist theory of social evolution, he discovered the spread of class struggle in the countryside, which had been subjected to intensified economic exploitation during the war. He further imagined that the subjective revolutionary factor of political consciousness was sure to reinforce the developing objective condition of social discontent when demobilized soldiers returned to their villages with the experience gained on battlefronts in foreign countries. This perspective of the process of revolutionary development in India, opened up by the new faith of Marxism, was analysed in his book, *India in Transition*, published two years later.[40]

On his way to Moscow, Roy had a brief sojourn in Berlin. There he met prominent German communists, such as Heinrich Brandler and August Thalheimer, who frequently invited him to secret meetings of communist leaders discussing the current problems of the revolution.[41] All of them treated Roy with kindness, affection and respect. But it was Thalheimer who took pains to give him the English rendering of the discussions and the support of the German leader won for Roy a place amongst the leaders of the communist party.[42]

Although no longer interested in the mission with which he had left India five years ago, having reached Berlin, Roy naturally wanted to establish contact with the members of the Indian Independence Committee. But before long, Roy discovered that the Berlin committee 'was not a happy family'.[43] He found Bhupendranath Datta, 'the only member of the committee present in Berlin, a sort of Rip van Winkle, who was still enjoying his blissful slumber'.[44] Moreover, Roy was annoyed when Datta asked him to account for the large amount of money he had received from agents of the German government. In Berlin, therefore, no heartening relationship could develop between Roy and the Berlin committee.

At long last when Roy arrived in Moscow, the Commission on the National and Colonial Questions of the second congress of the Communist International was in session under Lenin's chairmanship. It was in this meeting that Roy met Lenin for the first time.[45]

ROY, LENIN AND THESES ON NATIONAL AND COLONIAL QUESTIONS

At the second congress (19 July–7 August 1920), which was to formulate the ideological–tactical guidelines for communist movements in the colonial and semi-colonial countries, Roy, representing not India but Mexico, played an extremely important role.[46] The most crucial question which presented itself in the congress was that of the character of struggle in the colonial and semi-colonial countries and the strategy to be pursued for the promotion of proletarian revolution in those areas. What sort of revolution was to be brought about in those countries where the people were simmering with discontent against the prevailing order? Was it to be a bourgeois-democratic revolution or a social revolution or both in quick succession, as in Russia? What was to be the ideological orientation of the struggle of the colonies against imperialism? What was the relevance of the theory of class struggle to these colonies? Were the bourgeois-democratic movements in the colonies to be supported in their struggle for national liberation or was social antagonism to be aroused and a struggle to be carried on simultaneously against imperialism and the native bourgeoisie?

In regard to these crucial questions, a sharp controversy took place when two conflicting theses were presented before the congress, one by Lenin and another by Roy.[47] The entire controversy centred around the question whether socialists should support the national liberation movements led by the national bourgeoisie in the colonial and semi-colonial countries. In fact, as pointed out by Roy, there was a long-standing controversy inside the Bolshevik Party on this issue.[48] Opposing the contention of a section of socialists that as the national bourgeoisie could not have the sympathy of the working classes, any support to the bourgeois-nationalist movements would not only deprive the working classes of the benefits of social revolution but would also deliver them 'to the tender mercies of the reactionary nation-alist bourgeoisie',[49] Lenin maintained that the new counter-revolutionary social forces, unforeseen in original Marxism, were the result of colonial expansion and as such the unsuccessful revolt of the colo-nial peoples, even if led by the national bourgeoisie, was a condition for the overthrow of capitalism in the subjugated countries. The strategy of international proletarian revolution should, therefore, include active support of the national liberation movements in the colonial countries. This view was set forth in Lenin's famous *Theses on the National and Colonial Questions*. According to Roy, while presenting the theses to the second congress of the Communist International, Lenin declared that the Socialist International (1889–1916, also known as the Second International) was not a truly international organ-ization, because it excluded the oppressed masses of Asia and Africa. By including in its programme the question of the promotion of the national liberation movements in non-European countries, the Communist International would be a true world organization—the 'General Staff of the World Revolution'.[50]

But although Roy found Lenin's contention theoretically sound, he 'had misgivings about the practice of the theoretically-plausible programme'.

How was the colonial national liberation movement to be supported? It was the question of the ways and means. The resolutions of the Second International were not necessarily insincere. But it had no means to enforce them. In that respect, the Communist International was in an entirely different position. Its founder and leader, the Russian Bolshevik Party, was the ruler of a large country with vast resources. Its resolutions, therefore, had a powerful sanction. They could be carried out. Lenin said that the historic significance of the Russian Revolution was that it made the resources of at least one country available for the promotion of the world revolution. Once he went to the extent of declaring that having captured power before others the Russian proletariat had won the privilege of sacrificing itself for the liberation of the oppressed masses of the world. In the capitalist countries, there were communist parties which could be helped with the confidence that they were dedicated to the cause of social revolution. But in the colonial countries similar instruments were absent. How could then the Communist International develop the national liberation movement there as part of the World Proletarian Revolution?[51]

According to Roy, Lenin's views were based on ignorance of the relation of social forces in the colonial countries.[52] Justifying his stand on 'the old doctrinaire ground',[53] Lenin argued that imperialism was responsible for the colonial countries' feudal social conditions which not only hindered the development of capitalism but also thwarted the ambition of the native bourgeoisie. He pointed out that historically the national liberation movements of the colonial countries had the significance of the bourgeois-democratic revolution. Every stage of social evolution being historically determined, the colonial countries must go through bourgeois-democratic revolution before they could enter the stage of proletarian revolution. It was, therefore, necessary for the communists to regard the nationalist bourgeoisie as a revolutionary force and help the liberation movement under its leadership.[54] In reply to this 'orthodox defence of the infallibility of Marxism', Roy pointed out that the nationalist movement was ideologically reactionary because as a class the bourgeoisie even in the most advanced colonial countries, such as India, was not economically and culturally differentiated from the feudal social order. The triumph of the national liberation movement, therefore, would not necessarily mean a bourgeois-democratic revolution. Refuting Lenin's contention that as the inspirer and leader of a mass movement, Gandhi was a revolutionary, Roy maintained that being a religious and cultural revivalist, he was bound to be reactionary socially; however, revolutionary he might appear politically.[55]

Refuting Lenin's contention that as the proletarian movement in the colonial countries was 'still in its embryonic state', it was necessary for all communist parties to render assistance to the bourgeois-democratic liberation movement. Roy further pointed out that in the colonial countries there existed two distinct movements, the bourgeois-democratic nationalist movement with a programme of political independence under the bourgeois order and the mass action of the poor and ignorant peasants and workers for their liberation from all sorts of exploitation. Roy argued that the real strength of the liberation movements in the colonies was no longer confined to the narrow circle of bourgeois-democratic nationalists. In most of the colonial countries, he pointed out, there already existed organized revolutionary parties and the relation of the Communist International with the revolutionary movements in the colonies should be realized through these parties since they were the vanguard of the working class in their respective countries. The communist parties of different imperialist countries must work in conjunction with these proletarian parties and through them give all moral and material support to the revolutionary movement in general. Roy then averred that the revolution in the colonies was not going to be a communist revolution in the first stage, but if from the very outset the leadership was in the hands of a communist vanguard, the revolutionary masses would not be led astray.[56] Summing up the line of argument propounded by Roy, a Russian newspaper at that time observed:

> Comrade Roy arrives at the conclusion that it is necessary to eliminate from point 11 of the theses[57] on the national problem the paragraph according to which communist parties must assist any bourgeois-democratic liberation movement in eastern countries. The Communist International should assist exclusively the institution and development of the communist movement in India, and the Communist Party of India [CPI] must devote itself exclusively to the organization of the broad popular masses for the struggle for the class interests of the latter.[58]

According to Gene D. Overstreet and Marshall Windmiller, Roy, still a mere tyro in revolutionary strategy, had impugned the wisdom of Lenin, one of the greatest legatees of Marx, for the following reasons. First, Roy might have had the feeling that being Asian himself he was more competent than any non-Asian, even if it was no less a person than Lenin, to understand Asian conditions. And it was not in his nature to keep quiet in a situation that galled his pride.[59] Second, his views sprang primarily from his own assessment of the Indian situation. Although circumstances had drawn him to the international communist movement, intrinsically he still remained an Indian with his extreme views on national liberation struggle in India. He had always been opposed to the moderate policies of the INC and true to his grain he disliked a policy which would credit the INC with more revolutionary potential than any other Indian organization. Third, Roy was conscious that if the Communist International decided to support India's struggle for freedom under the INC leadership, then Virendranath Chattopadhyaya, who had some connections with the INC, would be the logical choice to control the Communist International's policies in regard to India. Roy definitely did not like this idea.[60]

Whatever considerations might have impelled Roy to put forward an alternative thesis on the national and colonial questions, he had the satisfaction of getting Lenin's wordings modified in the final resolution of the second congress. After considerable excursus in the congress, the crucial paragraph took the following shape:

> With regard to those states and nationalities where a backward, mainly feudal, patriarchal or patriarchal–agrarian regime prevails, the following must be borne in mind: All communist parties must give active support to the revolutionary movements of liberation, the form of support to be determined by a study of existing conditions, carried on by the party wherever there is such.[61]

The inclusion of the term 'revolutionary movements of liberation' instead of 'bourgeois-democratic liberation movement' as originally proposed by Lenin, was of paramount significance insofar as it was on the basis of this reversal of policy that the second congress of the Communist International decided upon the following course of action in regard to communist movements in the colonial countries:

1. As national liberation movements in these countries were of bourgeois-democratic character, the Communist International would extend its support to the 'revolutionary national bourgeoisie' in its struggle against imperialism.
2. Even if it were revolutionary in character, the bourgeois national–democratic movements were not to be given a communist label.
3. As vanguards of 'revolutionary movements of liberation', communist parties had to be formed and their independent course of struggle promoted at all costs.
4. In order to carry on a successful revolutionary movement in the colonies, the working class must join hands with the mass of peasants.
5. In order to eliminate reformist elements from the leadership of labour movements, communists must actively participate even in conservative trade unions.[62]

By forcing Lenin to make concessions in favour of his views, Roy had acquired a tremendous prestige as an able dialectician and a clever analyst of revolutionary strategy. He had, therefore, little difficulty in hewing his way to a position of considerable importance in the Communist International.

BAKU CONGRESS AND ROY'S REVOLUTION BLUEPRINT

When the Executive Committee of the Communist International (ECCI) elected by the second congress set up a subcommittee of five which came to be known as the Small Bureau, Roy was co-opted as a member of this all-powerful body, the supreme policy-making and executive organ of the Communist International.[63] Meeting shortly after the second congress, the bureau passed two resolutions, first to hold the first Congress of the Peoples of the East in Baku, and second to set up the Central Asiatic Bureau of the Communist International in Tashkent.[64] The three members of this bureau were Roy, G.Y. Sokolnikov and G.I. Safarov.[65]

Although Roy opposed the idea of a congress in Baku on the ground that it could serve no useful purpose, he felt that as a symbolic gesture of mass demonstration against imperialism, 'the projected show would have some significance'. He, however, decided not to join 'the picturesque cavalcade to the gates of the mysterious Orient'. He was eager for more serious organizational work, which would reinforce the position of the proletariat in the colonial countries. For this reason, he attached greater importance to the resolution to set up the Central Asiatic Bureau of the Communist International, charged with the responsibility of carrying through the revolution in Turkestan and Bokhara and then of spreading it to the adjacent countries, particularly India. Obsessed with this idea, he stubbornly opposed the plan of the Baku congress, characterizing it as a wanton waste of time, energy and material resources in frivolous agitation and went to the extent of calling it 'Zinoviev's Circus'.[66]

The Congress of the Peoples of the East met from 1–20 September 1920 in Baku, in a place where 'a monument had already been raised to commemorate the martyrdom of the victims of imperialist violence'.[67] Apart from lofty panegyrics and minatory speeches from Grigory Zinoviev, Bela Kun and Karl Radek, the only work of the congress was the formation of a Council of Propaganda and Action of the Peoples of the East, consisting of 47 members representing 20 nationalities and the establishment of a paper called the *Peoples of the East*. But both the council and the paper were destined to be short-lived.[68]

As a period of slackness began to follow the hectic days of the second congress of the Communist International, Roy became impatient to go to Tashkent where in October 1920, a military school for training Indians was set up and an India House established. Roy's plan was not only 'to supply the frontier tribes with the sinews of war so that they could make trouble' for the British Indian government but also to raise, equip and train an army in Afghanistan where thousands of Muslim *muhajirs* (pilgrims) from India had congregated in the hope either of joining Mustafa Kemal's army in Turkey or failing this, to take up residence in a Muslim country. Roy hoped that with the help of these *muhajirs*, he would be able to form a liberation army, and using the frontier territories as the base of operation and with the mercenary support of the tribesmen would march into India and occupy some territory where a civil government should be established as soon as possible.[69] According to Roy:

> The first proclamation of the revolutionary government would [be to] outline a programme of social reform to follow national independence. It would call upon the people to rise in the rear of the enemy, so that the liberation army could advance further and further into the country. The appeal should be addressed particularly to the industrial and transport workers. The entire adult population of the liberated territory would be armed, some for defence and others for enlarging the liberation army. The programme of social reform outlined in the proclamation issued on the establishment of the revolutionary government would be enforced in the liberated territories; consequently, the masses would enthusiastically support the new regime. The concrete picture of freedom would have a strong appeal to the vast majority of the people, giving them the incentive to strive for it. The vested interests throughout the land might be opposed to the revolutionary implications of the national liberation; but the imperialist power, weakened by the consequences of the World War [I], and shaken by a popular uprising, would not be able to offer any protection to the upper-class minority, who would wish to stem the tide of the democratic national revolution.[70]

Accordingly, accompanied by two trainloads of arms, gold bullion and Indian currency and with a number of Indians, Persians and other Middle Easterners, who formed what was described as the first International Brigade of the Red Army, Roy left Moscow for Tashkent.[71]

MUHAJIRS ABROAD AND FORMATION OF CPI

On 18 April 1920, the Khilafat Conference was held in Delhi to demonstrate the Indian Muslims' indignation at British perfidy against Turkey, the seat of the Islamic *khilafat*. The conference decided that British tyranny could no longer be tolerated and that the only option for Indian Muslims was to leave the country to go on *hijrat*. As a result of this decision, 18,000 *muhajirs*, that is, those who joined the *hijrat*, left India for Afghanistan.[72]

The journey of the *muhajirs* was a tortuous one. Crossing the Hind Kush mountain range, they reached Tirmiz, now in Uzbekistan, from where they were crossing the river Amu Darya by boat. Here, they were attacked by a group of rebel Turkmen who were armed and financed by the British. Only the timely arrival of the Red Army saved their lives. Reacting sharply to the fact that although they were Muslims they were attacked by Muslim Turkmen, they took up arms along with the Red Army to defend the Kirkee fort against the counter-revolutionaries.[73]

Rafiq Ahmad recalled:

It was now time for us to leave Kirkee. A steamer had come with an armed escort and all sixty of us got on board. This steamer took us to Charjao. Red Army soldiers played their band at the steamer jetty to welcome us. We stayed three days in Charjao and received lavish hospitality. It was while we were there that we could get to know one another well. Till then we could never be sure what was in the mind of the other fellow. Charjao was a railway junction, trains from many directions passing through. About half of our group expressed the desire to go to Anatolia, and arrangements were made by the Soviet authorities accordingly. The rest of us took the train for Tashkent.[74]

Soon after their arrival of the *muhajirs* in Tashkent in September 1920,[75] Roy, Evelyn, Abani Mukherjee and his Russian wife Rosa Fitingov and Muhammad Shafiq came to see them.[76] And it was on their advice that the *muhajirs* immediately started to take lessons at the newly established Indian Military School in Tashkent. But when the school was closed in May 1921 as a result of an agreement between Britain and the Soviet Union,[77] they proceeded to Moscow and joined the Communist University of the Toilers of the East, which was established in April 1921, to teach Marxism–Leninism to the peoples of the Orient.

It is important to note here that the level of political consciousness of most of the *muhajirs* was not very high. As Roy has pointed out, most of them were ignorant masses moved by religious fanaticism, while only a few educated youths, who constituted the driving force of the Khilafat Movement, were politically motivated.[78] When Roy met them in Tashkent, he found them 'a refractory lot, moved only by a religious fanaticism, which ought to have been shaken by their own experience'.[79] According to Roy, although they were decidedly anti-British, 'most of them were not even nationalists [and] none of them had any idea of democracy'.[80] Roy discussed this problem with the educated minority of the group and persuaded them to receive 'a course of political training before a military school for training the soldiers of the Indian revolution could be founded'. Roy felt that before they could proceed to anything fruitful with the emigrants, it was necessary to differentiate the educated minority from the fanatical mass. Accordingly, he set himself to the task of politically educating the educated few.[81]

Rafiq Ahmad also admitted that among the *muhajirs* there were all kinds of people, many of whom were moved by religious zeal and only a few of whom nursed the idea that from abroad they could discover some way of striking at British rule in India.[82] But Muzaffar Ahmad did not agree with Roy that the *muhajirs* were politically ignorant. According to Muzaffar Ahmad, it was a 'worthless statement'. He argued that events in India during 1919–20, such as the Jallianwala Bagh massacre, the horrors of martial law in Punjab and the countrywide working-class strikes, must have had some influence on the minds of the young *muhajirs*. He further argued that as the Non-Cooperation Movement emerged out of the Khilafat Movement, it would have been incredible that many of the *muhajirs* whom Roy confronted remained ignorant of bourgeois democracy.[83]

After studying for some time in the Communist University of the Toilers of the East, the *muhajirs* came to accept Marxism as their creed and according to Rafiq Ahmad, they formed the CPI in 1921. Rafiq Ahmad added:

As a matter of fact the Communist Party of India [CPI] had been set up towards the end of 1920 in Tashkent, though some of us did not join it. Now we formed the party though we were away from home, we did so because we felt it was necessary.[84]

After the émigré CPI had been organized in Moscow, it was affiliated to the Communist International. Muhammad Shafiq was the party's first secretary and M.N. Roy, Shafiq and Abani Mukherjee constituted its working committee. Rafiq Ahmad pointed out:

Roy could represent India in Moscow only on account of the formation of this émigré Communist Party of India [CPI]. Otherwise, he could have remained in the Communist International only in his capacity of an individual leader, but not as the special representative of India.[85]

Rafiq Ahmad's account of the formation of the CPI abroad has not been wholly corroborated by David N. Druhe. According to Druhe, it was among the students of India House in Tashkent that the CPI was formed in early 1921.[86] But Rafiq Ahmad is emphatic that the CPI was formed in Tashkent in either October or November 1920. Muzaffar Ahmad argued:

This stress on the party being set up in October or November 1920 is significant, in spite of Rafiq Ahmad's not having the distinction of being among the first members of the party. M.N. Roy's *Memoirs*, as published in the *Radical Humanist*, are so phrased that any odd date would do. This being so, it will not be unfair to accept Rafiq Ahmad's version. It may certainly be taken for granted that the Communist Party of India [CPI] was first set up in Tashkent in October or November 1920.[87]

This émigré CPI was affiliated to the Communist International in the first half of 1921 and therefore, concluded Muzaffar Ahmad, 'the date of the party's foundation, if it was not 1920, could not have been later than early 1921'.[88]

Anyway, after having formed the CPI in Tashkent and studying for nine months at the Communist University of the Toilers of the East, the *muhajirs* were anxious to return home, for they felt that their field of work lay only in their country. But although it was by no means easy for them to go back the way they had come, they were determined somehow to return to India. And, as Rafiq Ahmad pointed out, there was only one rather inaccessible route which they could think of—the Pamir route. The Communist Party of the Soviet Union (CPSU) was in charge of all arrangements for their journey, which was described by Rafiq Ahmad as the hardest experience of their lives.[89]

PESHAWAR CONSPIRACY CASE

The return journey of the newly converted Indian communists, however, ended in failure. While passing through Chitral, which was within Indian territory, they were apprehended by the Indian police and brought to Peshawar for trial in what later became famous as the Peshawar Conspiracy Case (1922–23). The accused were tried under Section 121-A of the Indian Penal Code which was an offence of conspiracy to 'deprive the King-Emperor of his sovereignty over India'.[90] In the magistrate's court, the accused did not defend themselves. They employed a lawyer only to see to it that the magistrate or the government's advocate did not violate any legal provision.

In the judgement which was delivered in the second week of May 1923, Ghulam Muhammad and Fida Ali Zahid, who had made guilty pleas, were released; Mian Muhammad Akbar Shah and Gawhar Rahman Khan were sentenced to two years' rigorous imprisonment and the rest to a year's hard labour. The accused did not appeal against the conviction and thus came to an end the first communist conspiracy case in India.

ROY AND BERLIN INDIAN INDEPENDENCE COMMITTEE

Early in 1921, Roy was called to Moscow to take part in a conference of Indian revolutionaries for the purpose of setting up an effective machinery for propaganda and organizational work in India. Also invited to take part in the conference were the members of Indian Independence Committee in Berlin with Agnes Smedley as their driving force. There followed a bitter disagreement between Roy and the Berlin committee over the leadership of the communist movement in India. Roy, however, carried the day and most of the members of the Berlin delegation left Moscow in disgust. Immediately after the Berlin revolutionaries left Moscow, the third congress of the Communist International met in Moscow in June–July 1921 and put stress on the necessity of formation of indigenous communist parties in countries where there were none. Believing that he had the mandate of the Communist International, Roy now set out to contact Indian revolutionaries in India and abroad.

COMMUNIST GROUPS IN INDIA

A movement was already afoot in India for the formation of a CPI as a result of which a number of amorphous groups were operating in different parts of the country. These groups, as pointed out by Zinoviev at the fifth congress of the Communist International, were more propaganda societies than parties in the real sense of the term. Communism in India was still in the realm of ideas and these groups drew sustenance from the seething discontent of the masses at the end of the war.[91]

Of the communist groups that lay scattered around the country, most active were those in Bombay, Calcutta, Madras, Lahore and Cawnpore (Kanpur). The leader of the Bombay group was S.A. Dange who, even while a student, attained considerable distinction as a radical political worker. Under the patronage of an opulent Bombay flourmill owner, R.B. Lotvala, and inspired by M.N. Roy, he had organized socialist study centres in Bombay and published a good number of Marxist tracts.[92] His first experience of political agitation was in 1915 when he organized a successful students' strike against the principal of his college. Thereafter, he joined the Non-Cooperation Movement under the leadership of Gandhi. After breaking away from Gandhism, he turned to Marxism and began to participate in labour movements during 1919–20. It was at this time that he was influenced by the writings of M.N. Roy and R. Palme Dutt.[93] In August 1922, he became the editor of an English-language weekly called *Socialist*. It was, indeed, a very bold endeavour of Dange because, as pointed out by Muzaffar Ahmad, no journal under this name had ever been brought out in India before.[94]

In Calcutta, Muzaffar Ahmad, who had 'neither any money nor any means of livelihood'[95] and whose 'knowledge of Marxism was very superficial', was the guiding force of communist workers in Bengal. According to Muzaffar Ahmad's own account, when he took the leap into the unknown, he counted on two things—his faith in the people and his unqualified loyalty to the directives of the Communist International.[96]

In 1920, when Muzaffar Ahmad became a full-time worker for a Bengali literary association, he came into contact with Kazi Nazrul Islam, then a *havildar* (sergeant) in the 49th Bengali Regiment, who was later to become a famous poet idolized by people. Although Islam was involved when plans were being made in Calcutta regarding the formation of a communist party, he did not join the party because he thought that he would not be able to abide by party discipline.[97] During this period, A.K. Fazlul Huq, then known as a Leftist leader, decided to produce a Bengali evening daily *Nava Yug* which came out under the joint editorship of Islam and Muzaffar Ahmad. The paper gained tremendous popularity from the very first day of its publication owing to the forceful pen wielded by Islam. He was more than a rebel—he became the soul of the young generation of Bengal, the epitome of a spirit that flared up unconsciously and ignited people's dormant anger with the message of revolt. He had become the symbol of violent protest against all kinds of oppression, exploitation and social bondage. And he appeared at a moment when the minds of the young were most receptive. According to Muzaffar Ahmad, *Nava Yug* was distinct from other Bengali dailies in that it contained news mostly about workers, peasants and the sailors who worked on the steamers which plied the river routes in Bengal. But Muzaffar Ahmad could not have imagined at that time that through these writings he was being slowly drawn towards communism.[98] In 1922, Muzaffar Ahmad came in contact with Abdur Razzak Khan, Abdul Halim and Qutubuddin Ahmad who, in collaboration with the eminent nationalist leader Maulana Abul Kalam Azad, had been running two Urdu weeklies—*Al Hilal* and *Al Bilagh*. In those days, Muzaffar Ahmad observed, it was very difficult to get Marxist literature in Calcutta and even if anything was available, the communists did not have the means to buy it. It was Qutubuddin Ahmad who used to buy a lot of such literature and it was because of him that others also had the opportunity to read Morgan Philips Price's *My Reminiscences of the Russian Revolution*, the first book available in India on the Russian Revolution.[99]

In Madras, a small communist group was organized around Malaypuram Singaravelu Chettiar, a senior lawyer, who, after proclaiming himself a communist in 1922, joined the workers' movement and courted arrest. In the Gaya session of the INC (1922), he moved the resolution on national independence. Chettiar claimed that he was the first man to address the AICC as 'comrades' in 1923.[100]

In Lahore, organizational work was being carried on by Ghulam Hussain, a lecturer in economics in the Islamia College of Peshawar. During the First World War, when a number of students from Lahore had fled India to prepare themselves for revolutionary work, Hussain gave up his job and came to Lahore to build up the CPI. From there, he began to publish a monthly paper in Urdu called *Inquilab*. At this time, he also became the secretary of the famous North Western Railway Employees' Union.[101] He was one of the accused in the Cawnpore Conspiracy Case (1924) in which he became an approver and charges against him were withdrawn.

In Cawnpore and other parts of Uttar Pradesh, except for some good work by Shaukat Usmani, nothing very remarkable was done.

COMMUNISTS AT HOME AND ABROAD

It was by no means an easy task for Roy and other communists abroad to draw together these widely dispersed Indian communists with their exiguous understanding of Marxism and world communist strategy both organizationally and ideologically and to link them directly to the Communist International. The problem of developing and perfecting workable channels of communication with the Indian communists was, perhaps, the most excruciating of all. But in spite of many difficulties, Roy continued to maintain contacts with comrades in India with great assiduity. According to reports of the Intelligence Bureau of the Government of India, his contacts with the communists in India were well known and his correspondence with them had been an unfailing source of information of proved accuracy as to the movement of men, money and literature.[102] In fact, there was very little that the Intelligence Bureau did not know about what went on between communists at home and abroad.

Apart from strict police vigilance, another problem for Roy was to discover people in India through whom he could communicate safely. Unfortunately for him, with the exceptions of Dange and Muzaffar Ahmad, he could not find many trusted friends in India. R.C.L. Sharma, a resident of Pondicherry, through whom Roy tried to route his correspondence proved utterly unsuitable for the delicate work. Before he started working as a liaison between Roy and Indian communists, Sharma had offered his services to the Intelligence Bureau but was not employed because, in the words of the director of the

Intelligence Bureau, 'he was constitutionally incapable of playing straight'.[103] Even after he began to work for Roy, the police were confident that he would undoubtedly 'sell them reasonably cheaply'. Although Roy had a little better luck with Chettiar, their clandestine arrangements with him lasted only until August 1923.[104]

Despite communication difficulties, some attempts were made during this period to form the ambivalent communist groups into an articulate political movement and to create an all-India organization. In 1921, on Roy's suggestion, a conference of the representatives of the Indian working class was convened by Samsuddin Hassan and Ghulam Hussain in Lahore with 'the object of organizing a political party of the Indian working class'.[105] The conference, however, could not be held on account of organizational inadequacies. But Roy still continued to urge the Indian communists to organize the working classes on the basis of their immediate grievances and to form a revolutionary party, by leading them through a series of strikes and agitations for the realization of their demands, thus making them conscious of their class solidarity.[106]

Encouraged by Roy's propaganda that a revolution in India could be brought about only by organizing communist vanguards, in February 1923, Chettiar issued a manifesto calling upon the communists from all over the country to meet in an all-India conference. Copies of this manifesto were sent to almost all prominent Indian communists, including Roy, Dange, Ghulam Hussain, Muzaffar Ahmad and Manilal Maganlal Shah. On receipt of the manifesto, Shah, with Abani Mukherjee's connivance, made some modifications and reissued it as their own. When Hussain received this modified version of the manifesto, he promptly responded by convening a conference in Lucknow on 30 June 1923, to organize what he called 'Dr Manilal's Manifesto Party'.[107] This counter-move by Shah made Chettiar furious and he immediately protested to Hussain pointing out that what Shah and Mukherjee called 'Dr Manilal's manifesto' was no more than a re-framing of his original manifesto. When Manilal's manifesto reached Roy in Europe, he immediately detected Abani Mukherjee's hand in it and lost no time in denouncing it as a 'spurious' document. Roy also wrote to Dange requesting him to get in touch with Chettiar without delay because, Roy told Dange, he was 'the best man available to be the figurehead of the legal party'.[108] In order to dispel the confusion created by Manilal's counter-manifesto, on 5 June, Roy issued a memorandum to the communists in India wherein he suggested that the purpose of an all-India conference should be to organize two parties—'a mass party to be called the Workers' and Peasants' Party and an illegal communist party'. Roy added that as the communist party would be the 'illegal apparatus' of the legal Workers' and Peasants' Party (WPP), the members of the former would *ipso facto* be members of the latter. Roy also suggested that it was the WPP which should send a delegation to the Communist International since the communist party would not be recognized as a true communist party. Roy then pointed out that the Indian communists should leave out of their propaganda the controversy of violence versus non-violence and cultivate a 'working alliance' with bourgeois-nationalist parties during the anti-imperialist struggle, availing themselves of 'every opportunity for striking an agreement' in order to put pressure on the bourgeois-nationalist movement and bring out its 'revolutionary significance'. He averred: 'That will be the best tactical move we can make without giving the lie to our programme.'[109]

CAWNPORE CONSPIRACY CASE

However, not only did the proposed conference not take place but all efforts to organize a communist party suffered a terrible setback when the government cracked down on the leading Indian communists and framed charges of 'conspiracy to establish throughout British India a branch of a revolutionary organization known as the Communist International with the object of depriving the King of the Sovereignty of British India'[110] against Roy, Nalini Gupta, Muzaffar Ahmad, Shaukat Usmani, Dange, Ghulam Hussain, R.C.L. Sharma and Chettiar. However, when the famous Cawnpore Conspiracy Case began in April 1924, proceedings were launched against only four—Gupta, Usmani, Dange and Muzaffar Ahmad. Roy was in Europe and there was no question of bringing him to the court. Sharma dodged prosecution by securing protection of the French government in Pondicherry. Hussain became an approver and Chettiar was excused on grounds of ill health.

In course of the hearings, Dange admitted that he had been in correspondence with Roy but insisted that it was for the purpose of gathering materials for study and journalistic writings. He also declared that he disapproved of Roy's programme and differed with him on the question of resorting to violent means for political ends. He claimed the right to preach socialism which, he argued, had been accorded to communists in other parts of the empire including Great Britain.[111] The other defendants denied all charges against them and pleaded innocence. But evidence against all of them was so compelling that the judge, H.L. Holme, who earned considerable notoriety by sentencing 172 people to death in the Chauri Chaura Case,[112] sentenced each of them to four years' rigorous imprisonment. When the accused appealed to the Allahabad High Court, the appeal judges, while describing the alleged conspiracy as absurd and unbelievable, came to the conclusion that the defendants had acted 'in the most serious spirit'. Consequently, the appeal was dismissed.[113]

SATYABHAKTA AND INDIAN COMMUNIST PARTY

In spite of the fact that the Cawnpore Conspiracy Case had greatly damaged the embryonic communist movement and demoralized the communists, efforts to build up a legal party had continued unabated. During the hearing, 'a certain person could be seen sitting occasionally in the visitors' gallery. His name was Satyabhakta.'[114] Immediately after the conclusion of the case, he 'announced in the newspapers that he had formed the Indian Communist Party'[115] in Cawnpore on 1 September 1924. Satyabhakta himself was the secretary of the party and among its members were Maulana Hasrat Mohani, V.H. Joshi, Rama Shandar Avasthi and Ram Gopal.[116] At the initial stage, this party did not attract much attention and by December 1924, it could claim only a modest membership of 78, including 3 women.[117]

After announcing the formation of the party, Satyabhakta circulated its provisional constitution which proclaimed that the object of this party, named the Indian Communist Party, was the establishment of complete *swaraj* and transformation of the Indian society on the basis of common ownership and control of the means of production and distribution of wealth 'in the interests of the whole community of India'.[118] In the declaration of principles of the party, it was pointed out that there existed a wide hiatus in Indian society between those who owned their means of livelihood and those who were deprived of it. As this cleavage inevitably gave rise to class antagonism, the primary object of the party would be the abolition of all class distinctions by emancipating the working class from oppression and exploitation. But Satyabhakta made it clear that it was essentially a nationalist party with nothing to do with the Communist International. This declaration notwithstanding, the government grew suspicious of Satyabhakta's activities and thrice raided the office of his party in Cawnpore.

In the meantime, Nalini Gupta and Muzaffar Ahmad were released from jail, the latter on grounds of poor health; and having found nothing worthwhile to do, they decided to attend the conference of Satyabhakta's Indian Communist Party, which was also the first communist conference in India, scheduled to take place on 26 December 1925, in Cawnpore, concurrently with the annual session of the INC. On reaching Cawnpore, Muzaffar Ahmad found that other comrades, including C.K. Iyengar, K.N. Joglekar, S.V. Ghate, R.S. Nimbkar, J.P. Bergarhatta, Ajodhya Prasad and Meer Abdul Majeed, had already arrived.

The chairman of the reception committee of the conference was Maulana Hasrat Mohani and the president-elect was Chettiar, who after the conviction of the accused persons in the Cawnpore Case, had presented himself at the court, although the government did not proceed further with the charges against him.[119]

The proceedings of the conference did not go smoothly because from the very outset a bitter controversy arose among the delegates as to the name of the new party. Satyabhakta contended that this party 'would be a party of Indian pattern, that is, a nationalist party, and hence the name would be Indian Communist Party'.[120] Both Mohani and Chettiar agreed with this view. Mohani pointed out: 'Our organization is purely Indian, our relation with similar parties of other countries will be only that of sympathy and mental affinity to all these in general and to the Third International [Communist International] in particular'.[121]

Chettiar was even more candid when he said:

Indian communism is not Bolshevism, for Bolshevism is a form of communism which the Russians have opted in their country. We are not Russians; Bolsheviks and Bolshevism may not be needed in India .... We are one with the world communists but not with Bolsheviks.[122]

Criticizing this attitude, Muzaffar Ahmad and a few others argued that 'according to the practice of the Communist International', the name of the party should be the Communist Party of India. Finally, Satyabhakta left the conference in a huff with his papers and files.

Denouncing the 'non-communistic' attitude of Satyabhakta, Mohani and Chettiar, Roy averred from Europe that those who maintained and propagated such points of view were the 'veritable enemies of the Indian working class'.[123] Roy pointed out that communists would betray their historic role 'if they failed to recognize the international character of the class struggle. A national communist is an enemy of the proletariat.'[124] Roy then added:

A communist that [who] does not fight for national independence of a subject people, does not lead an agrarian revolution against feudal landlordism, is opposed to international affiliation, preaches that the proletariat should not act till they are hundred per cent organized, does not have any idea about militant labour organization, does not believe in revolution, is hostile to armed insurrection and eager to do justice to possessing classes, such a communist party can receive justice from the British, but will never be the party of the Indian working classes—the vanguard in the struggle for freedom.[125]

FIRST CENTRAL COMMITTEE AND CONSTITUTION OF CPI

Despite such sharp differences of opinion over the ideological orientation of the party, a central committee was constituted consisting of Joglekar, Ghate, Nimbkar, Muzaffar Ahmad, Meer Abdul Majeed, Bergarhatta and Iyengar and the first constitution of the CPI was published towards the end of 1926. Ghate and Bergarhatta became joint secretaries of the central committee and Muzaffar Ahmad and Iyengar were appointed secretaries for their areas.[126] Bergarhatta was eventually found to be a police informer and left the party of his own accord. Ghate then became the general secretary and he held this post up to 20 March 1929.[127]

The newly constituted central committee of the CPI met in several secret sessions between 1926 and 1929 to work out a programme of action for the organization of communist movement in India. But the party was not yet affiliated to the Communist International because, as Muzaffar Ahmad put it: 'The party was a small one.' The Communist International, however, used to give recognition to the members of the party and at the sixth congress, which met in Moscow from 17 July to 1 September 1928, two of its members were elected alternate members of the ECCI. It was in 1930 that the party was formally affiliated to the Communist International.[128]

STRUGGLE FOR LEADERSHIP: ROY VERSUS CPGB

Although the central committee had provided the Indian communists with the much-needed centralized and coordinated leadership, its proper functioning continued to be stalled on account of the complete lack of consensus among its members on ideological, organizational as well as tactical questions. Paucity of funds also proved to be a serious problem. But the cardinal factor that stood in the way of formulation of a well-planned programme of action was the plethora of conflicting directives that started to pour in from abroad. This was symptomatic of a struggle for leadership between Roy on the one hand and the Communist Party of Great Britain (CPGB) on the other. The cumulative effect of all these factors was to create in the ranks of the Indian communists a persistent conflict and confusion.

Disagreement between Roy and the leaders of the CPGB first came to the surface in July 1925, when, in a meeting organized by the Colonial Bureau of the Communist International in Amsterdam, the representatives of the CPGB disapproved of Roy's policy and decided to take upon themselves the task of directing the movement in India. Although both the contending groups were expected to abide by the guidelines laid down by the Communist International, their disagreement was fundamental enough to defy an immediate compromise. This controversy found expression to a nicety in two books published during this period—Roy's *The Future of Indian Politics* and R. Palme Dutt's *Modern India*.

In *The Future of Indian Politics*, Roy made a clear distinction between 'the nationalist bourgeoisie' and 'the revolutionary masses' and maintained that the former was characterized by its desire to make a united front with the imperialist forces in order to safeguard the country against any possible revolution. The big bourgeoisie, therefore, was to be eliminated from the struggle for national liberation. Neither could the middle class be expected to play a revolutionary role because, in Roy's words, it was 'in hopeless political bankruptcy'. Roy, therefore, argued that the future of Indian politics would be determined by the social forces composed of workers, peasants and the petty bourgeoisie which remained and would always remain antagonistic to imperialism even in the new era dominated by 'the higher ideals of *swaraj* within the empire'.[129] He further argued that both the leadership and the organizational form of a revolutionary party would be determined by the social character of the movement. And the social elements that would henceforth compose the movement for national liberation were petty intellectuals, artisans, small traders, peasantry and the proletariat. As in the existing condition of Indian society, these elements belonged to the exploited class, the movement for national liberation would take place on the basis of the class struggle between them and their exploiters.[130] As for tactics, Roy suggested that in view of the anti-revolutionary character of the existing political organizations in India, the immediate task for all anti-imperialist elements would be to form a 'party of the people' which should be broad enough to accommodate all the forces of national revolution. The proletariat would be in it, said Roy, but it would not be a proletarian party. In this party, the proletariat would stand side by side with the petty bourgeois and peasant masses as the most advanced democratic class.[131]

R. Palme Dutt was broadly in agreement with Roy so far as the assessment of the Indian situation was concerned. But he did not see eye to eye with him on the question of strategy and tactics. From the point of view of strategy, Dutt was prepared to concede that the struggle for national liberation was a struggle of many social strata—of workers, peasants, the lower middle class, the intelligentsia and even of a section of the bourgeoisie.[132] Tactically, therefore, the Left nationalist elements 'should gather themselves round a popular national programme' and 'carry on a battle of clarification within the existing movement and organization'.[133] Therefore, Dutt insisted that there was no immediate need for the formation of a party of the people. In this regard, his advice to the Indian communists was to wait for the time when 'new forces will have to find their form and expression'.[134] Dutt averred that it was 'a matter of indifference' as to how that would arise, whether through the existing forms of the INC or the Swaraj Party or by the combination of these and other elements.[135]

It is interesting to note in this connection that by the beginning of 1927, Dutt had veered around to Roy's position having found in the Indian bourgeoisie a 'counter-revolutionary force' and admitted that only a mass movement based on the joint front of workers and peasants would 'bring new life' to Indian politics.[136] Dutt also maintained that in order to prevent the social revolution 'that would follow on national independence', the Indian bourgeoisie had 'made their terms with the imperialists'. Dutt pointed out that the imperialists had dangled the 'bait of industrial development and [made] promises of gradual constitutional reforms'.[137]

But before Dutt had accepted Roy's thesis, the CPGB began to send its emissaries to India in a bid to capture the leadership of the movement. First to come was Percy E. Glading who arrived on 30 January 1925, contacted a few communists and left India on 10 April, only to report that there was no communist party in India. Glading was followed by George Allison, a member of the same party and a representative of the Red International of Labour Unions (RILU). He arrived in Bombay on 30 April 1926, and engaged himself in organizing a Left-wing group inside the All India Trade Union Congress (AITUC). However, on 23 January 1927, he was arrested on the charge of entering India with a forged passport and was deported from India on the expiry of 18 months' prison term.

By this time, the CPGB had already sent another envoy, Philip Spratt, who arrived in Bombay on 30 December 1926, in the guise of a representative of a London bookseller. The object of his visit, according to his own version, was that of a messenger and reporter.[138] Before coming to India, Spratt had secretly met Communist International's representative to Britain David Petrovsky who instructed him to write a tract on China urging India to follow the example of the Kuomintang.[139] After his arrival in India, Spratt's most important task was to get in touch with the leading Indian communists and along with them to organize a WPP which would serve as a legal cover for the CPI.[140] His next task, as revealed in the Meerut Conspiracy Case, was to make an attempt to infiltrate the INC by placing the communists in leadership positions.[141]

In the middle of January 1927, came two more emissaries—Mardy Jones, a representative of the Workers' Welfare League of India and Shapurji Saklatvala, a communist member of the British Parliament. Although Saklatvala's object was clear enough, he was not commissioned by the CPGB to visit India. According to Spratt, his visit might have had something to do with his rivalry with the Dutt brothers for the leadership of the Indian communist movement.[142] On the face of it, Saklatvala's visit was a resounding success because during his brief sojourn he was able not only to cultivate a close relationship with the Indian communists but also to evoke tremendous public enthusiasm for his cause. But his attempt to impress upon the people that Gandhism was politically degenerating and 'a moral plague' was a failure.[143]

While the British communists were thus busy in promoting the communist movement in India, Roy was far away from the Indian scene because early in 1927 he was sent by the Communist International on a mission to China. And his absence from Europe provided the CPGB with an excellent opportunity to have a free hand in Indian affairs and assume leadership of the movement. Roy's position was further compromised by the fact that the Indian communists, under the influence of the emissaries from Britain, began to impugn his authority. But the indefatigable Roy was not to be daunted by his waning influence and in his anxiety not to lose contacts with the Indian communists, he dispatched to India one of his most trusted comrades, Fazal Elahi Qurban. But apart from meeting a few communist leaders in Calcutta, Madras, Delhi and Bombay, he could achieve little in India. From the very first day of his arrival, the police kept close surveillance on his movements and on 5 April 1927, he was arrested under Section 121-A of the Indian Penal Code and sentenced to five years' imprisonment.[144]

Meanwhile, Benjamin F. Bradley (also known as Ben Bradley), another member of the CPGB and the most successful of the foreign emissaries in India, arrived on the scene. He came in the guise of an engineer representative of his brother's firm, the Crab Patent Underdrain Tile Company,[145] and immediately set about the task of organizing the communist movement. Together with Spratt, he took the reins of the CPI and began to ride it with a vigorous stride.

ROY ON FORMING WORKERS' AND PEASANTS' PARTY

One of the principal points on which M.N. Roy laid repeated stress during the early years of the Indian communist movement was that the primary goal of the communists in India should be to form a party of the people, whether a peoples' party, a party of the masses, a republican party, a national revolutionary party or a WPP, as a rallying ground for all the revolutionary elements.[146] In a letter to Bergarhatta dated 22 October 1924, Roy expressed the opinion that the immediate task of the communists in India was 'not to preach communism' but to organize the national revolutionary movement on the basis of mass action and a national revolutionary party.[147] According to him, the paramount importance of a peoples' party lay in the fact that it was only under the leadership of such a party representing the workers and peasants that the national movement, which had been betrayed at Bardoli, could be 'restored on a new basis'.[148] In the fourth congress of the Communist International which met in Moscow and Petrograd from 7 November to 3 December 1922,[149] Roy warned that the counter-revolutionary bourgeoisie which was 'not pitted against the old order of social production'[150] would surely betray the revolutionary movement and 'unless we are prepared to train politically the other social elements, which is objectively more revolutionary, to step into their places and assume the leadership, the ultimate victory of the nationalist struggle becomes problematic for the time being'.[151] Therefore, the crying need for India was not bourgeois political parties but 'mass organizations which would express and reflect the demands, interests and aspirations of the mass of the people, as against the kind of nationalism which merely stood for the economic development and political aggrandizement of the native bourgeoisie'. Roy concluded: 'We have to develop our parties in these countries in order to take the lead in the organization of the united anti-imperialist front.'[152]

Although Roy had some doubts about the efficacy of a party which would serve merely as a legal cover for the communist party, he laid great stress on the need for a WPP 'through which the communists could function legally, through which agitation and propaganda could be carried on legally and the workers and peasants could be organized to defend the interests of their class'.[153] Moreover, such a party would be an excellent agency through which the communists could find their way to the masses.

At first, some leaders of the Communist International did not like the idea of workers' and peasants' parties broached by Roy 'because of the dangers inherent in them from a pure proletarian class point of view'. But when such parties began to come into being, the leaders of the Communist International 'not only did not oppose their spontaneous formation but also encouraged them when they started taking concrete shapes'.[154] Urging the communists to identify themselves with these parties, Dmitry Manuilsky told the fifth congress of the Communist International that the communists should not ignore these new phenomena 'which were revolutionising the East'.[155] In his message to the CPGB, Philip Spratt also said that the CPI should launch a WPP as a legal cover and its members should get into the trade unions and obtain the leadership of them.[156]

The growth of WPPs in India and other colonial countries called for some tactical imperatives which were set forth by Roy in a letter to the Indian communists dated 30 December 1927. This letter later became famous as the 'Assembly Letter' because an intercepted copy of it was read into the records of the Indian Legislative Assembly. In this letter, Roy clearly outlined the organizational forms and tactical guidelines of the projected WPP.[157] He maintained that the CPI and the WPP should operate side by side—the former would be illegal and the latter legal. The CPI, he pointed out, could exist legally in India only if it abstained from preparations to wage war against the British, that is, legality could be had 'at the expense of the very *raison d'etre*' of the CPI.[158] The WPP, on the other hand, would be a legal party serving as a rallying ground of all the exploited social elements—the proletariat, the peasantry and petty bourgeoisie. Roy suggested that the communists in the WPP should be the driving force of the party 'by virtue of their being the conscious vanguard of the working class'.[159]

As to the question of international affiliation, Roy maintained that while the communist party would unquestionably remain a section of the Communist International, the WPP should affiliate itself with the League Against Imperialism whereby it would obtain all necessary aid without being condemned as having connections with Moscow. Roy then took the opportunity to warn the Indian communists against the activities of the CPGB in India. He pointed out that the centres in Berlin and Paris were the agencies of the Communist International looking after the Indian affairs and that the CPI's relations with the Communist International would be maintained through these centres and not through London. Therefore, any representative of the CPGB could come to India and work there only under the supervision and in accord with the CPI. No CPGB representative had superior right unless he came with a mandate from the Communist International. He then added that the Indian communists in exile were members of the CPI, and were automatically members of the WPP and that they expected to be treated by their comrades at home as such. They should not be looked upon as outsiders who could serve only as financial agents. As members of the same party nationally and internationally, it was necessary for all of them to coordinate their efforts.[160]

WORKERS' AND PEASANTS' PARTIES ACROSS COUNTRY

In accordance with the policy line laid down by the Colonial Commission of the fifth plenum of the ECCI that the Indian communists should work in the INC and in the Left wing of the Swaraj Party and that all nationalist organizations should be formed into a mass revolutionary party,[161] the first WPP in India was formed in Bengal on 1 November 1925. Originally it was known as the Labour Swaraj Party of the INC and in the opinion of Muzaffar Ahmad, it was inspired neither by the Communist International nor by M.N. Roy.[162] According to Muzaffar Ahmad, the four original founders of the Labour Swaraj Party were Kazi Nazrul Islam, Qutubuddin Ahmad, Hemanta Kumar Sarkar and Samsuddin Hussain.[163] The objective of this party was to launch a vigorous struggle for national liberation by organizing the workers and peasants of the country and to fight for their class interests in the Legislature. When the news of the formation of this mass organization reached Roy in Europe, he congratulated its founders on their courage in breaking away 'from the politics of vested interests'.[164]

At the initiative of the Labour Swaraj Party, a peasants' conference was held at Krishnagar (also known as Krishnanagar), Bengal, on 6 February 1926, and it was here that the name of the party was changed to the Peasants' and Workers' Party of Bengal. Originally it was proposed that the new party should be called the WPP of Bengal but, as Muzaffar Ahmad explained, because there were more peasant representatives in the conference, the word 'workers' could not be put at the beginning of the name of the party. In a later conference, the name of the party was again changed to the WPP.[165] A weekly Bengali journal of the Labour Swaraj Party called *Langal* (plough) now came under the editorship of Muzaffar Ahmad and its name was changed to *Ganavanee* (the voice of the people) since *Langal* did not symbolize all the toiling masses but only the peasantry.[166] Although the CPI was not illegal at that time, it was difficult for the communists to work under its banner openly and therefore the programmes of the CPI were conveniently put into practice from the platform of the WPP. Even the WPP manifestos were drafted by the central committee of the CPI.[167]

When the second annual conference of the WPP of Bengal was held in February 1927, under the presidency of Atul Chandra Gupta, it could claim only 40 members, mostly confined to Calcutta, with the exception of a branch in Mymensingh which was known as Bangiya Krishak O Shramik Dal. But by the time the third annual conference took place at Bhatpara in March 1928, the party had on its rolls about 125 members and a little over 10,000 affiliated members. In this conference, attended by only 80 members, a resolution was passed demanding a Constituent Assembly, complete independence and immediate redress of all social and economic grievances of the masses. The resolution also called the workers and peasants to play a more active role in the struggle for national liberation.

The example of Bengal was followed by Bombay where in February 1927 the existing Congress Labour Group was transformed into the WPP under the leadership of S.S. Mirajkar who also became its secretary. In April 1927, the party began to publish a weekly in the Marathi language named *Kranti* (revolution) with an editorial board consisting of Joglekar, Mirajkar, Nimbkar and Ghate. According to the organizers of this party, its formation was necessitated by the fact that the INC was dominated by vested interests and as such it could not represent the exploited workers and peasants of the country. The workers and peasants should therefore look after their own interests by uniting under the banner of a mass party and putting pressure on the INC leadership to make a common cause with the toiling masses. The party adopted a resolution proclaiming that the time was ripe for the creation of a WPP capable of guaranteeing the social, economic and political progress of these classes, of standing up for their demands in the INC, helping them with the organization of trade unions and emancipating them from alien influence.[168] The party formed an executive committee and divided itself into several groups, such as the trade union group, propaganda group, peasants' group, youth group and so on, so as to enable its workers to concentrate effectively on their respective fields of activity. Their activities, however, were confined mainly to industrial workers and to a lesser extent to the peasants.

In the same year, a WPP was also formed in Punjab at the initiative of Meer Abdul Majeed, Sohan Singh Josh, Santokh Singh and Bhag Singh Canadian. Majeed was a tireless trade union leader who, along with some of his close associates, did some excellent organizational work among the railwaymen and textile workers in Lahore. He used to publish an Urdu weekly called *Mihnatkash* (worker) and was one of the founders of the famous Naujawan Bharat Sabha (New Youth Indian Association) of Punjab.[169] Santokh Singh, a member of the Ghadr Party, came to India after receiving training from the Communist University of the Toilers of the East in Moscow and founded a weekly called *Kirti* (worker). This journal was published in both Punjabi and Urdu with Josh and Ferozuddin Mansur as their respective editors. In 1927, at a conference of the AITUC, they came into contact with other communists from various parts of the country and as a result the Kirti Kisan Party (WPP) was formed. Josh and Majeed were its secretary and joint secretary, respectively. The newly formed party held its first annual conference in April 1928, and proclaimed that its aim was to free the country from the bondage of British imperialism, to emancipate the exploited workers and peasants from all kinds of social, political and economic slavery and finally to establish a United Socialist Republic in India. Unlike the WPP of Bombay, its activities were confined mostly to the peasants of Punjab.

The next WPP was formed in Meerut at a conference of the Mazdoor and Kisan Sangh (Workers' and Peasants' Association) held in October 1928, under the presidency of K.N. Sehgal. Among the prominent communist leaders who attended this conference were Muzaffar Ahmad, Philip Spratt, Meer Abdul Majeed, Sohan Singh Josh and P.C. Joshi.[170] In this conference, a resolution was passed demanding national independence, abolition of native states, recognition of the workers' right to form trade unions, abolition of the feudal system, land for landless peasants, establishment of agricultural banks, eight-hour working day and minimum wage for industrial workers. The party brought out a paper, *Krantikari* (revolutionary), which first appeared on 17 November 1928, with the banner headline 'We Are Revolutionaries! The Banner of Revolt Is In Our Hands!'[171]

Thus, having formed WPPs in Bengal, Bombay, Punjab and Uttar Pradesh, the Indian communists issued 'a call to action' in October 1928, and decided that in the last week of December an all-India conference of all the WPPs would be convened in Calcutta where they would be consolidated into one All India WPP.[172] In this conference, presided over by Sohan Singh Josh and attended by over 300 communists and other Left-wing elements, it was decided that a national executive committee would be constituted with the following members: Muzaffar Ahmad, D. Goswami, H.K. Sarkar, K.N. Joglekar, R.S. Nimbkar, S.A. Dange, S.V. Ghate, Sohan Singh Josh, Bhag Singh Canadian, Ferozuddin Mansur, Meer Abdul Majeed, P.C. Joshi, L.N. Kadam, Gouri Shankar and B.N. Mukherjee.[173] The conference resolved that the party would make all possible efforts to give momentum to the workers' and peasants' movement by clarifying ideas and streamlining its organizational apparatus. It also emphasized the international character of the working-class movement and highlighted the need for the party's affiliation with such international organizations as the League Against Imperialism, the Pan-Pacific Trade Union Secretariat (PPTUS) and the RILU. As to the party's relation with the INC, it was decided that henceforth it would play a definitely independent role because a mass movement based on the doctrine of class struggle could not identify itself with the counter-revolutionary bourgeois leadership of the INC. However, it was pointed out that while the WPP remained relatively weak and unorganized in the country, it would be necessary to follow the traditional policy of forming factions within the INC organizations for the purpose of agitation, of exposing the reactionary leadership and of drawing the revolutionary sections towards the WPP. But the WPP could have no intention of dominating or capturing the INC. The function of its members within the INC was purely critical. They could not be allowed to take office in the INC organizations because the object of the WPP was to build up its own independent organization so that it could, as soon as possible, dispense with the necessity of agitation within the INC.[174]

From the very beginning, international communism was somewhat chary in its attitude towards the emergence of WPPs in India. Although the Communist International leaders did not openly oppose their growth, they refused to consider them a substitute for the CPI. They also apprehended that too much attention to these parties would inevitably delay and retard the development of the communist movement in India. It was further thought that the very nature of these parties revealed a dual class character of the toiling masses which was not in conformity with the Marxist–Leninist conception of a vanguard of the people. It was for this reason that these parties, no matter how revolutionary they might appear to be, could all too easily be transformed into petty-bourgeois organizations.[175] What was more harmful, as pointed out by R. Page Arnot, was that some of the Indian communists actually regarded these organizations as communist parties 'in an Indian shape' and did not 'see the need for the creation of a separate communist party'.[176] In his report to the sixth world congress of the Communist International, Otto Wilhelm Kuusinen also said that the formation of 'labour and peasant' parties as a substitute for CPI was not advisable, particularly in the colonial and semi-colonial countries, because such parties would tend to transform themselves into petty-bourgeois parties, to move away from the communists, thereby failing to help them to come in contact with the masses.[177]

Disagreeing with Kuusinen, Clemens Dutt told the sixth congress that it would be a mistake to dismiss too lightly the role of the WPPs. He pointed out that in the existing stage of development in India, the characteristic feature of the WPPs was that they were opening up an important route through which the communists could find their way to the masses.[178] Saumyendranath Tagore, who was actively connected with the WPP of Bengal, agreed with Dutt and added:

> It seems to me that some of the comrades are scared with the nightmare which is the result of their own irrational fantasy that the Workers' and Peasants' Party [WPP] is a substitute of the Communist Party [CPI]. Nobody has ever put forward that the Workers' and Peasants' Party would be a substitute for the Communist Party. The petty-bourgeois elements in the country who have been proletarianized are sometimes more proletarian than the proletariat themselves. The petty-bourgeois intelligentsia, the urban petty bourgeoisie have to play a role in the revolutionary movement in the colonies. What should be the organizational expression of the anti-imperialist front of the petty-bourgeois elements? Can we afford to swamp the Communist Party with such petty-bourgeois elements? We cannot. On the other hand, the Communist Party of India [CPI] should utilize the revolutionary energies of the petty bourgeoisie. I think it is clear that this anti-imperialist front can only take the organizational form of a Workers' and Peasants' Party composed of the urban intelligentsia and the petty-bourgeois elements, under the leadership of the proletariat .... We have been able to take over some trade unions from the reformist leadership, to organize peasants' unions: now we are told to liquidate all those Workers' and Peasants' Parties. This is pure and simple professorial dogmatism against which Lenin warned us so many times.[179]

Among other Indian delegates who took part in the debate, Usmani, Masood Ali Shah (Raza) and Habib Ahmad Nasim (Mazut) favoured the liquidation of the WPPs in India and blamed the Communist International leaders for their indecisive attitude towards these parties. Usmani averred that the WPPs existed as a result of 'wrong tactics and instructions of the Comintern [Communist International]'.[180] Raza emphasized that he, Usmani and Mazut should criticize the policy of the Communist International towards the WPPs and for 'altogether ignoring' the organization of the CPI. This was just putting 'the cart before the horse [and] this policy must be revised'.[181]

Despite such bitter controversy about its *raison d'être*, the WPP of India continued to operate as a projection of the CPI until its virtual disintegration as a result of the Meerut Conspiracy Case in 1929.

The Meerut Conspiracy Case, far from stamping out communism in India, made martyrs of the communists and gave them a unique niche in Indian political life. By playing upon anti-British emotions of the people, they evoked nationwide sympathy and could enlist for their legal advice the services of such prominent nationalist leaders as Jawaharlal Nehru, Farid-ul-haq Ansari and Kailash Nath Katju. And with this trial, which belonged to class of cases of which the Mooney trial and the Sacco–Vanzetti case in America, the Dreyfus case in France, the Reichstag fire case in Germany were supreme instances,[182] the first chapter of communism in India came to a close and communist ideology 'came to be established in India'.[183]

ROY'S EXPULSION FROM COMMUNIST INTERNATIONAL

Curiously enough, the historic trial in Meerut came to synchronize with the expulsion of M.N. Roy from the Communist International. On 13 December 1929, the *International Press Correspondence* formally announced Roy's expulsion in the following words:

> In accordance with the resolution of the X plenum of the ECCI [on the International situation and the tasks of the Communist International, Para 9] and the decision of the presidium of the ECCI of 19.12.1929, according to which adherents of the Brandler organization cannot be members of the Communist International, the presidium of the ECCI, declare that Roy, by contributing to the Brandler press and by supporting the Brandler organization, has placed himself outside the ranks of the Communist International and is to be considered as expelled from the Communist International.[184]

The ECCI preferred five charges against Roy. First, he misled the communists at home by directing them to set up WPPs. Second, he had instructed the Indian communists to work within the INC thereby making them 'a tool in the hands of the compromising and betraying bourgeoisie'. Third, he had broached the theory of 'decolonization' contrary to the policy of the Communist International. Fourth, he had betrayed the revolutionary movement in China. And last, he had associated himself with the anti-Communist International German communist leaders Brandler and Thalheimer in opposing the Communist International's policies in the Reich.[185] The Indonesian delegate, Musso, told the plenum: 'Roy is no longer our comrade, he is rather a comrade of Gandhi, or at least a comrade of Brandler and Thalheimer.'[186] Among the delegates from India, G.K.A. Lohani and Saumyendranath Tagore also denounced Roy for his 'indiscipline, uncomradely behaviour, forgery and misappropriation of funds'. Tagore wrote:

> It is clear that Roy's expulsion from the Communist International was not due to any political difference with Stalinism. Roy, the careerist, always served the man in power. He was always the most servile agent of Stalin and is still a Stalinist with the hope that the wheel of fortune may turn in his favour and he again may be reinstated in his former position by Stalin. Roy joined the Brandler opposition in Germany only after his expulsion from the Communist International. And he did that only to give a political colouring to his expulsion.[187]

Muzaffar Ahmad also opined that 'Roy had a certain thirst for leadership [and] he could not maintain the revolutionary dignity of his position and the reason was his lack of integrity which dragged him down.'[188]

But as the authors of these charges could neither substantiate their allegations against Roy nor extricate themselves from their own self-interest in the matter, it may be presumed from the way they spouted venom against Roy that he fell a prey not to thirst for leadership or lack of integrity but to a violent factional strife which had earlier claimed Leon Trotsky. After all, the man who had the courage to cross swords with Lenin could not possibly be accused of having served the man in power. On the contrary, it is possible that 'they were jealous of the Bengali because he had succeeded in obtaining the favour of Lenin and held a high place in the communist hierarchy'.[189]

Roy's own version of the episode bears this out. In an article entitled 'My Crime', he wrote:

> For sometime I have been standing before the 'sacred guillotine' the mad application of which is causing such a havoc in the international communist movement. I have stood in that position for nearly a year, not shuddering with fear for my head, but aghast at the incompetence of those who have usurped the leadership of the movement and amazed at the temerity with which this incompetent and irresponsible leadership is driving the movement to rack and ruin.[190]

He further said:

> The crimes attributed to me, I have not committed. My offence is that I lay claim to the right of independent thinking, and that is not permissible in the present critical period through which the Communist International is passing. I was not declared a 'renegade' and placed outside the pale of the official International, so long as I did not speak out my disagreement. The gag of silence was imposed upon me, the all mighty apparatus depriving me of all the means of expression. In other words, for the unpardonable crime of independent thinking. I would have been quietly buried into oblivion, had I not dared raise my voice. But the duty of a revolutionary sometimes transgresses the narrow limits of arbitrary discipline .... I was placed in a position where I found it was my revolutionary duty to join the Opposition against the present leadership which is ruining the International.[191]

As to the 'Indian Question', Roy added:

> I disagree with all the resolutions of the sixth congress, not only with that on the Indian Question. If the mistake were on one particular question, it might be advisable to wait hoping that it would be corrected in course of time. But the mistaken line pursued in India is but a small part of a huge blunder. Therefore,

it is not permissible to keep quiet. The International is in a crisis which is manifested by the composition and exercise of its leadership.[192]

Again, in his last letter to Stalin, Roy said: 'I cannot reconcile myself to the idea that decency, loyalty and honesty should have no place in the catalogue of Bolshevik virtues.'[193]

B. POLITICAL WILDERNESS

SIMON COMMISSION, CALL FOR COMPLETE INDEPENDENCE AND CIVIL DISOBEDIENCE MOVEMENT

About the same time the communist leaders were removed from the political scene and brought to Meerut for trial, the country was aroused from the soporific torpor into which it had slumped after the suspension of the Non-Cooperation Movement and once again all was set for blood and sweat for the freedom fighters of India. The politics of the INC was no longer in the doldrums and a buoyant optimism pervaded the political atmosphere. This mood burst forth in righteous indignation against the Simon Commission and all political leaders, irrespective of party affiliation, decided to boycott it. On 3 February 1928, the day of the arrival of the commission in India, a general strike was observed all over the country, mammoth public meetings denounced the commission in the bitterest language and huge processions took to the streets waving black flags and banners with the words 'Go Back Simon' inscribed on them. On 16 February, Lala Lajpat Rai moved a resolution in the Central Assembly impugning the commission and this was greeted with tumultuous cry of *Bande Mataram* from every corner of the hall. On 30 October while leading an anti-Simon demonstration in Lahore, Rai was mercilessly beaten by the police and his death on 17 November, believed to be due to the severe injuries suffered in the beating, sparked off a wave of violent reaction in all parts of the country. On 8 April 1929, two young men, Bhagat Singh and Batukeshwar Dutt, hurled bombs at the Legislative Assembly with the intention, as they put it later, 'not to kill, but to make the deaf hear'.[194] This was followed by a chain of terrorist activities and the consequent police atrocities. A large number of young men were arrested from all over the country and an All India Conspiracy Case was started in Lahore in the middle of 1929. People's anger, however, reached boiling point when these young prisoners went on hunger strike to protest against the deplorable treatment meted out to them in jail and when one of them, Jatin Das, died on 13 September after a two-month fast. The death of Jatin Das reignited the flames of revolutionary struggle. Youth and student organizations sprang up all over the country and conferences were held in Calcutta, Poona, Ahmedabad, Lahore, Nagpur and at many other places.[195] Verbal condemnation of British oppression was followed by chemical explosives. While acts of sporadic terrorism continued unabated, a band of Bengali revolutionaries raided the Chittagong armoury on 18 April 1930. The entire nation was agog with excitement.

In this tense atmosphere, charged with enthusiasm and expectancy, the annual session of the INC was held in Lahore in December 1929 under the presidency of Jawaharlal Nehru. Nehru was an embodiment of youthful spirit and courage and his election to the presidency added a special significance to the INC session.[196] On his arrival in Lahore he received a welcome, which, as described by *The Tribune*, 'even the kings might envy'.[197]

B.R. Nanda added:

He was the first president-elect of the Congress [INC] to ride a horse—a white charger followed by a detachment of Congress [INC] cavalry. The capital of the Punjab wore festive look; the streets were canopied with bunting and sparkled with coloured lights. The procession swelled as it surged the narrow streets of Lahore. Windows, roofs and even trees were crowded with spectators .... The Congress [INC] was meeting again in the Punjab exactly after ten years. The Amritsar Congress [Amritsar session of the INC] had been held in December 1919, Non-Cooperation had followed in 1920. Was history going to repeat itself?[198]

History was indeed going to repeat itself, for the historic Civil Disobedience Movement followed the resolution adopted in Lahore which declared that the supreme goal of India's struggle was not dominion status but complete independence. The resolution, while acknowledging the efforts of the viceroy towards a settlement 'of the national movement for *swaraj*', pointed out that nothing was to be gained in present circumstances by the INC being represented at the proposed Round Table Conference. It also declared that in pursuance of the resolution passed at its Calcutta session (1928), the word *swaraj* would henceforth mean complete independence and it expressed the hope that all Congressmen would devote their exclusive attention to the attainment of complete independence for India. As a preliminary step towards organizing the campaign for independence and in order to make the INC policy as consistent as possible with 'the change of creed', it resolved upon a complete boycott of the central and provincial Legislatures and committees constituted by the government and called upon Congressmen and others taking part in the national movement to abstain from participating in future elections and directed the present INC members of the Legislatures and committees to resign their seats. The resolution then appealed to the nation to prosecute the constructive programme of the INC and authorized the AICC to launch a programme of civil disobedience, including non-payment of taxes, whether in selected areas or otherwise and under such safeguards as might be considered necessary.[199]

The Lahore session was a victory for the Left wing of the INC. The momentous decision to discard the goal of dominion status in favour of complete independence was celebrated with befitting solemnity. An epic grandeur was added to it when, as the clock struck midnight on 31 December 1929 and the date of ultimatum issued by the INC expired, the president of the INC came out in solemn procession to the banks of the Ravi and hoisted the tricolour flag of Indian independence in the presence of a huge gathering that endured the biting cold of Lahore to witness the historic scene. As the flag went up the staff, a thrill of joy shook the vast audience and they saw a distant vision of the glorious future of India. There were scenes of exuberance and Nehru danced around the flagstaff.[200]

The Congress Working Committee (CWC) had decided that 26 January 1930 should be observed as Independence Day all over the country. On that day, every Indian was called upon to take the pledge to shake off foreign domination and restore national independence. 'The Pledge of Independence' declared that it was the inalienable right of the Indian people, as of any other people, to have freedom and to enjoy the fruits of their toil and have the necessities of life so that they might have full opportunities of growth. If any government deprived the people of these rights, then the people had the right to defy it. And as the British government had not only deprived the Indian people of their freedom but had based itself in the exploitation of the masses and had ruined India economically, politically, culturally and spiritually, India must sever all British connections and attain complete independence.[201]

Although the government brusquely dismissed the nation's resolve to win complete independence as 'stage lightning and teapot thunder',[202] the symbolic act of observing Independence Day evoked unprecedented enthusiasm. On 26 January at numerous meetings throughout the country, the tricolour was unfurled and the pledge of complete independence taken. On 14 January, the CWC met at Sabarmati and decided to launch the Civil Disobedience Movement. The resolution adopted by the committee declared that civil disobedience should be initiated and controlled by those who believed in non-violence as an article of faith. But as the INC had in its organization also those who accepted non-violence as a policy, the CWC authorized Gandhi and those who believed in non-violence as an article of faith to start Civil Disobedience as and when they desired and in a manner and to the extent they might think fit. The CWC expressed the hope that when the campaign was actually in action, all Congressmen and others would extend to the civil resisters their full cooperation and that they would observe complete non-violence notwithstanding any provocation that might be offered. The CWC further hoped that in the event of a mass movement taking place, all those who were rendering voluntary cooperation to the government, such as lawyers, and those who were receiving so-called benefit from it, such as students, would withdraw their cooperation or renounce benefits as the case might be and would throw themselves into the final struggle for freedom. The committee finally hoped that in the event of the leaders being arrested and imprisoned, those who were left behind and had the spirit of sacrifice and service in them would carry on the INC organization and guide the movement to the best of their ability.[203]

The Civil Disobedience Movement was formally launched on 12 March 1930, when Gandhi, along with a band of 79 followers, started his historic march to Dandi, on the coast 200 miles away from Sabarmati, to manufacture salt in defiance of law.[204] Amid thunderous ovations all along the trek, Gandhi reached Dandi on 5 April and next morning he dipped into the sea water, returned to the beach and picked up some salt by the waves.

The technical violation of the salt law by Gandhi was a signal to the country for mass civil disobedience—open violation of all oppressive laws, boycott of British goods, non-payment of taxes and all other anti-British activities. In Calcutta, mayor J.M. Sen Gupta violated the law of sedition by publicly reading out seditious literature. The whole nation was astir. Thousands of ladies, high and low-born, came out of the seclusion of their homes, valiantly fought the battle of freedom and courted imprisonment. Never before had the country witnessed such a spontaneous national awakening. And for over three years, India convulsed in a desperate struggle defying the most ruthless repression by the government.

CHINESE EXPERIENCE AND ULTRA-LEFT POSTURE

While the country was in the throes of this gigantic struggle, the communists were in the wilderness. Far from identifying themselves with the national upsurge, they turned their backs on the mass anti-imperialist movement and kept themselves aloof from the 'well-spring of Indian political life'.[205]

This policy of remaining aloof from the mainstream of the national movement was in consonance with the tactical–ideological guidelines laid down by the Communist International in 1928. According to the thesis adopted by the sixth congress of the Communist International, liberation movements in the colonial and semi-colonial countries under bourgeois-nationalist leadership were nothing but attempts 'by means of empty nationalist phrases and gestures' to keep the petty-bourgeois masses under the influence of the leadership and to induce imperialism to grant certain concessions. It was, therefore, necessary for the communists in such countries to isolate and emancipate themselves from the influence of the bourgeois-nationalist movements. In accordance with this policy, it was decided that the 'communists must unmask the national reformism' of the INC and oppose the *Swarajists*, Gandhists and so on and their talk of passive resistance.[206]

This ultra-Left posture of the Communist International was outlined in unmistakable terms in an 'Open Letter' from the Young Communist International to the Indian workers, peasants and youth. The letter asked the Indian working class and other revolutionary elements to recognize that by championing reformist movements, the INC was actually retarding the revolutionary movement and as such it could not lead the struggle of the Indian people against British imperialism. Therefore, it was the duty of the Indian communists to sever all contacts with the INC and similar organizations, such as the League of Independence, to disclose the falseness and treachery of the assistants of British imperialism and to drive the traitors and 'phrasemongers' out of their ranks.[207]

That this ultra-Leftism had its root in the China experience was clear from the following observation by Radek in June 1930:

> When the earnest revolutionary struggle of the workers and peasants begins, the national reformists will inevitably stand on the other side of the barricade .... To have even the slightest doubt about that, after

what we have seen in China, and to fail to prepare ourselves and the masses for this inevitable change of front on the part of the national reformists, would mean a frivolous and criminal abandonment to defeat of the workers and peasants.[208]

The conclusion which automatically followed from this argument was that the INC under the leadership of Gandhi was like the Kuomintang of China. Both were tools of imperialism. And the communists must oppose all movements under Gandhi's leadership in order to guarantee the victory of the revolution.[209]

In December 1930, the *International Press Correspondence* published the 'Draft Platform of Action of the C.P. of India [CPI]'—an important document containing a detailed analysis of the Indian political situation and the programme of the CPI. After highlighting the fact that the Indian people were groaning under the yoke of British imperialism which had exploited its political and economic supremacy and taken billions of rupees year after year out of the 'miserable income of India', thus bringing the toiling masses to the state of famine, perpetual poverty and slavery, the 'platform' declared that it was only through merciless and violent overthrow of British imperialism that the working masses of India would succeed in achieving their real independence and creating the conditions necessary for the development and reconstruction of society on the basis of socialism.[210]

The 'platform' then went on to identify the collaborators with British imperialism in the enslavement of the Indian people—the native princes, the landlords, the moneylenders, the merchants and above all the national bourgeoisie. As to the role of the INC, it declared that by consistently following the policy of compromise with British imperialism, the INC had betrayed the revolutionary struggle of the masses. The greatest threat to the victory of the Indian revolution was the fact that the masses still harboured illusions about the INC and had not realized that it represented the class interests of the exploiters against the fundamental interests of the toiling masses.

Criticizing Gandhi, the 'platform' pointed out that under the cloak of vague statements about love, meekness, modesty, national unity, the historic mission of Hinduism and so on, he preached the inevitability and the wisdom of the division of society into rich and poor, the eternal social inequality and exploitation. He preached the interests of the capitalist development of India built 'on the bones and the sweat of the working masses of the people', in collaboration with world capitalism.

Analysing the class character of the INC, the 'platform' pointed out that the INC not only supported the manufacturers against the workers during the textile strikes but also assisted in the passing of anti-labour legislation. It was the INC, which not only refused to support the fight of the railwaymen against British imperialism but also opposed the peasantry in their struggle against the moneylenders, the big landlords and the native princes. Moreover, the 'platform' felt that the INC had produced the Motilal Nehru Report on Constitutional Framework in alliance with the liberals, the landlords and manufacturers in order to preserve the landlords, the princes and the moneylenders as 'junior partners of British imperialism'.

Describing the Delhi Manifesto of 2 November 1929 as a 'programme of the chambers of commerce and similar associations', the 'platform' declared that the INC and particularly its Left wing had done and were doing all in their power to contain the struggle of the masses within the framework of British imperialist constitution.[211]

In Part II of the 'platform', entitled 'The Fight for Partial Demands of the Revolutionary Movement', the attention of the Indian communists was drawn to the fact that the 'propaganda of non-violence' by Gandhi, Nehru and other Congressmen was intended to prevent a general national armed insurrection of the toiling masses against British imperialism. By his own admission, it was pointed out, Gandhi took part in the armed suppression of the Zulu peasants' uprising in Africa and assisted 'the British robbers in their fight against the German capitalists for the right to exploit the colonial peoples'. Gandhi also recruited Indian peasants for the British army and sent to their deaths hundreds of thousands of Indian workers and peasants in the interest of the 'British robbers'.

> And today Gandhi tells the workers and peasants of India that they have no right to, and must not, revolt against their exploiters. He tells them this at the very time when the British robbers are making open war on the Indian people in the North West Province and throughout the country.[212]

The Left-wing leadership of the INC was also bitterly castigated as an appendage of imperialism and an enemy of the toiling masses. The most harmful and dangerous obstacle to the victory of the Indian revolution, said the 'platform', was the agitation carried on by the Left elements of the INC led by Jawaharlal Nehru, Subhas Chandra Bose and others. Under the cloak of revolutionary phraseology, they carried on the bourgeois policy of confusing and disorganizing the revolutionary struggle of the masses and helped the INC to come to an understanding with British imperialism. Particularly blackguardly and harmful was the part played by the national reformists in the labour movement in which they tried in every possible way to substitute the methods of class collaboration for the methods of class struggle. The treacherous part played by the INC as regards the peasantry had once again shown itself in the appeal of its Left leaders to the British governor-general of Bengal to send troops to crush the peasants' revolt at Kishoreganj.

> In these circumstances, some of the Left national reformists [supporters of Roy and others], who realized that the masses are becoming disillusioned in the Congress [INC], has cleverly put forward the advice to win the National Congress [INC] from within. Nominally their object is to revolutionize the Congress [INC], in reality it is to restore the prestige of the Congress [INC] by replacing the old treacherous leaders by new leaders who are no better than the old.[213]

On the basis of this analysis, the communists came to the conclusion that there could be no compromise between the counter-revolutionary nationalist leadership and the revolutionary masses.[214] Some of the extremist elements went a step further and diagnosed the mass upsurge during the Civil Disobedience Movement as a manifestation of growing confrontation between bourgeois nationalism and a revolutionary mass movement of the workers and peasants. According to the *Labour Monthly*, as the INC led by Gandhi represented the dissatisfied Indian bourgeoisie, it was not a 'part and parcel of the vast mass agitation' taking place in the country, however much it might appear that the INC leaders were the 'instigators of the present revolt'. The prime interest of the INC in this mass movement was not to accelerate it but to prevent it from developing into a revolutionary movement.[215] Therefore, 'the real struggle was not between the Congress [INC] and the British imperialism, but between the Congress [INC] and the Indian revolutionary movement.'[216]

In these circumstances, what were the main tasks of the Indian communists? The 'platform' declared:

> The exposure of the Left Congress [INC] leaders who may again undertake to set up a new party or organization like the former League of Independence in order once again to mobilize the mass of the workers is the primary task of our party. Ruthless war on the Left national reformist is an essential condition if we are to isolate the latter from the workers and the mass of the peasantry and mobilize the latter under the banner of the Communist Party [CPI] and the anti-imperialist agrarian revolution in India …. On every occasion they must expose the treacherous part played by the National Congress [INC]. Against the bourgeois compromise front established by the national reformists, they must create the united front of the toilers from below, on the basis of definite proletarian revolutionary demands and activities.[217]

ORGANIZATION IN TATTERS

Apart from the confusion over tactical guideline, the factor that contributed most to the slump in communist activity during the post-Meerut years was the crippled condition of the party organization. Although it was proudly claimed that the Meerut trial had 'placed communism on a sure footing in India',[218] there is no denying the fact that the imprisonment of front-ranking leaders had a traumatic effect on the organizational apparatus of the party. The task of building a centralized and well-coordinated party machinery which could harness the revolutionary forces in India still remained a pipe dream and to make things worse, factional quarrels between different communist groups threw the entire party organization into a state of disarray. To complicate matters yet further, Roy had returned to India in 1930 and made a bid for the leadership of the revolutionary movement. At this time, the Communist International also temporarily withheld affiliation of the CPI and it was little wonder that 'chaos and disintegration in the party all over the country appeared in an acute form'.[219] Thus, quarantined from the nationalist movement, disintegrated organizationally and torn into warring factions, the CPI lay marooned with little prospect of an early salvage.

Despite their imprisonment, the old-guard communist leaders continued to make frantic efforts to maintain control over the party organization and direct the movement from behind their prison bars. They managed to smuggle a number of documents out of jail and as already noted, addressed an appeal to the Communist International to rescue the party. But in the meantime, a new leadership had emerged outside jail to take charge of the party organization. Chief among these new leaders were Abdul Halim, Ranendra Nath Sen and Somnath Lahiri in Calcutta and S.V. Deshpande, B.T. Ranadive and Suhasini Nambiar in Bombay. While other party centres in Punjab, Uttar Pradesh and Madras remained virtually paralyzed, the Calcutta group had been continuing to work under the name of the Calcutta Committee of the CPI[220] and the Bombay group busied itself in trade unions and propaganda activities. Marxist literature was published in regional languages; a paper named *Workers' Weekly* was brought out and *Kranti* was revived. But although the leaders of both the Calcutta and Bombay groups felt the urgency of coordinating their activities in order to set up a centralized party organ, every attempt in that direction failed to produce tangible results mainly on account of sharp disagreement among the leaders on questions of organizational forms and operational tactics. Halim and Deshpande, both moderates, had doubts about the rationale of the ultra-Left policy line and argued that their activities should be carried on within the confines of the law. They were satisfied with such propaganda work as the publication of Marxist literature and the formation of socialist study centres. But the militant section of the leadership, represented by Ranadive, was inclined to follow a hard line and wanted to organize countrywide strikes and demonstrations of workers and peasants.[221] The differences between factional groups also centred around such vital issues as the attitude towards the INC and civil disobedience, the nature of trade union activities and so on and so forth.

These factional quarrels were responsible for the complete lack of coordination between various communist groups. Muzaffar Ahmad complained that 'in spite of repeated requests from the Calcutta Committee to give an all-India shape to the Communist Party [CPI], there was no response from the party leaders in Bombay.' The Calcutta Committee, therefore, 'started sending reports to the Communist International through various channels'.[222] In fact, such allegations and counter-allegations were made by every group of the party and each claimed direct relations with the Communist International. And to make things worse, the Communist International 'welcomed them all but bound itself to none'.[223]

ROY'S BID FOR LEADERSHIP

It was at this period of endemic factionalism that Roy appeared on the Indian scene in a bid to capture the leadership of the communist movement. Immediately after his expulsion from the Communist International, he had sent two of his close associates, Tayab Shaikh and Sundar Kabadi, to India to prepare the ground for his campaign for leadership. Shaikh and Kabadi had with them a manifesto addressed to the 'revolutionary vanguard of the toiling masses of India' in which Roy broached the thesis, contrary to his earlier stand, that success of communism in India lay through the national revolution and that the Indian communists 'must work through the national mass organizations and volunteer corps'.[224] When Shaikh was arrested and Kabadi returned to Europe, Roy himself arrived in India in December 1930, defying the warrant of arrest issued against him in connection with both the Cawnpore and Meerut Conspiracy Cases. For seven months, Roy successfully managed to dodge the police and established contacts with almost all political parties, trade unions and youth organizations upon all of which he made a very favourable impression. Roy had to move under extremely difficult circumstances because every step of the way he was dodged by the police. Moreover, he had to face a hostile group of communists who viewed Roy's movements and activities with great suspicion. But despite all this, Roy did some excellent work in a very short period of time. At Jawaharlal Nehru's special invitation, he attended the Karachi session of the INC in March 1931, and it was widely believed at that time that the resolution on fundamental rights and economic policy adopted by the INC was Roy's handiwork.[225] In short, until his arrest in July 1931, Roy was in a large measure successful in his attempt to persuade a good number of Indian communists to eschew their ultra-Left posture towards the anti-imperialist struggle under the INC leadership.

Commenting on Roy's activities during the seven months he was at large, British Intelligence observed:

> There is no gainsaying the fact that … Roy did very considerable mischief, despite the fact that the police were continually hot on his heels. His doctrines gained many adherents in Bombay and the United Provinces, and at a later date also in Calcutta and its environs. He made serious and by no means unsuccessful endeavour to impregnate the Congress [INC] with his views and was received, and well received, by several of the Congress [INC] leaders in different parts of India. Even Mr Gandhi was aware of his presence in the Congress [INC] *pandal* [dais] in Karachi. Judged from the intellectual standpoint, Roy, ever a realist, stands out heads and shoulders above all other Indian communist leaders with the possible exception of Dr G.M. Adhikari, and his continuous exhortations to 'eschew the disastrous ultra-Left policy' were calculated in the end to win over many more adherents to communism than [S.V.] Deshpande's vaporous thundering could ever have done.[226]

EMISSARIES OF COMMUNIST INTERNATIONAL

The Communist International, now disturbed at Roy's activities in India, could no longer allow the CPI to drift aimlessly in search of an anchorage. The growing disorganization of the party became a singular source of concern and embarrassment for the Communist International was clearly indicated by the publication of numerous articles on India in its journals and also by the arrival of its emissaries in India.

In addition to the 'Open Letter' and the 'Draft Platform of Action of the C.P. of India [CPI]', one more manifesto was addressed to the Indian communists by the central committee of the Communist Party of China in July 1933.[227] Expressing deep concern at 'the slowness of the process of the formation' of the CPI and giving examples from the work of the communist parties of the Soviet Union and China, the Chinese leaders pointed out that the 'chief decisive question' for the Indian communists was 'the formation of a militant mass Indian communist party' which should be 'a model of Bolshevik organization and iron discipline'. The party, it was emphasized, would not be a peaceful one, but 'a militant, bold and revolutionary party'. They praised the work of the Calcutta Committee of the CPI which

> energetically took up the call for the formation of an All India Communist Party, which understood the necessity to shift the centre of gravity of party work to activities to an all-India scale and which proposed to put an end to the pitiful chapter in the history of the Communist Party of India [CPI], the chapter of petty squabbles and splits, and to open a new page by the formation of a powerful united Communist Party of India [CPI].[228]

In regard to tactics, the Chinese leaders asked the Indian comrades to eschew ultra-Left policy because, they argued, the struggle against Left national reformists did not mean refusal to work in the reformist trade unions and therefore, it would be a great mistake to continue the practice of self-isolation from workers' meetings and the mass trade unions which were under the influence of the reformists. The retrogression from ultra-Leftism was in line with an earlier article carried by the *International Press Correspondence* which declared that the task of taking the initiative in the building of trade unions did not contradict but presupposed active work in mass reformist trade unions. Therefore, a sectarian policy of withdrawal from the trade unions would only strengthen the position of the bourgeoisie and their agents.[229]

To salvage the CPI from the morass in which it had become bogged, the Communist International also sent a number of emissaries to India. First to arrive was Prem Lal Singh, an Indian student who had just completed a course at the Kazan Imperial University, which was then renamed as Lenin University. Apart from establishing contacts with the Meerut prisoners, he could achieve practically nothing in India and after six months' sojourn, he returned to Moscow empty-handed. At about the same time, an American couple, William Nathan Kweit and Helen Howlen, arrived, and they were joined in July 1930 by another American, Harry Somers. But they were soon arrested under the Foreigners' Act, 1864, and deported in September 1930. In 1931, the Communist International dispatched Muhammad Seppasi, a former colleague of Roy, with the express instruction to counteract Roy's activities in India. Seppasi planned to reach India along with the homecoming Indian Muslims from Mecca. But as the pilgrims had left Mecca before he could join them, he came back to Moscow frustrated. Then yet another American, Henry G. Lynd, arrived with considerable funds and instructions for the Indian communists. In fact, soon after his arrival, the Bombay group received a sum of 12,000 rupees through him. Considerable amounts of money were also smuggled through John Magnus Clark, William Bennet and Constance Marry Sargent. But all of these emissaries were arrested by the police and deported. March 1931 saw the arrival in India of the most successful of all the emissaries, Amir Haider Khan, described by the British government as 'a most dangerous individual'. Khan came to India in the guise of a seaman and dodging the police for over a year contacted prominent Indian communists, organized communist groups in a number of textile mills, formed the Young Workers' League and even sent one of his comrades to Moscow for training. He was arrested on 7 May 1932, and after his trial, was sentenced to two-and-a-half years' rigorous imprisonment.

About the activities of the Communist International's emissaries in India, the following comments were recorded in a report prepared by the British Intelligence:

> It cannot be claimed, of course, that all of Moscow's emissaries to India have been objects of official attention, but it may be accounted fortunate indeed that so many of them have come under the watchful eye of the police. Except for Amir Haider Khan, none has any practical achievement to his credit. This is due to variety of reasons, not least of which is the preventive action, which the authorities in India have been able to take. But another important reason is the inferior stamp of the agents themselves, and it was a strange freak of fortune which placed substantial funds in the hands of those who were incapable of

spending to the best advantage but kept an energetic enthusiast like Amir Haider Khan in penury to the detriment of all his ambitious schemes. The Meerut convicts are known to have made complaints to Moscow on this score and to have specifically asked that British citizens be sent in the future. If therefore, the Comintern [Communist International] repeats its former mistakes in this respect, it will have only itself to blame.[230]

By the end of 1933, almost all the Meerut prisoners had been released from jail and a concerted effort was made to pull the party from the rut. As a result of this effort, a conference was held in Calcutta in December 1933, and a new statute of the CPI was adopted. A central committee was also formed with G.M. Adhikari as the general secretary. Ben Bradley immediately left India to report the formation of the all-India party to the Communist International and soon afterwards the CPI again became a section of the Communist International. But at this juncture, the government formally declared the party illegal under the Criminal Law Amendment Act of 1908.

C. THE ANTI-IMPERIALIST UNITED FRONT

SHIFT IN SOVIET POLICY AND COMMUNIST INTERNATIONAL'S MODERATE LINE

Immediately after assuming the powers of the presidency on Paul von Hindenburg's death, on 2 August 1934, Adolf Hitler declared: 'To forge a mighty sword is the task of internal political leadership, to protect the forging and seek alliance in arms is the task of foreign policy.' The inner dynamics of this policy made war a precondition for peace and prosperity. That in the list of possible victims the Soviet Union figured high was made clear by Joseph Goebbels' crusade against communism. He averred: 'The problem of Bolshevism is once more brought to the fore in all severity and today all of civilized humanity faces anxiously the question whether or not it will be possible, once more, to save Western civilization from being flooded from the Eastern steppes.'

At about the same time, Benito Mussolini, still holding the blood-soaked dagger that struck in the back of Ethiopia, declared: 'We reject the absurdity of eternal peace. We must always be stronger. We raise the banner of anti-Bolshevism.'[231]

On 25 July 1927, in a memorandum to the emperor, Premier Baron Tanaka outlined the foreign policy of Japan. He pointed out:

> Japan cannot remove the difficulties in Eastern Asia unless she [it] adopts a policy of blood and iron .... If we want to control China, we must crush the United States .... But in order to conquer China, we must first conquer Manchuria and Mongolia. In order to conquer the world, we must first conquer China .... Having China's entire resources at our disposal, we shall proceed to conquer India, the Archipelago, Asia Minor, Central Asia and even Europe. But to get control of Manchuria and Mongolia is the first step if the Yamato race wishes to distinguish themselves.[232]

Manchuria was seized in September 1931. On 25 November 1936, the warlords of Japan joined the Nazi Reich in signing the Anti-Comintern Pact[233] and embarked on outrages in Manchuria and Mongolia against the Soviet Union.

In the face of this scourge of fascism, the Soviet Union could remain in isolation only at its peril. Consequently, it sought alliance with other states, joined the League of Nations on 18 September 1934, championed the cause of disarmament and collective security and shelving all anti-democratic campaigns, embarked upon the policy of a united front of all communists, socialists and liberals against fascism.

The sudden shift in Soviet foreign policy was soon followed by the abandonment of the Communist International's ultra-Left policy towards the nationalist movements in the colonial and semi-colonial countries. When the seventh congress of the Communist International met in Moscow on 1 August 1935, the tasks of the Indian communists in the new circumstances were outlined by the Chinese delegate, Wang Ming, in his thesis entitled 'The Revolutionary Movement in the Colonial Countries'. In this thesis, Ming pointed out that the isolation of the Indian communists from the mass anti-imperialist struggle was due to two factors. First, they had suffered for a long time from Left-sectarian errors and did not participate in the mass demonstrations organized by the INC. Second, they did not possess sufficient forces independently to organize a powerful anti-imperialist movement. For a long time, the small, scattered groups of communists could not even be united and by their sectarian policy these small communist groups objectively helped to retain the influence of Gandhism and national reformism over the masses.

Ming further pointed out that although the Indian communists had now begun to rid themselves of their sectarian errors and were taking the first step towards the creation of an anti-imperialist united front, they had shown a great lack of understanding of the united front tactics. This was borne out by the fact that in attempting to establish a united anti-imperialist front with the INC they put forward such demands as 'the establishment of an Indian Workers' and Peasants' Soviet Republic, confiscation of all lands belonging to the feudal lords without compensation, a general strike as the only effective programme of action' and so on. Such demands on the part of the Indian communists, he averred, could serve as an example of how not to carry on the tactics of the anti-imperialist united front.

Ming observed:

> The Indian communists should in no case disregard work within the National Congress [INC] and the national revolutionary and national reformist organizations affiliated with it, maintaining at the same time their complete political and organizational independence. Both within and without the National Congress [INC], the Indian communists must consolidate all the genuine anti-imperialist forces of the country.[234]

Elucidating his arguments, he asked the Indian communists to take lessons from the fellow travellers in China and Brazil where the communists followed the strategy of the united front with all the anti-imperialist forces—the working class, peasantry, petty-bourgeoisie and the national bourgeoisie. The Indian communists, he said, would do well to broaden and strengthen their party organization by enlisting support of the various political blocs representing the four classes and—while keeping complete independence—must strive to forge a broad anti-imperialist coalition in collaboration with the national revolutionary and national reformist organizations. In effect, therefore, Ming urged the Indian communists to pursue simultaneously the tactics of a united front from above and a united front from below, that is, to make a common cause with the nationalist leadership with the ulterior motive of ousting it from the national revolutionary movement.

In regard to the concrete programme of action, Ming advised the Indian communists to denounce the 'slave constitution' embodied in the Government of India Act, 1935,[235] to agitate for the release of all political prisoners and the abolition of all repressive laws and decrees, to fight against low wages, high land rents and confiscation of peasants' land for non-payment of debts and to fight for the vindication of people's legitimate democratic rights and liberties.

The tactical guidelines formulated by Ming were supported by Georgi Dimitrov who declared in the seventh congress of the Communist International that the Indian communists must 'carry on active work inside the organizations which take part in the Indian National Congress [INC], facilitating the process of crystallization of the national revolutionary wing among them for the purpose of further developing the national liberation movement'.[236]

As the two Indian delegates, S.V. Deshpande and S.S. Mirajkar, were arrested by the police in Singapore on their way to Moscow, the CPI was not represented in the seventh congress of the Communist International. Therefore, the task of working out the full import of the new policy line devolved upon the leaders of the CPGB.

DUTT–BRADLEY THESIS

Before the new policy line was formally intimated to the Indian communists, R. Palme Dutt and Ben Bradley came out with a thesis 'The Anti-Imperialist People's Front in India', published in the *International Press Correspondence* and the *Labour Monthly* in February and March 1936, respectively.

After reviewing the critical phase of the nationalist movement resulting from the failure of the Civil Disobedience Movement and the imposition of the new constitution, Dutt and Bradley pointed out that the INC under the leadership of Gandhi had 'given up for the time [being] the attempt to direct the struggle' and it was now time for radicalization of the entire national leadership on the basis of the broadest possible anti-imperialist united front. The united front, however, did not mean the abstract unity of the 'entire Indian population' because there were classes and elements in the Indian society—the princes, the landlords, the moneylenders and other reactionary religious–political groups, which could never be the partners of any anti-imperialist struggle. The united front would be forged with all the progressive elements that stood 'for the policy of irreconcilable struggle with imperialism, for the advancement of the programme to reflect the growing influence of socialist ideas'. The thesis called upon every Indian patriot to recognize that the first need for the powerful advance of the Indian nationalist movement was the unity of all anti-imperialist forces in a common front. This was the indispensable condition for the successful fight against the ever-sharpening forces of reaction and oppression.[237]

Summarizing the role of the INC in the national movement and the communist attitude thereto, Dutt and Bradley observed that the INC was already the united front of the Indian people in the national struggle because it had achieved a gigantic task by uniting wide forces of the Indian people against imperialism and remained the principal mass organization of diverse elements seeking national liberation. For this reason, nothing should be allowed to weaken the degree of unity that had been achieved by the INC. They then pointed out that the communists had many times criticized the policy, programme and ideology of the INC because they believed that it was dominated by the bourgeois leadership whose interests often conflicted with the interests of the masses and with the interest of the revolutionary anti-imperialist struggle.[238]

The primary task of the Indian communists was, therefore, to oust the right-reactionary leadership of the INC and join hands with its Left-wing leadership represented by the newly formed Congress Socialist Party (CSP) so as to transform the INC into a mass platform of anti-imperialist national revolutionary movement.[239] The Dutt–Bradley thesis said that the Congress socialists, trade unionists, communists and Left Congressmen should all be able to unite on the essentials of a minimum programme of anti-imperialist struggle for complete independence. They pointed out that in this struggle, the CSP could play an especially important part and for this reason every effort should be made to clarify questions of programme and tactics in the CSP.

Dutt and Bradley also expressed the opinion that the Indian communists should no longer decry the nationalist demand for a Constituent Assembly and insist on the establishment of Soviets instead. Although they made it clear that the Constituent Assembly was no substitute for the Soviets, they thought that under the prevailing conditions of the national movement the demand for a Constituent Assembly would be an effective slogan for the mobilization of the masses against imperialism.[240] The demand for a

Constituent Assembly was the expression of the people's urge for political liberation and, therefore, the communists must identify themselves with the national aspiration, for there could be no socialist revolution without political freedom.

To sum up, in consonance with the new line of the Communist International laid down by Wang Ming, Dutt and Bradley called upon the Indian communists to isolate the 'Right-reactionary' leadership of the INC and to make a common cause with all the Left elements of the country and thus to forge a *front populaire* against imperialism.

RESURGENCE OF CONGRESS LEFT WING

The political situation in India during the years following the Civil Disobedience Movement was decidedly conducive to the formation of a united front of the communists and other Left-wing nationalists. The failure of the Civil Disobedience Movement and the consequent wane of Gandhi's influence was followed by the emergence of the CSP which now began to rally not only the radical elements inside the INC but also the younger sections of the people in general. Its initial appeal lay in the fact that it appeared on the Indian political scene at a time when both non-violent civil disobedience and revolutionary terrorism had lost their charm.[241]

The resurgence of the radical Left wing under the banner of the CSP was accompanied by an unprecedented awakening of the workers, peasants and students. It was at this time that the AITUC, which had experienced two successive splits in Nagpur and Calcutta, was once again unified. Similarly, for the first time, a centralized peasants' organization, called the All India Kisan Sabha (AIKS), was formed under the leadership of Swami Sahajanand Saraswati. The students' movement also got a new momentum when it was centralized under the banner of the All India Students' Federation (AISF).[242]

The growing radicalization of nationalist opinion was indicated beyond doubt by the following observation of Jawaharlal Nehru:

> I do believe that fundamentally the choice before the world today is one between some form of communism and some form of fascism, and I am all for the former, that is, communism. I dislike fascism intensely and indeed I do not think it is anything more than a crude and brutal effort of the present capitalist order to preserve itself at any cost. There is no middle road between fascism and communism. One has to choose between the two and I choose the communist ideal.[243]

Again, in his presidential address at the Lucknow session of the INC in April 1936, Nehru declared that socialism was not only an economic doctrine but a vital creed to which he held with his head and his heart. He worked for Indian independence because the nationalist in him could not tolerate alien domination and he worked for it even more because for him it was the inevitable step to social and economic change. He wanted the INC to become a socialist organization and to join hands with all other forces in the world in order to bring about the 'new civilization'. But he realized that the majority in the INC might not be prepared to go this far. Nationalism, he added, was too narrow an objective even for the limited goal of political independence. Yet, most Congressmen hesitated to take steps which might frighten the vested interests. Most of these interests, he pointed out, were already ranged against the masses and nothing could be expected from them except opposition even in the political struggle.[244]

In December 1936, the annual session of the INC was held at Faizpur where the atmosphere was charged with socialist slogans emphasizing the rights of the workers and peasants and denouncing the forces of imperialism and fascism. In accordance with this spirit, the socialists demanded at the Subjects Committee that the INC should declare solidarity of the Indian people with the enslaved peoples of the world and with the people of the Soviet Union. But by then, observed Pattabhi Sitaramayya, Jawaharlal Nehru had somewhat resiled from his enthusiasm for communism as a result of the 'schooling that the president of Lucknow [session of the INC] had had for well neigh a year in the university of life'.[245] Nehru now took the stand that the INC stood for democracy in India and he fought for a democratic state, 'not for socialism'.[246]

GANDHI–BOSE CONFLICT

There being no annual conference of the INC in 1937, its 51st session was held at Vithalnagar in Haripura in 1938 and Subhas Chandra Bose was elected president. The election of Bose not only indicated the growing strength of the Left-wing forces inside the party but also precipitated his conflict with the Right-wing leadership represented by Gandhi. As pointed out by Bose himself, his endeavour to stiffen the opposition of the INC to any compromise with Britain caused annoyance 'in the Gandhian circles' who were then looking forward to an understanding with the British government. A further cause of exacerbation for Gandhi was the formation by Bose of the National Planning Committee for drawing up a comprehensive plan for national economic development, particularly industrialization. Gandhi was opposed on principle to the industrialization of the country and could not reconcile himself to any such programme being adopted by the INC. Moreover, when Bose began to make preparations for a massive national struggle which was to synchronize with the coming war in Europe, Gandhi and his followers objected because, so it seemed to Bose, they 'did not want to be disturbed in their ministerial and parliamentary work [and] were at that time opposed to any national struggle'.[247]

But Gandhi ultimately won the field. On the eve of the next session of the INC to be held at Tripuri in March 1939, 13 members of the CWC tendered their resignation leaving Bose and his elder brother Sarat Chandra Bose isolated. Soon afterwards, Govind Ballabh Pant and 160 other members of the AICC gave a formal notice to the president expressing their intention to move a resolution in the ensuing INC session reposing their fullest confidence in the leadership of Gandhi. The proposed resolution inter alia declared that in view of the critical situation that might develop during the coming years and in view of the fact that Gandhi alone could lead the country and the INC during such crisis, the AICC regarded it as imperative that the president should nominate the CWC in accordance with his wishes.[248]

In the face of such stiff opposition from the Right wing, it became impossible for Bose to continue as the INC president. Bose's proposal in March 1939, that the INC should issue an ultimatum to the British government demanding complete independence within six months was rejected by Gandhi and his followers including Nehru. Thus, a situation arose in which the Gandhian wing began to oppose Bose in every conceivable way with a view to make it impossible for him to function. This resulted in a complete deadlock within the INC. Bose now felt that as any compromise through direct negotiation had proved to be abortive, the deadlock could be resolved only if the Gandhian wing gave up its obstructionist policy or if he submitted to them. The Gandhian wing, observed Bose, was determined neither to accept his leadership nor to allow him to control the INC machinery. He would be tolerated only as a puppet president. According to Bose, the Gandhian wing had the tactical advantage of being the only organized party within the INC acting under a centralized leadership, whereas the Left wing had no such centralized leadership. Although the CSP was at that time the most important platform of the radical nationalists, its influence was limited primarily because of the absence of any centralized leadership commanding general confidence. To make matters more difficult for Bose, as his conflict with Gandhi became increasingly serious, 'even the CSP began to vacillate'. Thus, when Bose found that he could neither 'agree to be a puppet president', nor come to a compromise with the Right wing, he resigned the presidency on 29 April 1939.[249]

Bose was finally forced to resign because Gandhi turned his weapon of non-cooperation not against the British but against the president of the INC. Curiously enough, after the resignation of Bose, the followers of Gandhi, while denouncing Bose as a fascist, celebrated their 'victory' by raising slogans comparing Gandhi with Hitler. By doing so, they probably intended to extol Gandhi's firmness in dealing with his opponents, but such reckless action shocked many people both in and outside the INC. Even Rabindranath Tagore deprecated this fascist tendency among the INC Right-wingers.[250] Bose also said that 'if fascists meant Hitlers, super-Hitlers or budding Hitlers, then one may say that these specimens of humanity are to be found in the Rightist camp.'[251] Michael Edwardes commented:

> Gandhi, whom so many both in India and abroad believed to be compounded only of sweetness and light, had, by the use of his overwhelming prestige and the sort of intrigue one would expect from Tammany Hall, succeeded in disposing of the only real opposition to his leadership.[252]

GOVERNMENT OF INDIA ACT, 1935: CONGRESS LEFT VERSUS RIGHT

After Civil Disobedience Movement, the emergence of the CSP brought about a definite alignment of political forces and polarization of the nationalist leadership. At the Lucknow session of the INC (1936), Nehru openly identified himself with the Left and included in the CWC Subhas Chandra Bose, Jayaprakash Narayan, Narendra Deva and Achyut Patwardhan. He also exposed himself to the odium of the Right-wing leadership by proposing the affiliation of mass organizations of workers and peasants to the INC. The viability of the nationalist movement, he emphasized, lay in the identification of the INC with the economic struggle of the exploited masses. Although under the pressure of the Left-wing elements two subcommittees were formed to look into the problem of workers and peasants, Nehru's proposal for collective affiliation of their organizations to the INC was thrown out in the Subjects Committee and a Mass Contacts Committee was set up instead.

Another bone of contention which put the Left at loggerheads with the Right was the question of participation in the forthcoming elections and acceptance of office under the new constitution. Although the Left-wing leaders agreed that revolutionary parliamentarianism was 'an integral part of the national freedom',[253] they were not in favour of accepting office under the Government of India Act, 1935. Nehru opined: 'If the Congress [INC] decided to accept office under the new Act, I am quite sure to that extent it will cooperate with and strengthen British imperialism.'[254] Rightist opinion in the INC, however, argued that refusal to accept office would not only weaken opposition to the new Constitution but would also mean 'playing the game according to British rules'. The issue was debated furiously in the AICC meeting held in Delhi in March 1937. After two days of prolonged discussion, the amendment, opposing acceptance of office was defeated and a resolution was passed authorizing acceptance of office in provinces where the INC commanded a majority in the Legislature provided the INC in the Legislature was satisfied that the governor would not use his special powers of interference in regard to constitutional activities.[255]

Having decided to participate in the elections, the next controversy centred around the question of the programme to which the INC would commit itself in the election manifesto. The Leftist elements vehemently stressed the need for drawing up a radical socio-economic programme which would give expression to the demands and aspirations of the masses. In the AICC meeting held in Bombay, the Congress socialists pointed out that only a concrete programme aiming at the removal of the economic grievances of the masses could strengthen the popular base of the INC. The communists also prepared two draft manifestos, one for the consideration of the INC and another for their own party, wherein they demanded democratic rights and liberties for the workers and peasants, the right to strike, an eight-hour day, complete independence, confiscation of British capital, abolition of native states and establishment of a Workers' and Peasants' Soviet Republic.[256]

The election manifesto which was ultimately adopted by the INC was more or less in line with the Leftist position, insofar as it laid great stress on the necessity of mass movements in the struggle for freedom. To the workers, the manifesto promised to secure a decent standard of living, reasonable hours of work, protection against unemployment, help for old age, disability and sickness and a suitable machinery for the satisfactory settlement of industrial disputes. It also recognized the workers' rights to form unions and to strike for the safeguard of their legitimate interests. For the amelioration of the condition of the peasantry, the manifesto pledged to bring about radical land reforms including equitable distribution of land, relief to small cultivators by way of reduction of land revenue and total exemption of rent from uneconomic holdings. The manifesto also promised to solve the problem of rural indebtedness by declaring a moratorium, scaling down debts and making provisions for cheap credit facilities.

In regard to the new Constitution, the manifesto reiterated its entire rejection of the Government of India Act, 1935 and the Constitution that had been imposed on India against the will of its people. Any cooperation with the Constitution, it declared, was a betrayal of India's struggle for freedom and a strengthening of the hold of British imperialism and further exploitation of the Indian people who had already been reduced to direst poverty under imperialist domination. Therefore, the INC was determined neither to submit to this Constitution nor to cooperate with it but to combat it, both inside and outside the Legislature. It further declared that the INC would not recognize the right of any external power or authority to dictate the political and economic structure of India and every such attempt would be met by organized and uncompromising opposition of the Indian people.[257]

That the manifesto evoked great popular enthusiasm was evident from the fact that in the elections the INC obtained an absolute majority in five provinces. And overwhelmed by this success, some of the Leftists relented from their earlier stand and decided to take office. According to Jawaharlal Nehru, the opinion of the majority in the INC was in favour of acceptance of office, but it was even more strongly and unanimously in favour of the basic INC policy of fighting the new Constitution. They would go to the Assemblies not to become partners in the imperial firm but to try to prevent the federation from materializing, to stultify the Constitution and prepare the ground for the Constituent Assembly and independence, to strengthen the masses and wherever possible, in the narrow sphere of the Constitution, to give some relief to them.[258]

According to Michael Edwardes, there was another reason behind the eagerness of the INC to go to the Legislatures and accept office. During the three months in which the Act had been in force without INC participation, the interim ministries had exercised a large measure of real power and many Congressmen wanted the prerequisites of that power without being baulked by 'Left-wing intransigence'. And once in power, they 'began to show signs of enjoying it' and became, as Nehru saw it, 'involved in petty-reformist activities'. They forgot not only the main issue of national independence but also the promise of specific social and economic reforms contained in the election manifesto. At the same time, they 'found themselves under pressure from their constituents to get on with the job of translating promises into reality'. This posed a great dilemma, since to initiate radical socio-economic reforms would alienate 'special interest groups essential to Congress [INC] and failure to do so would alienate the masses'. Moreover, as pointed out by Edwardes:

> It would be a denial of Congress's [INC] avowed reasons for claiming that Indians could rule themselves better than the British. The strains inside Congress [INC] soon became severe and there is no knowing what might have happened if the outbreak of the Second World War had not given Congress [INC] ministries an excellent excuse to resign. Otherwise, disillusionment would inevitably have grown and Congress [INC] itself might well have split.[259]

CPI AND CSP: ALLIANCE AND CRACKS

It was in this piquant situation that the communists set about translating their policy of a united front into positive and purposeful action. Initially, the Indian communists, split into many quarrelling groups, were reluctant to follow the new line of the Communist International because they still shuddered at the idea of collaborating with the national-reformist leadership of the INC. Therefore, when Dutt and Bradley urged them to put the united front tactics into practice, many of them were inclined to ignore the advice.[260] But when the CSP unilaterally took the decision to accept communists in its ranks, they decided to eschew their Left-sectarian stand and thought it prudent to become partners of an anti-imperialist united front. The task of formulating the new tactical line was admirably executed by general secretary P.C. Joshi under whose energetic stewardship the CPI once again found a role to play in Indian politics.[261]

The idea of a socialist–communist alliance was first mooted by the leaders of the CPGB—Harry Pollitt, R. Palme Dutt and Ben Bradley—who discussed the question with one of the founder members of the CSP, M.R. Masani, who happened to be in Moscow during the seventh congress. But the dialogue was cut short when Masani insisted that such an alliance could be brought about only if the CPI dissolved and severed all connections with the Communist International.[262]

The socialist–communist alliance, however, took concrete shape through the enthusiasm and initiative of Jayaprakash Narayan, the general secretary of the CSP. At the second national conference of the CSP held in Meerut in January 1936, Narayan emphasized the need for a common front of all 'groups and individuals who stood by Marxism'[263] and suggested that in view of the shift in the policy of the Communist International, the communists should be admitted to the membership of the CSP. And despite the fact that there had been as yet no indication of an approval from the CPI, the national executive of the CSP unilaterally adopted a resolution to that effect, in the belief that the communists would reciprocate the socialist gesture.[264]

True to this expectation, the communists, in line with the new policy of the Communist International, seized the opportunity offered by the CSP and at Joshi's directive, large numbers of them came forward to accept membership of the CSP.

Within a very short time, the communists had infiltrated the ranks of the CSP and captured many important positions in both its central and local units.[265] Among those who occupied the most prominent positions in the CSP organization and leadership were Sajjad Zaheer, Z.A. Ahmed, K.M. Ashraf, E.M.S. Namboodiripad, P. Sundarayya, A.K. Gopalan, P. Ramamurthi and P. Jeevanandham.[266]

Sajjad Zaheer, who later became the founding member and secretary of the Communist Party of Pakistan and was convicted in the famous Rawalpindi Conspiracy Case, was made joint secretary of the CSP. Z.A. Ahmed, a teacher from Sindh, actively participated in INC politics during the early 1930s and was elected to the Sindh Provincial Congress Committee in 1936 and to the AICC in 1937. An excellent organizer, he later joined the CPI and after joining the CSP became a member of its executive committee. K.M. Ashraf, another member of the executive committee of the CSP, was also an active member of the INC during the 1930s and directed its Political and Economic Information Department in 1937. E.M.S. Namboodiripad also started his political career during the Civil Disobedience Movement and courted imprisonment. After his release from jail, he came under the influence of K. Pillai, A.K. Gopalan and K.P.R. Gopalan and embraced Marxism. He, thereafter, joined the CSP and became one of its joint secretaries. Similarly, Sundarayya also responded to Gandhi's call to join the national movement and participated in the *satyagraha* movement under his leadership. He joined the CPI in 1932. After the formation of the CSP, he was entrusted with the charge of its Andhra unit. A.K. Gopalan, one of the most active communist leaders since 1939, also entered the INC politics under Gandhi's leadership during the late 1930s. In 1935, he joined the CSP. He was elected president of the Kerala Provincial Congress Committee and from 1936 to 1939 was a member of the AICC. P. Ramamurthi was a member of the

AICC for long seven years and joined the CPI in 1936. After accepting membership of the CSP, he took charge of its Madras unit. P. Jeevanandham, who earned distinction during the anti-*Brahmin* movement in Madras during the 1930s, was in charge of the Tamil Nadu branch of the CSP.

However, the socialist–communist alliance began to run into difficulties when reports reached the CSP national executive that the communists were sowing seeds of discord by asserting that the party had not developed along true Marxist lines. It was alleged that they were trying to convert the socialist members to communism. Another serious allegation against the communists was that they were secretly manoeuvring to capture local CSP units and labour organizations. But although the CSP national executive took serious note of the communists' disruptive activities, it did nothing more than expressing its resolve to combat such factional tendencies, 'if necessary by resorting to disciplinary action'.[267]

The socialists also found themselves at loggerheads with the communists when the latter began to broach the idea that the Left forces should support 'the struggle of the Indian capitalists against the domination of the British financial capital' and declared that all the 'four classes' should unite under the banner of anti-imperialism.[268] This Rightist turn in communist policy was confirmed by a resolution adopted by the CPI politburo in February 1937, which declared that not only the Left forces but even the 'Indian merchants and industrialists' should be accommodated in the anti-imperialist united front.[269] In bitter indignation, the socialists denounced the resolution as a betrayal of Marxism. But the communists defended their stand by accusing the socialists of 'Left sectarianism' and pointing out that the four classes envisaged by the politburo did not include the 'pro-imperialist bourgeoisie or the landlords and princes'.[270] But despite these explanations, the socialists had little doubt that by their disruptive activities, both on the organizational and ideological fronts, the communists were undermining the very spirit of the Lucknow Agreement which, they held, stipulated the eventual merger of the two parties into a single political organization. The communists, on the other hand, alleged that socialists were hounding out the communists from the CSP ranks by branding them as 'disruptors'. In these circumstances, they declared that 'united action was practically impossible'.[271]

That the crack in the socialist–communist alliance was beyond repair became evident in the meeting of the CSP national executive in Patna in 1937, where the two groups violently clashed over an alleged secret CPI document, which had somehow fallen in the hands of the socialists. When the document was read in the meeting, the socialists were shocked to hear that the communists did not consider the CSP as a true socialist party and that the communists wanted to cooperate with it only to use it as a convenient platform of action. In great indignation at this 'Trojan horse strategy' of the communists, the CSP national executive formally declared the Lucknow Agreement as dead and unanimously decided not to admit any more communists into its ranks. However, the CSP national executive not only took no disciplinary action against the communists but also allowed them to continue to dominate over the Tamil Nadu and Kerala branches of the party.[272]

The communists attempted to refute these charges by reiterating their allegiance to the Lucknow Agreement and as a proof of their sincerity, proposed immediate merger of the two parties. But socialists rejected the proposal. Some socialist leaders, however, later felt that the decision not to expel the communists was a grave mistake.[273]

Another secret CPI document, which touched off a furore, was published by M.R. Masani in 1938. This document, 'The Communist Plot Against the CSP', contained a detailed plan of work for the utilization of the united front to promote communist interests. It instructed the communists to enter the CSP for the purpose of wrecking it from within, and asked them to indoctrinate the socialist ranks in order to win them to the fold of the CPI.[274] This was to be done 'without making much noise about it'. The document also contained

an analysis of the success of infiltration in various provinces, the number of persons won over to communism and who would vote communists on specific issues. Specific tasks were detailed for communists in all provinces, depending on whether the communists were now in a majority or minority, whether they held responsible positions in the executive [CSP national executive] or constituted the rank and file.[275]

After bringing this secret document to light, Masani demanded strong disciplinary action against the communists. But once again the CSP national executive failed to take any drastic measure against the communists. Commenting on this episode, Jayaprakash Narayan observed that although for many socialists this document was the last straw, the national executive allowed things to drift simply because it was reluctant 'to face an unpleasant task'. Such policy of drift, he regretted, not only created a good deal of confusion but also delivered the CSP into the hands of the communists and drove some of the leading members of the national executive to resign. Naturally, this produced a great consternation in the ranks of the CSP 'though it was welcomed by the CPI and its Trojan Horses and stooges'.[276]

Indeed, the communists were so much encouraged by the weakness and vacillation of the CSP national executive that at the Lahore conference of the party in 1938, they made an attempt to capture the national executive itself. Describing this climacteric event in the history of the CSP, Masani observed that things came to a head as a result of his presidential address in the course of which he 'made friendly but firm criticism of the Soviet dictatorship and the dubious policies it was pursuing in Spain and elsewhere, and stressed the necessity of adhering to democratic and clean methods for the achievement of a socialist society'. Masani said:

> Stung to action by an awareness of the clarification which the presidential address would produce in the ranks of the CSP, the communists decided to strike before the tide turned against them. They made an attempt at nothing less than complete capture of the CSP.[277]

When the question of the election of the new national executive for the next year came up, two lists were submitted before the conference—one by Jayaprakash Narayan and another by the communists. Narayan's list consisted of the old national executive with minor alterations and gave the communists no less than one-third of the seats. The list produced by the communists, on the other hand, showed that they were not satisfied with one-third of the seats but wanted an absolute majority in the national executive. Narayan and other leading members of the CSP thereupon made it clear that if the communist list were accepted, a split would become inevitable. However, the Lahore conference, by a narrow majority, voted for Narayan's list 'thus maintaining a precarious balance of power in the organization'.[278]

Although the communists failed in their bid to capture the national executive, they succeeded in precipitating a situation which forced four of the founding fathers of the CSP—Achyut Patwardhan, Ram Manohar Lohia, Ashoka Mehta and M.R. Masani—to resign. All these leaders had advocated expulsion of the communists from the CSP; but general secretary Jayaprakash Narayan, hoping against hope, thought that such an action would do more harm than good to the cause of socialism in India.[279]

After the Lahore conference, the two parties found very little ground for joint action and the socialist–communist alliance limped on at an uncertain pace until 1940 when the national executive finally expelled the communists from the CSP.

COMMUNIST INFLUENCE WITHIN CONGRESS

From the tactical point of view, the alliance with the socialists was of great significance to the communists, for it afforded them an opportunity to penetrate the INC of which the CSP was a constituent part. The communists avidly seized this opportunity and infiltrated the nationalist organization from its lowest level to the AICC. This not only broadened their base of mass contact but also gave them a new elan in

Indian politics. Of those who succeeded in occupying important positions in the INC, the most notable were Mian Iftikharuddin, Swami Sahajanand Saraswati and Indulal Yagnik.

From the very beginning of their united front with the INC, the communists vigorously pursued the tactics of united front from below against the Right-wing nationalist leadership with a view to 'moving the active sections of the Congress [INC] rank and file out of the reactionary "constructive programme" of Gandhism'.[280] The success of this policy was evident not only from the growing influence of the communists in the local units of the INC but also from the fact that by 1939 they claimed as many as 20 seats in the AICC.[281]

Emboldened by this success, the communists attempted to resolve the issue of violence versus non-violence by moving an amendment at the Faizpur session of the INC (1936) which declared that *swaraj* could be achieved only by 'an uncompromising revolutionary mass struggle' against imperialism. Although the amendment was defeated, the communist influence inside the INC was amply demonstrated by the fact that in the AICC, it was supported by 45 members out of 128 and in the full session by 262 members out of 713.

CPI VOLTE-FACE: GANDHI OVER BOSE

After the election of Subhas Chandra Bose as the INC president, the Leftists had fondly hoped that they had at last found an answer to Gandhi. But when Gandhi accepted the challenge and forced Bose to resign, they realized that Gandhi could not be fobbed off as easily as they thought. The communists, therefore, decided to trim their sails to the wind and chose to side with Gandhi against Bose. Throwing aside all their revolutionary pretensions, they declared that Gandhi commanded 'the greatest mobilizing power' and that the anti-imperialist struggle 'demanded not the exclusive leadership of one wing but a united leadership under the guidance of Gandhi'.[282] Explaining this shift in the communist policy, S.G. Sardesai observed that in the new conditions it was unnecessary for the Leftists to continue their old attitude towards Gandhism and Gandhian leadership. They had exposed the shortcomings of Gandhism sufficiently in the past and now, with the new strength at their command, the time and opportunity had come for them 'to weld even Gandhism with the new nationalism'. This necessitated a very close study and emphasis on every positive aspect of Gandhism particularly during its militant anti-imperialist phase between 1919 and 1920. Sardesai declared: 'This is the Gandhism that we have to resurrect, burnish and replenish.'[283]

This strange volte-face of the communist leaders not only created confusion and indignation among many of their followers but the image of the CPI also stood badly tarnished. Denouncing the leaders who were responsible for this somersault, Ajoy Ghosh asked:

> Has not Tripuri [session of the INC, 1939] meant the smashing up of the entire Left including the communists? Did not the communists follow a tailist policy throughout the session? Were they not obsessed with the ideas of unity and did they not, therefore, try to placate everybody and end by placating none? Did they not in their eagerness for unity vacillate at every step, renounce their entire political line and even their fundamental principles?[284]

The renunciation of the entire policy line hitherto advocated by the communists was in fact necessitated by the turn of events in the international situation which was swiftly escalating towards a crisis. With the mounting danger confronting the socialist fatherland, it was now important for the CPI to concentrate its attack against the enemies of the Soviet Union. The Neville Chamberlain government in Britain was nothing but an ally of fascist Germany and as such the communists must do everything to strengthen the anti-British movement in India. And for this purpose, an alliance with the INC under Gandhi's leadership was imperative.[285]

While the Indian communists transformed Gandhi overnight from an imperialist stooge to a powerful anti-imperialist force, the leaders of the socialist fatherland transformed Hitler from a fascist scourge to an apostle of peace. On 23 August 1939 came the stunning news that the Soviet Union had concluded a 10-year neutrality and non-aggression pact with Germany.

D. COMMUNIST PARTY OF INDIA AND THE SECOND WORLD WAR

RUSSO-GERMAN ENTENTE AND INDIAN RESPONSE

The Russo-German entente presented an awkward problem to the communists in Great Britain, France and India. It put the patriotism of the British and French communists to a severe test because they were now confronted with the embarrassing task of opposing the war efforts of their own national governments in order to suit the expediency of Russian diplomacy.

Describing the international situation as a 'tangled knot', the *Labour Monthly* commented that the situation placed different tasks according to their conditions before different sections of the international working-class movement in pursuit of their common aim and that this would require correspondingly different tactics at successive stages of development according to the sharp changes in the alignment of international forces. The communists, it said, were now in a new type of situation, which would stretch the capacity of the leadership of the working-class movement.[286]

As for the Indian communist's, although the Russo-German pact took them by complete surprise, they were saved from embarrassment by the rising tide of anti-war feeling in India.[287] In fact, as pointed out by M.R. Masani, it would have been more embarrassing had they supported war and had Russia joined the Allies against Germany.[288] They could now ride the waves of anti-war sentiment among the people and pledge their identity of interest in the common struggle against British imperialism. They could reiterate what Sundarayya said a year before the Soviet Union concluded its Non-Aggression Pact with Germany that the immediate issue before the Indian communists was not the fight against fascism but the fight for a true democracy in India. India's part in the coming international struggle, he said, was the struggle for its independence.[289]

Vacillation in the INC and the frankly pro-British attitude of leaders, such as Gandhi and Nehru, provided the Indian communists with an excellent opportunity for launching a vigorous campaign against the imperialist war. Although at Haripura and Tripuri sessions, the INC passed resolutions castigating British foreign policy as a calculated betrayal of democracy, Gandhi, 'from a purely humanitarian standpoint', now appealed for unconditional support for British war efforts. He declared: 'I am not just now thinking of India's deliverance, it will come, but what will be worth if England and France fall or if they come out victorious over Germany [only to be] ruined and humbled?'[290] In the same vein, Nehru also said that it was wrong to approach the problem with a view to taking advantage of Britain's difficulties. In the conflict between democracy and fascism, he pointed out, India's sympathy must lie on the side of democracy and it was for this reason that India should throw all its resources into the struggle against fascism.[291] In sharp contrast to these views, Subhas Chandra Bose, now leader of the newly formed Forward Bloc, declared that he 'did not want Britain to win the war because only after the defeat and break-up of the British empire could India hope to be free'.[292]

Amidst this controversy, the CWC met to discuss the question of India's role in the war and on 15 September 1939, adopted a resolution which categorically declared that India could not associate itself with a war said to be for democratic freedom, when that very freedom was denied to it. The resolution then demanded that the British government must declare in unequivocal terms what their war aims were in regard to democracy and imperialism, and the new order that was envisaged, in particular how those aims were going to apply to India.[293]

The INC resolution, which, in effect, proclaimed that as long as imperialism existed and India was held in subjection, the war was an 'imperialist war', vindicated the communist stand and also confirmed the wisdom of their united front policy. But the question of whether the policy would be pursued to its logical end depended on the future course of events in the international situation on the one hand and the attitude of the various Indian parties on the other. For the present, however, as long as the Soviet Union remained neutral, the communist strategy would be to mobilize all anti-imperialist forces against British imperialism.

RAMGARH RESOLUTION

With the outbreak of hostilities, the INC began to resile from its earlier stand of opposition to India's participation in the war. It now began to show signs of moderation. Under the shadow of German blitzkrieg in Europe when the collapse of Britain seemed almost imminent, the INC met at Ramgarh in March 1940, and adopted a resolution pledging support for the Allies in return for national independence. The resolution demanded a Constituent Assembly for the purpose of framing a constitution and asked the provincial Congress committees (various state committees of the INC) to convert themselves into *satyagraha* committees and to prepare for civil disobedience in case their demand for independence was not conceded by the British government. But Gandhi still insisted on unconditional support to Britain in its war against Germany. He said:

> I am not spoiling for a fight. I am trying to avoid it. Whatever may be true of the members of the Working Committee [CWC], I wholly endorse Mr Subhas Chandra Bose's charge that I am eager to have a compromise with Britain if it can be had with honour.[294]

Although the Ramgarh resolution proclaimed that 'nothing short of complete independence' could be accepted by the people of India in return for their support for Britain's war efforts, many regarded it as a volte-face on the part of the INC. Even a section of Congressmen resented that their leadership was bargaining for a compromise. This gave an opportunity to the communists to apply the tactics of united front from below, that is, to denigrate the leadership by making common cause with the rank and file. In a pamphlet issued at a time when the INC was in session at Ramgarh, they declared that with the outbreak of the war and with the consequent sharpening of the conflict between the bourgeoisie and the proletariat, Gandhism had entered into its last and most reactionary phase. Gandhi was no longer, even in a restricted sense, the 'unifier of the people's movement'. Gandhism now meant the policy of compromise and such a compromise was the biggest danger that faced the national movement in India. The pamphlet then added:

> This does not mean organizational break from the Congress [INC] which is even today dominated by Gandhites, but it does mean ruthless struggle against and exposure of Gandhism as a political line, as a technique and as an organizational principle; it does mean sharpest opposition to Gandhian leadership and determined effort to smash its influence.[295]

CAUTIOUS LEFT LINE

It was, in fact, to conform to Russia's interest that the Indian communists did not want an organizational break from the INC. From the outbreak of hostilities, the Soviet Union recognized that Britain might attack them using India and Iran as the jumping-off point of aggression.[296] It was, therefore, of paramount importance for the Indian communists not only to intensify anti-British campaign but also to unify and sustain all anti-imperialist forces in India, including the vacillating INC. It was for this reason that, while castigating the Right-wing leadership of the INC, they carefully refrained from attacking the INC itself. They also condemned the CSP and the Forward Bloc for disrupting national unity by following the tactics of a united front from above. When Bose organized the Anti-Compromise Conference at Ramgarh in 1940, P.C. Joshi, then secretary of the CPI, observed that the struggle to be initiated by the committee would neither be national nor a struggle. Far from leading the INC on to the path of mass struggle, he pointed out, it would only disunite and weaken the INC, 'the only organization capable of conducting a truly national campaign'.[297]

While laying such great stress on the need for unity under the INC, the communists called upon all anti-imperialist forces to set about the task of the 'revolutionary utilization of the war crisis for achieving national freedom'. A resolution adopted by the CPI politburo in November 1939 declared that in the new situation, the central task before the national forces was the revolutionary utilization of the war crisis which brought out in the sharpest manner and intensified a thousand fold the conflict between the Indian people and British imperialism and opened up the prospect of transformation of the imperialist war into a war of national liberation. Capture of power, it declared, was the immediately realizable goal, a goal for which preparations must be made in earnest.[298] Again, in the 'Independence Day' manifesto of January 1940, the CPI declared that the world was on the brink of mighty upheavals and the old order was tottering, shaking and falling to pieces. In the midst of the horrors of war and starvation, a new world was being born and it was the most opportune time for the revolutionary forces to strike at the root of imperialism. The manifesto said: 'If that opportunity is wasted … we shall commit a crime against our national movement, a crime against humanity. History will never forgive that crime.'[299]

In May–June 1940, when Germany had overrun West Europe, Bose passionately appealed to Gandhi 'to come forward and launch his campaign of passive resistance—since it was now clear that the British empire would be overthrown and it was time for India to play her [its] part in the war'.[300] But Gandhi contended that 'the country was not prepared for a fight and any attempt to precipitate it would do more harm than good to India'. To him the issue was 'one of pacifism, and not India's freedom'.[301] He said: 'We do not seek our independence out of Britain's ruin.' In the same strain, Nehru also echoed: 'Launching of civil disobedience at a time when Britain is engaged in life and death struggle would be [an] act derogatory to India's honour.'[302]

Gandhi's attitude created such resentment among a section of Congressmen that INC President Abul Kalam Azad angrily claimed that the party was not a pacifist organization but one for the achievement of India's freedom. He also pointed out that the people had every right 'to take to the sword if they had no other alternative'.[303] Similar views were also expressed by INC leader Chakravarti Rajagopalachari, who indignantly remarked that he thought that the party was a political organization pledged to win political independence of the country. It was not an institution for organizing world peace.[304] This feeling of resentment and dismay was reflected in a resolution adopted by the members of the CWC in June 1940, which declared that they were fully unable to support Gandhi although they recognized that he should be free to pursue his great ideal in his own way. They, therefore, absolved Gandhi from responsibility for the programme, which the INC had to adopt, namely the parallel organization of self-defence and maintenance of public security all over the country by Congressmen on their own account.[305] A month later, in July, the CWC met again and reiterated the demand for complete independence and proposed the establishment of a provisional national government which should be such as to command the confidence of all elected members in the Central Legislature as well as the closest cooperation of the provincial governments. The CWC further declared that if these measures were adopted, it would enable the

INC to throw its full weight behind the efforts for the effective organization of the defence of the country.[306]

But the British government refused to grant independence to India. Instead, it offered to enlarge the Viceroy's Executive Council and to accept a number of Indian representatives in it, to set up a War Advisory Council, to give full weight to the views of the minorities and after the war was over, to set up a representative body to decide on a new constitution. In substance, the famous August Offer had nothing more to offer than what had been offered by Lord Irwin 11 years ago.[307]

The INC rejected the August Offer and turned once again to Gandhi because it was felt the civil disobedience as contemplated in the Ramgarh resolution could be carried on only under his leadership. The radical elements now hoped that the movement would be 'organized on the largest possible scale' and might develop into a national revolt. But Gandhi would have nothing of the kind. Again he made it clear that to him the issue was pacifism and not the struggle for independence. The issue, he said, was not the freedom of India but the right 'to state freely what we feel about the war'. He declared: 'I claim the liberty of going through the streets of Bombay and saying that I shall have nothing to do with this war, because I do not believe in this war and in the fratricide that is going on in Europe.'[308]

Thus, the Civil Disobedience Movement was resumed without much enthusiasm on the part of Gandhi. According to Bose, Gandhi may have hoped that by following a mild policy, he would be able to open the door to a compromise with the British. The British government, however, mistook his goodness for weakness and continued to exploit India for the purpose of war.

Gandhi's unshakable pacifism frustrated the communists' hope of converting the Civil Disobedience Movement into a revolutionary mass insurrection. In great disappointment, they condemned the movement as a non-violent suicide and abject surrender to British imperialism. Criticizing Gandhi's attitude, the *Communist* observed:

> Human ingenuity could not have drawn up better rules for sabotaging all struggle and for dashing the national movement to pieces …. Every Congressmen must be made to realize that this *satyagraha* can only lead to our prostration before the enemy …. That we have a leadership that can offer such a plan is the supreme tragedy of the situation.[309]

Having failed to move the INC towards revolutionary mass action, the communists now directed their attack with greater virulence not only against the Right-wing leadership of Gandhi but also against the bourgeois-reformist character of the INC. In a major policy statement during this period, P.C. Joshi declared that it was only 'an explosive struggle with gloves off' that could achieve the goal of national liberation. Blaming the INC for its failure to move on to decisive mass action, he averred that Indians had failed to have a national struggle because the bourgeoisie was at the top of the national movement. The 'obvious course', therefore, would be to free the national front from the influence of bourgeois reformism and to develop the political strength of the proletariat 'within the common front' so as to overwhelm and isolate the cowardly bourgeoisie.[310] Apart from excising the bourgeois-reformist elements from the national movement, the course of action recommended by the CPI comprised 'storming military and police stations by armed bands of national militia in rural and urban areas, destruction of government institutions', and an extensive offensive against the armed forces of the government.[311]

In consonance with this militant line and as a first step towards the 'proletarian path' of armed insurrection, the communists began to organize a 'political general strike' in major industries as a result of which most of the textile mills in Bombay were completely immobilized.[312] In this way, the communists 'showed that they could disrupt a major industrial centre and thus translated into action at least part of their proposal for [an] all-out attack on the British'.[313]

It is important to note here that by the time Gandhi had launched the Civil Disobedience Movement, the Communist International's policy towards the INC had also taken a sharp Left turn. In a number of articles published in the Communist International's journals, the leaders of international communism vouched for the CPI's ultra-Left course of action and endorsed its tirade against Bose and the CSP leaders. From these articles, the most authoritative of which was one by G. Kochariants in *Bolshevik* in July 1940, it became evident that the united front was now as dead as a doornail and that the Indian communists were determined to 'ride the revolutionary wave to power even at the risk of isolation from the mainstream of the nationalist movement'.[314]

The CPI's minatory pronouncements and indiscriminate attack on nationalist parties and leaders of all stripes brought inevitable consequences—isolation from the nationalist movement and repression by the government. After breaking with the communists, Jayaprakash Narayan declared that the CPI had finally removed its mask and stood revealed 'as the sworn enemy of the Congress Socialist Party [CSP] and of every other progressive organization with which it had worked before'. As such, he concluded: 'It is desirable once [and] for all to give up vague talk of unity with the Communist Party [CPI].'[315] Subhas Chandra Bose also said that by attempting to utilize the Left Consolidation Committee (LCC) 'for popularizing their own organization' and by carrying out 'reprehensible propaganda' against the Forward Bloc, the communists had cast off all sense of shame.[316]

The government's response to the communist plan of 'organized assault on the very citadel of imperialism' by mass insurrection was also drastic. On 15 March 1940, a government announcement pointed out that it took a serious view of the subversive activities of the communists who were attempting to prejudice the international peace of India and interfere with the efficient prosecution of the war by impeding supplies of men and material.[317] Accordingly, by February 1941, the police had rounded up as many as 480 persons who were, as reported by Sir Reginald Maxwell, acknowledged communists or active supporters of the communist programme of violent mass revolution. The communists, however, were not brought to trial because, as Sir Reginald explained, that would have involved 'the disclosure of secret information' to the detriment of the government's war efforts.[318]

SOVIET–BRITISH ALLIANCE AND PRO-BRITISH COMMUNIST POLICY

The astonishment of the Indian communists detained in the Deoli Detention Camp knew no bounds when, on 22 June 1941, they heard the news that German bombers had struck at Soviet air fields and Nazi armies were on their march towards Moscow, Leningrad and Kharkov. Bewilderment was followed by confusion as the Nazi onslaught on the socialist fatherland forced the latter into the 'imperialist camp'.

In the face of the new alignment of forces, a revision of communist policy in countries fighting against imperialism appeared to be a tricky problem. But the communist logic was simple enough. Although the Soviet Union was fighting side by side with the imperialist forces and the interest of British imperialism coincided with that of the Soviet Union, the supreme aim of communist policy remained Russian victory, even if this meant jettisoning the nationalist objective of political emancipation. Explaining the rationale of this new policy, the *Labour Monthly* wrote that the primary concern of the proletariat in the imperialist as well as colonial countries must be the defence of the Soviet Union whose defeat would be a terrible blow not only to the proletariat of all countries but for humanity in general. Every act of proletarian struggle, it said, had to be subordinated to this supreme aim of Russian victory which would mean a great stride forward of the people's cause in every country.[319] In regard to the question of India's struggle for freedom, it was argued that 'the victory of the alliance of the peoples in association with the Soviet Union means not only the liberation of nations enslaved by fascism but the most favourable world conditions for the final liberation of the Indian people and all nations under foreign domination'. The path of India's independence, therefore, lay through the victory of the Soviet Union and its Allies over fascism.[320]

Caught in the whirlwind of war, the Soviet commentators had little time to devote to the question of India's role in the changed perspective of international relations. The only article on the 'Indian Question' during the entire war period was one by Soviet historian I.M. Lemin, published in the *Bolshevik* in September 1941. In this article entitled 'The Role of British Empire in the Current War', Lemin, neglecting to say a word about the liberation movement in India, praised the British empire for its courageous role in the war against fascism and went to the extent of assigning to it 'the highest place side by side with the USSR [Soviet Union]'. In regard to India's position in the new situation, Lemin had only this to say that the German attack on the Soviet Union was a menace to India since Germany had always considered an attack on the Ukraine and the Caucasus as the beginning of further attacks on Mesopotamia and India. Therefore, he said, India would serve its own interest only by mobilizing all its moral and material forces in support of the British government's war efforts.[321]

The burden of Lemin's argument was explained by R. Palme Dutt who brusquely pointed out that freedom or no freedom, the Indian communists must rally round the British government in order to secure victory of the Soviet Union. He averred that the interest of the people of India and Ireland and of all the colonial countries, as of all peoples of the world, was bound up with the victory of the Soviet Union against Germany. That victory, he pointed out, was absolute and unconditional and did not depend on any measures 'their rulers promise or concede'.[322]

Despite such clear instructions from abroad, the question of cooperation with the British government touched off a bitter controversy between the two fragments of the CPI—the inner core of the leadership interned at Deoli and those who remained outside. While the Deoli group, which included veterans, such as Dange, Muzaffar Ahmad, Mirajkar, Ranadive and Ajoy Ghosh, decided to follow the policy set forth by the Soviet and British commentators, underground party leaders, such as P.C. Joshi, contended, in accordance with the prevailing nationalist opinion, that their goal was the liberation of all oppressed people from both British imperialism and German fascism—a goal which could be achieved only by converting the imperialist war into a revolutionary war. This policy was spelt out in a pamphlet entitled 'Soviet–German War', issued by the CPI politburo in July 1941. It declared that the only way in which the Indian people could help in the 'just war' fought by the Soviet Union was by fighting all the more vigorously for their own emancipation from the imperialist yoke. Therefore, the communists must intensify the struggle against British imperialism. There could be no change in this policy until a people's government, which unequivocally renounced imperialist aims was established in India and other colonial countries. And for this reason, solidarity with the Soviet Union must be coupled with 'the exposure of the imperialist hypocrisy' of Winston Churchill and Franklin Roosevelt.[323] The pamphlet then declared:

> Reliance on the people, on the working class and not on the imperialists, this is the core of a truly internationalist policy .... They are false internationalists and deceivers of the people who say that we can side with the Soviet or win the war for the people by aiding the British government's war efforts.[324]

Elucidating the significance of this policy, the CPI politburo pointed out that 'a worldwide victory of the people' could be achieved not by harbouring the illusion that 'British and American aid will bring Soviet victory and a new world' but by waging 'a ceaseless struggle to expose the imperialist war aims of the British and American rulers to isolate them and to mobilize the people for seizing power'.[325]

The anti-imperialist policy of the underground communists was in tune with the mood of the nationalist sentiment which found expression in Nehru's observation that as long as Britain continued to keep India in subjection, the Indian attitude would be governed by the supreme nationalist objective of political emancipation. It was a war, he opined, ultimately for survival for each country that was involved in it and India could play its role only as a free nation.[326] In the same strain, a CWC resolution, adopted at Bardoli on 23 December 1941, also declared that the sympathies of the INC lay with the people who were subject to aggression and who were fighting for their freedom. Only a free and independent India, it further said, could be in a position to undertake the defence of the country on a national basis and be of help in the furtherance of larger causes that were emerging from the storm of war.[327]

Whitehall, however, made no secret of the fact that the British had no intention of fulfilling India's aspiration for a free existence. In August 1941, Britain and the United States jointly proclaimed the Atlantic Charter which declared that they respected the right of all people to choose the form of government under which they would live and that they wished to see sovereign rights and self-government restored to those who had been forcibly deprived of them. But in September, Churchill told the House of Commons that the principle embodied in the Atlantic Charter had no application in India, 'though in his opinion, it was in full accord with British policy in India as embodied in the August Offer'.[328] This amazing declaration at a time when India's cooperation was of paramount importance to British war efforts, created such consternation among all sections of public opinion in India that even those who were in favour of giving unconditional support to Britain in its hour of crisis now came to realize that it was futile to cooperate with the 'perfidious Albion'.

Such naked exposure of British imperialist intentions notwithstanding, the CPI, including its extremist underground elements, finally veered around the international policy line and decided to mobilize all their forces in the service of the British rulers. What actually prompted the hitherto uncompromising underground communists to abandon their anti-imperialist staunch so tamely is not easy to explain. But it was widely believed by many at that time that the dramatic switch was caused by a letter from Harry Pollitt to the Indian communists.[329] Immediately after Pollitt's letter reached the Indian communists, courtesy of Sir Reginald Maxwell, the CPI politburo came out with a new thesis which regretted its earlier 'bourgeois-nationalist deviation' and declared:

> We are a practical party, and in a new situation it is our task not only to evolve a new form of struggle for it, but also to advance new slogans appropriate to the new stage, suiting the new form of our national movement. The key slogan of our party, which guides all our practical political activity, is: Make The Indian Play A People's Role In The People's War.[330]

It was indeed an excruciating task for the Indian communists who had so long drawn sustenance from the strong anti-British feeling of the masses 'to turn around to the same audience and convince it that British imperialism had overnight become a "prisoner in the people's camp" and that the main enemy of India was no longer Britain but Germany and Japan'.[331] But in a desperate bid to justify the sudden reversal of their anti-imperialist policy in favour of the notion of a 'people's war', the communists put forward the argument that under the guidance of the Soviet Union, the war against fascism would not only assume a revolutionary character but that once the war was over, it would usher in a new world order. Under Soviet inspiration and leadership, the people of the world 'would advance arm in arm with one common aim of destroying Hitler, fascism and its allies, of smashing up the very structure of world imperialism, which bred the plague of fascism and imperialist war, and of replacing it by a world of free peoples'.[332] It was argued that India could achieve its goal of independence if all nationalist forces rallied together on the side of the Allies. In the very act of uniting for war, the Indian people could gather strength to wrench away their freedom from imperialist Britain. Therefore, the CPI urged all patriotic parties and groups to raise the slogan: 'National Unity for National Defence and National Government'.

Having laid down the basic guidelines of the new policy, the communists now started a vigorous campaign for stepping up production on the one hand and strengthening national unity on the other. Campaign for accelerating the productive forces was of paramount importance, because apart from maximizing India's contribution to British war efforts, it would unify the various economic forces—workers and capitalists, peasants and landlords. With this end in view, a resolution was adopted by the plenum of 1942, which, while putting forward some demands on behalf of the industrial workers, laid great stress on the need for uninterrupted industrial production and declared that strikes should be resorted to only under the greatest compulsion.[333] But soon afterwards, this cautious approach to industrial relations gave way to fervent calls for production at all costs. In his report to the first congress of the CPI in Bombay in 1943, Ranadive declared that although the condition of the workers was 'intolerable', their grievances should be redressed not by resorting to strikes but in close collaboration with the employers and government agencies. Repudiating all revolutionary rights of the industrial proletariat, Ranadive then added that production was a 'sacred trust' and that 'conditional support to production was nothing but a Left-nationalist deviation'.[334]

Similarly, the peasants were exhorted not to clamour for land reforms but to cooperate with the landlords and rural traders in an all-out effort to maximize agricultural production.[335]

It is important to note here that the communists avidly carried on the production campaign with the ulterior object of strengthening their own party organization. S.G. Sardesai frankly admitted that the acid test of the success of their production campaign was the extent to which it strengthened the party 'numerically and politically'. He argued that building the party through the food campaign was 'not at all seeking a sectarian, selfish advantage for the organization' at the cost of other countrymen. It was, on the contrary, the highest service the communists rendered to every Indian and every other patriotic party because to build the party was 'the only unfailing guarantee for the salvation of our motherland'.[336]

Side by side with the economic campaign for production, the CPI also carried on political campaign for national unity. The most significant aspect of this campaign was that in contrast to its earlier policy of unity within the INC, it now called for national unity on the basis of cooperation between the INC and the Muslim League. Describing the Muslim League as 'the premier political organization of the second largest community' in India, P.C. Joshi declared that for the sake of national unity the INC must 'concede the sectional demands of the Muslim League', that is, the demand for a separate sovereign state for the Muslims.[337] With characteristic casuistry, the communists thus not only admitted the communal basis of Indian politics but also advocated national unity for the purpose of eventual disunity.

By wooing the Muslim League and giving it pride of place in Indian politics, the CPI plainly discounted the express declaration of the British communist leaders that the league was a creation of British imperialism and that only the INC had the right to speak on behalf of the Indian people.[338] This inconsistency, however, was soon removed when the CPGB fell in line with the CPI, and endorsed the 'absolute correctness' of Joshi's reappraisal of the Muslim League.[339] Supporting the CPI's campaign for national unity on the basis of INC–League collaboration, R. Palme Dutt appealed to the INC to bury the hatchet and make 'far-reaching concessions to the Muslim League'.[340]

By broaching the idea that national unity could be achieved only on the basis of a rapprochement between the INC and the Muslim League, the communists not only demoted the former 'to the role of a spokesman of [/for] the Hindus of the subcontinent'[341] but also promoted the latter overnight from an appendage of British imperialism to an anti-imperialist democratic force. Praising the Indian Muslims for their awakening under the banner of the Muslim League, Sajjad Zaheer wrote:

> It is a good and fine thing, a happy augury, for the Indian Muslims and for India as a whole that the Muslim League continues to grow and gather around it millions of our liberty-loving people. In the increasing strength and capacity of the League to move the Muslim masses on the path of progress and democracy lies the salvation of millions of our Muslim countrymen and the possibility of a Congress [INC]-League unity.[342]

Chiding the INC leaders for their 'unsympathetic attitude' towards the Muslim League, Zaheer observed that Congressmen not only failed to see the anti-imperialist and liberationist role of the Muslim League but also failed to see that the demand for Muslim self-determination for Pakistan was a 'just, progressive and national demand'. The demand of the Muslims for Pakistan, he pointed out, was a positive expression of the very freedom and democracy for which Congressmen had striven and undergone so much suffering.[343]

Having elevated the Muslim League to the position of a progressive and anti-imperialist liberation force, the communists argued that the initiative for a compromise with it must come from the INC. According to Joshi:

> The Congress [INC] is the majority party. It has to deliver the goods. Gandhi's responsibility is greater. It is enough for the League [Muslim League] to formulate its demands. Clearly, it is the organization of the minority; it had every right to feel suspicious of the majority. He [Gandhi] has to think harder than Jinnah *saheb*. He has to work out a new platform for the Indian national movement which satisfies the League [Muslim League] and leads to Congress [INC]-League united front.[344]

By taking up the cudgels for the Muslim League, the communists provoked nationalist opinion in such a manner that it became increasingly difficult for them to keep up even a show of good relations with the INC. But they also realized that tactically nothing would be more harmful than completely breaking with the INC. Therefore, to salve the pique of the INC leaders, the CPI issued an 'open letter' to the CWC waxing eloquent on the great role of the INC in the struggle for freedom. The letter said:

> You are the respected leadership of our proud national movement, represented by the great Congress [INC], which has been built up with the blood of our martyrs, which is supported by the countless millions of our people .... We communists are 15 years old, born in the womb of the same broad national movement and we have endeavoured our very best to strengthen it. All of us proudly carry our Congress [INC] membership card, as treasured possession of our national heritage, as a living inspiration to fight the battle of India's freedom, shoulder to shoulder with our fellow patriots.[345]

Despite such panegyrics, the communists' ceaseless campaign for a compromise with the Muslim League had little impact on the INC, which, after the failure of the Cripps Mission, was forced into a desperate struggle against the British government.[346] In fact, after the failure of the Cripps Mission, all hope of an amicable settlement with the British faded away and the political atmosphere of India became choked with frustration, discontent and unrest. Even Gandhi, so long the chief advocate of cooperation with the Allies, began to show intransigence in his attitude towards the British government. In an article in *Harijan*, he, for the first time, aired the opinion that cooperation or friendly understanding between India and Britain was still far away.[347] This expressed the general feeling among the INC leaders. In a resolution adopted by the CWC on 2 May 1942, the INC made it clear that it was impossible for it to consider any scheme or proposal which retained, even in partial measure, British control and authority in India. The resolution further added that not only the interest of India but also Britain's safety and world peace demanded that Britain must abandon its hold on India and that it was on the basis of independence alone that India could deal with Britain or any other nation.[348] Immediately after the meeting of the CWC, on 3 May, Gandhi declared:

> The time has come during the war, not after it, for the British and the Indians to be reconciled to complete separation from each other .... I must devote the whole of my energy to the realization of this supreme act .... The presence of Britain in India is an invitation to Japan to invade India. Their withdrawal removes the bait. Assume however, it does not; free India will be better able to cope with the invasion. Unadulterated non-cooperation will then have full sway.[349]

On 7 June, Gandhi finally made up his mind to take the offensive. Gandhi declared:

> I have waited and waited until the country should develop the non-violent strength necessary to throw off foreign yoke. But my attitude has now undergone a change. I feel that I cannot afford to wait. If I continue to wait I might have to wait till doomsday. For the preparation that I have prayed and worked for may never come, and in the meantime I may be enveloped and overwhelmed by the flames that threatened all of us. That is why I have decided that even at certain risks which are obviously involved I must ask the people to resist slavery.[350]

On 14 July 1942, the CWC passed the famous Quit India Resolution, which reiterated the demand that the British must withdraw from India and warned that if the British turned a deaf ear to this demand, the INC would be 'reluctantly compelled' to launch a massive movement for the vindication of political rights and liberty of the people of India. After the resolution was passed at Wardha, Gandhi declared:

> There is no room left in the proposal for the withdrawal or negotiation. There is no question of one more chance; after all, it is an open rebellion .... I shall take every precaution I can to handle the movement gently, but I would not hesitate to go to the extreme limit, if I find that no impression is produced on the British government or the Allied powers.[351]

Then came Gandhi's clarion call to the nation:

> Everyone of you should from this moment onwards consider yourself a freeman or woman and act as if you are free .... I am not going to be satisfied with anything short of complete freedom .... We shall do or die. We shall either free India or die in the attempt.[352]

Welcoming the Quit India Resolution, Gandhi further said:

> The voice within me tells me I shall have to fight against the whole world and stand alone .... Even if the United Nations oppose me, even if the whole of India tries to persuade me that I am wrong, even then I will go ahead, not for India's sake alone but for the sake of the world .... I cannot wait any longer for Indian freedom. I cannot wait until Mr Jinnah is converted .... If I wait any longer, God will punish me. This is the last struggle of my life.[353]

But the British were in no mood to quit India. Instead, they arrested Gandhi and all the members of the CWC. The news of arrest of the leaders immediately triggered off a national upsurge the magnitude of which even the government could hardly anticipate. According to Michael Edwardes, to quell the uprising the government 'used British troops and aircraft against mobs, machine-gunning crowds from the air on at least five occasions'.[354]

The communists also joined the battle but on the side of the British. Criticizing the Quit India Resolution, the CPI weekly *People's War* wrote:

> After nine days of labour the working committee [CWC] has brought forth an abortion. The resolution it has produced has bankruptcy writ large upon it. From the rut of inactivity it now seeks to lead the nation into the politics of blind desperation and disaster.[355]

P.C. Joshi added that the CWC had 'tied the rope round the neck of the nation and handed over its ends to the imperialist bureaucracy. This was the lead that was being glorified as "national struggle".'[356] This stand of the CPI was in full accord with the policy of the CPGB outlined by R. Palme Dutt in a letter addressed to the Indian communists:

> By the time this reaches you, events will have moved very much further and you may be in the midst of big issues. The general line is clear—maximum mass mobilization against fascism; full cooperation in practical action with all who oppose fascism irrespective of political differences; no action of the present rulers so long as they stand by the Alliance to resist fascism, should deflect us from this line, which is in

the interests not merely of the world front of the peoples, but for the Indian people whose future cannot be separated from the world front of the peoples.[357]

As mass mobilization in favour of British war effort was impossible so long as the entire people, irrespective of caste, creed and political differences rallied around Gandhi, the communists attempted to weaken the Quit India Movement by driving a wedge between the Hindus and the Muslims. On 9 August 1942, *People's War* wrote:

> Vivisection of India is a sin, says Gandhi. And this sums up the opinion of the national leadership and emphasizes the gulf that must be bridged before it is too late … Nationalist opinion has been loud in its proclamation that under a free India, there must be no oppression of the minority by the majority. But a minority which distrusts the majority cannot be satisfied with such assertions. Its fear must be completely allayed. Its equal status must be guaranteed in a form easily understood. It must be given the right to secession, the right to form an independent state …. To look upon the right of secession as a special fad of Jinnah, as the conspiracy of a few communists to divide in the interests of British imperialism is to ignore the new Muslim awakening, as also of other nationalities, e.g. Andhras, Karnatakis, Maharastrians etc., the awakening of a distinct nationality to a new life, individual consciousness.[358]

At the same time, the communists also started an organized campaign to denigrate all parties, groups and individuals who were straining every fibre to free the country from imperialist bondage. A resolution adopted by the CPI on 23 May 1942 declared:

> The groups which make up the fifth column are the Forward Bloc, the party of the traitor [Subhas Chandra] Bose; the CSP, which betrayed socialism at the beginning of the war and pursued a policy of opportunism and disruption and ended in the camp of the Trotskyite traitors; and finally the Trotskyite groups which are criminal gangs in the pay of the fascists. The Communist Party [CPI] declares that all these three groups must be treated by every honest Indian as the worst enemy of the nation and driven out of political life and exterminated.[359]

Supporting the resolution, *People's War* wrote:

> The CSP, Forward Bloc and Trotskyites are parties organized on the basis of a fifth columnist policy …. We communists call these parties fifth-column parties …. The fifth-column groups want the deadlock to continue because under cover of this they hope to organize their cadres so that when the time comes for Japanese invasion they may blow up the rear to help the Japs and deliver our people to Jap enslavement.[360]

It is significant that although the communists denounced the Quit India Resolution as 'pernicious', 'misguided' and 'a national suicide',[361] they carefully refrained from equating the leaders of the INC with those of other 'fifth-column groups'. On the contrary, they tried to mollify the INC by deploring the government's repressive policy and demanding the release of the INC leaders. Blaming the government, they pointed out that by resorting to a policy of repression the government had not only plunged the country into a 'grave and perilous crisis' but had also done irreparable damage to the cause of anti-fascist struggle. They, therefore, appealed to the government to release Gandhi and other national leaders, stop repression, lift the ban on the INC and start negotiations for a permanent settlement.[362]

The sole purpose behind the CPI's conciliatory attitude towards the INC leaders was to prove its bona fides in the face of mounting criticism against its 'dubious anti-national role' during the Quit India Movement.

DEFECTION OF S.S. BATLIWALA

The profoundly pro-British orientation of their wartime policy had exposed the communists to the odium of the Indian public opinion at large. The image of their party was also badly tarnished when it was openly alleged that in collusion with the government the communists had attempted to sabotage the national movement. The most serious of these charges was made by S.S. Batliwala, a member of the central committee of the CPI, who, while explaining the reason for his defection from the party, observed:

> I became thoroughly convinced that I could not trust the bona fides of my comrades or rely on them to work honestly in the movement for the achievement of Indian freedom. I also realized that there was no possibility of overthrowing the unholy leadership to the top by fighting inside the party framework. I therefore decided to sever my connection with the party.[363]

Referring to the clandestine correspondence between party General Secretary P.C. Joshi and Home Minister Sir Reginald Maxwell during 1942–44, Batliwala alleged that 'an alliance existed between the politburo of the Communist Party [CPI] and the Home Department of the Government of India, by which Mr Joshi was placing at the disposal of the Government of India the services of party members'. He further alleged that Joshi

> detailed certain party members without the knowledge of the central committee or the rank and file of the party to be in touch with the Army Intelligence Department and supplied the C.I.D. [Crime Investigation Department] chiefs with such information as they would require against nationalist workers who were connected with the 1942 struggle [Quit India Movement] or against persons who had come to India on behalf of the Azad Hind Government of Netaji Subhas Chandra Bose.[364]

On 17 March 1946, in a letter to a columnist in the *Bombay Chronicle*, Batliwala repeated these charges and pointed out that during the war, Joshi had not only offered his 'unconditional help' to the government and the Army General Headquarters to fight the underground workers of the Quit India Movement and the Azad Hind Fauj (Indian National Army or INA) but had also offered

> to help retain the morale of the Indian soldiers by performances staged by the Indian People's Theatre Association [a communist drama front] in the front lines in Burma and Assam—when sons and daughters of the soil will sing, dance and recite in the language of the sepoy himself with the aid of folk music—so that he will be convinced that he is fighting a patriotic war.[365]

This offer, however, was rejected by the South East Asian Command on the ground that military authorities could not utilize the services of a political party.[366]

By playing marionette to the British government during the memorable days of the Quit India Movement, the CPI isolated itself from the national movement. But the communists made yet another attempt to recover lost ground by trying to restore good relations with the INC. When the communists were being expelled from the provincial committees of the INC, Joshi bemoaned:

> It is the Congress [INC] that planted the banner of Indian freedom; it is from Congress [INC] leaders that we got our early lessons in patriotism and it is today Congressmen who want to deny us the privilege of fighting shoulder to shoulder with them for the cause they taught us to accept as our aim of life.[367]

Joshi also made a fervent appeal to the INC leaders, saying that the policy of the CPI was not 'dictated from outside' but it 'decides its own policy as it understands the interests of its own people and of the people of the world'. Gandhi, while admiring the energy and discipline of the communists, dismissed Joshi's arguments as unrealistic.[368]

It was now clear that there was absolutely no possibility of a compromise between the INC and the CPI. But the final rupture came only when the CWC set up a subcommittee composed of Jawaharlal Nehru, Vallabhbhai Patel and Govind Ballabh Pant and on its recommendation expelled the communists from all elective offices of the INC.[369]

Meanwhile, the people's war had been won and the Second World War came to a close. But it was a pyrrhic victory for the Indian communists because although they had emerged from illegality as far back as 1942, they now stood thoroughly isolated from the national movement.

E. COMMUNIST VIEW OF INDEPENDENCE AND PARTITION

TURMOIL IN POST-WAR BRITAIN

The victory of the Grand Alliance left Great Britain facing appalling problems. Nazi Germany had suffered a mortal blow, but Britain was reduced from 'the greatest of powers' to a poor third. The war had violently shaken the entire British economy, exports were reduced to a fraction of their pre-war volume, war had liquidated 80 per cent of British investments abroad and the abrupt termination of the lend-lease programme threatened catastrophe. Under these circumstances, 'British politics at home and abroad was a business of wrestling with the spectre of bankruptcy and finding no permanent means of laying the ghost.'[370]

Chastened by these stark realities, the British people as well as their government finally came to realize that they could no longer hold on to the empire in India and that it was time for them to quit India with good grace. Even the diehards at home conceded, grumblingly and reluctantly, the need to accord to India the same free-nation status which Britain fought to achieve in Europe. The British troops, clamouring to go home, could no longer hold the country against open revolt. The war had exposed Britain's weakness and its power and prestige had been shattered. It would never again be able to demonstrate that strength which had for so long enabled it to rule millions of Indians.

As the stage was being set for the transfer of power, events in India began to move forward in an atmosphere of frenzied excitement. Historian R.C. Majumdar observed:

> The real struggle for freedom was over, and the battle for India's freedom was henceforth to be fought round the council table, the principal combatants being Hindus and Muslims and not the Indians and the British. The British were now sincerely anxious to grant freedom to India but the Indians were slow to take it, for they could not decide among themselves what form it should exactly assume. The role of the British was that of a mediator between two disputants, sometimes degenerating into that of a judge in a boxing bout between two prizefighters.[371]

INA TRIALS, NAVY MUTINY AND CABINET MISSION

While tortuous negotiations were going on between the INC, the Muslim League and the British government, 'the ghost of Subhas [Chandra] Bose, like Hamlet's father, walked the battlements of the Red Fort, and his suddenly amplified figure overawed the conferences that were to lead to independence.'[372] After the war, when the members of the INA of Bose, who had acquired the halo of martyrdom and virtual apotheosis, returned to India, the British government decided to court martial them for 'waging war against the King Emperor'. A military tribunal was constituted and the historic trial began in the Red Fort of Delhi. This was the last act of ineptness on the part of the British government for, as pointed out by Nehru, the trial of the INA heroes once again 'dramatized …the old contest: England versus India. It became in reality not merely a question of law … but rather a trial of strength between the will of the Indian people and the will of those who held power in India'.[373] The masses were once again excited and a wave of indignant protest against the trial of the heroes of Indian freedom swept the country. The INC had set up a defence committee with such celebrities as Bhulabhai Desai, Sir Tej Bahadur Sapru and Jawaharlal Nehru. Liberal contributions were made to the INA Defence Fund and flag days were observed. Finally, although the accused were sentenced to transportation for life (which in British India meant exile to Andaman), the government quailed before the storm of popular demonstrations and remitted the sentence.

Countrywide popular unrest on the issue of the INA trial was followed by a mutiny of a section of Indians in the Royal Indian Navy on 18 February 1946. These events created such a sensation all over the country that the British government realized that a settlement of the 'Indian Question' brooked no more delay. Therefore, on 19 February 1946, Lord Pethick-Lawrence in the House of Lords and Prime Minister Clement Attlee in the House of Commons simultaneously announced the government's decision to send to India a special mission consisting of three cabinet ministers—which would be known as the Cabinet Mission—to seek an agreement 'on the principles and procedure relating to the constitutional issue'. The members of the Cabinet Mission were secretary of state for India Lord Pethick-Lawrence, president of the Board of Trade Sir Stafford Cripps and first Lord of the Admiralty A.V. Alexander.[374]

The Cabinet Mission arrived in Delhi on 24 March 1946, and for three months carried on negotiations with the leaders of all shades of Indian opinion. During this short period, 182 parleys were held in which as many as 472 representatives of different political parties and groups were interviewed. The problems that faced the Cabinet Mission were many, but there is no doubt that the spectre of communism and the Soviet Union also haunted its members.

> Would there be a civil war if Britain left, having handed over power to Congress [INC]-dominated centre? If there was a civil war, there were men and nations who might take advantage of it. Britain's wartime honeymoon with Russia was over and the old fears had returned. In Tsarist days, Russia had always been the main threat to India, and only the strength and the unity that Britain had imposed had protected the country from invasion from the North. The Soviet Union, which had revived a good deal of Tsarist legend to boost morale during the war, might also revive the Tsarist dream of conquering India. Even if this idea were merely a nightmare, civil war would be sure to affect British business interests in India just when they were most needed to bolster the tottering economy of a war-exhausted Britain.[375]

Despite such apprehensions and many other complicated questions churned up by different political groups and leaders during talks of settlement, the Cabinet Mission had no doubt that it had to settle issues with the two major parties—the INC and the Muslim League. The elections to the Central and Provincial Legislative Assemblies held towards the end of 1945 and in early 1946 had clearly shown that only these two parties really counted in the country and any scheme for the transfer of power must be acceptable to both.

Nevertheless, after intensive confabulations with the Indian leaders, the Cabinet Mission put forward its own plan for the settlement of the Indian constitutional problem. It ruled out the idea of handing over power 'to two entirely separate sovereign states' and instead proposed an Indian Union, including both the British India and the Indian states, which should deal with foreign affairs, defence and communication and should also have powers necessary to raise finances required for these roles. The Union shall have an Executive and a Legislature consisting of representatives from both British India and the Indian states. The provinces would be free to form groups and each group could determine the provincial subjects to be taken in common by that group. The plan also proposed the setting up of a constitution-making body and the formation of an interim government in which all portfolios would be held by the Indian leaders. The British government, the Cabinet Mission assured, would give full cooperation to the interim government in matters of administration and in bringing about a rapid and smooth transfer of power in India.

The Cabinet Mission's plan could satisfy neither the INC nor the Muslim League. The INC would accept nothing short of transfer of power to a united India and the Muslim League was determined to oppose it. But the Cabinet Mission left nobody in doubt that the British really meant to quit India within a very short time.

CAUTIOUS SOVIET APPROACH TO INDIAN LIBERATION

In this state of flux, when events were fast building up towards a denouement, the Indian communists might have been expected to make a revolutionary utilization of the situation. In fact, during this period of headlong transition what they needed desperately but lacked was a sense of purpose and direction, a revolutionary strategy and a dynamic leadership. As a result, instead of responding forcefully to the challenge of events, communism in India 'evolved haltingly, trailing after events rather than anticipating them'.[376] Not surprisingly, therefore, the unique opportunity offered by the Indian situation slipped out of communist hands.

The helplessness of the Indian communists was the result of multiple factors. In the first place, during the years immediately after the close of the war, the Russian attitude was characterized by an amazing indifference, as a result of which the Indian communists could obtain no clear guidance from abroad. As pointed out by Overstreet and Windmiller, during this period,

> the Soviet commentary furnished only the most routine recognition of these tumultuous events. In the face of what might readily be interpreted as a revolutionary situation, the Soviet authorities were surprisingly passive. Far from offering a militant lead, their commentary on India was vague and cautious in the extreme.[377]

This Soviet indifference to Indian affairs was primarily due to the preoccupation of its leaders with such burning problems as the reconstruction of Russia, the absorption of East Europe and above all, the question of European political settlement.

That the Soviet leaders' enthusiasm for a communist revolution in India had significantly cooled down was first indicated in the speech of Russian Foreign Minister Vyacheslav Molotov at the World Security Conference in 1945 wherein he laid great stress on the role of the United Nations in solving the problems of post-war nations. After welcoming the British proposal that the 'representatives of India should be granted a seat at the conference', he declared that in the interest of international security the dependent countries should be granted national independence. But, he pointed out, this should be 'promoted' by a special organization of the United Nations 'which must act with a view to expediting the realization of the principles of equality and self-determination of the nations'.[378] The policy of bringing about a solution of the problems of colonial countries through the agencies of the United Nations was elucidated in clearer terms by a prominent Soviet commentator on Asian affairs, E. Zhukov, who maintained that although trusteeship under the United Nations was by no means an ideal, it could 'accelerate the progressive development of the colonies along the path of complete independence'. He also took a favourable view of the programme embodied in the Atlantic Charter and argued that it should be applied to the colonial countries. Zhukov, however, sounded a note of caution that if political freedom of the colonies were not accompanied by economic freedom, mere achievement of sovereign power by itself would not emancipate the colonial peoples from imperialist bondage.[379] Another Soviet commentator, A. Dyakov, showed greater temporization by simply stating that the task of maintaining international peace and security would be handicapped if the peoples of the colonial countries were not granted elementary political rights.[380]

In accordance with this moderate policy, the Soviet commentators on India urged the CPI to abandon its wartime policy of cooperation with the British and to return to the pre-war strategy of anti-imperialist struggle in collaboration with the Indian bourgeoisie 'with the exception of the feudal princes and a section of the big landlords'.[381] Their attitude towards the INC was also strikingly favourable. Emphasizing the important role of the INC in India's national movement and indirectly conceding the failure of the communists to provoke revolutionary mass movements, Dyakov observed that as the social and political activity of the Indian people was at a very low level and as their degree of organization was inferior to that observed in other democratic countries, the INC was in a position to formulate in its programme 'a number of propositions' which had the support of the broad sections of the population.[382] In regard to the Muslim League and its demand for Pakistan, the Soviet commentators' approach was equally cautious. Although they admitted that the Muslim League was the 'most influential' political organization of the Muslims, they shared the progressive Indian opinion that the partitioning of the country would not solve the Hindu–Muslim problem. They held that the transformation of India into a 'federation of national administrative-political regions' would contribute far more to the interests of the country than its division on a communal basis.[383] Thus, Dyakov not only rejected the Indian communists' earlier plea for partition, but actually veered around the INC position.[384]

The Soviet commentators' cautious approach towards the post-war Indian situation clearly superseded their earlier enthusiasm for revolutionary mass movements and there was nothing in their analysis which could provide the Indian communists with any effective guidance.

1946 ELECTION MANIFESTO

In the absence of any clear guidelines from abroad, the Indian communists were in a dilemma, torn between the legacy of the past and the demands of the future. As a result, although the new situation offered them a unique opportunity to play a decisive role during the closing years of the freedom movement, they failed to make a revolutionary use of that unprecedented opportunity.[385] That they had nothing significant to offer to the people in their hour of glory was clear from the CPI's 1946 election manifesto when the party was entering an election as a legal party for the first time in its history. The manifesto contained little that could catch the imagination of the people and inspire their revolutionary zeal. In line with the cautious approach outlined by the Soviet commentators, the manifesto clearly sought a compromise with the nationalist bourgeoisie.

Giving up its earlier uncompromising attitude towards the national reformists, the manifesto declared that the communists would concentrate all their 'fire against the imperialist rulers of our common motherland' because it was 'a crime to waste one word or lose one comrade in internal factional warfare'. It further declared: 'The only call of our party is: Indians must not fight Indians but all Indians together must fight the British enslavers.' Thus, just when the British rulers were about to quit India, the communists put to the forefront 'not claims about their own worth, not differences with other parties, but the need to overthrow the British rule'.[386] Appealing to the bourgeoisie to join hands with the workers and peasants, the manifesto said:

> The Communist Party [CPI] shall seek the wholehearted cooperation and close alliance of the middle class and shall struggle to build its alliance with the working class …. The Communist Party appeals to the revolutionary middle class to see in our party the unifier of the middle class with the working class in the towns and the peasantry in the villages.[387]

In regard to the party's economic policy, the manifesto showed great moderation by declaring that industrial planning should be implemented through 'free and equal cooperation between the representatives of the state, management and labour'. In the agrarian field, although the manifesto demanded abolition of the feudal system, it fixed the size of a maximum landholding at 100 acres and declared that the party would 'not touch the small *zamindars* [landlords] or the rich peasants'.[388] Thus, in their manifesto, the communists not only called upon the workers, peasants, middlemen, employers and others to rally for a planned national development but also went so far as to declare that under this economic programme the rich peasants would derive more benefit than the poor peasants.[389]

NATIONALITY POLICY

While these astonishingly moderate pronouncements disappointed a section of radicals both inside and outside the party, the communist nationality policy outlined in the manifesto had alienated virtually all shades of progressive public opinion in the country. As a solution to India's constitutional problems, the manifesto broached the idea that power should be 'transferred not to one or even two Indian governments [Indian and Pakistani] but to seventeen interim sovereign national Constituent Assemblies, correspond- ing to the "nationalities" as defined by the party in 1942, with one addition—the Beluchis'. Curiously, however, the manifesto did not suggest how the boundaries of these states were to be delimited or how the Constituent Assemblies were to be constituted. But the manifesto left no doubt that

> they were to constitute independent entities, possessing full and real sovereignty and enjoying the 'unfettered right to negotiate, formulate and finally to decide their mutual relations within an independent India, on the basis of complete equality'. Each Assembly would send delegates to an all-India Constituent Assembly to debate the final constitutional settlement, but [the] manifesto declared that these delegates should have no more authority than that of plenipotentiaries.[390]

The communist advocacy of regional particularism, in total disregard of the Indian nationalist sentiment, exposed the CPI to such public odium that the party was threatened with a split on the issue. The absur- dity of the scheme was also laid bare by R. Palme Dutt who came to India accompanying the Cabinet Mission as a special correspondent of the *Daily Worker*. In his 'Travel Notes' published in the *Labour Monthly*, he put great stress on the need for a rapprochement between the CPI and the INC and squarely dismissed the party's nationality policy as impractical and reactionary. Dutt averred: 'The unity of India is desirable from a progressive point of view and partition would be a reactionary step.'[391] He also put forward the suggestion that power should be transferred to a provisional Government of India with representatives of both the INC and the Muslim League and, in the event of a lack of compromise between these two parties, with INC representatives alone. He then added that the task of framing a constitution should be entrusted to a Constituent Assembly the members of which would be directly elected by the people.[392]

As a result of Dutt's counsel, the CPI forthwith gave up its demand for the partition of the country into 17 states and submitted a memorandum to the Cabinet Mission which, without saying a word about Pakistan, declared that the CPI was firmly convinced that the best interests of the Indian people would be served by their remaining together in one common union.[393]

AUGUST RESOLUTION: EXTREMISTS VERSUS MODERATES

But that Dutt's counsel for moderation did not satisfy the extremist leadership of the party represented by Ranadive, Adhikari and Ajoy Ghosh soon became evident when the CPI central committee adopted the August Resolution in 1946.[394] This resolution pointed out that while the INC represented 'the mainstream of the independence movement', the Muslim League had behind it 'the bulk of the anti-imperialist freedom-loving Muslim masses' and the CPI represented 'the bulk of the organized workers and peasants'. The resolution then declared that a 'joint front' of these three main patriotic parties—the INC, the Muslim League and the CPI—was essential for launching the final struggle against imperialism. The resolution criticized the compromising attitude of both the INC and the Muslim League, called for bold action and declared that the paramount task of the CPI was to 'come forward as the organizer of this new phase of the Indian revolution and lead it to victory'.[395]

Far from overcoming the breach between the moderate and extremist elements, the August Resolution only aggravated their differences, and by the end of 1946 the central leadership of the CPI was in complete disarray. As a result, when the interim government headed by Jawaharlal Nehru was formed in September 1946, the two factions came out with conflicting policy statements. The extremist point of view was put forward by Adhikari who held that the interim government was nothing but an imperialist design and impugned the leadership for surrendering to vested interests. The communists, he said, must expose the 'appeasers of vested interests' and build the 'revolutionary unity of the Indian people for the final fight for independence and democracy'.[396] The moderate attitude found expression in the draft resolution moved by Somnath Lahiri, a communist member of the Constituent Assembly, which categorically asserted that the interim government had the overwhelming support of the people and called upon all progressive forces of the country to cooperate with it.[397]

As Lahiri's resolution reflected the majority opinion of the party, the extremists were forced to capitulate to the moderate line. In the preface of the publication embodying Lahiri's resolution, Adhikari himself admitted that despite the compromising policy pursued by the nationalist leadership, the Constituent Assembly could assert the will of the Indian people.[398] But although the extremist leadership had veered around to the soft line, some ultra-revolutionaries in provincial units refused to budge from their militant posture and began to foment insurrections in various parts of the country, particularly in South India. Their violent activities created such a serious situation in Telangana in Hyderabad that the authorities had to take stern measures to quell widespread disturbances.[399] A large number of party workers and trade union leaders were arrested and the CPI was declared illegal in Madras.

The adventurism of the ultra-Left groups in the wake of India's independence not only created further confusion in the party ranks but also considerably neutralized whatever advantage was beginning to be achieved by the moderate group under P.C. Joshi's leadership. The repressive measures of the government crippled the party apparatus, and during the crucial days of early 1947 when events began to unfold in a rising crescendo, the communists remained pathetically subdued and isolated.

SILENCE OF CPSU AND CPGB

Throughout these critical months, guidance from abroad also remained conspicuously perfunctory in nature. Since their departure from India, the British communist leaders had said nothing of any significance about the climacteric situation in India. The Soviet commentators were equally reticent. Their commentaries during this period conveyed little more than routine reiteration of diatribes against British imperialism which, said Zhukov, was 'patterned on the relationship between the United States and the Philippines whereby the latter had received only formal independence while remaining under the economic and military control of the U.S. [United States]'.[400] Soviet commentator Dyakov discreetly hailed Nehru as a 'Left-wing progressive' leader and commended the role of the Indian delegation to the United Nations.[401] It became evident that for the time being the Soviet commentators had modified their posture to conform to the political realities of the moment and their primary concern was whether India would follow a really independent policy or join the imperialist bloc like the Philippines had done.[402]

MOUNTBATTEN PLAN: SOVIET AND INDIAN INTERPRETATIONS

The Soviet temporization, however, came to an abrupt end when, following the announcement of the Mountbatten Plan, a virulent attack was once again launched both against British imperialist policy and the Indian nationalist leadership. Denouncing the plan as an imperialist manoeuvre calculated to tighten its noose around the Indian subcontinent, Dyakov declared that by accepting it the nationalist leaders had surrendered to the pressure of the Indian bourgeoisie who were anxious to exploit the domestic market in league with the imperialists.[403] In the same vein, Zhukov came out with a hard-hitting article in which he identified the nationalist leadership of the INC with the big bourgeoisie and averred that by accepting the imperialist terms of settlement, the INC leadership had capitulated to the conspiracy hatched by British imperialism and domestic-monopoly capitalism. He regretted that even a progressive leader, such as Nehru, had gone over to reactionary camp. Significantly, Zhukov concluded his article by indirectly justifying the Muslim League's demand for Pakistan and openly repeating the CPI's earlier demand for the right of self-determination of the various Indian 'nationalities'.[404]

The change in the Soviet attitude took clearer shape at a conference of the Academy of Sciences of the Soviet Union in July 1947, where leading experts on Indian affairs, Zhukov, Dyakov, V.V. Balabushevich and S.M. Melman, reviewed the Indian situation in detail and deplored the bourgeois leadership of the INC for betraying the people by going over 'to the camp of reaction and imperialism'.[405] Although there were considerable differences of opinion among these spokesmen regarding the strategy and tactics to be followed by the CPI, they agreed that the leaders of both the INC and the Muslim League represented the reactionary big bourgeoisie and their compromise with British imperialism clearly revealed 'the cupidity and treachery of the Indian bourgeoisie, which for the sake of its profits is prepared to sacrifice the independence of its country'. They also asserted that the scheme of partition of the country was 'the result of a deal between the Indian bourgeoisie and landlords and British imperialism'. The Soviet theoreticians then underlined the glorious role of the Indian working class in the anti-imperialist national liberation movement and declared:

> The toiling masses of India, under the leadership of the Indian working class and its party, the Communist Party of India [CPI], are conducting a resolute struggle against the reactionary bloc of imperialists, bourgeoisie and landowners for complete independence, for liquidation of all remnants of feudalism, for people's democracy.[406]

Ironically, this scathing criticism of the INC leadership could not have come at a less inopportune moment for the Indian communists. Totally ignorant of what was transpiring in Moscow and following a meeting of the central committee of the CPI in Bombay, the party came out at almost the same time with a diametrically opposite analysis of the Indian situation. In striking contrast to the Soviet appraisal of the INC leadership, the CPI in its June 1947 resolution described the INC as the main national organization and urged its leadership to implement rapidly and consistently the declared anti-imperialist democratic programme. The resolution also added that the CPI would fully cooperate with the national leadership in the proud task of building the Indian Republic on democratic foundations, thus paving the way to Indian unity. The cooperation, the resolution pointed out, could be achieved only by a 'joint front' of all the progressive forces of the country.[407] Overstreet and Windmiller observed:

> The predominant theme of the June [1947] resolution was the aspiration toward unity—the unity of the multifarious political and religious elements of the subcontinent. The party [CPI] was fully confident, the resolution declared, that with such unity the imperialist intrigues can be decisively defeated and that India could pass on to genuine national independence.[408]

The CPI's attitude towards the Mountbatten Plan was also remarkably soft. Although it was contended that the Mountbatten Plan was the culmination of a two-faced policy 'which, while making concessions to the national demand to transfer power, [also] sets in motion disruptive and reactionary forces to obstruct the realization of real independence', the resolution also admitted that the plan contained 'important concessions to India's nationalist aspirations and opened up new opportunities for national advance'.[409] The resolution then affirmed that these concessions had been 'extracted through the continuous pressure of the Congress [INC] leadership for transfer of power'.

Endorsing the CPI resolution, R. Palme Dutt described the Mountbatten Plan as an 'enforced retreat of imperialism' and declared that the time had come for the INC and the CPI to bury the hatchet and set about the task of laying the foundations of new India. Dutt said:

> Now more than ever, the situation reveals the urgent need increasingly recognized on both sides, to endeavour to overcome the past phase of sharp division between the Congress [INC] and the CPI in order to march forward together upon a common programme of democratic advance, for the achievement of full independence and eventual all-India democratic union, and for the fulfilment of the economic and social demands, land reforms, measures of nationalization and planned industrial development, for which the workers and peasants and masses of the Indian people are looking.[410]

Thus, on 15 August 1947, when the INC under Nehru's leadership fell heir to power in India, the Indian communists came to realize that they could put little premium on the prospect of a violent revolution in India. All they could now strive for was some respectability in the politics of new India.

NOTES AND REFERENCES (CHAPTER 3)

A. EARLY YEARS OF THE COMMUNIST MOVEMENT: FORMATION OF CPI

1   Lala Har Dayal, *Forty-four Months in Germany and Turkey, February 1915 to October 1918: A Record of Personal Impressions* (London: P.S. King and Son, 1920), 68.
2   For an account of the activities of the Ghadr Party, see Randhir Singh, *The Ghadr Heroes* (Bombay: People's Publishing House, 1945).
3   Prabhat Kumar Mukhopadhyay, *Bharate Jatiya Andolan* (Bengali; Calcutta: Granthan, 1960), 287–88.
4   Gene D. Overstreet and Marshall Windmiller, *Communism in India* (Bombay: Perennial Press, 1960), 20.
5   Born on 1 December 1886, in a rich family of Aligarh in Uttar Pradesh, Mahendra Pratap joined the national movement at an early age. In 1906, he attended the Calcutta session of the INC and took active part in the Swadeshi Movement. In 1912, he became an ardent follower of Gopal Krishna Gokhale. In 1914, he left India 'on a voluntary exile' and reached Geneva through Marseille. While in Geneva, he came in contact with Lala Har Dayal, Shyamji Krishna Varma and Virendranath Chattopadhyaya with whom he went to Germany in 1915. For a detailed account of his life, see Mahendra Pratap, *My Life Story of Fifty-five Years* (Dehradun: World Federation, 1947).
6   Giles Tyler Brown, *The Hindu Conspiracy and the Neutrality of the United States, 1914–1917* (California: University of California—Berkeley Press, 1941), 40–52. Also see John Price Jones and Paul Merrick Hollister, *The German Secret Service in America* (Boston: Small, Maynard and Company, 1918), 264–67.
7   M.N. Roy, *Memoirs* (Bombay: Allied Publishers, 1964), 3–4.
8   Ibid., 4.
9   Ibid., 'Introduction' by G.D. Parikh, vi.
10 There is some controversy regarding the exact date of Roy's birth. L.P. Sinha in his book *Left Wing in India* (Muzaffarpur: New Publishers, 1965) stated that Roy was born in 1887 (p. 69). According to Gene D. Overstreet and Marshall Windmiller, Roy was born in 1886. But they admitted that they were unable to establish Roy's exact date of birth with precision. It was a cousin of Roy, they pointed out, who stated that he was born in the Bengali year 1293, that is, 1886–87 AD. See Overstreet and Windmiller, *Communism in India*, 20 and *Radical Humanist*, XVIII, Calcutta, 7 February 1954, 78. However, I accept the year given by G.P. Bhattacharya in his book *M.N. Roy and Radical Humanism* (Bombay: J.B.H. Wadia, 1961). Also see Roy, *Memoirs*, 567.
11 M.N. Roy, *Letters from Jail* (Dehradun: The Indian Renaissance Association, 1943), 204.
12 Roy, *Memoirs*, 'Epilogue' by V.B. Karnik, 567. A revolutionary in those days described at a later period Roy's baptism in revolutionary nationalism in the following words:

> Narendra, almost a boy, hardly fourteen, and yet virile and energetic, full of revolutionary enthusiasm, rushed into a little room in which we were holding an informal talk on the problems then facing us in Bengal and elsewhere. He had a talk with us. After this, he offered himself as a whole-timer for the cause of liberty of India from the foreign yoke. He declared an oath that he would be prepared to do the impossible; for there was nothing impossible for a revolutionary. Soon after, he joined us; he proved to be of very great value to our movement and possessed rare qualities found only in a great leader of men.

Also see A.K. Hindi, *M.N. Roy—The Man Who Looked Ahead* (Ahmedabad: Modern Publishing House, 1938), 8. (M.N. Roy's aide Tayab Shaikh actually took the pen name A.K. Hindi).

13 Hindi, *M.N. Roy—The Man Who Looked Ahead*, 20–21.

14 Roy, *Memoirs*, 5.

15 Ibid., 5.

16 Roy, *Memoirs*, 22. Also see Sir Cecil Kaye, *Communism in India, 1920–1924* (Delhi: Government of India Press, 1926), 4.

17 Roy, *Memoirs*, 22.

18 Ibid.

19 Ibid., 29. M.N. Roy related an incident which ultimately made him interested in the philosophy of Marx. One evening when Lala Lajpat Rai was addressing a socialist meeting, a questioner asked: 'How did the nationalists propose to end the poverty of the Indian masses?' What happened thereafter in the meeting has been described by Roy as follows:

> There followed a lively exchange of words between the speaker and the interrogator. The former grew impatient and excited when his evasive answer—'Oh, let us first be masters of our house'—failed to give satisfaction. The latter pressed his point to the extent of asking provocatively: 'What difference would it make to the Indian masses if they were exploited by native capitalists instead of foreign imperialists?' Lalaji flew into a towering rage and retorted: 'It does make a great difference whether one is kicked by his brother or by a foreign robber.' The audience was surprised into a frigid silence. In the beginning, I shared Lalaji's indignation at the cheekiness of the hoboes [a derogatory designation for the extreme Left-wingers in the American labour movement]; but I also felt rather uncomfortable; there was something wrong in our case. Suddenly, a flight flashed through my mind—it was a new light.

See Roy, *Memoirs*, 28.

20 Chandra Chakraberty, *New India* (Calcutta: Vijoyakrishna Brothers, 1951, 34. In his *Memoirs*, Roy denied that Chakraberty made any arrangement for his journey to Germany on the *Deutschland*. On the contrary, he said that his failure to proceed to Germany from New York 'was due to the oiliness of the leader in New York'. Roy remarked: 'I could not imagine that the impostor was deceiving me … but he knew that he was betraying the cause he presented to represent'. See Roy, *Memoirs*, 67.

21 Roy, *Memoirs*, 23.

22 Ibid., 58.

23 Ibid., 59.

24 Ibid., 184.

25 Ibid., 109.

26 Ibid., 213.

27 Ibid., 107.

28 Ibid., 549.

29 Ibid., 550–51.

30 M.N. Roy, *La India: su Pasado, su Presente y su Porvenir* (Spanish; Mexico, 1918), 122.

31 Roy, *Memoirs*, 194.

32 Ibid., 195.

33 Ibid.

34 Ibid., 204.

35 Ibid., 205–06.

36 Ibid., 211.

37 Ibid., 223.

38 Ibid., 219–20.

39 Ibid., 237.

40 Ibid., 237–38.

41 Ibid., 277.

42 Ibid.

43 Ibid., 294.

44 Ibid., 293.

45   See ibid., 341–47 for a vivid description of M.N. Roy's first interview with Lenin.

46   The Indian delegation to the second congress of Communist International (1920) consisted of Abani Mukherjee who had been sent to Japan about the same time Roy first went to Java, and M.P.T. Acharya who had left India in 1908 and had widely travelled in Europe and America in search of support for India's struggle for freedom. But of the Indians attending the congress, only Roy had a vote, accorded to him as head of the Mexican delegation. Evelyn, Mukherjee and Acharya had only consultative votes. Roy, it may be noted here, continued to travel on a Mexican passport as late as 1925. See Overstreet and Windmiller: *Communism in India*, 27. Also see *Masses of India* (February–March 1925), 2.

47   In his *Memoirs*, Roy said that it was at Lenin's behest that he ventured to write an alternative thesis on the 'National and Colonial Questions'. Roy recalled:

> I was reluctant to oppose Lenin publicly. Our discussions were carried on in private. The delegates whispered, mostly in awe, that the Indian upstart had dared question the wisdom of Lenin and cross verbal swords with the master of polemics. But Lenin's attitude was very kind and tolerant. In the beginning, he appeared to be amused by the naiveté of a novice. But before long he was impressed by my arguments, and could not dispute the authenticity of the facts I cited … Lenin finally amazed me by proposing that after a general discussion in the commission set up to examine the question, he would move that his theses as well as mine should be recommended for adoption by the congress [of the Communist International]. I agreed to formulate my critical notes and positive ideas in a document which, I insisted, should be presented not as the alternative but as the supplementary theses. Lenin agreed with the remark that we were exploring a new ground and should suspend final judgement pending practical experience.

See Roy, *Memoirs*, 380–81.

48   Ibid., 376.

49   Ibid.

50   It may be noted here that before 1920, the leaders of international communism, anticipating an impending proletarian revolution all over the world, felt that all anti-imperialist national liberation movements should be supported and coordinated with the international communist movement. In 1919, while addressing the Second All-Russian Congress of Communist Organizations of the Peoples of the East, Lenin declared that the revolutionary movement of the peoples of the East would develop effectively only in direct association with the revolutionary struggle of the Soviet Republic against international imperialism. After pointing out that '1905 was followed by revolutions in Turkey, Persia and China and that a revolutionary movement developed in India', Lenin concluded: 'Now our Soviet Republic has to group around it all the awakening peoples of the East and together with them, wage a struggle against international imperialism'. See V.I. Lenin, *The National Liberation Movement in the East* (Moscow: Foreign Languages Publishing House, 1957), 220 and 233–34.

51   Roy, *Memoirs*, 378–79.

52   Ibid., 379.

53   Ibid., 376.

54   Ibid., 379. In 1916, Lenin wrote:

> Socialists must not only demand the unconditional and immediate liberation of the colonies without compensation—and this demand in its political expression signifies nothing else than the recognition of the right to self-determination; they must also render determined support to the more revolutionary elements in the bourgeois-democratic movements for national liberation in these countries and assist their uprising— or revolutionary war, in the event of one—*against* the imperialist powers that oppress them.

See V.I. Lenin, *Collected Works*, Vol. XXII (Moscow: Progress Publishers, 1964), 151–52.

55   Roy, *Memoirs*, 379. Roy's arguments were well summarized by Franz Borkenau in the following words:

> The irruption of modern industry in the East was bound soon to lead to an alignment of forces considerably nearer to the typical situation of the West than that existing in the East before the war. The bourgeoisie, while growing richer, would somehow coalesce with the feudal classes and both together would tend to come to a compromise with Western imperialists against proletariat and peasantry.

See Franz Borkenau, *The Communist International* (London: Faber and Faber, 1938), 292.

56 *The Second Congress of the Communist International: Proceedings of Petrograd Session of July 17th and Moscow Sessions of July 19th–August 7th, 1920* (Moscow: Communist International, 1920), 578.

57 In paragraph 11 of his 'Draft Theses on National and Colonial Questions', Lenin wrote:

> In respect to the more backward countries and nations with prevailing feudal or patriarchal and patriarchal–peasant relations, it is necessary to bear in mind especially: The necessity of all communist parties to render assistance to the bourgeois-democratic liberation movement in such countries; especially does this duty fall upon the workers of such countries upon which the backward nations are colonially or financially dependent.

See ibid., 478.

58 *The 2nd Congress of the Communist International as Reported and Interpreted by the Official Newspapers of Soviet Russia: Petrograd–Moscow, July 19–August 7, 1920* (Washington, DC: United States Department of State, Government Publishing Office, 1920), 43.

59 In this connection, it is interesting to note that a British communist named J.T. Murphy, who met M.N. Roy at the second congress of the Communist International, described him as 'a tall fine figure of a man, with black hair and glittering eyes, handsome *brahmin*. ... Of all Indians I have met he was the most arrogant'. See J.T. Murphy, *New Horizons* (London: John Lane at the Bodley Head, 1941), 240.

Another Indian communist who knew Roy during this period, described him as 'self-important and ill-tempered in discussion, he was often vehement in seeking to impose his opinion upon others'. Abdul Qadir Khan in *The Times* (London, 25–27 February 1930). Khan had written a three-part series of articles in *The Times* on 25, 26 and 27 February 1930.

In his *Memoirs*, Roy himself confessed: 'It is true that I have always been rather stiff, if not arrogant. In the earlier days of my contact with modern ideas and modern culture, it was the expression of inferiority complex. But in course of time, experience taught tolerance and modesty'.

60 Overstreet and Windmiller, *Communism in India*, 30–31.

61 *The Second Congress of the Communist International: Proceedings of Petrograd Session of July 17th and Moscow Sessions of July 19th–August 7th, 1920*, 574.

62 Sinha, *Left Wing in India*, 37.

63 Roy, *Memoirs*, 390–91. Explaining Roy's exclusion from the ECCI, Overstreet and Windmiller observed:

> The first concerns the delicate state of Anglo–Soviet relations brought about by British charges that the Russians were interfering in India. Roy may have been kept off the ECCI in order not to antagonize the British Foreign Office. The other possibility is that the Russians, at the time of the second congress, may not have been eager to channel all their efforts in India through him.

In this connection, it may be noted that Roy became a candidate member of the ECCI at the fourth congress in 1922, and a full voting member in 1924 when he also joined its presidium. See Overstreet and Windmiller, *Communism in India*, 33.

64 Roy, *Memoirs*, 391.

65 G.Y. Sokolnikov became the commander of the Red Army in Central Asia—of the Turk front perhaps at an age of less than 40. He was also the chairman of the Turkistan Commission of the Soviet government. A handsome youth,

> he was intellectually qualified to be the editor of the underground party organ *Pravada*, during the crucial period immediately preceding the capture of power by the Bolsheviks. ... In the struggle for leadership of the party after Lenin's death, Sokolnikov supported his former chief [Leon] Trotsky. On the latter's downfall, he sunk into political oblivion eventually to be among the numerous unfortunate children consumed by their blood-thirsty Mother, the Revolution.

The other member of the Central Asiatic Bureau of the Communist International, G.I. Safarov, was 'a prodigy of the party ... the bright young disciple of Lenin'. He won the reputation of 'an erudite Marxist, a prodigious writer and a brilliant journalist'. However, Roy also said that he was a fanatic.

> Once he believed that Trotsky was a counter-revolutionary; then he was convinced that Stalin was betraying the revolution. On both occasions, he was passionately sincere. Fanatical determination to save the purity of the faith and defend the integrity of the church ultimately cost him life ... Safarov was among the unnamed victims of the 1937 purge [also known as the Great Purge].

See Roy, *Memoirs*, 392–94.

66   Ibid., 391–92.

67   Ibid.

68   William Z. Foster, *History of the Three Internationals: The World Socialist and Communist Movements from 1848 to the Present* (New York, NY: International Publishers, 1955), 30–31. Commenting on the date of the end of the Baku congress, Muzaffar Ahmad observed: 'It must have been earlier than September 20, since it is known from the documents of the Communist International that on September 20, [Grigory] Zinoviev reported to its executive committee on the Baku congress'. See Muzaffar Ahmad, *The Communist Party of India and Its Formation Abroad* (Calcutta: National Book Agency, 1962), 64. Also see David N. Druhe, *Soviet Russia and Indian Communism* (New York, NY: Bookman Associates, 1959), 27–30.

69   Roy, *Memoirs*, 420.

70   Ibid.

71   Overstreet and Windmiller, *Communism in India*, 35.

72   The word *hijrat* means to go away leaving one's country and friends behind in order to save oneself form oppression. For a full account of the *hijrat* movement, see (a) Ahmad, *The Communist Party of India and Its Formation Abroad*, 11–55; (b) Shaukat Usmani, *Peshawar to Moscow* (Benaras: Swarajya Publishing House, 1927); (c) *Indian Annual Register*, (Calcutta, 1921), Part I, 206–10; and (d) L. Hutchinson, *Conspiracy at Meerut* (London: George Allen and Unwin, 1935).

73   Muzaffar Ahmad, *The Communist Party of India: Years of Formation, 1921–1933* (Calcutta: National Book Agency, 1959), 12–13.

74   Ahmad, *The Communist Party of India and Its Formation Abroad*, 27–28. Among those who set out for Tashkent were: Muhammad Akbar Khan (the leader of the group), Meer Abdul Majeed, Sultan Mahmud, Ferozuddin Mansur, Gawhar Rahman Khan, Mian Muhammad Akbar Shah, Abdul Qadir Sehrai, Fida Ali Zahid, Ghulam Muhammad, Jafar, Abdulla Safdar, Abdul Matin, Abdur Rahim, Shaukat Usmani, Tajuddin, Masood Ali Shah, Muhammad Hussain, Abdul Qayum, Rafiq Ahmad and others.

75   Ibid., 28.

76   In his *Peshawar to Moscow*, Shaukat Usmani stated that when they reached Tashkent, they found two groups of 'professional revolutionaries' there—one led by M.N. Roy, included Abani Mukherjee and Mohammad Ali, the other was led by Abdul Rab (also known as Abdur Rab), who was supported by M.P.T. Acharya and Khalil Bey, an uncle of Enver Pasha of Turkey. According to Usmani's account, some of the *muhajirs*, including Usmani himself, joined Roy, some joined Rab and others formed a 'neutralist' group. See Usmani, *Peshawar to Moscow* and Overstreet and Windmiller, *Communism in India*, 35.

77   Ahmad, *The Communist Party of India and Its Formation Abroad*, 30.

78   Roy, *Memoirs*, 420.

79   Ibid., 456.

80   Ibid., 461–62.

81   Ibid., 462. At the Communist University of the Toilers of the East in Tashkent, the *muhajirs* were taught issues such as historical materialism, class war, the French Revolution, the American Revolution and the evolution of capitalism. Also see Abdul Qadir Khan's article in *The Times*, 26 February 1930. Khan himself was a student at the university.

82   Ahmad, *The Communist Party of India and Its Formation Abroad*, 16.

83   Ibid., 73–74 and 78. Some of the students who took lessons at the Communist University of the Toilers of the East in Tashkent were: Mian Muhammad Akbar Shah, Gawhar Rahman Khan, Sultan Mahmud, Meer Abdul Majeed, Ferozuddin Mansur, Fazal Elahi Qurban, Abdulla Safdar, Rafiq Ahmad, Shaukat Usmani, Habib Ahmad Nasim, Fida Ali Zahid, Abdul Qadir Sehrai, Masood Ali Shah, Abdul Qayum, Abdul Hamid and Abdul Qadir Khan.

84   Ibid., 33.

85   Ibid., 34. In a letter to Muzaffar Ahmad dated 29 December 1958, Rafiq Ahmad stated that the earlier members of the party were: M.N. Roy, his wife Evelyn Roy, Abani Mukherjee, his wife Rosa Fitingov, Muhammad Shafiq and Masood Ali Shah. See ibid., 57.

86   Druhe, *Soviet Russia and Indian Communism*, 34.

87   Ahmad, *The Communist Party of India and Its Formation Abroad*, 65.

88 Ibid., 87–88. It should be noted here that Rafiq Ahmad's account of the formation of the CPI has been corroborated by Evelyn Roy. Jane Degras quotes her as saying that the CPI was founded in October 1920. See Jane Degras, *The Communist International Documents, 1919–1943*, Vol. II (London: Oxford University Press, 1956), 11.

89 For a first-hand description of their journey from Moscow to India, see 'The Story of Rafiq Ahmad's Travels' in Ahmad, *The Communist Party of India and Its Formation Abroad*, 35–50.

90 The accused in the Peshawar Conspiracy Case were: Mian Muhammad Akbar Shah, Gawhar Rahman Khan, Meer Abdul Majeed, Ferozuddin Mansur, Habib Ahmad Nasim, Rafiq Ahmad, Sultan Mahmud, Abdul Qadir Sehrai, Fida Ali Zahid and Ghulam Muhammad. The first nine were members of the émigré CPI, while Ghulam Muhammad had returned from Tashkent long ago and had never joined the CPI. His name was added to the list of the accused a few days after the case started. The object of the government was to secure him as an approver. From among the communists, Fida Ali Zahid turned out to be an approver.

91 *Fifth Congress of the Communist International: Abridged Report of Meetings Held at Moscow June 17th to July 8th, 1924* (London: CPGB, 1924), 11.

92 Indulal Yajnik, *Life of Ranchoddas Bhavan Lotvala* (Bombay: The Writers' Emporium, 1952), 54.

93 S.V. Ghate, 'Reminiscences', *New Age* (Delhi, 6 April 1958).

94 Ahmad, *The Communist Party of India: Years of Formation, 1921–1933*, 10.

95 Ibid., 8.

96 Ibid.

97 Ibid.

98 Ibid., 6.

99 Ibid., 9.

100 Philip Spratt, *Blowing Up India: Reminiscences and Reflections of a Former Comintern Emissary* (Calcutta: Prachi Prakashan, 1955), 33.

101 Ahmad, *The Communist Party of India: Years of Formation, 1921–1933*, 10–11.

102 Sir David Petrie, *Communism in India, 1924–1927* (Calcutta: Government of India Press, 1927), 127.

103 Kaye, *Communism in India, 1920–1924*, 91.

104 Ibid., 103.

105 Hindi, *M.N. Roy—The Man Who Looked Ahead*, 101.

106 Ibid., 125.

107 Kaye, *Communism in India, 1920–1924*, 79.

108 Exhibit No. 23 in Cawnpore Conspiracy Case evidence. *King Emperor Versus Nalina Bhushan Das Gupta, Muhammad Shaukat Usmani, Muzaffar Ahmad, and Shripat Amrit Dange, in the High Court of Judicature at Allahabad, Criminal Side* (Allahabad: Superintendent Government Printing, 1924), 9–11.

109 Overstreet and Windmiller, *Communism in India*, 64.

110 Cawnpore Conspiracy Case, 'Introduction', 5.
For a detailed account of the charges against the accused, also see *Indian Annual Register*, Vol. I (Calcutta, 1924), XVIII.

111 *The Socialist* (Bombay, 24 November 1924).

112 Ahmad, *The Communist Party of India: Years of Formation, 1921–1933*, 17.

113 L.F. Rushbrook Williams, *India in 1924–1925* (Calcutta: Government of India Central Publication Branch, 1925), 100.

114 Ahmad, *The Communist Party of India: Years of Formation, 1921–1933*, 16.

115 Ibid., 17.

116 *The Socialist*, 17 December 1924, 7.

117 Of the 78 members of the Indian Communist Party, 50 came from Uttar Pradesh, 11 from Rajputana, 7 from Central Provinces, 5 from Bengal and 2 from Bihar. Among these members, 16 were journalists, 11 'national workers', a few merchants—'but the working class elements in what were a communist party was negligible'. See *The Socialist*, 17 December 1924 and also Sinha, *Left Wing in India*, 155–56.

118   V.H. Joshi, 'The Constitution and Programme of the Indian Communist Party', *The Socialist*, 19 November 1924.

119   Initially, Shapurji Saklatvala, then in London, was requested to preside over the conference. But he could not come because the CPGB did not give him permission. See Ahmad, *The Communist Party of India: Years of Formation, 1921–1933*, 18.

120   Ibid., 19.

121   *Indian Annual Register*, Vol. II (Calcutta, 1925), 367.

122   Ibid., 371.

123   *Masses of India* (Paris, March 1926), 6.

124   Ibid., September 1926.

125   M.N. Roy, 'What is a Communist Party?' in *Masses of India* (January 1926).

126   Ahmad, *The Communist Party of India: Years of Formation, 1921–1933*, 21. Also see Meerut Sessions Court, *Judgement delivered by R.L. Yorke, Esq., I.C.S., Additional Sessions Judge, Meerut, on 16th January, 1933, in the Meerut Communist Conspiracy Case. Sessions Trial No. 2 of 1930. King Emperor Versus P. Spratt and Others*, Vols. I–II (Simla: Government of India Press, 1932–33), 343.

127   Overstreet and Windmiller, *Communism in India*, 78.

128   Ahmad, *The Communist Party of India: Years of Formation, 1921–1933*, 28–36.

129   M.N. Roy, *The Future of Indian Politics* (London: R. Bishop, 1926), 90.

130   Ibid., 95.

131   Ibid., 114.

132   R. Palme Dutt, *Modern India* (London: CPGB, 1927), 129.

133   Ibid., 148.

134   Ibid.

135   Ibid.

136   Ibid., 'Preface to the English Edition'.

137   Ibid., 17.

138   Spratt, *Blowing Up India: Reminiscences and Reflections of a Former Comintern Emissary*, 29.

139   Overstreet and Windmiller, *Communism in India*, 87.

140   Spratt, *Blowing Up India: Reminiscences and Reflections of a Former Comintern Emissary*, 29.

141   Meerut Sessions Court, *Judgement delivered by R.L. Yorke*, 98.

142   Spratt, *Blowing Up India: Reminiscences and Reflections of a Former Comintern Emissary*, 36.

143   Shapurji Saklatvala and M.K. Gandhi, *Is India Different? The Class Struggle in India: Correspondence on the Indian Labour Movement and Modern Conditions* (London: CPGB, 1927), 17.

144   Petrie, *Communism in India, 1924–1927*, 114.

145   Meerut Sessions Court, *Judgement delivered by R.L. Yorke*, 162.

146   *International Press Correspondence* (18 February 1929).

147   Meerut Sessions Court, *Judgement delivered by R.L. Yorke*, 67.

148   *Fifth Congress of the Communist International: Abridged Report of Meetings Held at Moscow June 17th to July 8th, 1924*, 196.

149   The Indians to whom invitation to the fourth congress was issued included M.N. Roy, S.A. Dange, Nanlini Gupta, Chiraranjan Das (son of Chittaranjan Das) and Subhas Chandra Bose. But eventually, only Roy had attended the congress and held India's only vote. See Kaye, *Communism in India, 1920–1924*, 27–28.

150   M.N. Roy, 'The Empire and the Revolution', *Labour Monthly*, Vol. III (London, October 1922): 224.

151   *Advance Guard* (Zurich, 15 January 1923), 3.

152   Ibid.

153   Meerut Sessions Court, *Judgement delivered by R.L. Yorke*, 29.

154   Sinha, *Left Wing in India*, 177.

155   *Fifth Congress of the Communist International: Abridged Report of Meetings Held at Moscow June 17th to July 8th, 1924*, 187.

156   Spratt, *Blowing Up India: Reminiscences and Reflections of a Former Comintern Emissary*, 29.

157   Meerut Sessions Court, *Judgement delivered by R.L. Yorke*, 180–89. Also see *The Times*, (London, 25 September 1928) and *The Statesman* (Calcutta, 18 August 1928).

158 Meerut Sessions Court, *Judgement delivered by R.L. Yorke*, 186.

159 Ibid., 187.

160 Ibid., 189.

161 *International Press Correspondence* (18 April 1925), 513.

162 Ahmad, *The Communist Party of India and Its Formation Abroad*, 153 and 165.

163 Ahmad, *The Communist Party of India: Years of Formation, 1921–1933*, 8–9 and 22. It may be noted here that Saumyendranath Tagore indicated that Muzaffar Ahmad was also one of the founders of the Labour Swaraj Party. See Saumyendranath Tagore, *Historical Development of the Communist Movement in India* (Calcutta: Red Front Press, 1944), 6.

164 M.N. Roy, 'A Step in the Right Direction', in *Masses of India* (Paris, February 1926), 3.

165 Ahmad, *The Communist Party of India: Years of Formation, 1921–1933*, 23.

166 Ibid.

167 Ibid., 24.

168 *The Communist International between the Fifth and the Sixth World Congresses, 1924–1928* (London: CPGB, 1928), 475.

169 Ahmad, *The Communist Party of India: Years of Formation, 1921–1933*, 24–25.

170 Ibid., 25.

171 *Krantikari* (Hindi; 17 November 1928).

172 Ahmad, *The Communist Party of India: Years of Formation, 1921–1933*, 26.

173 At this conference, numerous banners carried such slogans as: 'We Want Nothing But Complete Independence', 'Let Land Be Divided Among Cultivators', 'Let Simon Commission Go To Hell', 'Down With Nehru Report' (Motilal Nehru Report on Constitutional Framework), 'Down With Imperialism', 'Down With Capitalism and Landlordism' and 'Down With Bourgeois Nationalist Hypocrisy'. See Sinha, *Left Wing in India*, 188.

174 *Thesis of the Workers' and Peasants' Party of India*, Resolutions adopted by the first All India Workers' and Peasants' Party conference in Calcutta on 21st to 24th December 1928, *Labour Monthly*, Vol. II, No. 3 (London, March 1929).

175 'The Colonial Thesis of the Sixth Congress', *International Press Correspondence* (17 October 1928).

176 R. Page Arnot, *How Britain Rules India* (London: CPGB, 1929), 31.

177 Otto Wilhelm Kuusinen, 'The Revolutionary Movement in the Colonies', *International Press Correspondence* (4 October 1928).

178 *International Press Correspondence* (17 October 1928).

179 *International Press Correspondence* (8 November 1928).

180 Ibid.

181 Ibid.

182 Harold Laski's 'Preface' to Hutchinson, *Conspiracy at Meerut*, 8.

183 Ahmad, *The Communist Party of India: Years of Formation, 1921–1933*, 33.

184 *International Press Correspondence* (13 December 1929).

185 *International Press Correspondence* (29 October 1931). Also see Druhe, *Soviet Russia and Indian Communism*, 120.

186 *International Press Correspondence* (21 August 1929). Also see Overstreet and Windmiller, *Communism in India*, 140.

187 Tagore, *Historical Development of the Communist Movement in India*, 14.

188 Ahmad, *The Communist Party of India and Its Formation Abroad*, 66 and 154.

189 Druhe, *Soviet Russia and Indian Communism*, 47. Also see Roy, *Memoirs*, 581–84. Also see, *The Times* (London, 25 February 1930) 15.

190 Roy, *Memoirs*, 583.

191 Ibid., 584.

192 Ibid.

193 Ibid., ix.

B. POLITICAL WILDERNESS

194 It is significant that during his trial, Bhagat Singh gave a statement calling for a revolution that would establish in India 'the sovereignty of the proletariat'. See *Indian Annual Register* (Calcutta, 1929), 78.

195 R.C. Majumdar, *History of the Freedom Movement in India*, Vol. III (Calcutta: Firma K.L. Mukhopadhyay, 1963), 320.

196 Ibid., 325.

197 *The Tribune* (Lahore, 27 December 1929).

198 B.R. Nanda, *The Nehrus: Motilal and Jawaharlal* (London: George Allen and Unwin, 1962), 325.

199 Majumdar, *History of the Freedom Movement in India*, Vol. III, 325–26.

200 Ibid., 327. Also see Nanda, *The Nehrus: Motilal and Jawaharlal*, 326.

201 Pattabhi Sitaramayya, *The History of the Indian National Congress*, Vol. I (Bombay: Padma Publications, 1946), 363–64.

202 Michael Edwardes, *The Last Years of British India* (London: Cassell and Company, 1963), 52.

203 Sitaramayya, *The History of the Indian National Congress*, Vol. I, 368.

204 Nanda, *The Nehrus: Motilal and Jawaharlal*, 327–28.

205 M.R. Masani, *The Communist Party of India—A Short History* (London: Derek Verschoyle, 1954), 42.

206 Ibid.

207 *International Press Correspondence* (9 January 1930), 25.

208 Karl Radek, 'Problems of the Revolution in India', *International Press Correspondence* (26 June 1930).

209 Ibid. (31 July 1930), 666.

210 For the full text of the 'Draft Platform of Action', see *Indian Communist Party Documents, 1930–1956* (Bombay: Democratic Research Service, 1957), 2. Also see *International Press Correspondence* (18 December 1930).

211 *Indian Communist Party Documents, 1930–1956*, 3–4.

212 Ibid., 7.

213 Ibid., 8.

214 *Workers' Weekly* (Bombay, 24 April 1930).

215 *Labour Monthly* (London, May 1930).

216 *International Press Correspondence* (6 November 1930).

217 *Indian Communist Party Documents, 1930–1956*, 8–9.

218 Tagore, *Historical Development of the Communist Movement in India*, 21.

219 Ahmad, *The Communist Party of India: Years of Formation, 1921–1933*, 37.

220 Ibid., 37. Muzaffar Ahmad added: 'Once [Joseph] Stalin mentioned the work of the Calcutta Committee [of the CPI] either at an enlarged meeting of the central committee of the Communist Party of the Soviet Union [CPSU] or at the plenum of the Executive Committee of the Communist International [ECCI]'.

221 Sir Horace Williamson, *India and Communism* (Simla: Government of India Press, 1935), 161.

222 Ahmad, *The Communist Party of India: Years of Formation, 1921–1933*, 37–38.

223 Masani, *The Communist Party of India—A Short History*, 44.

224 Williamson, *India and Communism*, 163.

225 Jawaharlal Nehru, *An Autobiography* (Bombay: Allied Publishers, 1962), 266–67.

226 Williamson, *India and Communism*, 168.

227 *International Press Correspondence* (24 November 1933).

228 Ahmad, *The Communist Party of India: Years of Formation, 1921–1933*, 38–39.

229 'The Present Situation in India', in *International Press Correspondence* (22 September 1933).

230 Williamson, *India and Communism*, 179.

C. THE ANTI-IMPERIALIST UNITED FRONT

231 It is interesting to note that on 20 January 1927, Winston Churchill wrote to Benito Mussolini:

> If I had been an Italian, I am sure that I should have been whole-heartedly with you from the start to finish in your triumphant struggle against the bestial appetites and passions of Leninism … Your movement has rendered a service to the whole world … Italy has shown that there is a way of fighting the subversive forces which can rally the masses of the people, properly led, to value and wish to defend the honour and stability of civilized society. She [Italy] has provided the necessary antidote to Russian poison.

See Frederick L. Schuman, *International Politics: The Western State System and the World Community* (New York, NY: McGraw-Hill, 1958), 455.

232 Carl Crow, *Japan's Dream of World Empire (The Tanaka Memorial)* (New York, NY: Harper and Brothers, 1942), 9–10.

233 Schuman, *International Politics: The Western State System and the World Community*, 443.

234 Wang Ming, *The Revolutionary Movement in the Colonial Countries* (New York, NY: Workers Library Publishers, 1935), 64.

235 In a pamphlet entitled 'Transformation of Elections into Mighty Anti-Imperialist Demonstrations' issued by the central committee of the CPI on 5 December 1936, the Indian communists clarified their attitude towards the new constitution:

> Today the focal point of imperialist attack on India is the new constitution. To free ourselves from the new bondage should be the main flank of our political struggle. To concentrate all our forces, to mobilize all our energy, to fight the slave constitution, that is the task which confronts us … Transform the elections into a weapon to forge an anti-imperialist United Front! Form the United National Front Against Imperialism! Smash the New Constitution!

236 Georgi Dimitrov, 'The Offensive of Fascism and the Task of the Communist International for the Unity of the Working Class against Fascism', *International Press Correspondence* (20 August 1935).

237 *Communist* (The organ of the CPI central committee), Vol. I, No. 12 (September 1936), 2.

238 Ibid.

239 In an article entitled 'For the Ani-Imperialist People's Front: Long Live Soviet Hindusthan' published in *Communist*, it was pointed out that the bourgeois leadership of the INC was no longer united in its reformism but it was disintegrating. Referring to Jawaharlal Nehru's presidential address in INC's Lucknow session in April 1936, it said: '… it was a clear anti-imperialist call than had ever been made from the Congress [INC] chair'. See *Communist* (September 1936), 16.

240 In an undated pamphlet entitled 'The United National Front' issued by the CPGB, Harry Pollitt, R. Palme Dutt and Ben Bradley said:

> There can be no question of substituting the slogan of Constituent Assembly for the slogan of Soviet power. It was Roy who advanced the slogan of Constituent Assembly against Soviets, against revolution … Roy counterposes the slogan of Constituent Assembly to Soviets instead of counterposing it to the present slave constitution raising the illusion that the Constituent Assembly can fulfil the task of the Soviets.

241 Subhas Chandra Bose, *The Indian Struggle, 1935–1942*, Vol. II (Calcutta: Netaji Publication Society, 1952), 10.

242 Ibid., 16–17.

243 Ibid., 430.

244 Jawaharlal Nehru, *India's Freedom* (London: George Allen and Unwin, 1965), 36. It may be noted here that during this period, Nehru became so much critical of M.K. Gandhi that he described him as 'amazingly backward' and observed that 'much that he says seems to fit in with a medieval Christian and not at all with modern psychological experience and method'. Also see Jawaharlal Nehru, *Nehru on Gandhi* (New York, NY: John Day Company, 1948), 78 and 91.

245 Sitaramayya, *The History of the Indian National Congress*, Vol. II, 31.

246 Ibid., 33.

247 Bose, *The Indian Struggle, 1935–1942*, Vol. II, 17.
248 Sitaramayya, *The History of the Indian National Congress*, Vol. II, 110–11.
249 Bose, *The Indian Struggle, 1935–1942*, Vol. II, 19–20.
250 Mukhopadhyay, *Bharate Jatiya Andolan*, 213–15.
251 Edwardes, *The Last Years of British India*, 67.
252 Ibid.
253 Sinha, *Left Wing in India*, 430.
254 Jawaharlal Nehru, *Eighteen Months in India: 1936–1937* (Allahabad: Kitabistan, 1938), 20.
255 Majumdar, *History of the Freedom Movement in India*, Vol. III, 560.
256 *Communist* (September 1936).
257 V.P.S. Raghuvanshi: *Indian Nationalist Movement and Thought* (Agra: L.N. Agarwal, 1951), 276.
258 Edwardes, *The Last Years of British India*, 65.
259 Ibid., 65–66.
260 Overstreet and Windmiller, *Communism in India*, 162.
261 *Indian Communist Party Documents, 1930–1956*, Document No. 9, 66.
262 M.R. Masani, 'The Communist Party in India', *Pacific Affairs*, Vol. XXIV (March 1951), 21–22.
263 Jayaprakash Narayan, *Socialist Unity and the Congress Socialist Party* (Bombay: CSP, 1941), 3. In this connection, Masani commented:

> The United Front tactics of the communists were greatly facilitated by the enthusiasm of Jay Prakash Narayan ... who had become an intellectual adherent of the Comintern [Communist International] during his years as a student in the U.S.A. The reason for this attitude was the same as elsewhere—lack of understanding of communist tactics and intellectual surrender to Marxism.

See Masani, *The Communist Party of India—A Short History*, 67.
264 Yusuf Meherally, ed., *Jayaprakash Narayan, Towards Struggle* (Bombay: Padma Publications, 1946), 170.
265 In this connection, it may be noted that the exact number of the communists who joined CSP cannot be ascertained correctly because of the fact that the CPI was still illegal and admission had to be granted secretly.
266 Masani, *The Communist Party of India—A Short History*. 68. Also see, 'Party News', *The Congress Socialist* (26 December 1936).
267 *All India Congress Socialist Party Circular Letter No. 4 to Provincial Secretaries* (Patna, 31 March 1937), 2.
268 *Communist* (March 1937), 18.
269 Ibid., 5.
270 Ibid. (April 1937), 25.
271 Ibid. (June 1937), 25.
272 Masani, *The Communist Party of India—A Short History*, 69.
273 Meherally, *Jayaprakash Narayan, Towards Struggle*, 172–74.
274 For a full text of this document, see *Indian Communist Party Documents, 1930–1956*, Document No. 3, 36.
275 Masani, *The Communist Party of India—A Short History*, 70.
276 Narayan, *Socialist Unity and the Congress Socialist Party*, 26.
277 Masani, *The Communist Party of India—A Short History*, 71.
278 Ibid.
279 See Sajjad Zaheer's article entitled 'Unity is Strength' in *The Congress Socialist* (5 March 1938). In this article, Zaheer denied that the communists had any intention of capturing the CSP. He argued that the two mass movements must work in unison and for this purpose, the communists should be allowed to work freely in the CSP.
280 *Communist* (February 1937), 7.
281 R. Palme Dutt, *India Today* (Bombay: People's Publishing House, 1949), 397.
282 *National Front* (19 March 1939), 96.
283 Ibid. (30 April 1939), 189.
284 Ibid. (19 March 1939), 101.
285 Overstreet and Windmiller, *Communism in India*, 170.

D. COMMUNIST PARTY OF INDIA AND THE SECOND WORLD WAR

286 *Labour Monthly* (London, 1 October 1939).

287 *Amrita Bazar Patrika* (Calcutta, 24 August 1939).

288 Masani, *The Communist Party of India—A Short History*, 77.

289 *National Front* (3 April 1938).

290 *Harijan* (9 September 1939).

291 *The Statesman* (Calcutta, 10 September 1939).

292 Subhas Chandra Bose, *The Indian Struggle, 1920–1934*, Vol. I (Calcutta: Netaji Publication Society, 1948), 28–29.

293 *Indian Annual Register* (Calcutta, 1939), 226–28.

294 *Harijan* (20 January 1940).

295 *Legislative Assembly Debates: Official Report*, Vol. I, No. 2 (Delhi: Manager of Publications, 12 February 1941), 122–23.

296 Michael Carritt, 'India Before the Storm', in *Labour Monthly* (London, May 1940), 194–95.

297 B. Asche, 'Nehru and the Question of Civil Disobedience in India', *World News and Views* (London, 8 June 1940).

298 P.C. Joshi, *Communist Reply to Congress Working Committee's Charges* (Bombay: People's Publishing House, 1945), 36.

299 For a full text of the Independence Day Manifesto, see *World News and Views* (London, 16 March 1940).

300 Bose, *The Indian Struggle, 1920–1934*, Vol. I, 33.

301 Abul Kalam Azad, *India Wins Freedom* (Delhi: Orient Longman, 1959), 33.

302 Ibid.

303 Ibid., 34.

304 Edwardes, *The Last Years of British India*, 70.

305 Majumdar, *History of the Freedom Movement in India*, Vol. III, 602.

306 Sir Reginald Coupland, *The Constitutional Problem in India*, Vol. II (Oxford: Oxford University Press, 1945), 239–40.

307 Ibid., 248.

308 Ibid., 247.

309 *Communist* (November 1940). Also see Joshi, *Communist Reply to Congress Working Committee's Charges*, 6.

310 P.C. Joshi, 'Whom, How and Why Does Bose Fight', in *Unmasked Parties and Politics* (Bombay: CPI, 1940), 186.

311 *Legislative Assembly Debates: Official Report*, Vol. I, No. 2, 122–23.

312 *Indian Annual Register* (Calcutta, 1940), 47.

313 Overstreet and Windmiller, *Communism in India*, 183.

314 Ibid., 186.

315 Meherally, *Jayaprakash Narayan, Towards Struggle*, 179.

316 Sita Ram Goel, *Netaji and the CPI* (Calcutta: Society for Defence of Freedom in Asia, 1955), 5–6.

317 *The Hindu* (Madras, 15 March 1940).

318 *Legislative Assembly Debates: Official Report*, Vol. I, No. 2, 121.

319 See article entitled 'Leading the World Against Hitler' by Quaestor in *Labour Monthly* (London, August 1941).

320 *World News and Views* (London, 18 October 1941).

321 I. Lemin, 'The Role of the British Empire in the Current War', *Bolshevik* (September 1941).

322 *Labour Monthly* (London, September 1941), 381.

323 Yusuf Meherally, ed., *Acharya Narendra Deva, Socialism and the National Revolution* (Bombay: Padma Publications, 1946), 152–53.

324 Pamphlet entitled 'Soviet–German War', issued by the CPI politburo in July 1941.

325 *Communist* (August 1941), 3.

326   J.S. Bright, ed., *Before and After Independence: A Collection of the Most Important and Soul-stirring Speeches by Jawaharlal Nehru, 1922–1950* (Delhi: Indian Printing Works, 1952), 223.

327   Sitaramayya, *The History of the Indian National Congress*, Vol. II, 310.

328   Majumdar, *History of the Freedom Movement in India*, Vol. III, 611.

329   Masani, *The Communist Party of India—A Short History*, 80.

330   Joshi, *Communist Reply to Congress Working Committee's Charges*, 45.

331   Masani, *The Communist Party of India—A Short History*, 80.

332   For a full text of the new policy statement by the CPI, see G.M. Adhikari, *From Peace Front to People's War* (Bombay: People's Publishing House, 1944), 347.

333   For a detailed account of the economic policy adopted by the plenum, see N.K. Krishnan, *National Unity for the Defence of the Motherland* (Bombay: People's Publishing House, 1943), 27–35.

334   B.T. Ranadive, *Working Class and National Defence* (Bombay: People's Publishing House, 1943), 34.

335   S.G. Sardesai, *People's Way to Food* (Bombay: People's Publishing House, 1943), 46.

336   Ibid., 34.

337   P.C. Joshi, *The Indian Communist Party: Its Policy and Work in the War of Liberation* (London: CPGB, 1942), 1.

338   Ben Bradley, 'India Threatened', *Labour Monthly* (London, May 1942).

339   Joshi, *The Indian Communist Party: Its Policy and Work in the War of Liberation*, 1.

340   R. Palme Dutt, 'Notes of the Month, *Labour Monthly* (London, September 1942).

341   Overstreet and Windmiller, *Communism in India*, 201.

342   Sajjad Zaheer, *A Case for Congress-League Unity* (Bombay: People's Publishing House, 1944), 1, 20 and 36.

343   Ibid.

344   Joshi, *They Must Meet Again* (Bombay: People's Publishing House, 1944), 30. According to Overstreet and Windmiller, the immediate purpose of the communist policy to befriend the Muslim League was 'to enlist the support of the [Muslim] League and the Muslim people for the war' and also to 'penetrate the Muslim population of the subcontinent'. See Overstreet and Windmiller, *Communism in India*, 215.

345   N.K. Krishnan, *Forgery Versus Facts: Communist Party Exposes the Fifth Column* (Bombay: People's Publishing House, 1943), 23.

346   *World News and Views* (London, 1 May 1942) and *Labour Monthly* (London, May 1942).

347   *Harijan* (19 April 1942).

348   Coupland, *The Constitutional Problem in India*, Vol. II, 288.

349   *Indian Annual Register* (Calcutta, 1942), 237–54. Commenting on the new attitude of M.K. Gandhi, Abul Kalam Azad said that his mind 'was now moving from the extreme of complete inactivity to that of organised mass effort'. See Azad, *India Wins Freedom*, 72.

350   Ibid., 237–54.

351   Majumdar, *History of the Freedom Movement in India*, Vol. III, 644.

352   Ibid.

353   Edwardes, *The Last Years of British India*, 81.

354   Ibid., 82.

355   *People's War* (19 July 1942).

356   Ibid., (16 August 1942).

357   Ibid., (2 August 1942).

358   Ibid., (9 August 1942).

359   Madhu Limaye, *The CPI: Facts and Fiction* (Hyderabad: Chetana Prakashan, 1951), 48–49.

360   *People's War* (12 September 1943). Also see Joshi, *Communist Reply to Congress Working Committee's Charges*, 10.

361   Joshi, *Communist Reply to Congress Working Committee's Charges*, 10.

362   Krishnan, *National Unity for the Defence of the Motherland*, 20.

363   Masani, *The Communist Party of India—A Short History*, 82.

364   Ibid., 83.

365   Ibid., 83.

366   Ibid., 82–84.

367   P.C. Joshi, *Congress and Communists* (Bombay: People's Publishing House, 1944), 2.

368   For a detailed account of the correspondence between Gandhi and P.C. Joshi, see M.K. Gandhi and P.C. Joshi, *Correspondence Between Mahatma Gandhi and P.C. Joshi* (Bombay: People's Publishing House, 1945).

369   *Indian Annual Register*, Vol. II. (Calcutta, 1945), 102 and 112–22.

E. COMMUNIST VIEW OF INDEPENDENCE AND PARTITION

370   Schuman, *International Politics: The Western State System and the World Community*, 580.

371   Majumdar, *History of the Freedom Movement in India*, Vol. III, 745–46.

372   Edwardes, *The Last Years of British India*, 93.

373   Ibid.

374   V.P. Menon, *Transfer of Power in India* (Calcutta: Orient Longman, 1957), 234.

375   Edwardes, *The Last Years of British India*, 102.

376   Overstreet and Windmiller, *Communism in India*, 223.

377   Ibid., 225.

378   Sitaramayya, *The History of the Indian National Congress*, Vol. II, 656.

379   E. Zhukov, 'The Colonial Question at the Present State', in *Marxist Miscellany*, Vol. II (May 1945), 118–19. Also see article entitled 'The Defeat of Japanese Imperialism and the National Liberation Struggle of the Peoples of East Asia', *Bolshevik* (December 1945), 86–87.

380   A. Dyakov, 'India After the War', *New Times*, 15 January 1946, 10.

381   A. Dyakov, 'Contemporary India', *Bolshevik*, February 1946, 41.

382   Dyakov, 'India After the War', 10.

383   Dyakov, 'Contemporary India', 48–51.

384   Overstreet and Windmiller, *Communism in India*, 227.

385   It is interesting to note here that in the 1946 elections, the CPI put up only 108 candidates for a total of 1,585 provincial Legislative seats and won only eight seats, seven of which were reserved for labour representatives. For a detailed account of the election results, see *Indian Annual Register*, Vol. I (Calcutta, 1946), 229–32.

386   P.C. Joshi, *For the Final Bid For Power: The Communist Plan Explained* (Bombay: People's Publishing House, 1946), 53. Also see Sinha, *Left Wing in India*, 548.

387   Joshi, *For the Final Bid For Power: The Communist Plan Explained*, 101–02.

388   Ibid.

389   B.T. Ranadive, *Jobs for All* (Bombay: People's Publishing House, 1945), 30. Also see G.M. Adhikari, *Food for All* (Bombay: People's Publishing House, 1945), 26.

390   Overstreet and Windmiller, *Communism in India*, 231.

391   R. Palme Dutt, 'India and Pakistan', *Labour Monthly* (London, March 1946), 92–93.

392   Ibid.

393   *Indian Annual Register*, Vol. I (Calcutta, 1946), 220–22.

394   For details of the CPI central committee's deliberations, see the party's pamphlet entitled *For the Final Assault: Task of the Indian People in the Present Phase of Indian Revolution* (Bombay: People's Publishing House, 1946).

395   Overstreet and Windmiller, *Communism in India*, 243.

396   G.M. Adhikari, *Resurgent India at the Crossroads* (Bombay: People's Publishing House, 1946), 24.

397   For the full text of the resolution, see *Declaration of Independence: Communist Party Resolution for the Constituent Assembly* (Bombay: People's Publishing House, 1946), 5–10.

398   Ibid., 2–4.

399   *People's Age* (2 February 1947), 12.

400   Overstreet and Windmiller, *Communism in India*, 249.

401   A. Dyakov, 'The Situation in India', *Soviet Press Translations* (28 February 1947), 6.

402   For a discussion of the Soviet attitude towards India during this period, see Gene D. Overstreet's thesis *The Soviet View of India, 1945–1948* (Columbia University, New York, NY, 1953).

403   A. Dyakov, 'The New British Plan for India', *New Times*, 13 June 1947, 12–15.

404   Overstreet and Windmiller, *Communism in India*, 255.

405   For a detailed account of this new policy line, see John H. Kautsky, *Moscow and the Communist Party of India* (New York, NY: John Wiley and Sons and the MIT Press, 1956), 24–26.

406   Overstreet and Windmiller, *Communism in India*, 257.

407   *People's Age* (29 June 1947), 6–7.

408   Overstreet and Windmiller, *Communism in India*, 261.

409   *Mountbatten Award and After: Political Resolution of the Central Committee of the CPI* (Bombay: People's Publishing House, 1947).

410   R. Palme Dutt, 'The Mountbatten Plan for India', *Labour Monthly* (London, July 1947), 210–19.

4

Growth of the Congress Left Wing

MASS APPEAL OF GANDHI

At the close of the First World War, the nationalist movement in India stood at a crossroads. Constitutionalism had lost its appeal, sporadic terrorism had spent its force and armed revolution, in the words of Subhas Chandra Bose, was sheer madness.[1] But the war had changed the national as well as the international perspective and brought about an unprecedented awakening of the masses which heralded an era of toil and struggle, lightning and thunder. And as dark clouds began to gather in the political sky of India, Gandhi appeared with a halo of saintliness round his head and became India's man of destiny.

> He knew himself—he knew his country's needs and he knew also that during the next phase of India's struggle, the crown of leadership would be on his head. No false sense of modesty troubled him—he spoke with a firm voice and the people obeyed.[2]

To many, Gandhi's asceticism, his loincloth and saintly way of living, his daily prayers, his penitential fasts, his adherence to non-violence and solicitude for truth, his fearlessness and his 'metaphysical conception of political freedom'—all combined to give him a unique spiritual élan and charged the nationalist movement with what might be called mysticism and supernaturalism. Many Congressmen began to look upon him not only as the undisputed leader of India's struggle for freedom but also as a religious preceptor and 'began to preach the cult of the new Messiah'. They 'gave up eating fish and meat, took the same dress as the Mahatma [Gandhi], adopted his daily habits like morning and evening prayer and began to talk more of spiritual freedom than of political *swaraj*'. Gandhi began to be worshipped as an *avatar* (incarnation of God) across the country. The madness around him reached such a point that in the Jessore Provincial Congress Conference in Bengal in 1923, a resolution was moved for the goal of the INC of 'not political *swaraj* but spiritual *swaraj*'. Even the warders in the service of the Prisons Department did not believe that he had been imprisoned by the British rulers. They would like to believe that since Gandhi was a *mahatma* (great soul), 'he would assume the shape of a bird and escape from prison any moment he liked.' Political issues

> would no longer be considered in the cold light of reason but would be unnecessarily mixed up with ethical issues …. And worst of all was the tendency on the part of the orthodox followers of the Mahatma to regard everything that he said as gospel truth without reasoning or arguing and to accept his paper *Young India* as their Bible.[3]

No wonder, therefore, that Gandhi became, in the words of Jawaharlal Nehru, 'the beloved slave driver'.

Thus, ever since 1920 Gandhi had been the sun in the Indian political sky and, as P.L. Lakhanpal observed, the gods of the INC did indeed shine mainly by the light and moved mainly by the power of the central sun of Gandhiji's personality. Still, by no means all of them were dolls and dummies. A C.R. Das [Chittaranjan Das] or a Pandit Motilal Nehru was a luminary that would not only adorn the political firmament of any country but also profoundly influence the destinies of any people. Such gods never shine in altogether borrowed light or move in altogether delegated power.[4]

Lakhanpal added:

But such gods have been the exception and not the rule. The common runs of Congressmen have had—even to this day to some extent—their own lights not only dimmed but practically extinguished by the light of the central sun. They have not only hidden their lights under a bushel of modesty but also smothered them under a pall of surrender. The pall has fortunately been a moral pall which has rendered the surrenderer into a kind of passive dignity.[5]

'RATIONALIST REVOLT' OF LEFT WING

The Left wing inside the INC emerged as a 'rationalist revolt' against Gandhi, his philosophy and his technique of nationalist struggle. The revolt came from those who held radical views on social, economic and political questions and who advocated an uncompromising, vigorous and activist policy for the attainment of India's freedom. In contrast to the subjectivism of Gandhi's philosophy and his introvert nationalism, the radical elements' ideas were socialistic, for they believed that *swaraj* must be interpreted in terms of the masses, providing to the purely political concept of freedom a social and economic content. For them, political emancipation was only the means to the ultimate end of emancipation from social and economic inequality, oppression and exploitation. Gandhi's supreme concern was the means than the ends; he was more interested in specific issues than in ultimate objectives and his approach to all issues, whether moral or political, was intuitive rather than intellectual. To the radicals, on the other hand, all means were rational and justified if they could fulfil the ultimate objective.

Explaining the significance of Leftism in the context of the anti-imperialist phase of the nationalist movement, Bose wrote that in the Indian political parlance in the post-First World War period, Leftism meant anti-imperialism. He further observed:

A genuine anti-imperialist is one who believes in undiluted independence [not Mahatma Gandhi's substance of independence] as the political objective and in uncompromising national struggle as the means for attaining it. After the attainment of political independence Leftism will mean socialism and the task before the people will then be the reconstruction of national life on a socialist basis. Socialism or socialist reconstruction before achieving our political emancipation is altogether premature. Genuine anti-imperialists, i.e. Leftists, have always to fight on two fronts. So also in India, they have to fight on the one side, foreign imperialism and its Indian allies, and on the other, our milk-water nationalists, the Rightists, who are prepared for a deal with imperialism.[6]

According to Bose, a compromise with imperialism would mean that an anti-imperialist national struggle would soon be converted into a civil war among the people themselves. In the event of a compromise with imperialism, he added, the task of the Leftists would be to fight not only imperialism but also its 'new-fangled Indian allies'. And this would mean that the national struggle against imperialism would be converted into a civil war among the Indians themselves.[7]

Thus, the Left wing inside the INC emerged when some radical nationalists committed themselves to the twin goals of complete independence and socialism. And these forces began to come to the surface after the suspension of the Non-Cooperation Movement in 1922.

SUSPENSION OF NON-COOPERATION MOVEMENT
AND DISSENT IN CONGRESS CAMP

The suspension of the Non-Cooperation Movement, which took place in the teeth of such bitter opposition and at a moment when every Indian was anxiously looking forward to the grand finale of their struggle for freedom, came like a bolt from the blue and sparked off a 'regular revolt in the Congress [INC] camp'. Bose recalled that Chittaranjan Das

> was beside himself with anger and sorrow at the way Mahatma Gandhi was repeatedly bungling. He [Das] was just beginning to forget the December blunder when the Bardoli retreat came as a staggering blow. Lala Lajpat Rai was experiencing the same feeling and it is reported that in sheer disgust he addressed a seventy-page letter to the Mahatma [Gandhi] from prison.[8]

Motilal Nehru was also 'furious' at the sudden suspension of the movement and remarked: 'This ends the movement; there is no need to call off the movement because some people in a big country like India lost their balance of mind and committed violence.'[9] Jawaharlal Nehru aptly gave expression to the general feeling of anger and disappointment when he remarked that if this was the inevitable consequence of a sporadic act of violence, then there was something basically wrong with the philosophy and technique of non-violent struggle.[10]

When the news of the suspension of the Non-Cooperation Movement and the impending showdown between Gandhi and his opponents reached Moscow, M.N. Roy remarked that as a political organization the INC was dead and its corpse needed 'either to be buried or resurrected by a new breath of life'.[11] The malady of the INC, he pointed out, lay in the fact that it had no definite economic programme and as such it could not 'count upon the conscious support of any social element'.[12] Therefore, the only course open to those who believed in revolutionary mass action was to form an opposition bloc within the INC. This opposition bloc, he suggested, should put forth a revolutionary programme in order to give a fresh impetus to the waning enthusiasm of the masses and thus to draw them into the political struggle.[13] In line with the policy of the Communist International adopted at the second congress, Roy maintained that the new mass party must not part company with the INC but would try to capture its leadership.[14]

According to Roy, the man who could fulfil the task of resurrecting the INC and leading the Indian revolution was Chittaranjan Das, whose deep humanitarianism and radical socio-economic ideas had earned him a unique position among the people. Hoping to make a fellow traveller out of Das, Roy now began to address letters and articles directly to him. Roy's agents in Bengal also contacted him and supplied him with Roy's literature. From the limited evidence available, although it is difficult to ascertain the extent of Roy's influence over Das, it is interesting to note that during this period some of Das' speeches echoed Roy's ideas as expressed through the pages of *Vanguard*. For example, while delivering the presidential address at a political conference in Dehradun on 1 November 1922, Das observed:

> The Liberals fight shy of revolution. What is revolution .... Revolution means complete change and we want complete change. I am sorry most of our non-cooperators are still enamoured of parliamentary government. I do not want the sort of *swaraj* which will be for the middle class alone .... I want *swaraj* for the masses, not for the classes. I do not care for the bourgeoisie. How few are they?[15]

In the same vein, he declared at the annual session of the AITUC held in Lahore in 1923, that the *swaraj* he was striving to win was not for a class of the people but for the masses who comprised 98 per cent of the population.[16]

As the first outburst of resentment against Gandhi subsided, a fresh storm of controversy was let loose by Das when he began to broach the idea that Congressmen should participate in the ensuing elections and go to the councils in order to boycott them 'more effectively from within'. But Gandhi and his followers maintained that the INC should have nothing to do with elections and councils. In view of such bitter dispute between Gandhi and Das, it was necessary for Congressmen to settle the issue in the annual session of the INC to be held at Gaya on 26 December 1922. And at this juncture, when a showdown between Gandhi and Das seemed inevitable, M.N. Roy, in line with the Leninist thesis that communists should work in collaboration with the nationalist organizations, decided to put the INC leadership to a test.

M.N. ROY'S 'PROGRAMME' FOR CONGRESS

On 1 December 1922, Roy offered through the pages of *Advance Guard* a comprehensive 'Programme for the Indian National Congress [INC]' which called upon Congressmen to overthrow British imperialism by means of a violent revolutionary struggle. While pointing out that 'premature resort to violent tactics may be playing into the hands of the enemy', Roy maintained that it was erroneous to think that there could be any such thing as a 'non-violent revolution', no matter how 'peculiar and abnormal' the situation in India might be. The cult of non-violence, he pointed out, was inseparable from an anti-revolutionary spirit and only the enemies of an Indian revolution pinned their faith on non-violent struggle. Roy also urged the INC to align itself with the exploited workers and peasants and called for complete national independence, universal suffrage, abolition of landlordism, nationalization of public utilities, recognition of the right of labourer to organize themselves, a minimum wage in industries, an eight-hour day, free compulsory education, abolition of a standing army and the arming of the entire people to defend national freedom.[17]

Five days before the INC session at Gaya, on 21 December 1922, *Reuters* cabled Roy's 'programme' to all the subscribing newspapers in India. This created an unprecedented furore among the nationalist leaders and many began to wonder why the semi-official news agency had given such extensive publicity to the 'programme' put forward by an 'impatient Marxist' and 'political adventurer' whose literature was known to be proscribed in India. Commenting on the 'programme', *The Times of India* indignantly remarked that it was given 'a publicity seldom accorded even to a Prime Minister's most serious utterances. Why should it have been thought worthwhile to cable three columns of Bolshevik delirium to this country?'[18] It is noteworthy that the nationalist daily *Amrita Bazar Patrika* was the only newspaper in India to give a favourable appraisal of Roy's 'programme'.[19]

According to Overstreet and Windmiller, *Reuters* had enthusiastically publicized Roy's 'programme' for 'the sole purpose of labelling it as Bolshevik'. In those days, Bolshevism had become a symbol of danger to many Indians and by branding the 'programme' as a Bolshevik plot, the British government wanted to discredit not only the ideas contained in it but also the leaders who had advanced them.[20]

As a result of the hostility of most of the Congressmen towards Roy's 'programme', Das retreated to a measurable extent from his earlier radical ideas and criticized both the Bolshevik Revolution and the violent means by which it was achieved. Describing the revolution in Russia as 'a very interesting study', he declared in his presidential address at the Gaya session that the fate of Russia was 'trembling in the balance' because Marxian doctrines and dogmas had been forced upon 'the unwilling genius of Russia'. The soul of Russia, he added, must struggle to free itself from 'the socialism of Karl Marx' because a revolution brought about by violence was bound to fail. The revolution of non-violence was 'slower but surer and it was the only method by which freedom could be achieved in India'. Finally, describing himself as 'one of those who hold to non-violence on principle', Das reminded the protagonists of violent revolution that apart from any question of principle, history had proved over and over again the utter futility of revolutions brought about by force and violence.[21]

RESIGNATION OF C.R. DAS AND FORMATION OF SWARAJ PARTY

Although Das' open pronouncement in support of non-violent struggle was a triumph for Gandhi, on the question of council entry, a split in the INC camp could not be avoided. In his address, Das made a vigorous plea for council entry and declared that as the idea of boycott implied something more than mere withdrawal, the only successful boycott of councils was either to mend them in a manner suitable to the attainment of *swaraj* or to end them completely.[22]

The followers of Gandhi, most prominent among whom was Chakravarti Rajagopalachari, stubbornly opposed this contention and when the issue came up for voting they won a thumping victory. The rejection of this policy by the INC made Das' position extremely anomalous and when the AICC met on 1 January 1923 to lay down its programme for the year, he announced his resignation, declaring that as there were 'at least two schools of thought with fundamental differences', he could not associate himself with 'most of the resolutions' passed by the party. He also announced his intention to work in future with those who shared his beliefs. Accordingly, the supporters of Das, notably Motilal Nehru, V.J. Patel, N.C. Kelkar, S. Satyamurti and M.R. Jayakar, issued a manifesto constituting themselves into a new organization within the INC, the Swaraj Party.

The defection of so many eminent leaders, including such stalwarts as Das and Motilal Nehru, foreshadowed a split in the INC camp. What was worse, when disagreement degenerated into ignoble squabbles, it became almost impossible to carry into effect the programme of action adopted by the INC. Party quarrels came to take up more time 'for the leaders than an active effort to carry out the Congress [INC] resolutions'.[23]

EMERGENCE OF LEFT AS A POWERFUL GROUP INSIDE CONGRESS

When the Swaraj Party was formed, wrote Subhas Chandra Bose:

> It had drawn elements both from the Right and from the Left. During the lifetime of the leader [Chittaranjan Das] the Left elements had the upper hand because he himself belonged to the Left. But in his absence the Right elements were able to raise their head.[24]

Following Das' death in 1925, the Left wing made an attempt to assert itself at the Madras session of the INC in 1927 when the youthful elements led by Subhas Chandra Bose and Jawaharlal Nehru successfully carried a resolution committing INC to the goal of complete national independence. Opposing the resolution, Gandhi opined that it was 'hastily conceived and thoughtlessly passed'.[25] But despite Gandhi's opposition, the growing strength of the radical elements was evident from the fact that three representatives of the Left wing—Subhas Chandra Bose, Jawaharlal Nehru and Shuaib Qureshi—were included in the CWC. Thus, the Madras session of the INC, in the words of Bose, 'may be regarded as standing for a definite orientation towards the Left'.[26]

The Madras session also revealed that within the INC there were two distinctly opposed groups— the orthodox elements who would be content with dominion status and the radicals who demanded complete national independence. Although at a meeting of the AICC held in November 1928, a compromise had been arrived at between the two groups, matters came to a head at the Calcutta session of the party in December when Gandhi moved a resolution suggesting that dominion status be accepted provided the British Parliament accepted the Motilal Nehru Report on Constitutional Framework in its entirety within a year. The resolution was opposed by the Left-wing leaders represented by Bose and (Jawaharlal) Nehru, who moved an amendment to the effect that the INC 'would be content with nothing short of independence, which implied severance of the British connection'.[27] But when the amendment was put to the vote, it was lost by 973 votes to 1350. According to Bose, as the followers of Gandhi made the vote a question of confidence, most of the members voted for his resolution not out of conviction but because they were unwilling to be party to forcing Gandhi out of the INC. But despite the defeat of the resolution, he pointed out, the voting demonstrated the strength and influence of the Left wing.[28]

The government took notice of the emergence of the Left wing as a powerful group within the INC. Describing the Calcutta session of the party as 'a clear triumph for extremism', a secret government circular dated 21 February 1929, observed:

> If the experience of the Calcutta Congress [Calcutta session of the INC, 1928] is any guide, the decision of future policy appears to lie almost entirely with the young men, notably Pandit Jawaharlal Nehru and Babu Subhas Chandra Bose. There is a tendency for the political and communist revolutionaries to join hands, and Pandit Jawaharlal, an extreme nationalist, who is at the same time genuinely attracted by some of the communist doctrines, stands almost at the meeting point …. The situation contains serious potentialities of danger …. If the extremist leaders press on with their programme, it appears to the Government of India that they should not have a free hand to develop their organization, and increase their following with a view to striking at the moment most favourable to themselves.[29]

The growing strength and influence of the Left wing was largely due to the fact that during this period, Jawaharlal Nehru began to tack close to the doctrines of Marx whose scientific method in analysing social and economic phenomena had made a deep impression on him. A study of Marxism, Nehru wrote in his *The Discovery of India*, produced such a powerful effect on his mind that he came to believe that the 'Soviet Revolution had advanced human society by a great leap and had lit the bright flame which could not be smothered, and that it had laid the foundations for that new civilization towards which the world could advance.'[30] Nehru was also convinced that this new civilization would spread to other lands and put an end to the wars and conflicts on which capitalism fed.[31] Nehru's predilection for Marxian doctrines found further expression when he admitted that class struggle was inherent in the capitalist system because the ruling or owning classes would never welcome any change of the socio-economic state of their lands.[32]

In February 1927, Nehru went to Brussels to attend the communist-sponsored Congress of Oppressed Nationalities and actively associated himself with the League Against Imperialism—a communist front which emerged from the deliberations of this conference. In Brussels, he came in close contact with many communists and for the first time got an insight into the inner conflicts of the capitalist world and the problems of the colonial and dependent countries. As a result of these personal contacts, Nehru 'turned inevitably with goodwill towards communism'. It was, however, not a doctrinal adherence because he did not know much about the 'fine points of communism'. His acquaintance with communism was limited to its broad features and what attracted him most were the 'tremendous changes taking place in Russia'. Nehru confessed that the communists often irritated him by 'their doctrinal ways, their aggressive and vulgar methods, [and] their habit of denouncing everybody who did not agree with them'. This reaction, he thought, was perhaps due to his 'bourgeois education and upbringing'.[33]

Nehru returned from Brussels with the conviction that India's problems needed to be judged in the broader context of the crisis of capitalism and imperialism. He realized that

> just as capitalism provided its own grave-diggers, so its spawn, imperialism, nurtured within itself the seeds of conflict and decay, and both systems had their roots in global trends which affected East and West, the white and coloured, the privileged and the dispossessed. Colonialism and capitalism were two faces of the same coin. Capitalism, with its hankering after cheap labour and cheap raw materials, leading ultimately to colonialism.[34]

This new realization led Nehru to believe that the nationalist leaders who continued to think 'within the narrow frame' of the existing sociopolitical structure were playing into the hands of the British government, which controlled that structure. They could not do otherwise, he averred, because, in spite of 'occasional experiments with direct action', their whole outlook was reformist. For this reason, they were incapable of offering the revolutionary solutions demanded by the Indian situation.[35] And unless far-reaching and revolutionary socio-economic changes were brought about in India, its political freedom would be meaningless.[36] Under his inspiration, the Uttar Pradesh Provincial Congress Committee adopted a resolution declaring that the misery of the Indian people was due not only to foreign exploitation but also to the socio-economic structure of society, which the alien rulers supported so that their exploitation might continue. Therefore, in order to remove the misery of the Indian masses, it was essential to make revolutionary changes in the existing socio-economic structure of Indian society.[37]

Jawaharlal Nehru's intellectual proclivity towards the radical socio-economic ideas of Marx created a flutter in the INC camp and many Right-wingers felt that 'vodka has gone to his head'.[38] Thus, Nehru found himself in a very awkward position in which while Right-wing Congressmen thought that he was playing Moscow's game, he was being denounced by the ultra-Left communists as a 'reformist of the worst type'. As a matter of fact, although he was attracted to Marxist ideas during this period, communism as a whole did not attract him greatly. As Nehru himself explained, he had been too much influenced by the humanist liberal tradition of the nineteenth century to abandon it and embrace communism. Although the philosophy of communism appealed to him, he disliked dogmatism and 'the treatment of Karl Marx's writings or of any other book as revealed scripture which cannot be challenged, and the regimentation and heresay-hunts which seemed to be a feature of modern communism', were anathema to him.[39] According to Subhas Chandra Bose, although Nehru's ideas and views were of a radical nature, in practice he was a loyal follower of Gandhi. Bose observed: 'It would probably be correct to say that while his brain is with the Left-wingers, his heart is with Mahatma Gandhi.'[40]

The truth of Bose's observation was revealed in the Lahore session of the INC in 1929 when, much to the chagrin of the Left wing, Gandhi won Nehru over and decided to back his candidature for the INC presidency. The Left-wingers did not want Nehru to play into the hands of Gandhi by accepting the presidency. They were fully aware of Gandhi's strength and were of the opinion that as they were not in a position to have their programme adopted by the INC, it was futile for Nehru, one of their outstanding spokesmen, to accept the presidency. But Gandhi played his cards extremely well and by sponsoring Nehru's candidature he was able successfully to 'beat down the Left-wing opposition and regain his former undisputed supremacy' over the INC. Nehru's submission to Gandhi proved to be unfortunate for the Left wing 'because that event marked the beginning of a political rapprochement between the Mahatma [Gandhi] and Pandit Jawaharlal Nehru and a consequent alienation between the latter and the Congress Left wing'.[41]

Thus, when the INC met in Lahore, nobody had a shred of doubt that Nehru 'was a figurehead', and that Gandhi would dominate the entire proceedings. Gandhi's position was further consolidated when, by advocating complete independence, he weaned away a section of the Left wing to his side. Such undisputed supremacy notwithstanding, a great furore was created when in his resolution Gandhi congratulated the viceroy on his 'providential escape' from the bomb hurled at his train. The Left wing regarded this clause not only irrelevant but also uncalled for in a political resolution. But Gandhi made it a question of confidence and it was passed by a narrow margin. Thereupon, on behalf of the Left wing, Bose moved a resolution to the effect that the INC 'should aim at setting up a parallel government in the country and to that end should take in hand the task of organizing the workers, peasants and youths'. Bose was indignant that this resolution was also defeated, with the result that though the INC

accepted the goal of complete independence as its objective, no plan was laid down for reaching that goal nor was any programme of work adopted for the coming year. A more ridiculous state of affairs could not be imagined, but in public affairs, we are sometimes inclined to lose not only our sense of reality but our common sense as well.[42]

Gandhi's victory in Lahore was complete with the expulsion of all the Left-wing elements, including Bose and Srinivasa Iyengar, from the CWC. Although there was considerable resentment over the expulsion of Bose and Iyengar, Gandhi made it clear that he would not accept a CWC that could not be of one mind. Once again he made it a question of confidence and Congressmen, reluctant to repudiate him, 'had no option but to give in to his demand'.[43]

After the setback in Lahore, the Left wing recovered some lost ground when the INC met in Karachi in March 1931, to ratify the Gandhi–Irwin Pact. The first phase of the Civil Disobedience Movement had by this time come to an end demonstrating, in the words of R.C. Majumdar, 'the awakening of political consciousness among the masses to a degree undreamt of before either by the friends or foes of India'.[44] Excitement of the younger section of the people also ran very high over the execution of the three revolutionaries—Bhagat Singh, Basabrao Rajguru and Sukhdev—the commutation of whose capital punishment Gandhi was unable to obtain when he took up the matter with the viceroy.[45] The executions filled the country with poignant grief and the younger section held Gandhi partly responsible because he did not agree with Bose's suggestion that he should break with the viceroy on the question. As a result, when Gandhi, along with president-elect Vallabhbhai Patel reached Karachi, they were met with hostile public demonstration.[46] Similar demonstrations were also held during the open session when Gandhi refused to endorse a resolution expressing admiration for the courage and sacrifice of Bhagat Singh and his comrades. Ultimately, although the resolution was adopted in a modified form 'disapproving of political violence in any shape or form', the whole episode somewhat tarnished Gandhi's image.

In Karachi, although the Left wing had decided not to approve of the Gandhi–Irwin Pact, they refrained from precipitating a split because, as Bose pointed out, the 'official party machinery' had managed the situation with such thoroughness that they could expect little support from the elected delegates 'who alone could vote' at the INC. Nothing would be gained, they felt, by creating a split in the INC particularly when the government was eager for a division in the party camp.[47] For this reason, although disapproving the Gandhi–Irwin Pact, the Left wing did not oppose it in the plenary session of the INC.[48]

However, the Left wing did have the satisfaction of getting the INC to pass a resolution on fundamental rights and economic policy which was new in that the party hereby recognized, for the first time in its history, that 'to end the exploitation of the masses, political freedom must include real economic freedom.'[49] Stressing the importance of this resolution, Nehru observed that by advocating nationalization of key industries and services and various other measures, the INC had taken 'a step, a very short step, in a socialist direction'.[50] Although the resolution was both 'mild and prosaic', there were those in the Government of India who foresaw the spectre of the 'Bolshevik stealing into Karachi and corrupting the Congress [INC] leaders'.[51]

FORMATION OF SOCIALIST GROUPS

The adoption of the resolution on fundamental rights and economic policy not only gave a socialist orientation to the INC objectives but also served to provide a powerful stimulus to the growth of socialist movement in the country. Among the various socialist groups formed during this period, the most important were those in Bihar, Uttar Pradesh, Delhi, Bombay and Punjab. The Bihar Socialist Party was formed in July 1931, by Jayaprakash Narayan, Phulan Prasad Varma and Rahul Sankrityayan[52] with the object of establishing a socialist state in India where private property and individual or class ownership of land and capital would be abolished.[53] The organizing committee of the party consisted of Abdul Bari, Phulan Prasad Varma and Rahul Sankrityayan. Under its auspices, the Socialist Research Institute was established in Patna in early 1934. In Uttar Pradesh, those who took prominent parts in organizing a socialist group were Sampurnanand, Paripoornanand Painuli, Kamalapati Tripathi and Tarapada Bhattacharya. In Bombay, similar groups were formed by eminent socialists, such as Yusuf Meherally, M.R. Masani, Achyut Patwardhan and Kamaladevi Chattopadhyay. The Punjab Socialist Party, however, sprang up as a splinter group of the Naujawan Bharat Sabha which was started as a thoroughgoing nationalist movement to fight communalism and religious fanaticism. Subsequently, it developed into a terrorist organization and when the All India Naujawan Bharat Sabha met in Karachi in March 1931, a section of the Punjab Naujawan Bharat Sabha declared that they were against terrorism and that they believed in mass action on socialist lines.[54] It was as a result of this dispute between the terrorists and socialists that the Punjab Socialist Party was formed in September 1933.

BIRTH OF CONGRESS SOCIALIST PARTY

The idea of the CSP first took shape in the Nashik Central Jail where a group of young socialists— Jayaprakash Narayan, Ashoka Mehta, Achyut Patwardhan, Yusuf Meherally, M.R. Masani, N.G. Gore, S.M. Joshi and M.L. Dantwala—came to realize that it was only by forming an effective opposition bloc inside the INC that the drift to neo-constitutionalism could be prevented and the nationalist movement resuscitated to a revolutionary purpose and with a mass base.[55] They also felt that to intensify the national struggle which had so far been 'a predominantly middle-class movement', it was necessary 'to broaden the basis of the movement by organizing the masses on an economic and class-conscious basis'.

Immediately after their release from prison, the socialists set about the task of implementing their programme and convened the first All India Congress Socialists' Conference at the Anjuman Islamia Hall in Patna on the eve of the AICC meeting on 17 May 1934. To mobilize Left-wing opinion, Narendra Deva in his presidential address said:

> Congressmen have so far been approaching the masses in the name of democracy and political freedom, but these high platitudes have never moved them out of their apathy and quiescence and the response accordingly has not been very satisfactory. These abstract ideas make no appeal to the masses because they have no meaning for them. They can, however, be made restive and class conscious and can come into the arena of active warfare only when an economic appeal is made to them.[56]

Deva went on to add that the national struggle was coming more and more to be identified with the struggle of the oppressed classes and a full recognition of this fact alone would enable Congressmen to formulate the correct policies for the future.

The socialists, however, agreed that the INC was the only political organization in the country from whose platform the national struggle for freedom could be carried on and to leave the INC would be to isolate themselves from the mainstream of the national movement.[57] As further explained by Deva, although the INC had many shortcomings, it was the greatest revolutionary force in the country. Moreover, as the existing stage of Indian struggle was that of the bourgeois-democratic revolution, it would be suicidal for the socialists to cut themselves off from the national movement that the INC represented. According to Deva:

> The one great quality of a true Marxist was that he was not dogmatic or sectarian in his attitude. He would never refuse to take part in the national movement simply on the ground that the struggle was being conducted by the petty-bourgeois elements of society although he would make ceaseless efforts to give it

a socialist direction. In the peculiar conditions of India, socialists could very well work within the Congress [INC] and combine national struggle with socialism.[58]

In his presidential address to the conference, Deva also expressed 'a genuine fear' that being deprived of the healthy influence of the revolutionary movement, the autonomous *swarajist* section of the INC would in course of time become a purely constitutional and reformist body and would develop a mentality which would run counter to the revolutionary character of the INC. He warned: 'Let it be remembered that the policy which has been adumbrated by the new Swaraj Party was quite different in spirit from that of its namesake which is associated with the hallowed names of Srijut C.R. Das [Chittaranjan Das] and Pandit Motilal Nehru.'[59] Deva then declared that in order to fight the 'policy of alternating between direct action in a revolutionary situation and constructive or legislative work according to one's temperament', the socialists would 'fervently and persistently agitate within the Congress [INC] for the adoption of an economic programme with a view to socialize the nationalist struggle'.[60]

The Patna conference, therefore, adopted a resolution urging the INC to formulate a programme that would be 'socialist in action and objective'. Political freedom, it said, must include real economic freedom of the starving millions.[61]

After accomplishing the task of uniting the socialists and other radical elements of the INC and formulating the broad outlines of their social, economic and political objectives, the Congress socialists met in Bombay on 22–23 October 1934, under the presidency of Sampurnanand to give birth to the CSP. The programme and the constitution of the party were also adopted in this meeting. Deva, Jayaprakash Narayan and M.R. Masani were elected as the president, the secretary and the joint secretary of its national executive, respectively.

The constitution of the CSP, as adopted in the Bombay conference, provided that the highest policy-making body would be the annual conference consisting of delegates of its provincial units. The annual conference would every year elect the executive committee consisting of one general secretary, four joint secretaries and eleven ordinary members.[62] The membership of the party would be open only to the members of the INC who would also be members of provincial CSP units, provided that they were not members of any communal organization or of any other political organization whose objects and programmes were, in the opinion of the party, inconsistent with its own.[63]

The Bombay conference also adopted a 'platform of the party' which declared that the main objects of the CSP were to be 'the achievement of complete independence in the sense of separation from the British empire' and 'the establishment of a socialist society' in India.[64] The significance of the first objective was clarified in a separate resolution which said that complete independence 'must mean the establishment of an independent Indian state' and 'refusal to compromise at any stage with British imperialism'.[65] According to L.P. Sinha:

> The demand for refusal to enter at any stage into negotiations on the constitutional issue with the British government was based on the assumption that freedom could not be achieved through negotiation and that freedom thus gained would not be a real freedom. This underlying assumption remained throughout the history of the CSP, moreover, it was an assumption which it shared with the communists and other Left groups.[66]

The establishment of a socialist society in India was to be achieved through the implementation of a 15-point programme:[67]

1. Transfer of all power to the producing masses.
2. Development of the economic life of the country to be planned and controlled by the state.
3. Socialization of key principal industries [such as steel, cotton, jute, railways, shipping, plantations, mines], insurance and public utilities, with a view to the progressive socialization of the instruments of production, distribution and exchange.

4. State monopoly of foreign trade.
5. Organization of cooperatives for production, distribution and credit in the unsocialized section of the economic life.
6. Elimination of princes and landlords and all other classes of exploiters without compensation.
7. Redistribution of land to the peasants.
8. The state to encourage and control cooperative and collective farming.
9. Liquidation of debts owned by peasants and workers.
10. Recognition of the right to work or maintenance by the state.
11. 'To everyone according to his needs' is to be the ultimate basis of distribution of economic goods.
12. Adult franchise which shall be on the functional basis.
13. The state shall neither support nor discriminate between religions nor recognize any distinction on caste or community.
14. The state shall not discriminate between the sexes.
15. Repudiation of the so-called public debt of India.

The 'platform' also outlined in detail the immediate demands of the party as well as its programme of action both inside and outside the INC. It was resolved that while the CSP's work inside the INC would be directed towards its acceptance of a socialist programme, work outside the INC would be devoted to the task of organizing the workers and peasants for the purpose of developing and participating in the day-to-day economic and political struggle for their class interests and thus intensifying the class struggle of the masses and of creating a powerful mass movement for the achievement of independence and socialism.[68]

The immediate demands of the CSP were: freedom of speech and of the press; freedom of association; the release of all political prisoners detained without trial and withdrawal of all orders of externment and internment or restrain on political grounds; free and compulsory primary education and the liquidation of adult illiteracy; drastic reduction by at least 50 per cent of the military expenditure of the Government of India; regulation and control of religious endowments; repeal of all anti-national and anti-labour laws; reinstatement of all farmers and tenants deprived of their lands owing to their participation in the movement of national independence; control and supervision by the state of industries subsidized or otherwise protected; control by the state of banking, key industries and ownership of mineral resources; municipalization of public utilities; full state control over exchange and currency; control of usury; a steeply graduated tax on all income including net income from agriculture above a fixed minimum and graduated death duties; freedom of labour from serfdom and conditions bordering on serfdom; the right to form unions, to strike and picket; compulsory recognition of unions by employees; a living wage; a 40-hour week and healthy conditions of work; insurance against unemployment, sickness, accident, old age and so on; one month's leave every year with full pay to all workers and two month's leave with full pay to women during maternity; prohibition against employment of children of school age in factories and women and children under 16 in underground mines; equal wages for equal work; elimination of the feudal system without compensation; encouragement of cooperative farming; liquidation of debts owned by workers and peasants; liquidation of arrears of rent, complete exemption from rents and taxes of all peasants with uneconomic holdings; reduction of rent and land revenue by at least 50 per cent; abolition of all feudal and semi-feudal levies on the peasantry; penalization of illegal exaction of rent or money decrees of homestead, agricultural resources and that portion of a peasant's holding which is just sufficient to maintain an average peasant family.[69]

The programme and demands of the Congress socialists clearly indicated that they sought to make an economic appeal to the producing classes for the purpose of mobilizing them on a class basis against both British imperialism and 'the forces of native reaction'. They felt that as foreign imperialism had attempted to entrench its position through the formation of a bloc with the forces of native reaction, it was necessary for them to rally all the radical elements of the country against the newly constituted bloc of imperialism and its native allies. Deva said: 'The capitalist class in India is not capable of leading the bourgeois-democratic revolution. Capitalism long ago ceased to be a revolutionary force.'[70]

ATTACK ON CSP FROM RIGHT AND ULTRA-LEFT CAMPS

The revolt of the socialists caused considerable annoyance to the Right-wing leaders who contended that the formation of a separate party within the INC was bound not only to strike at the root of the INC's organizational unity but also to disrupt the struggle for national emancipation. Socialism to them was antithetical to Indian nationalism because of the 'unique tradition and cultural heritage of the country'. Apart from their dislike for socialism, class struggle, revolution and the like, the Right-wing leaders feared that by working inside the INC, the new party would impair its unity.[71] Gandhi, however, welcomed the emergence of a socialist group inside the INC although he disapproved of its programme. He held that class struggle, as propagated by the socialists, implied violence and as such was against the fundamental principles of the INC.[72]

But according to Bose, the formation of the CSP represented 'a legitimate and natural reaction against the move towards the Right which the Congress [INC] policy adopted'. He argued:

> If there had not been a revolt within the Congress [INC] against a swing to the Right, then one would have been justified in thinking that the Congress [INC] was dying. But because the Congress [INC] was neither dead nor dying, the revolt did take place and the Congress Socialist Party [CSP] came into existence. To attempt to suppress the party [CSP] or browbeat its members with the threat of disciplinary action, shows a woeful lack of knowledge of the elementary principles of modern politics. This attempt was made in 1923 when the Swaraj Party was born and it only served to strengthen that party and add to its importance.[73]

Bose, however, pointed out that while the instinct that had urged the formation of the CSP was correct, there was 'some lack of clarity in the ideas of the party'. The very name of the party, he said, was an unhappy one because the term 'socialism' had different complexions and connotations to different people. There was hardly anything common between the socialism of Ramsay MacDonald and the militant ideology of the Spanish socialists.[74] He further added:

> The Congress Socialist Party [CSP] seems to be under the influence of Fabian socialism which was the fashion in England fifty years ago. Since then, much water has flown down the Thames and also down the Ganges. So many developments have taken place in different parts of the world since end of the Great War and so many socio-economic experiments have been and are being made that a modern party can not afford to hark back to the idea and shibboleths prevalent in Europe four or five decades ago.[75]

The Rightist misgivings about the radical socio-economic policy of the CSP found expression in a resolution of the CWC adopted on 17 June 1934. While welcoming the formation of 'groups representing different schools of thought', the resolution found it necessary to remind Congressmen that the Karachi resolution, as finally adopted by the AICC in Bombay in August 1931, neither contemplated confiscation of private property nor advocated class war. Confiscation of private property and class war, it said, were contrary to the INC creed of non-violence.[76] It was further contended by the Right wing that the Congress socialists were first and foremost internationalists and as such could not be wholly depended upon in the struggle for national liberation.[77]

Attack on the Congress socialists also came from the ultra-Leftists, including the communists, who branded them as 'social fascists'[78] and impugned their ideology as 'fake socialism' because of their affiliation with the INC. They pointed out that those who had so long remained under the spell of Gandhism could not be expected to accept true socialism as their creed.[79] The substance of their criticism, according to Deva, was that as socialism was the special task of the proletariat, only a workers' party could build it and that to accomplish the task it must act as an independent class force and must have an independent political organization. The CSP being organizationally connected with the INC had no independent existence and therefore it could not be expected to perform the task which it had set before itself.[80] Another criticism was that the CSP had come into existence as a result of a conspiracy hatched by the bourgeoisie and the INC which had split itself into two wings to deceive the masses and disrupt their struggle. Dismissing this charge as 'puerile' and 'naïve', Deva remarked that such formulae could be 'invented by a dullard who is incapable of understanding even a simple fact'. He did not feel the necessity to 'take into account further criticisms of a similar nature because they are so ludicrous that they need not be seriously considered'.[81]

DEFENCE OF JAYAPRAKASH NARAYAN AND NARENDRA DEVA

In view of such attacks both from the Right and the Left, the leaders of the CSP were impelled to clarify their ideological orientation and position vis-à-vis the INC and other Leftist parties.

Explaining the significance of the name of the party, Deva observed that in sharp contrast to communism, Congress socialism represented 'the Indian translation of the Russian social democracy' which implied the interdependence of two revolutions—one social, that is, economic emancipation, and the other political, that is, democratic freedom. Quoting Lenin, he pointed out that as socialist objectives could be realized only through the struggle for democracy, in colonial countries the national struggle was a democratic struggle. The socialists accepted the term 'Congress' because it symbolized the struggle for a democratic order in India. The CSP, he finally made clear, did not call itself the Social Democratic Party because that name had acquired a bad connotation after the betrayal of the European social democrats in the First World War.[82]

Replying to the criticism that if the Congress socialists wanted to establish socialism in India, they should have formed an independent party outside the INC, thus liberating themselves from the reactionary influence of the bourgeois leadership, Deva pointed out that they did not break away from the INC because that would have isolated them from the 'great national movement against British imperialism' which the INC symbolized.[83] Explaining the reason why the CSP was within the INC, he said that it came into existence when a group of Congressmen came under the impact of socialist ideas and saw that a crisis had come over democracy in the West and that parliamentary institutions were crumbling on all sides. They saw that capitalism was in a decadent condition and had entered its last stage, that is, imperialism. When the choice before the world lay between fascism and socialism, they found that in the midst of the surrounding gloom Russia alone was the hope of the poor, the oppressed and the downtrodden. And having studied the history of revolutions in other countries, they came to the conclusion that the programme of the INC should be fundamentally altered in order to combine national independence with socialism.[84]

The CSP was, therefore, formed not as a rival political organization to the INC, but 'to work within the Congress [INC], to strengthen it, to mould and shape its policies'.[85] Describing the INC as the only organization capable of 'waging a national struggle and maintaining national unity', Jayaprakash Narayan observed that it represented the widest, the strongest anti-imperialist front and if India were to wage war with imperialism with any chance of success, that battle had to be waged under the tricolour flag of the INC. The AIKS, the AITUC or the AISF, he said, could not hope to fight imperialism with any degree of success: that task unquestionably belonged to the INC.[86] From this appraisal of the role of the INC in the struggle for national liberation, Narayan concluded: 'The Congress [INC] alone is the country's salvation. And let us remember the Congress [INC] means the whole and not part of it. A limb torn from the body does not have its proportionate strength and ability. It merely dies.'[87]

Although the Congress socialists accepted the fact that the INC represented the mainstream of the nationalist movement, they also contended that the influence of reactionary forces over its leadership had rendered it incapable of leading a revolutionary struggle against British imperialism and its native allies. The INC no doubt represented the broad nationalist sentiment of the Indian people, but neither its constitution nor its programme could fulfil the aspirations of the oppressed and the exploited masses. Therefore, a radical change in the leadership and programme of the INC was needed. This alone could transform it into a mass anti-imperialist front. And the chief task to which the Congress socialists addressed themselves was of replacing the bourgeois-reactionary leadership of the INC by the leadership of revolutionary elements of the party. To achieve this, the Congress socialists found it necessary not only to separate 'the anti-imperialist elements from the bourgeois leadership but also to develop and broaden the Congress [INC] as to transform it into a powerful anti-imperialist front'.[88]

In his presidential address to the Bengal provincial unit of the CSP in September 1935, Narayan said that the work of the socialists inside the INC was governed by the policy of developing it into a true anti-imperialist body. It was not their purpose, he pointed out, to convert the whole INC into a full-fledged socialist party. All they sought to do was to change the content and policy of the INC so that it might emancipate the masses both from foreign power and the native system of exploitation.[89] In this connection, Deva also emphasized that all they wanted to do was to enhance the prestige of the INC and that they would do all that lay in their power to build it into a powerful organization and to make it a fit instrument for conducting the anti-imperialist struggle.[90] Deploring the fact that Gandhism had become 'a cloak for vested interests and selfish groups who have nothing in common with the Congress [INC] ideology of mass struggle', Deva declared that the ideal of the Congress socialists was to establish a classless society in India where there would be no exploitation, unemployment or starvation.[91] The socialist presence in the INC, he averred, should be a guarantee that it would follow a right course of action and this was possible only if they played their part well. 'Let us by our exemplary conduct and by constructive work among the masses broaden the basis of our struggle and thereby win the deliverance of our people and strengthen the progressive forces in all countries of the East.'[92]

The 'strategic' importance of the CSP, according to Narayan, lay in the fact that it had grown 'out of the very heart of the national movement'. But Narayan was distressed that this led other Leftist parties, particularly the CPI, to take advantage of its unique position; and when they failed to use the CSP to advance their own party interests, they sought to destroy it as an obstacle to the rise of others.[93]

From its inception, however, the CSP's desire was to forge a common platform of action with the CPI. As Deva pointed out, it wanted to cooperate with the communists in those labour sectors where the latter's influence was considerable while the communists were expected to cooperate with the socialists among the peasantry and other fronts where the influence of the INC was paramount. However, the communists were not only unprepared for such cooperation but also refused to accept the Marxist character of the CSP. Castigating the communists for their refusal to cooperate with the Congress socialists, Deva observed that while on the one hand the communists were clamouring for admission to the CSP, on the other they tried their best to destroy the organizations that the socialists had built up with tremendous efforts and wherein they gave the communists opportunities to work. These activities only served to demonstrate that the communists could not tolerate the influence of any party, except theirs, in the working-class movement. The communists, he said, wanted to enter the CSP not to foster socialist unity, but only to promote their own influence in areas where they had made little headway, particularly in the peasants' movement. On the question of the communists' persistent demand for their inclusion in the CSP, Deva pointed out that it was impossible for anyone to be honestly loyal to two political parties at the same time and no party could grow on suppression of varying tendencies and the creation of mechanical unity.

> Ideological differences often further the development of a party, but this does not mean that we throw open our doors to persons who directly or indirectly receive their instructions or draw their inspiration from another party. Those who press for the inclusion of communists in the CSP forget that the CSP is a political party and not a joint front, a national parliament embracing various sections and classes like the Congress [INC] .... It is time it is realized that the CSP is a political party with its distinct ideology, programme of work, approach and discipline.[94]

According to Narayan, the most fundamental difference between the CPI and the CSP—which precluded the possibility of any lasting unity between the two—was that while the former was a branch of the Communist International, the latter was an independent organization, the very existence of which was in opposition to the line of the Communist International. Moreover, the CPI was not only antagonistic to the INC but had also set up organizations in rivalry to it, such as the WPP and the League Against Imperialism. The CSP, on the other hand, supported the INC and made all efforts to strengthen it as an instrument of national struggle. The communists considered the INC as a bourgeois organization which they must shun and fight. But the Congress socialists looked upon the INC as a mass-national organization which they must support and develop along their own lines.

The second difference between the two parties was in regard to their respective roles in the trade union movement. While the Congress socialists believed firmly in the unity of the trade union movement and directed all their efforts to that end, the communists had split the movement by forming their own Red Trade Union Congress (RTUC). Narayan Observed:

> It is hardly necessary to point out what would become of the trade union movement and workers' solidarity if every little party were to form its own union. Workers in every industry and every factory would be split up into rival unions fighting among themselves. Even this elementary Marxism was unknown at that time to our communist friends, and if one may venture to suggest, to the Third [Communist] International too. Here again the policy of the Congress Socialist Party [CSP] was totally different, and it was truly Marxist policy.[95]

The third difference was in regard to the question of socialist unity. Here also, the Congress socialists stood firmly for close cooperation between all the socialist groups and the eventual growth of a united socialist party. But the attitude of the communists was not so conducive to such a unity because they regarded the CPI 'as the only true socialist party with right to exist and treated all others as enemies'. Narayan recalled:

> During those days, as now, the principal communist line of attack was that we were no socialists and had no understanding of Marxism. It was they who were the true interpreters of Marx and Lenin. It is, therefore, of interest to note here that it was not very long before these self-appointed priests of Marxism were eating all their words and repudiating all the fundamental policies which they had been asserting with such half-educated cocksureness. In less than two years they came running into the Congress [INC], disbanded their red trade unions [RTUC], joined the All India Trade Union Congress [AITUC], and at least in words, accepted the objective of socialist unity. The Marxism of Congress Socialist Party [CSP] proved sounder than the parrot-like dogmatism of the Communist Party [CPI].[96]

Thus, it was clear that there was no question of the CSP's affiliation with the Communist International. As pointed out by Narayan, although the CSP was neither anti-Communist International nor anti-Russian, the question of affiliation was beset with grave and insuperable difficulties. On this issue, Narayan said:

The Congress Socialist Party is not a party transplanted from outside. It is a growth of the Indian soil. It was not inspired by any outside force. It grew and developed out of the experience of the Indian people struggling for freedom. Its very formation was a protest and revolt against the line the Third [Communist] International pursued in India.[97]

Summing up the circumstances under which the CSP had grown and the part it played in putting socialism on the political map of India, Narayan wrote:

Before the party was formed in 1934, soon after the cessation of Civil Disobedience [Movement], socialism could hardly be said to have been in the picture of Indian politics. It had received a certain amount of publicity at the time of the Meerut Conspiracy Case; but it secured no place for itself in the political life of the country, and appeared to the people rather as an article of foreign importation. In 1931, Shri [Mr] M.N. Roy, when he returned to India secretly, formed a party of his own. But that party, too, remained practically unknown, and did not as much as create even a little ripple over the surface of Indian politics. The utterances of individual radical nationalist leaders, like Pandit Jawaharlal Nehru and Shri Subhas Chandra Bose, had attracted to a degree the attention of a section of the middle-class intelligentsia. But there was no organized movement worth the name. It would be no exaggeration, therefore, to say that it was the Congress Socialist Party [CSP] that in 1934 put socialism on the political map.[98]

THE SECOND WORLD WAR AND CSP

At Tripuri, instead of rallying all the Left-wing forces inside the INC under the leadership of Bose, the Congress socialists revealed their incapacity to come to grips with a situation that demanded unity of purpose and action. Their vacillation, described by Bose as a 'betrayal',[99] also showed that they were too anxious to abide by the discipline of the INC and maintain its unity under a composite leadership even if it meant going back upon the CSP's professed policy, laid down in the Faizpur Thesis, of replacing the INC leadership which was 'unable to develop within the framework of its conception and take the struggle of the masses to a higher level'. This anxiety for the unity of INC organization and leadership was once again demonstrated at the outbreak of the Second World War when at first the Congress socialists unconditionally rejected the idea of entry into the war, but soon afterwards accepted the INC position of support for British war efforts.

During the early years of the international crisis, the policy of the CSP was to utilize the situation for the intensification of the national struggle and awakening of the revolutionary spirit of the masses.[100] The Congress socialists regarded the war as a conflict between the partners of imperialism and as such there was no question of siding with either Britain or Germany even in lieu of India's independence. In his 'Statement at the Prosecution' at Jamshedpur in 1940, Narayan averred that India could in no way be a party to the war, because, both German Nazism and British imperialism were driven by 'selfish ends of conquest and domination, exploitation and oppression'. Narayan further said:

Great Britain is fighting not to destroy Nazism, which it had nurtured, but to curb a rival, who might no longer be allowed to grow unchallenged. It is fighting to maintain its dominant place in the world and to preserve its imperial power and glory. As far as India is concerned, Great Britain is fighting to perpetuate the Indian empire.[101]

Elucidating this stand, Deva pointed out that every war had to be studied separately and with reference to the historical background from which it arose because 'Marxism does not ask who declares a war but in what context of circumstances a war takes place. The present war [Second World War] is an outcome of "capitalist imperialism" and of "the policy of conquest" pursued by both groups of belligerent nations.' Deva further pointed out that the war was being fought for repartitioning the world in accordance with the new relationship of imperialist forces. He said that the mere fact that Russia had become a victim of German aggression would not change the character of the war. Russia was fighting a nationalistic war for the defence of the fatherland. The alliance of Russia with England had changed neither the character of the war nor the peace aims of England. It was, therefore, strange that Stalin praised England and America as defenders and liberators of Asia. But the truth of the matter was that each one of the Allies was fighting to safeguard its own national interest. A modern war between great powers, he pointed out, did not signify a conflict between democracy and fascism but a struggle of two imperial powers for the re-division of the world.[102]

The attitude of the CSP was first spelt out in a meeting of its national executive held on 6 September 1939. As a result of the deliberations of this meeting, two war circulars were issued by the party general secretary Narayan which not only rejected the idea of support to Britain but also stressed the need for carrying on 'a vigorous anti-war propaganda, including demonstrations and political strikes' and energizing the provincial party committees for such activities.[103] In accordance with this policy, the Congress socialists criticized the resolution of the CWC which declared that the INC was prepared to 'throw its full weight into the efforts for the effective organization of the defence of the country' if a provisional national government was formed as an immediate step to the declaration of complete independence. They argued that even if Britain agreed to this condition, it would remain an imperialist power and the war an imperialist war.[104] They also pointed out that independence could be achieved not by negotiations or compromise but by direct struggle for the masses—a golden opportunity provided by the war crisis.

In line with this uncompromising anti-war policy, the Congress socialists severely chided the communists for their 'people's war' strategy. A war, they argued, could be regarded as a 'people's war' only when it was fought by the subject people for national liberation or when they rose in revolt 'against the bourgeoisie and their national government, acting on the slogan "turn the imperialist war into a civil war."'[105]

Deva explained:

A genuine people's war should lead to the destruction of both imperialism of capitalistic democracy and of fascism. But he will indeed be a bold man who would say that the present war is being fought to destroy imperialism. That would mean that the British and American governments are waging war to destroy themselves.[106]

Refuting the communist argument that the participation of the Soviet Union in the war was in itself a guarantee of worldwide liberation from the imperialist order, Deva said that it would be wrong to consider everything from the point of view of the interests of the Soviet Union which was ranged on the side of the Allies fighting in self-defence against Hitler. It was, therefore, false propaganda to say that the war was being fought by any side for freedom and democracy.[107] He further added that those who were forced by their own contradictions to argue that the Indian people should help the imperialists because they were rendering full help to Russia were advocating not a people's policy, but an imperialist policy. By advocating such a policy, he said, the communists had not only betrayed socialism but also distorted Marxian dialectics. 'The revolutionary duty of the socialists was to expose those social-chauvinists who were exploiting the proletariat's sympathy for the Soviet Union.'[108]

Having thus analysed the character of the war from the Marxian point of view, Deva was of the opinion that in all probability the war would bring in its train a series of mass revolutions when people would take a direct hand in the shaping of things. Therefore, he declared: 'We have to prepare ourselves for that eventuality. Our task lies in that direction. We should awaken and develop the revolutionary spirit of the masses and prepare them for revolutionary action.'[109]

The Congress socialists then proceeded to implement the policy of preparing themselves for mass revolutionary activities and in pursuit of the decision of the Anti-Compromise Conference at Ramgarh, plunged into the struggle for India's demand for complete independence.

At this juncture, when Hitler had overrun West Europe and the collapse of the Allies seemed imminent, Gandhi and his followers began to show eagerness to cooperate with British war efforts, provided a reasonable assurance was given in regard to the declaration of independence. If a struggle had to be launched at all, they argued, it was to be strictly non-violent in character.[110]

REJECTION OF GANDHI'S NON-VIOLENCE PLEA

The leaders of the CSP as well as a section of younger Congressmen squarely rejected Gandhi's plea for non-violence and started violent mass revolutionary activities all over the country. In fact, the issue had almost led to a split in the INC camp. Narayan said:

> Coming to the question as it affects us, I would first remind you of the difference between Gandhiji's views on non-violence and those of the working committee [CWC] and the AICC, Gandhiji is in no event prepared to depart from non-violence. With him it is a question of faith and life-principle. Not so with the Congress [INC]. The Congress [INC] has stated repeatedly during this war that if India became free, or even if a national government were set up, it would be prepared to resist aggression with arms. But, if we are prepared to fight Japan and Germany with arms, why must we refuse to fight Britain in the same manner? The only possible answer can be that the Congress [INC] in power could have an army, whereas the Congress [INC] in wilderness has none. But supposing a revolutionary army were created or if the present Indian army or a part of it rebel, would it not be inconsistent for us first to ask the army to rebel and then ask the rebels to lay down arms and face British bullets with bared chest?[111]

This uncompromising attitude of the Congress socialists found expression in an instruction issued by Narayan who, after his sensational escape from prison in 1942, had assumed the leadership of the countrywide revolutionary movement. In his message to the revolutionaries, Narayan said:

> Dislocation is an infallible weapon for people under slavery and subjection and with which he has all along fought against the ruling power. To efface all such instruments as have been devised and adopted by rulers for keeping people in bondage and fleecing them, to dismantle all tools and machineries, to render ineffective all means of communications, to reduce buildings and store houses to ashes—all these are forms of dislocation. So, cutting wires, removing of railway lines, blowing up of bridges, stoppage of factory work, setting fire to oil tanks and also to *thanas* [police stations], destruction of government papers and files—all such activities come under dislocation and it is perfectly right for people to carry out these....[112]

Narayan also repudiated Gandhi's plea for non-violence in a letter addressed to all freedom fighters in which he pointed out:

> My own interpretation of the Congress's [INC] position—not Gandhiji's—is clear and definite. Congress [INC] is prepared to fight aggression violently if the country became independent. Well, we have declared ourselves independent, and also named Britain as an aggressive power; we are, therefore, justified within the terms of the Bombay resolution itself to fight Britain with arms. If this does not accord with Gandhiji's principles, that is not my fault.[113]

In the same vein, Narayan further said:

> I should add that I have no hesitation in admitting that non-violence of the brave, if practiced on a sufficiently-large scale, would make violence unnecessary, but where such non-violence is absent, I should

not allow cowardice, clothed in *shastric* [intricacies usually involved in the various interpretations of religious scriptures] subtleties, to block the development of this revolution and lead to its failure.[114]

Although the role of the Congress socialists during the Quit India Movement was in direct opposition to Gandhi's principle of non-violence, it is important to note that they never intended to repudiate the leadership or the unity of the INC. The unity of the INC, they maintained, was *sine qua non* for the unity of the national leadership and therefore to force a split in the INC was to strike at the root of the nationalist movement. Their strategy was to maintain the unity of the INC under Gandhi's leadership and at the same time to launch a mass revolutionary struggle under the banner of the INC. Deva said that this policy did not mean that the socialists had accepted the Gandhian philosophy of life or that they had come to regard the Gandhian technique as adequate and effective. In fact, they had put forward a revolutionary programme only to supplement the 'inadequacy and ineffectiveness of Gandhism'.[115] L.P. Sinha observed: 'The Congress socialists seemed to have been caught up in a situation where while the heart was with Gandhi, the head was with Marx; and though Gandhism was gradually having the upper hand, the ghost of Marx refused to disappear.'[116]

When the Quit India Movement came to an end, Narayan refused to admit that it was suppressed. He said: 'The history of all revolutions shows that a revolution is not an event. It is a phase, a social process.'[117] Attributing the failure of the movement to the 'lack of efficient organization and of a complete programme of national revolution', he felt that the INC

was not tuned to the pitch to which revolution was to rise. The lack of organization was so considerable that even important Congressmen were not aware of the progress of the revolt, and till late in the course of the rising, it remained a matter of debate in accordance with the Congress [INC] programme. In the same connection should be mentioned the regrettable fact that quite a considerable number of influential Congressmen failed to attune their mental attitude to the spirit of this last fight for freedom.[118]

He further pointed out:

After the first phase of the rising was over, there was no further programme placed before the people. After they had completely destroyed the British Raj in their areas, the people considered their task fulfilled, and went back to their homes, not knowing what more to do. Nor was it their fault. The failure was ours; we should have supplied them with a programme for the next phase.[119]

Narayan then went on to underline the task of all radical forces in the new situation brought about by the Quit India Movement:

With the implication of the last phase of the revolution clear in our minds, we have to prepare, organize, train and discipline our forces .... It is total revolt of the masses that is our objective. So, along with our immense technical work, we must do intensive work among the masses—peasants in the villages and the workers in the factories, mines, railways and elsewhere. We must do ceaseless propaganda among them and help them in their present difficulties, organize them to fight for their present demands, recruit from them selected soldiers for our various activities and train them technically and politically. With training, a few may succeed where thousands failed before. In every *fiska* [treasury] and *taluka* [administrative division] and *thana* [police station], in every considerable factory and workshop or other industrial centres, we must have a band of militants, mentally and materially equipped for the next rising.[120]

CONGRESS SOCIALISTS' STAND ON NEGOTIATION FOR INDIA'S FREEDOM

As the war came to a close and the Labour Party came to power in Britain, events in India, in the words of Lord Mountbatten, began to rush forward in a torrent. These events were marked by hectic negotiations between Indian leaders and the Labour government, which now realized that it was time to grant India its freedom not only in fulfilment of its promise but also in the interest of the British people themselves. From the point of view of the INC, freedom seemed just round the corner, but its form and pattern were at stake. And it was 'the time for civilized negotiation between men who', according to Michael Edwardes, 'spoke the same unapocalyptic language'.

Thus, when events began to shape themselves towards the victory of India's struggle for freedom, the Congress socialists refused to budge from their uncompromising stance and continued to oppose the idea of a negotiated settlement with the British imperialists on the question of independence. Complete independence, they maintained, could be achieved only when the last vestige of imperialism was overthrown by a revolutionary struggle of the masses, freedom won through negotiation and compromise would not be a freedom for the masses; rather, as Deva thought, 'it would be a self-delusion to think that the middle classes would, after winning freedom, willingly transfer all power to the toiling masses. This has never happened in history. India is no exception.'[121] Castigating the Right-wing leadership for betraying the masses, Deva contended that the INC could truly represent the masses only by championing their economic demands. The doors of the INC, he declared, would have to be thrown wide open to peasants and workers and all such elements as were opposed to the interest of the masses would have to be eliminated. The interest of the masses was supreme and every other interest that conflicted with the interests of the people would have to be discarded. Only if this were done, would class organizations become unnecessary. But a middle-class-dominated organization could not be expected to do this. For this reason, peasants and workers should be encouraged to have their own unions and nothing should be done to control their independent organizations. What the INC could do was to undertake the 'political schooling' of these organizations and to incorporate their demands in its policy and programme. The political and social emancipation of the people could be achieved only by such interaction.[122] Narayan also contended that the INC could uphold the cause of the exploited masses not only by championing their economic demands but also by renewing the demand to 'Quit India' and by mobilizing the people 'in the final challenge with the imperialist power'. He added:

> It is that power, which is our primary enemy and which instigates and supports the reactionary forces in this country. It is that power which has to be destroyed first :.... I believe that in the fire of revolution alone can be burnt down the edifices of imperialism together with the supporting edifices of communalism and feudalism.[123]

On the question of communal harmony, the Congress socialists held that Hindu–Muslim unity could be brought about not by temporary pacts or agreements but 'by laying emphasis on the economic issues which equally affect the Hindu and Muslim masses of the country'. Their economic interests were identical and a lasting unity could be forged only on the basis of their common struggle for common economic interests.[124]

But although the Congress socialists welcomed an early settlement of the communal problem, they were opposed to any compromise with the Muslim League so far as its demand for Pakistan was concerned. Narayan averred:

> In our country the only forces of freedom are those that are ready to fight and suffer for freedom. The Muslim League during its entire career has not once taken the path of struggle and suffering, nor is it ready to take the path today. India cannot win her [its] freedom without fighting for it. And when the Muslim League is not prepared to participate in the fight, a settlement with it in no way strengthens the forces of freedom .... It is necessary to grasp clearly that the [Muslim] League is in league with Britain. Mr Jinnah is a deliberate traitor to his country, a Mir Jaffer of the present day. He believes that he can get what he wants from Britain. But Britain is not accustomed to handing over parcels of her [its] empire to its tools.

There is no doubt that after she [Britain] has made the full use of Mr Jinnah she [it] will throw him into the dustbin of discarded tools as surely as she [it] has thrown others into it before .... Let Muslims remember that it is not the sons of Mir Jaffer who rule Bengal today but the dirty kin of Clive. Mr Jinnah no doubt considers himself a very clever person, but for all his conceit and Fuehrerian attitudes history will show him to have been made a historic fool .... The League's real politik is the ugly issue of imperialist machination and national treachery.[125]

When the INC accepted the partition of the country as the only basis for a peaceful settlement of the Hindu–Muslim problem, the Congress socialists were so disappointed and deeply moved by this 'act of surrender' that they not only blamed the INC leadership for this national calamity but also bemoaned their own failure to prevent it. A resolution of the CSP national executive, adopted on 3 June 1947, said:

Each act of surrender, perhaps not of much import by itself but of great effect as a link in the chain, and the refusal of the Congress [INC] leadership to prepare a position and hold on to it have brought us to this fateful situation. The Socialist Party [CSP] must also record its own failure and that of the wider revolutionary movement in working out an alternative and positive policy.[126]

NOTES AND REFERENCES (CHAPTER 4)

1 Subhas Chandra Bose, *The Indian Struggle, 1920–1934*, Vol. I (Calcutta: Netaji Publication Society, 1948), 294.
2 Ibid.
3 Ibid., 114–15.
4 P.L. Lakhanpal, *History of the Congress Socialist Party* (Lahore: National Publishers and Stationers, 1946), 4–5.
5 Ibid.
6 Bose, *The Indian Struggle, 1920–1934*, Vol. I, 409.
7 Subhas Chandra Bose's presidential address to the Anti-Compromise Conference, Ramgarh, March, 1940. For the full text of the address, see Subhas Chandra Bose, *Crossroads—Collected Works, 1938–1940* (Calcutta: Netaji Research Bureau, 1962).
8 Ibid., 74.
9 R.C. Majumdar, *History of the Freedom Movement in India*, Vol. III (Calcutta: Firma K.L. Mukhopadhyay, 1963), 830.
10 Jawaharlal Nehru, *Nehru on Gandhi* (New York, NY: John Day Company, 1948), 38–39.
11 *Advance Guard* (Zurich, 1 October 1922), 1.
12 Ibid. (Zurich, 1 November 1922), 3.
13 Ibid. (Zurich, 1 December 1922), 2.
14 Exhibit No. 7c in Cawnpore Conspiracy Case evidence. *King Emperor Versus Nalina Bhushan Das Gupta, Muhammad Shaukat Usmani, Muzaffar Ahmad, and Shripat Amrit Dange*, in the High Court of Judicature at Allahabad, Criminal Side (Allahabad: Superintendent Government Printing, 1924).
15 *The Tribune* (Lahore, 4 November 1922).
16 Bose, *Crossroads—Collected Works, 1938–1940*, 81–82.
17 *Advance Guard* (Zurich, 1 December 1922).
18 *The Times of India* (Bombay, 22 December 1922).
19 *Amrita Bazar Patrika* (Calcutta, 27 December 1922).
20 Gene D. Overstreet and Marshall Windmiller, *Communism in India* (Bombay: Perennial Press, 1960), 53–54.
21 P.C. Ray, *Life and Times of C.R. Das* (London: Oxford University Press, 1927), 267–68.
22 Majumdar, *History of the Freedom Movement in India*, Vol. III, 216–17.
23 Ibid., 219–20. Also see Bose, *The Indian Struggle, 1920–1934*, Vol. I, 117.
24 Bose, *The Indian Struggle, 1920–1934*, Vol. I, 117.
25 Ibid., 117 and 146.
26 Ibid., 117. About M.K. Gandhi's role in the Madras session (1927) of the INC, Jawaharlal Nehru wrote:

> Gandhiji was in Madras and he attended the open Congress [INC] sessions, but he did not take any part in the shaping of policy. He did not attend the meetings of the Working Committee [CWC] of which he was a member. That had been his general political attitude in the Congress [INC] since the dominance of the Swaraj Party. But he was frequently consulted, and little of importance was done without his knowledge. I do not know how far the resolutions I put before the Congress [session] met with his approval. I am inclined to think that he disliked them, not so much because of what they said, but because of their general trend and outlook.

See Jawaharlal Nehru, *An Autobiography* (Bombay: Allied Publishers, 1962), 167.

27 Bose, *The Indian Struggle, 1920–1934*, Vol. I, 157.

28 Ibid.

29 B.R. Nanda, *The Nehrus: Motilal and Jawaharlal* (London: George Allen and Unwin, 1962), 310.

30 Jawaharlal Nehru, *The Discovery of India* (London: Meridian Books, 1956), 15.

31 J.S. Bright, ed., *Important Speeches—A Collection of Speeches by Jawaharlal Nehru from 1922–1945* (Lahore: Indian Printing Works, 1945), 102.

32 Jawaharlal Nehru, 'From Lucknow to Tripuri—A Survey of Congress Politics, 1936–1939', in *The Unity of India—Collected Writings, 1937–1940* (New York, NY: John Day Company, 1942), 118.

33 Nehru, *An Autobiography*, 163.

34 Frank Moraes, *Jawaharlal Nehru—A Biography* (Bombay: Macmillan, 1956), 113.

35 Nehru, *An Autobiography*, 137.

36 J.S. Bright, ed., *Before and After Independence: A Collection of the Most Important and Soul-stirring Speeches by Jawaharlal Nehru, 1922–1950* (Delhi: Indian Printing Works, 1952), 223.

37 Jawaharlal Nehru, *Recent Essays and Writings on the Future of India, Communalism and Other Subjects* (Allahabad: Kitabistan, 1937), 33.

38 Patricia Kendall, *India and the British: A Quest for Truth* (London: Charles Scribner's Sons, 1931), 426.

39 Nehru, *An Autobiography*, 591.

40 Bose, *The Indian Struggle, 1920–1934*, Vol. I, 29.

41 Ibid., 169–70. In this connection, it may be noted that while proposing Jawaharlal Nehru's name for the post of the INC president, M.K. Gandhi said: 'I know that I am not keeping pace with the march of events. There is a hiatus between the rising generation and me'; See *Indian Annual Register*, Vol. II (Calcutta, 1929), 14. For the differences between Gandhi and Nehru, also see D.G. Tendulkar, *Mahatma: Life of Mohandas Karamchand Gandhi*, Vol. VIII (Bombay: Vithalbhai K. Jhaveri, 1951), 350–51.

42 Bose, *The Indian Struggle, 1920–1934*, Vol. I, 174.

43 Ibid., 175.

44 Majumdar, *History of the Freedom Movement in India*, Vol. III, 381.

45 According to Pattabhi Sitaramayya, peoples' admiration for these revolutionaries was so great that 'at that moment Bhagat Singh's name was as widely known all over India and was as popular as [M.K.] Gandhi'. See Pattabhi Sitaramayya, *The History of the Indian National Congress*, Vol. I (Bombay: Padma Publications, 1946), 456.

46 Majumdar, *History of the Freedom Movement in India*, Vol. III, 383–84.

47 Bose, *The Indian Struggle, 1920–1934*, Vol. I, 205–06.

48 It is interesting to note that when M.K. Gandhi asked Jawaharlal Nehru to move the resolution on the Gandhi–Irwin Pact (also known as the Delhi Pact) and the Round Table Conference, Nehru at first hesitated. Nehru said:

> It went against the grain and I refused at first, and then this seemed a weak and unsatisfactory position to take up. Either I was for it or against it, and it was not proper to prevaricate or leave people guessing in the matter. Almost at the last moment, a few minutes before the resolution was taken up in the open Congress [Karachi session of INC, 1931], I decided to support it.

See Nehru, *An Autobiography*, 266.

49 *Indian Annual Register*, Vol. I (Calcutta, 1931), 363.

50 Nehru, *An Autobiography*, 266.

51 Ibid., 266–67.

52 Rahul Sankrityayan, an erudite scholar in Oriental studies, was a professor of Sanskrit and Pali in Ceylon during 1926–28 and travelled extensively in Tibet and southern China. He joined the CPI in 1939 and was elected the president of the AIKS in 1940. He was imprisoned along with many other communists in the Deoli Detention Camp. In 1944, he was appointed the professor of Oriental languages at the Leningrad Academy of Sciences. He wrote extensively on the compatibility of Marxism with Oriental religions, especially Buddhism.

53 L.P. Sinha, *Left Wing in India* (Muzaffarpur: New Publishers, 1965), 305.

54 Bose, *The Indian Struggle, 1920–1934*, Vol. I, 160–61.

55   Yusuf Meherally, *Leaders of India*, Vol. II (Bombay: Padma Publications, 1946), 51–52. Also see Yusuf Meherally, ed., *Jayaprakash Narayan, Towards Struggle* (Bombay: Padma Publications, 1946), 9.

56   Yusuf Meherally, ed., *Acharya Narendra Deva, Socialism and the National Revolution* (Bombay: Padma Publications, 1946), 8–9.

57   It may be noted here that at the All India Congress Socialists' Conference in Patna, Rajani Mukherjee of Bengal moved a resolution to the effect that the CSP should be organized outside the INC. But the resolution was defeated.

58   Meherally, *Acharya Narendra Deva, Socialism and the National Revolution*, 4–5.

59   Ibid., xii.

60   Ibid., 26–29.

61   *Indian Annual Register* (Calcutta, 1934), 344.

62   The executive committee elected at the Bombay conference consisted of: general secretary Jayaprakash Narayan; joint secretaries M.R. Masani, Mohanlal Gautam, N.G. Gore and E.M.S. Namboodiripad; members Narendra Deva, Sampurnanand, Kamaladevi Chattopadhyay, Purshottam Tricumdas, P.Y. Deshpande, Ram Manohar Lohia, S.M. Joshi, Amarendra Prasad Mitra, Charles Mascarenhas, Achyut Patwardhan, Nabakrushna Chaudhury; and additional members Yusuf Meherally, Saurabh Batliwala, Farid-ul-haq Ansari, Rambriksh Benipuri and D. Mehta.

63   *All India Congress Socialist Party: Report of the First Conference* (Bombay: CSP, 1934).

64   See 'The Platform of the Party' adopted at the Bombay conference of the CSP (Bombay: CSP, 1934).

65   *All India Congress Socialist Party: Report of the First Conference*.

66   Sinha, *Left Wing in India*, 325.

67   See 'The Platform of the Party' adopted at the Bombay conference of the CSP. Also see Lakhanpal, *History of the Congress Socialist Party*, 39–40; Meherally, *Jayaprakash Narayan, Towards Struggle*, 101–02; Sinha, *Left Wing in India*, 325–26.

68   See 'The Platform of the Party' adopted at the Bombay conference of the CSP.

69   Lakhanpal, *History of the Congress Socialist Party*, 41. Also see Sinha, *Left Wing in India*, 327–28.

70   Meherally, *Acharya Narendra Deva, Socialism and the National Revolution*, 68.

71   Sinha, *Left Wing in India*, 317.

72   *Indian Annual Register*, Vol. II (Calcutta, 1934), 'News'.

73   Bose, *The Indian Struggle, 1920–1934*, Vol. I, 383.

74   Ibid., 383–84.

75   Ibid., 384.

76   *Indian Annual Register*, Vol. I (Calcutta, 1934), 300.

77   Meherally, *Acharya Narendra Deva, Socialism and the National Revolution*, 66.

78   M.R. Masani, *The Communist Party of India—A Short History* (London: Derek Verschoyle, 1954), 54.

79   Meherally, *Acharya Narendra Deva, Socialism and the National Revolution*, 76.

80   Ibid., 74.

81   Ibid., 66.

82   Ibid., 115–16. Also see Narendra Deva's article 'Problems of Socialist Unity' in *The Congress Socialist*, 9 April 1938.

83   Meherally, *Acharya Narendra Deva, Socialism and the National Revolution*, 4.

84   Ibid., 74–75.

85   Meherally, *Jayaprakash Narayan, Towards Struggle*, 137.

86   Ibid., 139.

87   Ibid., 139–40.

88   *The Faizpur Thesis of the Congress Socialist Party*, Resolutions adopted by the party at its third annual conference at Faizpur on December 23, 24 and 25, 1936. Minoo Masani Papers, National Archives of India, Delhi.

89   Meherally, *Jayaprakash Narayan, Towards Struggle*, 130.

90   Meherally, *Acharya Narendra Deva, Socialism and the National Revolution*, 73.

91   Ibid., 109.

92 Ibid., 87.
93 Meherally, *Jayaprakash Narayan, Towards Struggle*, 162.
94 Meherally, *Acharya Narendra Deva, Socialism and the National Revolution*, 117–18. Also see Narendra Deva's article 'Problems of Socialist Unity' in *The Congress Socialist*, 9 April 1938.
95 Meherally, *Jayaprakash Narayan, Towards Struggle*, 167–68.
96 Ibid.
97 Ibid., 183.
98 Ibid., 160.
99 Bose, *Crossroads—Collected Works, 1938–1940*, 113.
100 *All India Congress Socialist Party: Report of the First Conference*. Also see Meherally, *Acharya Narendra Deva, Socialism and the National Revolution*, 149.
101 Meherally, *Jayaprakash Narayan, Towards Struggle*, 203.
102 Meherally, *Acharya Narendra Deva, Socialism and the National Revolution*, 144.
103 CSP *War Circular No. 1* and *War Circular No. 2* (Lucknow: CSP, 1939). This was a mimeographed intra-party circular addressed to provincial party secretaries and party members.
104 *Indian Annual Register*, Vol. II (Calcutta, 1940), 332.
105 Meherally, *Acharya Narendra Deva, Socialism and the National Revolution*, 146.
106 Ibid., 147.
107 Ibid., 148.
108 Ibid., 153–54.
109 Ibid., 149.
110 Ibid., 245–46.
111 Meherally, *Jayaprakash Narayan, Towards Struggle*, 25–26.
112 K.K. Datta, *Freedom Movement in Bihar*, Vol. III (1942–1947), (Patna: Government of Bihar, 1957), 444; Majumdar, *History of the Freedom Movement in India*, Vol. III, 667–68; Meherally, *Jayaprakash Narayan, Towards Struggle*, 25–26.
113 Meherally, *Jayaprakash Narayan, Towards Struggle*, 25–26.
114 Ibid.
115 Meherally, *Acharya Narendra Deva, Socialism and the National Revolution*, 183.
116 Sinha, *Left Wing in India* (Muzaffarpur, 1965), 507.
117 Meherally, *Jayaprakash Narayan, Towards Struggle*, 20.
118 Ibid.
119 Ibid.
120 Ibid., 26.
121 Meherally, *Acharya Narendra Deva, Socialism and the National Revolution*, 180–81.
122 Narendra Deva, 'The Common Man and the Congress', *Janata* (Delhi, 10 February 1946).
123 *Janata* (Delhi, 26 January 1947).
124 Meherally, *Acharya Narendra Deva, Socialism and the National Revolution*, 158–59.
125 Meherally, *Jayaprakash Narayan, Towards Struggle*, 42–43.
126 *Indian Annual Register*, Vol. I (Calcutta, 1947), 259.

5

Labour and Peasant Movements

A. THE LABOUR MOVEMENT

CRISIS AFTER THE FIRST WORLD WAR

As a spearhead of Left-wing political movement, modern trade unionism came to India after the close of the First World War when to the complex political condition of the country had been added a number of serious socio-economic problems. Some of these problems were created by the war and others magnified by it.[1] On the economic front, the post-war years witnessed an unprecedented crisis resulting in worsening conditions of life and work for all Indian workers. While essential commodities became scarce and expensive, wages fell, working hours were extended and conditions of work were appalling. At the same time, industry was expanding and making enormous profits and under-fed and discontented industrial workers began to return to their villages where they hoped in vain to get food. In fact, the economic situation became so deplorable that it provoked eminent British labour leader A.A. Purcell to remark that the condition of the Indian labour had no parallel in the world. That such a state of affairs should exist in the nineteenth century after 150 years of British rule, he said, was a serious reflection upon everybody concerned.[2]

Apart from the economic consequences of the war, a number of other factors in post-war India combined to produce unrest among the broad masses of the people. All these were conducive to the growth of workers' organizations—a radical political movement, the enunciation of the doctrine of racial equality, soaring prices and consequent economic hardship and finally the influenza epidemic which resulted in a shortage of labour.[3] It was under this combination of circumstances that Indian labour felt it necessary to organize against the exploitation and oppression by their employers.

UNITY AGAINST OPPRESSION

It was not an easy task at that time for poor and illiterate workers to fight for their interests through organized trade unions. In the first place, there was opposition, oppression and victimization on the part of employers who placed all sorts of obstacles in the way of their workers forming trade unions. There was also the opposition of the government, many of whose officers regarded trade union work as a seditious activity. Workers' meetings and processions were not only restricted, sometimes they were altogether prohibited. The police used to blacklist, threaten and harass trade union workers. Arrests were not unknown and on many occasions prison sentences were imposed on workers for normal trade union work. Trade union activity under such circumstances was a courageous task. However, workers were able to organize a good number of unions and lay the foundation of the trade union movement because the pioneers of the labour movement possessed the virtues of infinite patience, determination and a keen sense of social service.[4] Further obstacles to the development of an organized trade union movement were the migratory character of Indian workers, lack of leisure, differences in language, employers' opposition and, above all, lack of education.[5]

In spite of these difficulties, a number of factors favoured the growth of trade unionism as an organized political movement. The most important of these was the tremendous political upheaval at the close of the war. B. Shiva Rao pointed out:

> It is difficult, perhaps, at this distance of time to realize how profoundly the war had stirred the imagination of the people. A Home Rule Movement was inaugurated in the early stages, and brought into play a technique which was both new and extremely effective in its results. Never before in Indian politics had there been a movement so widespread and carrying on such intensive propaganda by all the methods known in the West—pamphleteering, meetings, posters and demonstrations. Everywhere there was hope and expectation that the end of the war would mark the dawn for India, not merely of a political advance, but of a new status.[6]

The ferment did not leave the masses unaffected. In fact, in the urban areas it released forces which might otherwise have slumbered for years. The war had completely destroyed the hitherto unquestioned notion of the superiority of the white race and for the humble factory worker accustomed to bear untold insult and suffering without a protest, this was a thrilling experience. It was not just the vindication of legitimate rights; it was even more—the assertion of racial equality.

The war brought about a new outlook within the Indian labour. Indian soldiers who had been to Europe during the war had fought shoulder to shoulder with British and other European soldiers and came to realize that they were in no way inferior to others. When they came back home after the end of the war, they brought with them new ideas and aspirations. Through them, these ideas and aspirations spread in cities and villages and changed the outlook of workers and peasants. A new sense of confidence and a new awareness began to develop among them and they became ready to stand up for their rights and to resist insult and injustice. It was this new psychological atmosphere which helped the growth of the trade union movement.[7]

Into this new atmosphere, nationalist leaders emerged to champion the cause of the working class and 'to secure support for the political movement in which they were engaged' and which they wanted to be 'broadbased so that the end may not be the transfer of political power from the white to the brown bureaucracy'.[8] This sentiment was expressed by one of the early leaders of the trade union movement, B.P. Wadia, who declared that as without the masses there could be no democracy, the masses needed to be brought into line with the educated classes. The working class, he pointed out, did possess a political outlook, but they did not know the art of making themselves heard. Therefore, it was the duty of the educated class 'to persuade them into speed and action'. He further added that the labour movement was an integral part of the national movement, which could not succeed if the working classes were not encouraged to organize their force on a national basis. Unless this was done, Wadia said: 'Even the Montagu Reforms will not succeed in transferring power of the bureaucracy from foreign to native hands; that is not democracy'.[9] Thus, although at the initial stage the demands of the workers were essentially economic, their movement soon assumed political dimensions and they were drawn into the vortex of India's struggle for freedom. The leaders of the INC, who were in the forefront of the nationalist movement, also did not keep themselves aloof from the trade union movement. When the AITUC was formed in 1920, Lala Lajpat Rai, the then president of the party, was elected its first president. Subsequently, this position was held by eminent INC leaders, such as Chittaranjan Das, Sarojini Naidu, Jawaharlal Nehru and Subhas Chandra Bose. The close association of the nationalist leaders with the trade unions brought about a distinct political tendency in the outlook of workers and left a permanent mark on their movement.

INFLUENCE OF RUSSIA AND BRITAIN AND CONFLICT OF OPINION

The ideals of the British labour movement also played an important role in the awakening of the Indian working class to a new consciousness. During the war, in order to enlist the support of the Indian working classes, the government had given wide publicity to the achievements and sacrifices of the British working classes which not only made Indian workers aware of their important role but also inspired many Indian intellectuals, such as Rai, R.R. Bakhale and N.M. Joshi, to organize the working classes on the pattern of the British Trade Union Congress (BTUC).[10] In his address to the first session of the AITUC, Rai urged Indian workers to emulate the ideals of the British Labour Party and opined: 'We should adopt the aim of the British Labour Party as our own, start educating our people on these lines and formulate for them measures which will secure for them real freedom'.[11]

Meanwhile, as a result of the dichotomy in the international socialist movement which gave rise to a sharp conflict inside the world trade union movement between two rival conceptions of its purpose, British labour leaders also began to evince interest in the problems of the Indian working class.[12] The moderate leadership of the Indian trade union movement—represented by Rai, V.V. Giri, Diwan Chaman Lal, N.M. Joshi and others—took inspiration from these leaders, furthering their determination to model the Indian trade union movement after that of Britain.

But the most decisive and potentially most meaningful boost for the struggle of the Indian working class came from the ideals of the Russian Revolution, which not only sharpened the class-consciousness of the workers but also taught them to prioritize

> the need for a political revolution which would dispossess the capitalists and institute the workers' state and to insist that workers' control meant primarily political control by the working class as a whole, and only secondary control over particular industrial processes by the workers actually engaged in them.[13]

Inspired by this new revolutionary ideology, trade unionism developed as an international movement and as an 'instinctive answer to capitalist exploitation'.[14]

In effect, during the post-war years the struggle of the Indian working class suddenly leapt to a position of remarkable strength and trade unionism entered on a phase of vigorous growth in marked contrast to its previous inactivity outside a limited group of philanthropists and intellectuals. In a short period of time, a large number of trade unions were formed in almost all industrial centres of India. Among the most prominent of these were the Madras Labour Union (1918), the Indian Seamen's Union (1918), the Great Indian Peninsula Railwaymen's Union (1919), the Ahmedabad Textile Workers' Union (1920), the North Western Railway Employees' Union (1920), the Indian Colliery Employees' Association (1920), the Jamshedpur Labour Association (1920), the Bengal Nagpur Railway Indian Labour Union (1920), the East Indian Railway Labour Union (1921) and the Assam Bengal Railway Employees' Union (1921).[15]

FORMATION OF AITUC

In 1920, these trade unions drew together in a national organization—the AITUC—'to coordinate the activities of all labour organizations in all trades and in all provinces in India and generally to further the interests of Indian labour in matters social, political and economic'.[16] The first session of the AITUC was held in Bombay in October 1920 under the presidency of Rai and the prominent nationalist leaders who were present in the conference included Annie Besant, Motilal Nehru, Muhammad Ali Jinnah, Vithalbhai Patel, B.P. Wadia, Joseph Baptista, Diwan Chaman Lal, V.V. Giri, S.A. Brevli, V.M. Paver, N.M. Joshi and many others.

One of the factors which hastened the formation of the AITUC was the stipulation of the International Labour Organization (ILO) that the workers' delegation to it should be representative of the largest organization of the country.[17] This ILO decision provided the Indian working class with an opportunity to voice their grievances in an international forum. Bakhale said: 'The working class in India did not fail to realize the importance of the right that was bestowed on them and the harm that would be done if they did not organize themselves in order to exercise that right.'[18]

The AITUC quickly became the rallying ground for the various working class organizations for the redress of their urgent economic grievances. But controversy soon arose over the question of its ideological orientation and political role.

Ideologically, although there has always been a socialist strand in the trade union movement, its early leaders, as already pointed out, were deeply influenced by the social–democratic ideas of the British Labour Party. Influenced by the tradition of British socialism, they came to admire democratic values, methods and institutions and discarded the Marxian concept of violent revolution. Rai, for example, condemned capitalism as the precursor of the twin scourge of militarism and imperialism, but refused to accept the fundamental tenets of Marxism and to interpret trade unionism in terms of class struggle.[19] This non-Marxist attitude was spelt out in the manifesto of labour deputation to the governor of Bombay which declared that the policy of the AITUC was not to intensify class antagonism but to promote the well-being of workers on the basis of harmony between labour and capital.[20]

Politically, it was practically impossible for the AITUC to keep itself aloof from the struggle for national liberation because of the fact that the trade union movement had grown not only out of a desire for the collective defence of the economic interests of the workers but also as a direct response to the national movement which itself entered upon a new phase during the post-war years. In fact, all the nationalist leaders who were present at the first session of the AITUC recognized that the workers had a great role to play in the freedom movement.

However, N.M. Joshi, known as the father of the Indian trade union movement, was of the opinion that the political activities of labour organizations should not go beyond agitations for the amelioration of their economic grievances. He said:

> I feel that the trade unions in the country have a good share of political work before them in securing labour legislations passed through the central and provincial Legislatures. Labour legislation in our country is not as good, as advanced, as in some European countries. We have to put pressure upon the government to make our protective labour legislation up-to-date and modern. If the government does not do it, we shall have to induce some members of the Legislatures to promote such legislation.[21]

GANDHI'S ROLE IN TRADE UNION MOVEMENT

Like Joshi, Gandhi, whose concept of socialism corresponded to the anarchistic-communitarian ideology expounded by Pierre–Joseph Proudhon, John Ruskin and Leo Tolstoy, was also opposed to workers' participation in political movements. To him, trade union activity was 'a variety of constructive work which should have nothing to do with politics'.[22] Under his influence, the Mazdoor Mahajan of Ahmedabad stayed away from political movements organized and led by Gandhi himself. Dange wrote: 'The Mazdoor Mahajan preached that capitalists were their trustees as they were cleverer and workers ignorant. The capitalists were necessary for society. Capital and labour were two wheels of the social chariot on which life moved'.[23]

Commenting on Gandhi's role in the trade union movement, Gopal Ghosh observed:

> The participation of Gandhiji in the working-class movement at that time was highly significant. During long 30 years from the foundation of the National Congress [INC], its leaders did never come forward to take part in any way in the working-class movement. What, then, was the reason behind this sudden changeover? Another remarkable feature was that these Congress [INC] leaders came forward building-up unions in the industries manned and managed by the Indian capitalists.[24]

Adding that Gandhi first imported politics into the working-class movement in India, he further observed:

> At the dawn of the trade union movement in India, Wadia came forward with the political ideal of collaboration with the imperialists. Similarly, Mahatma Gandhi came to the scene as an upholder of the ideal of class-collaboration in Ahmedabad, the stronghold of Indian mill owners .... To form workers' union with the cooperation of the mill owners and on the basis of class collaboration was his political ideal in the working-class movement.[25]

INITIAL TRADE UNIONISM AND POLITICAL IDEOLOGIES

Although trade unionism in India as an organized movement was, to a large extent, the upshot of the impact of socialist ideas, the force of that impact was sought to be modified by the moderate attitude of nationalist leaders who were committed to an ideology which was more Fabian than Marxian. Although their professed goal was socialism, there was nothing of communism about it. Their aim was not to intensify the class struggle and exterminate the capitalist but 'to save him from himself, to use and transform him'. And it was as a reaction against such 'bourgeois-reformist influences' that revolutionary and militant trade unionism emerged in India. Describing the AITUC as 'a strange conglomeration of nationalism, utopianism and reformism',[26] M.N. Roy averred that the task before the AITUC was not reform but revolution. It was not conservative trade unionism based upon 'bankrupt theories of collective bargaining', but revolutionary mass action that could bring about social progress in India. For this reason, it was necessary for the AITUC to 'free itself from the leadership which believes in piecemeal reforms'.[27] Roy said: 'Our object is the economic reform of the producing classes. The ultimate goal will be attained after a long and bitter struggle. Therefore, our primary task is to organize the masses and lead them in the struggle for economic freedom.'[28] In the same vein, Roy also added that if the workers' position was to be improved and a sound trade union movement built up, it was necessary to attack and overthrow the leadership of the reformists in the trade unions.[29]

COMMUNISM AND TRADE UNIONISM

From the early 1920s, revolutionary trade unionism in India developed within the mainstream of the communist movement. That it drew inspiration and guidance from the international communist movement first became evident when at the first session of the AITUC in Bombay in 1920, Singaravelu Chettiar moved a resolution emphasizing the need for sending a workers' delegation to the Communist International.[30] Although the resolution was defeated, the Communist International continued to be the main source of inspiration of the Indian communists for their strategy and tactics on the trade union front. In a message to the Lahore session of the AITUC in 1923, the fourth congress of the Communist

International asked the Indian workers not to be content with a 'fair day's wage for a fair day's work' but to fight for the ultimate goal of the overthrow of capitalism and imperialism.[31] It also urged the Indian communists to bring the trade union movement under their influence and to 'organize it on a class basis and purge it of all alien elements'.[32] The Communist International's interest in the Indian trade union movement was actually first indicated when the RILU, set up by the Communist International in 1921,[33] sent a message to the second session of the AITUC held at Jharia in 1921 and appealed to the Indian organization 'to join in the new great world movement of international solidarity' for the overthrow of capitalism.[34]

It was after the suspension of the Non-Cooperation Movement, when India stood at a political cross-roads, that the communist strategy to bring over the entire working class to a policy of social revolution began to assume ever greater significance. Although this period was marked by general economic stabilization[35] following a decline in the political tempo and demoralization among industrial workers caused by the great strike wave of 1918–22, the communists intensified their attempts to enlist a broad spectrum of working-class support for their revolutionary cause and to develop their organizational apparatus within the trade unions. In this,

> they were aided and stimulated by the émigré Indians trained at Tashkent and Moscow in the strategy and tactics of revolutionary trade unionism and communism as well as by other communists belonging to international communism who sought to inspire action through letters, propaganda in the form of booklets and pamphlets, messages, appeals, financial aid etc.[36]

According to Overstreet and Windmiller,[37] it was after the arrival of George Allison in India in April 1926 that the communists began to 'ginger up' their activity in the trade union movement.[38]

Although the Cawnpore Conspiracy Case temporarily lowered the morale of the communists, during 1925–26 they resumed trade union work with renewed vigour and virulence. The factors which contributed to this remarkable recrudescence of militant trade unionism were the high tide of popular sympathy for the communists after the Cawnpore Conspiracy Case; the passage of the Trade Union Act of 1926 which, for the first time, gave legal recognition to the trade unions;[39] and the influence of 'certain visitors from abroad who created contacts in some of the industrial centres with likely adherents to the creed' and 'found it expedient to seek the shelter of the trade union movement and carry on their work through the affiliated unions'.[40] Moreover, as pointed by B. Shiva Rao, the fact that employers, such as the Bombay mill owners, and 'the agents of certain railways refused to countenance ordinary trade union organizations and methods, but showed a disposition to yield only when communist influence had gained considerable ground among the workers, was a powerful stimulus' to the growth of militant tendencies in the trade union movement.[41]

All these factors had set the conditions in which the communists could form a large number of labour unions all over the country. Their success was more remarkable among the cotton–textile workers and railwaymen of Bombay where they organized their largest and strongest unions—the Girni Kamgar Mahamandal—with a membership estimated at 54,000[42] and the Great Indian Peninsula Railwaymen's Union. The former was formed in August 1925 by two prominent trade union leaders of Bombay, A.A. Alve and D.R. Mayekar. However, when the two leaders fell out in 1928, Alve and his group broke off and organized a separate union under the name Girni Kamgar Union. S.A. Dange became the secretary and Ben Bradley, S.H. Jhabvala and R.S. Nimbkar were elected vice-presidents of the new organization.

As this was a period of intense nationalist agitation throughout the country, the communists took the opportunity to raise a number of political issues from their trade union platforms. These issues were as follows:

the inseparability of the working-class struggle from the struggle for political emancipation; the need for a working class party; leadership or at least hegemony of the proletariat in the national movement; struggle in respect of definition of the political goal of freedom to mean complete independence; alliance with the peasant masses and their struggles; persistent use of the strike weapon; overthrow of reformist trade union leadership; affiliation of the AITUC with the RILU and the League Against Imperialism and relations with the Pan-Pacific Trade Union Secretariat [PPTUS]; protests and demonstrations against the Simon Commission, the Whitley Commission and the Trade Disputes Act, [1929], and the danger of a new capitalist war against the Soviet Union; expression of friendship with the Soviet Union and China; criticism of the Motilal Nehru Report on Constitutional Framework; struggle against the ILO and the IFTU; Labour *swaraj* and labour constitution etc.[43]

Thus, industrial and political issues tended to mingle in one stream and in the following years a frenzied political excitement and feverish industrial unrest swept over the country.

By this time, the communists had successfully extended their activities to almost all industrial centres of India and, as B. Shiva Rao pointed out, 'from their standpoint, there was reason for satisfaction in the prolonged strike which had occurred in several parts of India during the year.'[44] They had also made determined attempts to capture the AITUC and since its seventh session in Delhi in March 1927, attended by Shapurji Saklatvala, the communist member of the British Parliament, 'they emerged as a distinct group with their own tactics, programme and ideology.'[45] Commenting on the increasing influence of the communists over the Indian working class, Soviet commentator Balabushevich observed that the Delhi resolution of the AITUC was a 'step forward' but bemoaned the fact that most of the Indian trade unions did not support class struggles but still believed in class collaboration.[46]

During the industrial unrest that overtook the country in 1928, the number of disputes were about 200—only half the number in 1921, but the loss of working days reached an all-time record, which was more than the total figure for all the previous five years.[47] The Government of India's annual report of 1928–29 to the British Parliament stated:

> During the years under review, the industrial life of India was far more disturbed than during the preceding year. The total number of strikes was 203, involving no less than 506,851 people, as compared with 129 strikes in 1927–28 in which 131,655 people were involved.[48]

During the industrial strikes of 1928, the Indian working class demonstrated magnificent solidarity and class-consciousness largely because they were inspired more by political ideas than immediate economic demands. This was clearly reflected in the editorial comment of the weekly journal *Kranti* after the strike of the Bombay textile workers was called off. It reminded its readers that 'the strike is not ended but it is only suspended. Although we go to the mills, we do so boiling with rage. There is no peace until capitalism is overthrown.'[49] On another occasion, *Kranti* averred:

> If a man, excited by the fire of *zoolom* [injustice], were to do any unlawful act, then he was not responsible for it, but capitalism which does this *zoolom* and brings mountains of unhappiness should be hanged. But how can capitalism be hanged by the court of the capitalists? The law throughout the world is the law of capitalism. The workman can't be happy unless and until capitalism is killed and ownership of factories and agriculture is in the hands of labour.[50]

Added to this revolutionary consciousness, in the words of L.P. Sinha,

> was an attempt to instil into the workers a sense of internationalism. In 1927, for the first time the question of international solidarity of labour was brought before the Indian workers by publicizing the trial in America of Sacco and Vanzetti and the efforts being made to secure their acquittal. The expression of friendship with the Soviet Union and China also became a theme at this time and the workers were asked to support the 'Hands off China movement'.[51]

IFTU AND RILU'S CONTROL BID

Meanwhile, the struggle for leadership inside the world trade union movement between the two international labour organizations—the International Federation of Trade Unions (IFTU) with its headquarters in Amsterdam and the RILU organized from Moscow—found its echo in India and plunged the Indian trade union movement into a crisis which threatened an open split between the supporters of the two wings. The rivalry between the two international bodies centred around fundamental ideological and tactical differences between the communists and the various social–democratic parties. The IFTU was a loose federation of independent national movements, each of which claimed the right to determine its own policy in accordance with respective national conditions, subject only to the broad and undefined claims of an international working-class solidarity of which each was its own interpreter. The IFTU at its conferences and through its bureau representing various countries issued pronouncements upon international policy and sought to prescribe a common line of action for national movements. But each national body remained free, in practice, to determine its policy and method of action: there was no presumption that any national movement would be prepared to take its orders from the IFTU. The RILU, on the other hand, was, in theory, an international movement, of which the national movements were only subordinate sections. In accordance with the Marxian principle of international class solidarity, the workers of the world as a whole were called upon to take up a common revolutionary programme and it was the duty of the national sections to carry this into effect.[52] Commenting on the rivalry between the IFTU and the RILU, Giri wrote:

> The sessions of the Congress [AITUC] during this period were lively. Most of the important resolutions [were] related to international policies and ideologies of the working-class movement. Heated discussions centred on the participation of the Trade Union Congress [AITUC] in the Geneva International Conference, the affiliation of the Trade Union Congress [AITUC] to the Third International [Communist International] at [/in] Moscow and the refusal to associate the Trade Union Congress [AITUC] with the International Federation of Trade Unions at [/in] Amsterdam. The two groups, with distinct leadership, lobbied in the Congress [AITUC] sessions for the ascendancy of their group. Renewed political activity also exercised the workers' minds and influenced the leaders of the two groups.[53]

Giri then added that 'the rival leadership confused labour and this resulted in the failure of many strikes' and that the 'employers took full advantage of the differences among the leadership'.[54]

The rivalry between the two international labour organizations for control over the Indian trade union movement was first evidenced at the Madras session of the AITUC held in January 1926. This session was attended by a representative of the British Labour Party, Major Graham Pole, who brought with him messages from the BTUC and the IFTU. The council of the trade unions of the Soviet Union and the RILU also sent messages soliciting close cooperation with the AITUC for fulfilment of common ends.

The question of international affiliation assumed greater importance when, at the Cawnpore session of the AITUC held in November 1927, the RILU and the IFTU openly clashed for control of the Indian organization. In its message to the conference, the RILU not only called upon the Indian working class to wage a 'relentless struggle against capitalist exploitation' but also urged them not to be 'misguided by the British labour leaders'. The executive bureau of the RILU was convinced, the message said, that the trade union leaders of India would be able to determine who were the enemies and who were the friends of the exploited classes. The message then hoped that the working classes of India would march shoulder to shoulder with those who had placed upon their banner the unity of the world trade union movement. The BTUC representative responded to this with a categorical declaration:

> It is the business of our delegation, it is our duty—a duty we are highly honoured and deeply grateful to perform—to do whatever is possible to relate, to link up, to coordinate this trade union movement with the BTU [British Trade Union] movement.[55]

The war of recrimination between the two wings of the international labour movement precipitated a split in the Indian trade union leadership and at the ninth session of the AITUC held at Jharia in December 1928, the communists made a desperate attempt to force the issue by 'seeking to commit the Congress [AITUC] definitely to their programme'.[56] Recalling the occasion, Jawaharlal Nehru wrote:

> I found the old tussle going on between the reformists and the more advanced and revolutionary elements. The main points in issue were the question of affiliation to one of the Internationals, as well as to the League Against Imperialism and the Pan-Pacific Union [PPTUS], and the desirability of sending represen- tatives to the International Labour Office [ILO] Conference at [/in] Geneva. More important than these questions was the vast difference in outlook between the two sections of the Congress [AITUC]. There was the old trade union group, moderate in politics and indeed distrusting the intrusion of politics in indus- trial matters. They believed in industrial action only and that too of a cautious character, and aimed at the gradual betterment of workers' conditions. The leader of this group was N.M. Joshi, who had often repre- sented Indian labour in Geneva. The other group was more militant, believed in political action and openly proclaimed its revolutionary outlook.[57]

Commenting on the imminent split between the two groups, Nehru observed that although the split was likely in any event, there was no doubt that many people actively worked for it and forced the issue. On the one side, there was the youthful enthusiasm of some members of the Left wing who wanted to go ahead regardless of consequences, and on the other, the deliberate attempt to push them on so as to widen the breach and thus get additional reasons for seceding.[58]

The 1928 Jharia session of the AITUC was attended by prominent labour leaders and political personalities including Nehru, Ben Bradley, Philip Spratt, representative of the League Against Imperialism J.W. Johnstone and Australian communist Jack Ryan, who represented the PPTUS. After the first day's proceedings, Johnstone was arrested, which provoked the delegates to take a prompt decision to affiliate the AITUC with the League Against Imperialism.[59] But the communist proposal to affiliate the AITUC with the Communist International-controlled PPTUS was rejected and the issue was postponed for the next session. Commenting on the defeat of the communist proposal, Ryan observed that by the time the next AITUC session would be convened, there was every reason to believe that the Left wing would no longer be in a minority and that the old conservative leaders would be defeated.[60]

MODERATES VERSUS EXTREMISTS: SPLIT IN AITUC

The trial of strength between the two groups and the consequent split ultimately took place at the 10th session of the AITUC held in Nagpur in 1929 under the presidency of Jawaharlal Nehru.[61] At this session, the radical group placed before the executive committee a series of resolutions relating to the boycott of the Whitley Commission and the International Labour Conference in Geneva, affiliation of the AITUC to the PPTUS and to the Communist International in Moscow, refusal to associate the AITUC with the IFTU and a number of other issues the implications of which were more or less similar. When these resolutions were adopted by the AITUC executive committee and ratified in the open session, the moderate group under N.M. Joshi's leadership withdrew from the AITUC with the declaration that it was impossible for them to cooperate with those who 'are determined to commit the Congress [AITUC] to a policy with which we are in complete disagreement'.[62] The moderates then decided to form a new organization under the name All India Trade Union Federation. Giri observed: 'However much one may regret the split, it was a process through which many progressive movements had to pass, and so did the All India Trade Union Congress [AITUC].'[63]

Although the split was the inevitable culmination of the bitter rivalry between the moderate and the radical groups, it did not put an end to dissension among the AITUC leadership. Shiva Rao said:

> There were dissensions of a personal character among its office-bearers, further aggravated by differences in views. One section was plainly for the methods recommended by the Third [Communist] International at [/in] Moscow, while the other favoured the adoption of tactics dictated by Mr M.N. Roy who at that time was in India without his presence being known to the authorities. But Mr Roy's conviction and long term of [prison] sentences in the course of the year deprived his followers of his services from behind the scenes. Moreover, Gandhi's Civil Disobedience Movement dislocated all organized activities in 1930. And when the Trade Union Congress [AITUC] met in the spring of 1931 in Calcutta, it split into two sections amidst scenes of wild disorder.[64]

As a result of this split, the communists under S.V. Deshpande and B.T. Ranadive seceded from the AITUC and formed a new organization namely the RTUC.

In December 1930, CPI issued a 'Draft Platform of Action' which called upon 'all class-conscious workers to concentrate every effort on the creation of a revolutionary trade union movement'. It then declared:

> The C.P. of India [CPI] deems it essential to organize trade unions based on factory committees, with the leadership elected directly by the workers and consisting of advanced revolutionary workers. The trade unions must become regularly functioning mass organizations, working in the spirit of the class struggle, and all efforts must be made to expel and isolate reformists of all shades, from the open agents of British capitalism, such as [N.M.] Joshi, [Diwan] Chaman Lal and [V.V.] Giri etc., to the sham Left national reformists, such as [Subhas Chandra] Bose, [Ramchandra Sakharam] Ruikar, [Sir Padamji Pestonji] Ginwala and other agents of the Indian bourgeoisie, who constitute a reactionary bloc for joint struggle against the revolutionary wing of the trade union movement. At the same time, the C.P. of India [CPI] works for the transformation of the All India Trade Union Congress [AITUC] into a fighting all-India centre of the labour movement on a class basis.[65]

In the concluding paragraph, the CPI declared that it was 'definitely against the principle of arbitration and interference by capitalist arbitration courts', because the 'sole means of winning any serious concessions on the part of the exploiters is resolute class struggle by strikes and mass revolutionary activities.[66]

DIVIDED LEADERSHIP AND BID FOR RAPPROCHEMENT

A sharp deterioration in the living conditions of workers as a result of nationalization, wage cuts, retrenchment and strikes revealed the limitations and weaknesses of a divided leadership in the trade union movement. A section of the trade union leadership came to realize that unless their movement was reunited, the struggle of the working class against exploitation would never be successful. Commenting on the situation, British labour leader Lester Hutchinson wrote:

> The great days of their unity and strength had passed with the collapse of the textile strike of 1929. Since then they had become divided among themselves by the unscrupulous activities of groups of adventurers and agent provocateurs, and at the mercy of opposing factions. But their enthusiasm at our reception showed that this was only a temporary phase, and that it would not take long for them to unite again in face of an attack, and present a strong, if not a stronger form than that with which they had astonished the world in 1928.[67]

Initiative for a rapprochement between the two contending groups came almost simultaneously from two unions, the All India Railwaymen's Federation (AIRF) and the Girni Kamgar Union, representing the moderate and the radical elements, respectively.

In pursuance of its decision, taken at a convention in May 1911, to formulate a draft programme for unity, the AIRF met in Madras in July 1932, and put forward a draft constitution underlining the principles on the basis of which a common platform of action was to be forged.

1. A trade union is an organ of class struggle, its basic task, therefore, is to organize the workers for advancing and defending their rights and interests; and although collective bargaining is the necessary implication of trade union and although in the transitional period to socialism, negotiations, representations and other methods of collective bargaining must remain an integral part of trade union activities, labour and capital cannot be reconciled in the capitalistic system.
2. That cooperation with the employing classes is not excluded if it is necessary in the interests of the working classes.
3. That the Indian trade union movement shall support and actively participate in the struggle for India's political freedom from the point of view of the working class. This would mean the establishment of a socialist state and during the interval, socialization and nationalization of all means of production and distribution as far as possible.
4. The Indian Trade Union Congress [AITUC] stands for: (a) freedom of the press, (b) freedom of speech, (c) freedom of assembly, (d) freedom of organization.
5. The Trade Union Congress [AITUC] shall send delegates to the International Labour Conference held under auspices of the League of Nations.
6. The methods of obtaining the objective of the trade union movement shall be peaceful, legitimate and democratic.[68]

The draft was not wholly acceptable to the radicals who pointed out that it not only failed to define the workers' role in the context of the class struggle but also ignored the most important issue, that is, the question of international affiliation. Some moderate elements within the AIRF, however, accepted the draft and decided to form a new organization, the National Federation of Labour, on the basis of the principles embodied in it. In April 1933, this new organization was amalgamated with the AITUC under the name of the National Trade Union Federation (NTUF), the aims and objects of which were declared to be the establishment of a socialist state in India, amelioration of the workers' social and economic conditions of life and active participation in the freedom movement 'from the point of view of the working class'.[69]

While the moderate elements were thus united under the banner of NTUF, the radicals also found a common ground of action on the basis of a 'platform of unity' produced by the Girni Kamgar Union. The most distinctive feature of this 'platform' was the categorical declaration that a trade union was a class organization of the workers whose interests were irreconcilable with those of the capitalists.[70] It also underlined the need for workers' participation in the struggle for national freedom because, it was pointed out, to compromise between the foreign and the Indian bourgeoisie for responsible government or dominion status could never change the condition of workers since the basic political demand of the Indian working class was the overthrow of imperialism and capitalism and socialization of the means of production.[71] This 'platform of unity' was formally accepted by the AITUC at its 13th annual session held in Cawnpore in December 1933.

CSP'S EFFORTS TO FORGE A UNITED FRONT

The stalemate that continued for some time with regard to the search for unity was broken when in 1934, the newly formed CSP came forward with a number of suggestions for bringing about a compromise between the moderate and the radical trade union leaders. These suggestions were:

There shall be joint action by the All India Congress Socialist Party [CSP], the All India Trade Union Congress [AITUC], the National Trade Union Federation [NTUF] and the Red Trade Union Congress [RTUC] on specific issues, such as the danger of another war, government repression, the Joint Parliamentary Committee Report and other issues which may arise from time to time; the nature of joint action being holding of meetings and demonstrations, observing of 'days' and anniversaries, issuing of statements and literatures etc.

There shall be joint action only if the following conditions are fulfilled by parties to the joint action:

1. There shall be no mutual criticism in speeches or by distribution of leaflets at joint functions.
2. There shall be no abuse of each other, nor imputations on the motives and honesty of either party.
3. Before every joint action there shall be joint agreement regarding the terms of resolutions and slogans, carrying of banners and flags and distribution of leaflets and literatures.
4. There shall be no advocacy of violence or non-violence by either party at joint functions.
5. At joint functions there shall be no appeal for support to either party or to enroll members or to draw any exclusive advantages to either party .... Each party to the United Front Agreement [i.e. the AITUC and the RTUC] reserves to itself the right to genuine and honest criticism of the political principles and policies of the other from its independent platform.[72]

One of the tangible results of the CSP's efforts to forge a united front of labour organizations was the amalgamation of the RTUC with the AITUC. At the 14th session of the AITUC held in Calcutta in April 1935, these two organizations were united and a joint manifesto was issued which called for (a) transfer of all power to the oppressed and exploited classes, (b) abolition of native states and parasitic landlordism, (c) freedom of the peasantry from all exploitation, (d) nationalization of all land, public utilities, mineral resources, banks and all other key industries and (e) institution of a minimum wage, limited hours of work and insurance against old age, sickness and unemployment.[73]

But in spite of these notable advances, the major task of uniting the National Trade Union Congress (NTUC), which represented the moderates, and the AITUC, which represented the Left elements, was yet to be achieved. Shiva Rao observed: 'The difficulty was not so much of evolving a common programme of work as of bringing the two sections into a single organic movement.'[74] Both the organizations held almost similar views in regard to such specific issues as workers' participation in the freedom movement and opposition to the Government of India Act, 1935. But the two vital questions over which there was no agreement were the interpretation of the concept of class struggle and international affiliation. While the moderates interpreted class struggle in terms of peaceful and democratic methods, to the radicals it implied direct action involving the use of force. Besides, the Left elements were opposed to not only the NTUC's affiliation to the IFTU but also the sending of delegates to the ILO.

Despite these differences, both the sections were eager to forge a common platform of action. Therefore, after long discussion between the leaders of the two groups, it was decided that a joint labour board would be constituted consisting of the representatives of the two bodies 'in order to press for certain reforms beyond the range of controversy and to facilitate common action during the strikes and boycotts'.[75]

Although the joint labour board never functioned satisfactorily, it paved the way for the eventual unity of the two organizations, which took place in Nagpur in April 1938.[76] The conditions of amalgamation were that the reconstituted AITUC

will not seek affiliation to any foreign organization, although affiliated unions are permitted this liberty on the condition that there is similarity of objects and methods. With regard to political questions and the declaration of strikes, it has been laid down that decisions will be conditional upon the support of three-fourth majority, though here again individual unions were absolved from being restricted in their actions by a mandate of that character.[77]

A joint general council was also set up with 44 member representatives from each section. It was also decided that the constitution of the AITUC would be that of the NTUF as well. The AITUC flag remained red, but without the hammer and sickle, which upset the extreme Left-wing elements.

With the outbreak of the Second World War, trade union movement in India took a new turn. At the 18th session of the AITUC held in Bombay in September 1940, Giri moved a resolution which said:

> As the present war between Great Britain on the one side and the fascist powers on the other is claimed by Britain to be waged for the vindication of the principles of freedom and democracy and not for any imperialistic purposes, India, without any sympathy either for imperialism or fascism, naturally claims for herself [itself] freedom and democratic government before she [it] can be expected to take part in the war. Participation in a war, which will not result in the establishment of freedom and democracy in India, will not benefit India, much less will it benefit the working class.[78]

When the resolution was adopted by a majority vote, a section of leaders, led by M.N. Roy, who stood for support to British war efforts, seceded from the AITUC and formed a new organization named Indian Federation of Labour. It is interesting to note here that in recognition of its support, the government sanctioned a monthly grant of Rupees 13,000 to this new organization.[79]

During the Quit India Movement, when almost all the nationalist leaders were either in jail or underground, the communists found an excellent opportunity to capture the trade union movement and soon the AITUC became a 'purely communist front masked only by the cooperation of Mr N.M. Joshi, its general secretary'.[80] Although by 1945, the communists had become discredited and isolated from the mainstream freedom movement, it impacted little in trade unionism as the nationalists failed to recapture the AITUC. As a result, the INC labour leaders, under the initiative of Vallabhbhai Patel, formed the Indian National Trade Union Congress (INTUC) on 3 May 1947, and called upon all the labour organizations under its influence to disaffiliate themselves from the AITUC and join the new organization.[81] And with the formation of the INTUC, the process of polarization of political forces in the trade union movement began to unfold in an entirely new context—independent India.

B. THE PEASANT MOVEMENT

FARMERS' AWAKENING FOLLOWING THE FIRST WORLD WAR AND NON-COOPERATION MOVEMENT

The socio-economic cataclysm brought about by the First World War not only ushered in a new era for Indian labour but also awakened the peasantry, long subjected to dumb misery and oppression, to a new political consciousness. The war and its effects, said Narendra Deva, had created conditions which helped the Indian peasants to make a resolute break with their inglorious past and to acquire a new confidence·in themselves. Their traditional passivity was broken, their deep-rooted conservatism was demolished and for the first time they began to feel their importance in India's struggle for freedom.[82]

Apart from the far-reaching effects of the war, another important factor in the awakening of the peasantry was the Non-Cooperation Movement launched by the INC under the leadership of Gandhi. In fact, it was during the Non-Cooperation Movement that the Indian peasants were drawn into the national movement and it was for this reason that the growth of the peasant movement in India can be traced to this period.

By drawing the peasants into the national movement, the INC had not only generated a spirit of revolt among them but also made a political issue of their economic grievances. The resolution adopted by the INC at its Nagpur session in 1920 calling for the 'no tax' campaign and urging the peasants to join the freedom movement clearly reflected the growing sympathy of the INC leaders for the peasants. When the Non-Cooperation Movement began, its message reached the remotest villages and the peasants began to look forward to the establishment of *swaraj* when 'all their grievances would be removed'. As a result of the INC preaching non-cooperation with the government, peasants were urged not to go to the courts to settle their disputes. Accordingly, litigations went down and rural democratic establishments or *panchayats* were set up for the settlement of disputes.[83]

But although the creed of non-violence was advocated by the INC, the peasants were in no mood to remain peaceful. Agrarian upheavals, as Nehru observed, were 'notoriously violent, leading to jacqueries, and the peasants of part of Oudh [Ayodhya] in those days were desperate and at white heat. A spark would have lighted the flame'.[84] This anger frequently burst into violence and the government quelled the uprisings with brutal force. Although the peasants had 'little staying power, little energy to resist for long', they faced oppression with great courage. Nehru found it surprising that

> they [the peasants] had shown for a whole year great power of resistance against the combined pressure of the government and the landlord. But they began to weary a little and the determined attack of the government on their movement ultimately broke its spirit for the time being. But it still continued in a lower key.[85]

One of the reasons why agrarian upheavals failed to gather momentum on an all-India scale was that although the INC leaders solicited the cooperation of the peasants in the national movement, they were unwilling to espouse their 'class demands'.[86] But in spite of the reluctance of the INC leaders to bring the class demands of the peasants to the forefront of the national movement, it was during the Non-Cooperation Movement that the traditional outlook of the Indian peasantry began to undergo a radical change; instead of accepting the landed aristocracy as their natural leaders, they now began to look to the new leadership of the middle class, as represented by the INC, for relief and leadership.[87] It was also during this period that young nationalist leaders, such as Nehru, began to take interest in the problems of the peasantry. Narrating his reaction after he visited some villagers, Nehru wrote:

> Looking at them and their misery and their overflowing gratitude, I was filled with shame and sorrow, shame at my easy-going and comfortable life and our petty politics of the city which ignored this vast multitude of semi-naked sons and daughters of India, sorrow at the degradation and overwhelming poverty of India. A new picture of India seemed to rise before me, naked, starving, crushed and utterly miserable. And their faith in us, casual visitors from the distant city, embarrassed me and filled me with a new responsibility that frightened me.[88]

After the withdrawal of the Non-Cooperation Movement, the interest of the INC leaders in the peasants began to cool down. But the peasants continued to fight for the removal of their economic grievances and gradually their movement began to intensify. In the state of Uttar Pradesh, notably in the districts of Hardoi, Kheri, Sitapur and Lucknow, their movement came to be known as Eka Andolan (individual protest) which was directed against the landlords and government officials who exploited the peasants by exacting more than what they were legally entitled to. There were two types of Eka Sabha (individual committee)—one dealt solely with economic questions, while the other had a political programme as well. The peasants used to discuss issues, such as *swaraj*, *swadeshi* and the boycott of law courts, in their meetings. The Eka Sabhas also launched agitation for the removal of ejectment laws that empowered landlords to eject their tenants at will in order to secure high premiums by settling land with other tenants. Such sort of exploitation and oppression sparked off widespread resentment among the peasants and they began to feel the necessity of forming independent class organizations of their own.[89]

But it was not easy for the Indian peasants to form any such organization. As a social class, they were characterized not only by the absence of homogeneity but also by deep-rooted conservatism, individualistic outlook and proverbial incapacity to organize.[90] Deva pointed out that the Indian peasants, trampled upon by tyranny and sunk deep in superstition, knew only one way of protest and that was to rush headlong into riotous conduct.[91]

In these circumstances, the peasantry could not but turn to the middle-class intelligentsia and individual political leaders for guidance and leadership. Although most of these leaders were Congressmen, they took up the cause of the peasants independently of the INC organization. And it was this factor which imparted an independent character to the peasant movement and initiated the process leading to the formation of separate peasants' organizations. The need for the formation of independent class organizations of the peasants was later explained by N.G. Ranga in the following words:

> We are advised by many Congress [INC] leaders not to aim at the development of any independent class or functional organizations as the Congress [INC] has been concerning itself most fully about all our needs and demands …. The peasants need only answer that it is just because of their blind reliance upon the chance help trickling from others that they are today so helpless, without their own organization, or class consciousness or any ability to stand up for their rights. How can they explain away their growing poverty and crushing burdens of taxation except by the failure of all our political forces to look after them?[92]

That the INC was not seriously interested in championing the cause of the peasantry became abundantly clear from the Bardoli resolution adopted in February 1922. The resolution asked the peasants to suspend the 'no tax' campaign and declared that withholding of rent to landlords was 'contrary to the Congress [INC] resolutions and injurious to the best interests of the country'. The resolution assured the landlords that the INC was in no way considering to attack their legal rights and that even where the *ryots* (tenant farmers) had genuine grievances, the INC wanted them to be redressed by mutual consultation and arbitration.[93]

No wonder, the Bardoli resolution sorely disappointed the peasants and they felt that the INC had left them in the lurch. And significantly, it was just at this time that communism appeared on the Indian political scene.

COMMUNIST INTERNATIONAL'S INTEREST IN INDIAN PEASANTRY

With the appearance of communism, revolutionary ideas began to steal their way into the peasant movement. The bulk of the peasants, however, were totally ignorant of the significance of those ideas. Slogans of socialism and revolution had caught the imagination of only a small section of peasant leaders who were stirred by Lenin's declaration[94] that the aim of the Bolshevik Revolution in Russia was to wrench the mills and factories from the hands of the private owners and to give ownership of the means of production and redistributed property to the whole people as well as to reconstruct agriculture on socialist lines by handing over all lands to the peasants.

During the early years of their movement, the Indian communists also failed to recognize the revolutionary significance of the peasant movement. They had interpreted the Bolshevik Revolution and Marxist preachings only in terms of establishment of a workers' reign and consequently worked only among them, while the peasants, in a predominantly agricultural country such as India, remained neglected. This happened despite the Communist International's insistence from the very beginning on the importance of work among peasants in the colonial and semi-colonial countries.[95]

The second congress of the Communist International, held in Moscow in 1920, adopted an agrarian programme calling upon the communists in colonial and semi-colonial countries to support peasant movements against landlords and all other remnants of feudalism. Emphasizing the role of the peasants in these countries, Lenin told the congress that every nationalist movement could be a bourgeois-democratic one, because the masses there were mostly peasants. It would be utopian to suppose, he pointed out, that the proletariat could carry on revolutionary activity without getting into definite relations with the peasants.[96] Similarly, the third (1921) and the fourth (1922) congresses of the Communist International also stressed the importance of the role of the peasants in the colonial countries such as India. The resolution adopted at the fourth congress declared that the agrarian question was of 'first-class importance in majority of the countries of the East'. The resolution pointed out that only agrarian revolutions aiming at the expropriation of large landowners could rouse the vast masses of peasants. The revolutionary movement in the colonial and semi-colonial countries of the East, it said, could not be successful unless it was based on the action of the mass of peasants.[97]

The interest of the Communist International in the Indian peasantry was further indicated when a special section of the Krestintern (the Peasant International, the peasant wing of the Communist International) was set up with the object of intensifying communist activity among Indian peasants. But as there was no well-organized communist party in India at that time, the Krestintern started its work through the CPGB. In 1926, a letter was sent to prominent CPGB member Arthur MacManus asking him to furnish the Krestintern with the names of Indian peasant leaders who could be contacted by the Communist International. The letter said: 'Our first task will be to get into touch with all the existing peasants' organizations of India even if the latter, by their programme, be at variance with our views as to the general aims and methods of work among peasants.'[98]

It was in line with this policy of the Communist International that the Indian communists felt that the time was ripe for the creation of a political WPP in order to mobilize these classes for revolutionary struggle against imperialism and capitalism.[99]

While the communists were thus trying to identify themselves with the social and economic grievances of the peasants, the world was caught in an acute agrarian crisis. Colonial countries, such as India, were especially hard hit because the imperialist countries shifted a considerable part of their burdens to the colonies. As a result, prices began to fall, reducing millions of agricultural producers to economic ruin. Whatever little surplus they had was used to pay land tax. The peasants' burden of indebtedness began to increase, leading to the virtual ruin of the middle and small peasants. In utter desperation, the peasants became restless and 'no tax' campaigns were launched in many places to secure relief from the government. In Uttar Pradesh, the peasant unrest assumed such serious proportions that the government was compelled to reduce rents.[100]

It was at this time, in December 1929, that the INC met in Lahore and decided to launch a programme of civil disobedience, including non-payment of taxes. When the movement was actually launched, the peasants joined it in the hope that this time the INC would bring their grievances to the forefront of the national movement. But they were bitterly disappointed when the movement was called off and the Gandhi–Irwin Pact was made without any reference to peasant problems and grievances. The peasants felt that once again they had been let down by the INC and they began to recognize the necessity of forming their own class organizations. Deva said:

> The question is often asked where is the need for the *kisan* [peasants] organization when the Congress [INC] membership predominantly consists of peasants and the Congress [INC] has in its agrarian programme of Faizpur and the Economic Rights Resolution of Karachi incorporated many of the demands of peasants in its programme.[101]

The answer, he pointed out, was that the INC being a multi-class organization, the peasants were unable to assert themselves in it. Their attitude towards other classes was hesitant and they found themselves lost in the mixed gathering. Therefore, to enable them to become bolder it was necessary to give them preliminary training in an organization of their own class. Peasants' organizations were necessary to exert revolutionary pressure on the INC to take the peasants' demands more seriously.[102]

Meanwhile, in December 1930, the CPI came out with its famous 'Draft Platform of Action' which not only denounced the 'treacherous part played by the National Congress [INC] as regards the peasantry' but also outlined their party's [CPI] policy towards the peasants' 'resolute class struggle' against imperialism and its native allies. It declared:

1. The C.P. of India [CPI] fights for the confiscation without compensation of all land and estates, forests and pastures of the native princes, landlords, moneylenders and the British government and their transference to the peasant committees for use by the toiling masses of the peasantry. The C.P. of India [CPI] fights for wiping out the whole of the land from the rubbish of the middle ages.

2. The C.P. of India [CPI] fights for the immediate confiscation of all plantations and their transference to revolutionary committees elected by the plantation workers. The allotments to which the planters assign their contract workers and also the land not in cultivation [is] to be handed over to the labourers and the poor peasants as their property. At the same time, the C.P. of India [CPI] is in favour of the nationalization of large-scale machinery equipped plantations, and workshops connected therewith, for utilization in the interests of the whole of Indian people.

3. The C.P. of India [CPI] fights for the immediate nationalization of the whole system of irrigation, complete cancellation of all indebtedness and taxes, and the transference of the control and supervision of the work of irrigation to revolutionary peasants' committees elected by the working peasantry.

4. In order to disorganize British rule and maintain revolutionary pressure against it, the C.P. of India [CPI] calls upon the peasantry and agricultural proletariat to engage in all kinds of political demonstrations and collective refusal to pay taxes and dues, or to carry out the orders and decisions of the government and its agents.

5. The C.P. of India [CPI] calls for refusal to pay rent, irrigation charges or other exactions, and refusal to carry out any labour services whatsoever [such as *begar* or forced labour] for the landlords, native princes and their agents.

6. The C.P. of India [CPI] calls for the refusal to pay debts and arrears to government, the landlords and the moneylenders in any form whatsoever.

7. As a practical watchword for the campaign among the peasantry, and a means of developing more political consciousness in the peasant movement, the C.P. of India [CPI] calls for the immediate organization of revolutionary peasant committees in order to carry on a fight to achieve all the revolutionary democratic changes required in the interests of emancipating the peasantry from the yoke of British imperialism and its feudal allies.

8. The C.P. of India [CPI] calls for the independent organizations of the agricultural proletariat, particularly the plantation workers, and its amalgamation with the proletariat as well as its representation in the peasant committees. The C.P. of India [CPI] is firmly convinced that the complete, thoroughgoing and permanent achievement of the above mentioned political and social changes is possible only by the overthrow of British domination and the creation of a Federal Workers' and Peasants' Soviet Republic.[103]

But in spite of this declaration, the Indian communists at that time could do very little to organize the peasantry under the banner of the CPI and as a result, the Indian peasants, without any class organization of their own, remained more or less isolated from the political movements carried on both by the INC and the CPI.[104]

FORMATION OF ALL INDIA KISAN CONGRESS

With the passing of the Government of India Act, 1935, the isolation of the peasantry was to a large extent broken. Under this Act, the peasants were enfranchised for the first time and when their feudal masters began to woo them for their votes, a spirit of self-confidence ran through the peasant masses. They shook off their apathy and began to develop a critical temper. A revolutionary change had come over their ways of thinking and they learnt to criticize those whom they rendered unquestioning obedience in the past. Their old frustration began to give way to buoyancy and traditional submissiveness and resignation to fate to a new hope and enthusiasm. The peasant masses were in motion and there were stirrings of a new life on all sides.[105]

As a result of this awakening, numerous peasants' organizations began to spring up in various parts of the country. The process gathered momentum in 1935 when several members of the Central Legislative Assembly formed a 'peasant group' to influence, according to its secretary, N.G. Ranga, 'public opinion from the forum of the Legislative Assembly on various peasants' problems'.[106]

Encouraged by these developments, the South Indian Federation of Peasants and Workers convened a conference of peasants to explore the possibilities of forming an all-India organization from whose platform the peasants could fight for their class demands.[107] At this conference, which was held in Madras in December 1935 under the presidency of N.G. Ranga, an organizing committee was formed to coordinate the activities of various provincial organizations as a first step towards the formation of an all-India peasant organization. It was also decided that the representatives of all peasants' organizations would meet in another conference in Meerut in January 1936. The Meerut conference, held under the presidency of Kamaladevi Chattopadhyay, outlined the aims and objectives of the peasant movement and formed an organizing committee with N.G. Ranga, Mohanlal Gautam and Jayaprakash Narayan as secretaries. The conference also decided that an All India Kisan Congress (AIKC) would be held in Lucknow in April 1936.

The Lucknow conference, held under the presidency of Swami Sahajanand Saraswati, laid the foundation of the AIKC. A manifesto was also issued wherein it was declared that the object of the *kisan* movement was to secure complete freedom from economic exploitation and the achievement of full economic and political power for the peasants and workers and other exploited classes.[108] The manifesto enumerated the minimum demands of the peasants as abolition of feudalism, cancellation of all arrears of rent and revenue, reduction of rent and revenue by at least 50 per cent, right of permanent cultivation for the peasants, graduated income tax, death duty and inheritance tax upon all agricultural revenue of landlords, minimum wage for agricultural workers, development of irrigation facilities, establishment of village *panchayats* and adult franchise. Emphasizing the peasants' role in the national movement, the manifesto declared that the *kisan* movement stood for the achievement of ultimate economic and political power for the producing masses through the active participation in the struggle for national freedom.[109]

From the moment of its inception, the AIKC was subjected to pulls and pressures both from the Right and the Left. Right-wing leaders of the INC, such as Vallabhbhai Patel, viewed the formation of a separate peasants' organization with misgivings and maintained that as the INC itself was a peasants' organization, the formation of the AIKC was not only unnecessary but also injurious to the national movement.[110] Left-wing INC leaders, such as Jawaharlal Nehru, on the other hand contended that the INC was a multi-class national organization and as such it could not represent the class interests of the peasants. Nehru, however, was of the opinion that the AIKC could serve the peasants best by affiliating itself with the INC.

Explaining the reasons why the AIKC was formed outside the INC, Deva observed that in many places the INC was controlled by professional men, merchants and moneylenders of the city and as they could not identify themselves with the rural population, they could not be expected to safeguard the interests of the peasantry. The result was that there was acute antagonism between the town and the country. And as the INC had very little hold on the masses of the rural areas, the peasants had to break away from it in order to have their own organ of struggle.[111] Urging the INC leaders to fraternize with the peasants in order to prevent them from developing ultra-Left tendencies, Deva averred that the INC leaders should accept that their indifference to the peasants was in no way conducive to the growth of INC's influence in the rural areas and for this reason they should do all that lay in their power to fraternize with the peasants and espouse their cause. And this would be possible only if there was a change in the local leadership of the INC. Deva then hoped that the INC would become a true representative of the peasants in the foreseeable future.[112] He felt that as Congressmen they would have to ensure that the INC did not 'become a dumping ground of all sorts of opportunists and self-seekers'. In similar vein, he urged the peasant leaders as well to make it sure that their organization did not 'provide shelter to malcontents and disgruntled persons who want to use it as a springboard'.[113]

The question of alliance between the INC and peasants' organizations was highlighted in the Andhra Provincial Ryots' Conference held at Nidubrolu in June 1936. In his presidential address to the conference, Ranga said that although the INC was the 'greatest asset' in Indian political life and although the peasants had contributed much towards the growth of its enormous prestige, it was not the peasants' organization. The time, however, had come for the peasants to make the INC their own political party which could be achieved only if functional representation was permitted within the party structure. The peasants, he declared, could not be content with the mere hope that the INC might accept their suggestions. They must insist upon it as a condition of their alliance with the INC. He concluded: 'Let it be remembered that the Indian National Congress [INC] stands to gain everything and nothing to lose by its conscious and wholehearted alliance with the workers and peasants. Its alliance with high finance has only weakened it, while spelling disaster upon the masses.'[114]

The controversy regarding the relationship between the INC and the peasants' organizations continued until 1938 when in its Haripura session the INC recognized the right of the peasants to form their own class organizations. In his presidential address to the INC, Subhas Chandra Bose pointed out that the organizations of workers and peasants existed as objective facts and 'since they have come into existence and show no signs of liquidating themselves, it should be manifest that there is historical necessity behind them'. He further said:

> I am afraid that whether we like it or not, we have to reconcile ourselves to their existence. The only question is how the Congress [INC] should treat them. Obviously, such organizations should not appear as a challenge to the National Congress [INC], which is the organ of mass struggle for capturing political power. They should, therefore, be inspired by Congress [INC] ideals and work in close cooperation with the Congress [INC] …. I feel that this could easily be done without landing oneself in conflict or inconsistency. Cooperation between the Congress [INC] and other two organizations could be facilitated if the latter deal primarily with the economic grievances of the workers and peasants and treat the Congress [INC] as a common platform for all those who strive for political emancipation of their country.[115]

On the question of affiliation of workers' and peasants' organizations to the INC, Bose said that personally he held the view that the day would come when the INC would have to grant this affiliation in order to bring all progressive and anti-imperialist organizations under its influence and control. But, he pointed out, there were bound to be differences of opinion as to the manner and the extent to which affiliation should be given. The character and stability of such organizations would also have to be examined before affiliation could be agreed to. In Russia, he said, the united front of the Soviet of workers, peasants and soldiers played a dominant part in the Bolshevik Revolution, while in Great Britain the BTUC exerted only a moderating influence on the national executive of the British Labour Party. In India, the

INC leaders would have to consider carefully what sort of influence organizations, such as the AIKS and the AITUC, would exert on the INC in case affiliations were granted.

BID TO CONTROL KISAN MOVEMENT AND TRIUMPH FOR LEFT

After the formation of the AIKC, all the Leftist elements—the communists, the Congress socialists and the Left Congressmen—began to vie with each other to gain control over the peasant movement. Although all these elements were united in their opposition towards the Right-wing leadership of the INC, they differed as to the aims and objectives of the *kisan* movement. In the words of L.P. Sinha:

> An ideal posited by the moderates and many Left Congressmen was that of the *Kisan–Mazdoor Raj* [rule of peasants and workers] but the communist elements and to a lesser extent the Congress socialists looked askance at this goal. To them, the difficulties of reconciling the concept of *Kisan–Mazdoor Raj* with that of socialism were wide enough. The conception of socialism was that of a society in which the ownership of means of production, distribution and exchange are socially owned. The ultimate stage of socialism preclude all remnants of private property whether in land or in other means of production. The conception of *Kisan–Mazdoor Raj*, on the contrary, was democratically conceived [in the liberal sense]. Behind the vague idealizing of the *Kisan–Mazdoor Raj*, as expressed in the writings and speeches of certain Kisan Sabha [AIKS] leaders, was the hard core of the retention of peasant proprietorship.[116]

Describing this conception as 'peasantism', Deva said that it looked at all questions from the narrow and sectional viewpoint of the peasant class. Its tenets were derived from the ideal that India's economic evolution would necessarily have to retain its specific peasant character. It believed in rural democracy, which meant a democracy of peasant proprietors. It had the outlook of the middle peasant, who had been influenced by modern ideas and was based on petty-bourgeois economy. In its crude form, it would mean a kind of narrow agrarianism and 'an insatiable desire to boost the peasant in all possible places'. Such an outlook, he said, was unscientific and betrayed a mentality which gave exaggerated importance to small peasants.[117]

Despite differences as to the aims and objects of the peasant movement, the Left-wing peasant leaders were united in their opposition to the dominant leadership of the INC. They were thoroughly dissatisfied with the performance of the INC in bringing about agrarian reforms which, they alleged, was being delayed for no good reason. According to Deva:

> The process [of agrarian reforms] was slow and though Congress [INC] governments enjoyed the backing of the masses, there was in evidence in certain provinces a feeling of hesitation to go fast for fear of the vested interests. Though the measures hitherto taken were only in the nature of palliatives and did not foreshadow any radical change on the social basis of the landowning class, yet the hue and cry was raised by the landed aristocracy as if changes of revolutionary dimensions were being incorporated in the statute. The economic situation was so desperate that drastic measures were needed to bring relief to the masses. All that the Congress [INC] governments did was only to ease a few of the more iniquitous burdens that the peasant was made to bear, but his [the peasant's] condition is so miserable that the remaining burdens will prove irksome and heavy and he will make insistent and imperative demand to be relieved of them as well.[118]

As a result of this dissatisfaction, differences between the INC and the peasant organizations began to grow and at the Comilla session of the party in 1938, the AIKC changed its name to AIKS. It adopted the red flag as the symbol of peasants' struggle, which many Right-wing INC leaders looked upon as a challenge to the national flag.

This was a triumph for the Left, particularly for the communists who tended increasingly to look upon the AIKS as a 'subsidiary of the CPI'.[119] This attitude, however, created deep resentment among non-communist peasant leaders, such as Indulal Yagnik and Swami Sahajanand Saraswati, who resigned from the AIKS in 1943 and 1945, respectively. At the end of the war and on the eve of independence, both the INC and the CSP promoted their own peasant organizations and the AIKS remained with the communists.

NOTES AND REFERENCES (CHAPTER 5)

A. THE LABOUR MOVEMENT

1   The political and economic condition of India at the close of the First World War has been discussed in Chapter 1 of this book.
2   A.A. Purcell and J. Hallsworth, *Report on Labour Conditions in India* (London: Trade Union Congress General Council, 1928), 6.
3   B. Shiva Rao, *The Industrial Worker in India* (London: George Allen and Unwin, 1939), 19.
4   V.B. Karnik, *Indian Trade Unions: A Survey* (Bombay: Labour Education Service, 1960), 21.
5   On the question of the migratory character of the Indian labour, the Royal Commission on Labour in India commented: 'Those who are frequently leaving an industrial centre, even for short spells and are frequently changing their employer, are less inclined than more permanent workers to maintain a constant interest in any organization'. See *Report of the Royal Commission on Labour in India* (Calcutta: Government of India Press, 1931), 321.
6   Rao, *The Industrial Worker in India*, 18.
7   Karnik, *Indian Trade Unions: A Survey*, 16–17.
8   V.B. Karnik, 'Trade Unions: Progress Towards Democracy', in *Studies in Indian Democracy*, ed. S.P. Aiyar and R. Srinivasan (Bombay: Allied Publishers, 1965), 659.
9   Rao, *The Industrial Worker in India*, 14–15.
10 M.N. Roy, *Indian Labour and Post-War Reconstruction* (Lucknow: A.P. Singh, 1943), 13. Also see *Indian Annual Register* (Calcutta, 1921), 266.
11 *Report of the First Session of the AITUC* (Bombay: AITUC, 1920), 203–04.
12 For the policy of the British Labour Party towards the working class organizations of the colonies, see the party's pamphlet, *Labour and the New Social Order: A Report on Reconstruction* (London: Labour Party, 1918).
13 G.D.H. Cole, *British Trade Unionism Today* (London: Gollancz, 1939), 170.
14 Ibid., 262.
15 R.K. Das, *Labour Movement in India* (Berlin: Walter de Gruyter and Company, 1923), 30–40.
16 *Draft Constitution and Rules: Report of the First Session of the AITUC* (Bombay: AITUC, 1920), 75.
17 Rao, *The Industrial Worker in India*, 149.
18 R.R. Bakhale, ed., *The Directory of Trade Unions* (Bombay: AITUC, 1925), 1.
19 *Report of the First Session of the AITUC*, 18. For Lala Lajpat Rai's views on capitalism and Marxism, see Lala Lajpat Rai, *The Political Future of India* (New York, NY: B.W. Huebsch 1919), 200–02.
20 *Report of the First Session of the AITUC*, 50–55.
21 Karnik, 'Trade Unions: Progress Towards Democracy', in *Studies in Indian Democracy*, ed. Aiyar and Srinivasan, 659–60.
22 Ibid. M.K. Gandhi's attitude towards trade unionism may be summarized as follows:

    (i)   The cause of strike must be just.
    (ii)   Strikers should never resort to violence.
    (iii) They should never molest blacklegs.
    (iv)   They should be in a position to maintain themselves during strikes.

(v)   They should never depend upon funds or charity.

(vi)   They should remain firm even if the strike is long.

(vii)   They should be absolutely united because strike is no remedy if substitute labour is available.

(viii)   Workers must not resort to strike without the consent of their union.

(ix)   Strike should be the last resort: It could be resorted to only after negotiations with employers have failed.

See G.N. Dhawan, *The Political Philosophy of Mahatma Gandhi* (Bombay: Popular Books Depot, 1946), 254–55; V.B. Singh, ed., *Economic History of India, 1857–1956* (Bombay: Allied Publishers, 1965), 573.

23   Gopal Ghosh, *Indian Trade Union Movement* (Calcutta: T.U. Publications, 1961), 71.

24   Ibid.

25   Ibid., 70–71.

26   M.N. Roy, 'Where Are the Masses?', *International Press Correspondence* (9 May 1923), 333.

27   M.N. Roy, *Political Letters* (Zurich: The Vanguard Bookshop, 1924), 19–20.

28   Ibid., 72.

29   B.F. Bradley, *Trade Unionism in India* (London: Modern Books, 1932), 13.

30   M.N. Roy, *The Future of Indian Politics* (London: R. Bishop, 1926), 104.

31   See *Resolutions and Theses of the Fourth Congress of the Communist International* (London: CPGB, 1922), 15.

32   See 'Report on India', *From the Fourth to the Fifth World Congress: Report of the Executive Committee of the Communist International* (London: CPGB, 1924).

33   E.H. Carr, *The Bolshevik Revolution, 1917–1923* (London: Macmillan, 1950), 399–401.

34   S.D. Punekar, *Trade Unionism in India* (Bombay: New Book Company, 1948), 91.

35   Cole, *British Trade Unionism Today*, 69–71.

36   L.P. Sinha, *Left Wing in India* (Muzaffarpur: New Publishers, 1965), 116.

37   Gene D. Overstreet and Marshall Windmiller, *Communism in India* (Bombay: Perennial Press, 1960), 369.

38   Philip Spratt, *Blowing Up India: Reminiscences and Reflections of a Former Comintern Emissary* (Calcutta: Prachi Prakashan, 1955), 32.

39   Rao, *The Industrial Worker in India*, 222.

40   Ibid.

41   Ibid., 151–52.

42   Ibid., 152. For a detailed account of the Bombay textiles unions during this period, see *Report of the Bombay Strike Enquiry Committee, 1928–1929* (Bombay: Government Central Press, 1929).

43   Sinha, *Left Wing in India*, 123.

44   Rao, *The Industrial Worker in India*, 152.

45   Ibid.

46   *International Press Correspondence* (9 June 1927).

47   Rao, *The Industrial Worker in India*, 188.

48   *India in 1928–1929* (Calcutta: Government of India Central Publication Branch, 1930), 7. It is a statement prepared for presentation to the Parliament with the requirements of the 26th section of the Government of India Act.

Industrial Labour in India, International Labour Office, Studies and Reports Series A, No. 41 (London: P.S. King and Son, 1938), 344.

49   Ahmad Mukhtar, *Trade Unionism and Labour Disputes in India* (Bombay: Longmans, Green and Company, 1935), 215–16.

50   Ibid., 216.

51   Sinha, *Left Wing in India*, 127.

52   Cole, *British Trade Unionism Today*, 267.

53   V.V. Giri, *Labour Problems in Indian Industry* (Bombay: Asia Publishing House, 1959), 13.

54   Ibid.

55   *Report of the Eighth Session of the AITUC* (Bombay: N.M. Joshi, 1928).

56   Rao, *The Industrial Worker in India*, 153.

57 Jawaharlal Nehru, *An Autobiography* (Bombay: Allied Publishers, 1962), 186.

58 *Indian Annual Register*, Vol. II (Calcutta, 1929), 429.

59 *Indian Annual Register*, Vol. II (Calcutta, 1928), 503–04.

60 *The Far Eastern Bulletin* (16 January 1929), 5.

61 According to some observers, there were three factions at the Nagpur session of the AITUC—the communists, the reformists and the 'nationalists'. The election of Jawaharlal Nehru to the presidency was said to be the result of a compromise between the communists and the 'nationalists'. See Nehru, *An Autobiography*, 187. Also see S.K. Vidyarthi, 'The Trade Union Movement in India', *Revolutionary Age* (29 August 1931), 3–4. It may be mentioned here that while serving prison term at Bareilly Central Jail during 1931–36, M.N. Roy had taken the pseudonym of S.K. Vidyarthi to continue writing against the establishment. Around this time, he also wrote a book titled *China in Revolt* under the pseudonym of S.K. Vidyarthi, which was published from Bombay by Vanguard Publishing Company.

62 *Indian Annual Register*, Vol. II (Calcutta, 1929), 363. Also see Rao, *The Industrial Worker in India*, 154.

63 Giri, *Labour Problems in Indian Industry*, 14.

64 Rao, *The Industrial Worker in India*, 154–55.

65 *Indian Communist Party Documents, 1930–1956* (Bombay: Democratic Research Service, 1957), 10–12.

66 Ibid.

67 L. Hutchinson, *Conspiracy at Meerut* (London: George Allen and Unwin, 1935), 142.

68 Mukhtar, *Trade Unionism and Labour Disputes in India*, 164–65.

69 Rao, *The Industrial Worker in India*, 155.

70 *Indian Annual Register*, Vol. II (Calcutta, 1933), 407.

71 Ibid.

72 M.R. Masani, *The Communist Party of India—A Short History* (London: Derek Verschoyle, 1954), 54–55.

73 *Report of the Fourteenth Session of the AITUC* (Calcutta: AITUC, 1935).

74 Rao, *The Industrial Worker in India*, 156.

75 Ibid.

76 Ibid.

77 Ibid.

78 Giri, *Labour Problems in Indian Industry*, 20.

79 *International Labour Review*, Vol. 57 (Geneva: International Labour Office, 1948), 19.

80 Masani, *The Communist Party of India—A Short History*, 85.

81 Singh, *Economic History of India, 1857–1956*, 592.

B. THE PEASANT MOVEMENT

82 Yusuf Meherally, ed., *Acharya Narendra Deva, Socialism and the National Revolution* (Bombay: Padma Publications, 1946), 34.

83 Nehru, *An Autobiography*, 58–59.

84 Ibid.

85 Ibid., 62.

86 Meherally, *Acharya Narendra Deva, Socialism and the National Revolution*, 34.

87 Ibid., 35.

88 Frank Moraes, *Jawaharlal Nehru—A Biography* (Bombay: Macmillan, 1956), 66.

89 Meherally, *Acharya Narendra Deva, Socialism and the National Revolution*, 61.

90 A.R. Desai, *Social Background of Indian Nationalism* (London: Oxford University Press, 1948), 35.

91 Meherally, *Acharya Narendra Deva, Socialism and the National Revolution*, 7.

92 N.G. Ranga, *The Modern Indian Peasant* (Madras: Kisan Publications, 1936), 1–2.

93 Pattabhi Sitaramayya, *The History of the Indian National Congress*, Vol. II (Bombay: Padma Publications, 1947), 392.

94   V.I. Lenin, *Alliance of the Working Class and the Peasantry* (Moscow: Progress Publishers, 1965), 222.

95   Sinha, *Left Wing in India*, 176.

96   *The Second Congress of the Communist International: Proceedings of Petrograd Session of July 17th and Moscow Sessions of July 19th–August 7th, 1920* (Moscow: Communist International, 1920), 56.

97   *Resolutions and Theses of the Fourth Congress of the Communist International*, 56.

98   *Communist Papers, Documents Selected from Those Obtained on the Arrest of the Communist Leaders on the 14th and 21st October, 1925*, Parliamentary Publications, 1926, Vol. XXIII (London: His Majesty's Stationery Office, 1926), 104.

99   *The Communist International Between the Fifth and the Sixth World Congresses, 1924–1928* (London: CPGB, 1928), 475.

100 Meherally, *Acharya Narendra Deva, Socialism and the National Revolution*, 35.

101 Ibid., 42.

102 Ibid.

103 *Indian Communist Party Documents, 1930–1956*, 13–14.

104 Commenting on the impact of communism on the Indian peasants, Pattabhi Sitaramayya wrote:

> They found a cause, a flag and a leader. The cause of the *kisan* was not a new one but had all along been upheld by the Congress [INC]. The flag they chose to favour was the Soviet flag of red colour with hammer and sickle. The flag came more and more into vogue as the flag of the *kisan* and the communists. ... Really it was less of socialism and perhaps more of communism that was gradually permeating the atmosphere...

See Sitaramayya, *The History of the Indian National Congress*, Vol. II, 73.

105 Meherally, *Acharya Narendra Deva, Socialism and the National Revolution*, 36–38.

106 *Indian Annual Register*, Vol. II (Calcutta, 1936), 288.

107 It may be noted in this connection that some radical peasant leaders of Bihar initially opposed this move on the part of the South Indian Federation of Peasants and Workers because they apprehended that it was motivated more by political considerations than by genuine sympathy for the peasants. This apprehension was caused by N.G. Ranga's statement emphasizing the need for carrying the peasants' struggle to the parliamentary front. See N.G. Ranga, *Kisans and Communists* (Bombay: Pratibha Publishers, 1949), 60.

108 *Indian Annual Register*, Vol. II (Calcutta, 1936), 280.

109 Ibid.

110 Ibid., 286.

111 Meherally, *Acharya Narendra Deva, Socialism and the National Revolution*, 50.

112 Ibid., 50–51.

113 Ibid., 46.

114 Ranga, *The Modern Indian Peasant*, 7–11.

115 Subhas Chandra Bose: *Selected Speeches of Subhas Chandra Bose* (Delhi: Government of India Publications Division, 1962), 90.

116 Sinha, *Left Wing in India*, 397.

117 Meherally, *Acharya Narendra Deva, Socialism and the National Revolution*, 51.

118 Ibid., pp. 39–40.

119 Overstreet and Windmiller, *Communism in India*, 385.

6 Growth of Other Leftist Parties

One of the most important elements contributing to the strength and vitality of the INC during the nationalist movement was its ability to accommodate and reconcile conflicting interest groups and ideologies within the party. As a result, inside the INC there had always been a number of groups whose ideologies were at variance with those of the dominant leadership under Gandhi. Many of the erstwhile terrorists and revolutionaries who joined the INC during the Non-Cooperation Movement were deeply impressed by Gandhi's hold upon the masses and felt the necessity of transforming the party into a revolutionary mass organization. Although they worked within the organizational framework of the INC, they accepted neither the creed of non-violence nor the broad ideals and objectives of the party. Most of them were imbued with Marxian ideas and wanted the INC to become a revolutionary organization in the Marxian sense of the term. Political scientist Myron Weiner observed:

> There was thus a nationalist movement operating parallel to Congress [INC] which was prepared to use violence…a movement which broadly accepted the leadership of Gandhi and the Congress Party [INC] but which was prepared to use its own methods. This movement continued to prod Gandhi and the Congress Party [INC] to move faster and to intensify its activities. It urged complete independence even while the Congress [INC] leadership was prepared to accept dominion status; and it urged Civil Disobedience Movement when the Congress [INC] leadership still hoped that further negotiations would bring concessions from the British rulers.[1]

After the suspension of the Civil Disobedience Movement and the subsequent break-up of the Left unity following the Tripuri session in March 1939, some of these groups broke away from the INC and emerged as independent political organizations. Similarly, a few groups had also emerged from the communist movement. In fact, during this period, India witnessed the emergence of different shades of Leftist parties all of which were characterized by their opposition to the Gandhian leadership of the INC and their adherence to Marxian ideas. Apart from the CSP, the most notable of these parties were the Forward Bloc, the Revolutionary Socialist Party (RSP), the Revolutionary Communist Party of India (RCPI), the Bolshevik Party of India (BPI), the Bolshevik Leninist Party and the Radical Democratic Party.

THE FORWARD BLOC

After his release from internment in March 1937, when Subhas Chandra Bose came to attend the AICC meeting at Haripura the following year, he found that the Leftists, instead of gaining in strength, had lost much ground. This setback, he felt, was due to the fact that 'there was something wanting in the policy and the line of action hitherto pursued by them'. Analysing the composition of the INC, he could distinguish a number of groups inside the party, namely, the official bloc led by Vallabhbhai Patel, Rajendra Prasad, Maulana Abul Kalam Azad and others; the Congress socialists; the ultra-Leftists and the followers of M.N. Roy. In between these groups, there were other radical anti-imperialist elements who could not join hands with the official bloc and 'for reasons of their own did not like to join any of the existing Leftist parties or groups'. Bose felt that unless and until these elements were organized on a definite platform, 'the Leftist movement was not likely to gather further accession of strength to an appreciable degree.' It was, therefore, suggested that a new bloc should be organized within the INC on the basis of a minimum programme so as to enable all the unorganized radical elements to unite on a common platform. Accordingly, a draft manifesto, prepared by an ultra-Leftist leader and amended by a prominent Congress socialist, was sent out to a number of radical Congressmen to ascertain their opinion. At this stage, however, opinion in the socialist circle began to change and some Congress socialists openly declared themselves against the idea of forming a Left bloc inside the INC. In view of this attitude on the part of the Congress socialists, the proposed move could not be launched immediately. The idea of a Left bloc, however, persisted and the enthusiasts once again formulated a programme and adopted it provisionally at the Tripuri session of the INC in March 1939. It was also decided that a final decision would be taken at the next AICC session.[2]

Although from the very beginning Bose was in favour of this move, he felt that he could best serve the public cause by keeping out of the proposed Left bloc while maintaining a friendly attitude towards it.[3] However, this changed soon afterwards when after the Tripuri session of the AICC in March 1939 he came to realize that his differences with Gandhi were irreconcilable and he not only resigned from the INC presidency on 29 April the same year but also proceeded to form a radical and progressive party 'with a view to rallying the entire Left wing under one banner'. Thus, the Forward Bloc of the INC, as it was then known, was formed on 22 June 1939. Bose became its president and journalist Sardul Singh Kavishar (also known as S.S. Cavesheer) its vice-president.[4]

Describing the formation of the Forward Bloc as a 'new phenomenon in Indian politics', Bose maintained that neither personal factors nor accidental circumstances could account for the birth of the new party. The same inner urge for national emancipation, he said, which gave birth to the INC was also responsible for the formation of the Forward Bloc.[5]

Although Bose hoped that the Forward Bloc would provide a platform for all radical anti-imperialist and progressive elements, the new party became a target of bitter attack both from the Right and the Left. While the Right-wing INC leaders argued that the new party would cause a split in them and destroy national unity, the Left-wing leaders pointed out that it was formed purely on personal grounds and as such it had no sound ideological basis.[6]

Replying to these criticisms, Bose drew a distinction between real unity and false unity and averred that those who had raised the slogan of unity at any price and under any circumstances had lost dynamism and revolutionary urge.[7] He asked:

> Did the formation of the Gandhi Seva Sangha create a split and destroy national unity? If it did not, then why should the formation of the Forward Bloc do so? Left consolidation will, in my view, be a stepping-stone towards real national unity, which is unity of action and not unity of inaction. Without Left consolidation, I do not see how we can arrive at real national unity.[8]

In regard to the question as to why he was creating 'an internal crisis' within the INC by forming a new party, Bose pointed out that an internal crisis, today or tomorrow, was inevitable in view of the uncompromising attitude of the INC high command. He said:

> We can avert the internal crisis today only by surrendering completely to them. But what shall we gain by postponing the crisis through a surrender? Why put off the evil day? We are fast approaching an external crisis. It would be disastrous to have an internal crisis when the external crisis overtakes us. It would be much more desirable to face the internal crisis now, go through it and emerge out of it before the external crisis seizes us.[9]

Bose then pointed out that it would be a fatal mistake to think that a split, even when it was temporary, was an unmixed evil. On the contrary, a temporary split was sometimes necessary for the sake of political advancement. The secession of the moderates in 1918 and of the non-cooperationists in 1920 was not an unmixed evil. Taking example from abroad, he pointed out that the growth of the Bolsheviks would never have been possible but for the split in the Russian Social Democratic Labour Party in 1903. Bose further emphasized:

> It should not be forgotten that the Left within the Congress [INC] believes in national unity more than the Right. That is why the Left stands for a composite cabinet, while the Right stands for a homogeneous one. Consequently, the Left within the Congress [INC] will always work with the object of establishing real national unity. The present move in the matter of forming the Forward Bloc at this juncture has been forced by unavoidable circumstances and by the uncompromising attitude of the Congress [INC] high command.[10]

As for the attitude of the new party towards the INC, Bose declared:

> The Forward Bloc will function as an integral part of the Congress [INC]. It will accept the present constitution of the Congress [INC]—its creed, policy and programme. It will cherish the highest respect and regard for Mahatma Gandhi's personality and complete faith in his political doctrine of non-violent non-cooperation. But that will not mean that the Forward Bloc will necessarily have confidence in the present high command of the Congress [INC].[11]

Explaining its attitude towards other Leftist parties, Bose said that the Forward Bloc—being a platform for all anti-imperialist, radical and progressive groups—would naturally have a friendly attitude towards all the existing Leftist groups and parties in the INC and it would not do anything to weaken or undermine them.[12]

The twofold task of the Forward Bloc, Bose declared, would be 'to instil life and revolutionary impulse into the existing programme of the Congress [INC]' and 'to prepare the country for the coming struggle through countrywide agitation and through an advanced radical programme'. In order to mobilize 'all available revolutionary energy of the nation', the Forward Bloc would raise a Congress Volunteer Corps on an all-India basis and develop closer and intimate contacts with other anti-imperialist organizations, such as the AIKS, the AITUC, Youth League and student movements.[13]

Although initially almost all the Leftist parties were bitterly critical of the Forward Bloc, their attitude began to soften shortly afterwards and as a result the party joined the LCC as a separate unit. Both the communists and the Congress socialists now regarded the Forward Bloc not as a disruptive force but as a platform of radical Congressmen who were neither communists nor socialists. It, therefore, represented a progressive force with which a united front could be forged.

The honeymoon between the Forward Bloc and other Leftist parties was, however, short-lived. In October 1939, the Congress socialists withdrew from the LCC and in December the communists followed suit denouncing the Forward Bloc as a counter-revolutionary organization of the disgruntled petty bourgeoisie.[14]

Meanwhile, the Second World War had been formally declared and the Forward Bloc launched upon its programme of uncompromising struggle against British imperialism. At this juncture, Bose felt, what was of paramount importance for India was national unity. In his presidential address at the first conference of the All India Forward Bloc in Nagpur in June 1940, he said:

> The wheels of history are grinding on, quite regardless of what we may be doing in India. But in order to fully utilize the opportunity, which international events have presented to us, we must have sufficient unity and solidarity among ourselves. If India could speak with one voice today, our demand indeed would be irresistible. It follows, as a consequence, that while we should think of intensifying the national

struggle and widening its scope, we should at the same time try to develop national unity and solidarity to the maximum limit.[15]

Outlining India's role in the war, Bose openly declared that India must not cooperate with British war efforts because only after the defeat and break-up of the British empire could India hope to be free. As a protest against the decision of the INC to offer cooperation to Britain, the Forward Bloc launched an all-India campaign of civil disobedience and 'many among the rank and file of the Congress [INC], especially the volunteers, joined the campaign.'[16]

Taking alarm at Bose's militant anti-British activities, the government banned the Forward Bloc, arrested almost all its prominent leaders and raided its offices across the country. Bose himself was arrested on 2 July 1940, under Section 129 of the Defence of India Rules, 1939, and was detained in the Presidency Jail, Calcutta. On 26 November, he addressed a long letter to the governor of Bengal conveying his decision to go on hunger strike for an indefinite period. He started his fast on 29 November and as his condition began to deteriorate rapidly, he was released on 5 December only to be interned in his house in Calcutta. But on 17 January 1941, he secretly disappeared from his house and left India. [17]

The ban on the All India Forward Bloc was lifted just ahead of the provincial elections in 1946 and a meeting of the party working committee was held in Bombay on 10 June in absence of Bose. A draft manifesto was adopted in the meeting wherein it declared the Forward Bloc to be a socialist party with an ideology and programme based upon the concept of militant class struggle.[18]

The party contested the provincial elections and its leader Hari Vishnu Kamath won a seat in the Constituent Assembly, while Jyotish Chandra Ghosh, Hemanta Kumar Basu and Lila Roy won seats in the Bengal Legislative Assembly.[19] The second national conference of the party was held in Arrah, Bihar, in January 1947, where Kavishar was elected the president and former Congressman Sheel Bhadra Yajee the general secretary.[20] The leaders present in the session denounced the negotiations for the transfer of power between the INC and the British government as 'bogus'. They also said that the INC, driven by the frightened bourgeoisie, had entered into a partnership with British imperialism to defeat the revolutionary upsurge of the people.

At a subsequent special session near Calcutta in April 1947, the party decided to boycott the Constituent Assembly and asked its members to resign from it. Kamath was dissociated as he did not agree to resign, while the three other elected members followed the party line. The resolution called upon the toiling masses and all other patriotic forces to carry on relentless struggle for the seizure of power for the Indian people.[21]

THE REVOLUTIONARY SOCIALIST PARTY

The origin of the RSP can be traced to the Anushilan Samiti, a terrorist organization that sprang up in Bengal in 1905.[22] After a lull in the activities of the Samiti for over a decade, it was revived in the early 1920s when a conference of the revolutionaries was held in Kanpur in October 1924. At this conference, an all-India revolutionary organization was formed under the name of the Hindustan Republican Association. This organization, which subsequently styled itself as the Hindustan Socialist Republican Army, was originally started after the failure of the Non-Cooperation Movement by two Bengali revolutionaries in Uttar Pradesh. The object of the association was declared to be the establishment of a 'federated Republic of the United States of India by an organized armed revolution'. The association had a central committee with branches almost all over the country. Each provincial organization was to have its various departments and each was to focus on violent crimes with a view to collect money and arms; assassination was made permissible for the enforcement of discipline. From its inception, the association was very loosely knit; at times it seemed almost to disappear, but following its reinvention in Kanpur in 1924 it came to attention more frequently and was established in Madras. It also functioned in Bihar, Uttar Pradesh, Punjab and Delhi.[23] The guiding spirit of the association was Jogesh Chatterjee who, like M.N. Roy, belonged to the early batch of terrorists and was later influenced by socialist ideas. During the Civil Disobedience Movement, Chatterjee was arrested for taking part in violent activities and remained in jail till 1937.

Most of the revolutionaries were arrested and imprisoned after the Chittagong Armoury Raid in 1930. While in prison, they began to read Marxist literature and very soon were completely imbued with socialist ideas. Even while in jail, some of them prepared a thesis, which they issued after their release in 1937.[24] With the adoption of this thesis by fellow revolutionaries, a new political group had emerged on the Indian political scene. This group styled itself as the RSP of India at the time of the Ramgarh session of the INC in 1940.[25]

The thesis prepared by the revolutionaries in jail recognized the proletariat allied with the peasantry and the lower middle class as the 'only consistently revolutionary class' and declared that the goal of the new party was the violent overthrow of British imperialism and the establishment of communism and a classless society. The final victory of the proletariat over imperialism and its allies, it said, would assume the form of a dictatorship because it was 'inevitably bound' to rely on military forces, on the arming of the masses and not on institutions established by 'lawful' and 'peaceful' means. The immediate programme of the new party included the achievement of self-determination, the formation of a Constituent Assembly, the total annulment of foreign debts, agrarian reforms, abolition of princely states, liquidation of rural indebtedness, nationalization of key industries and foreign concerns and social insurance for the working classes.[26] Although the thesis recognized the Soviet Union as the 'base of the coming socialist world revolution', it pointed out that the ideal of internationalism presupposed the development of the revolutionary movement in one's own country.[27] Thus, ideologically, the RSP was closer to the CSP than to the CPI.

As a matter of fact, although the RSP had its own tradition, thesis, organization, leaders and allegiances and loyalties, it started working as an organized group within the CSP. But differences between the two parties began to develop when the RSP decided to support Bose against Gandhi in Tripuri session of the INC in 1939.[28] As the CSP had remained neutral in the Gandhi–Bose conflict, the revolutionary socialist leaders became disillusioned at the passivity and pro-Gandhian attitude of the Congress socialists. This difference of attitude was a fundamental one because the issue involved was not just a contest between two wings of the INC to capture the leadership but the policy which the INC would adopt towards the coming international crisis—whether a mass movement against British rule should be launched in anticipation of the war or whether it should be postponed in view of the threat of war. On this question, the RSP took the stand in favour of the immediate launch of a massive anti-imperialist struggle and denounced the neutrality of the Congress socialists as betrayal of Marxism–Leninism and surrender to 'social Gandhism'.[29] And it was on this issue that the RSP broke away from the CSP and set itself up as a separate political party.

All through the war, the RSP steadfastly held to its anti-war policy.[30] Even after the German attack on the Soviet Union, it continued to follow this policy and declared that in spite of the Soviet Union's alliance with the Allies, the character of the war had not changed. The RSP believed India could help the Soviet Union only after it achieved independence. When the Quit India Movement was launched, the RSP endorsed the 'Quit India' slogan of the INC and enthusiastically took part in it.[31]

After the war when negotiations began for the transfer of power, the RSP declared that both the transfer of power and the partition of the country were nothing but a 'backdoor deal between the treacherous bourgeois leadership of the Congress [INC] and imperialism'. And although the transfer of power was now a *fait accompli*, the party decided to carry on the 'half-baked, truncated and unfinished' struggle against British imperialism.[32]

THE REVOLUTIONARY COMMUNIST PARTY OF INDIA

Although as a distinct political organization the RCPI emerged on the Indian political scene in 1942, its genesis can be traced to the late 1920s when Saumyendranath Tagore, who had joined the communist movement during the years of its formation, fell out with both the CPI and the Communist International.

Born in the famous Tagore family of Bengal in 1901, Saumyendranath took part in the Non-Cooperation Movement. After the withdrawal of the movement, he parted company with the INC under Gandhi's leadership and was drawn to the communist movement. In June 1927, Tagore, a leader of the Bengal WPP, went to Moscow to apprise the leaders of the Communist International of the state of affairs of India's communist movement. During his conversation with Osip Piatnitsky, the general secretary of the central committee of the Communist International, Tagore alleged that the leaders of the Communist International were being misled by M.N. Roy regarding 'the work of the communists in India'. Commenting later on the conversation with Piatnitsky, Tagore observed:

> It was evident from the talk that a quite different picture of the communist activities had been presented to the Comintern [Communist International] by M.N. Roy. Piatnitsky had an idea that there were hundreds of communists in India in those days … which [actually] did not exceed more than a dozen.[33]

Tagore also alleged that although the Communist International had placed enormous sums at the disposal of Roy, 'hardly any money had been received in India and the growth of the communist movement was tremendously handicapped due to the lack of money and literature.'[34]

However, a clash took place between Tagore and the leaders of the Communist International during the sixth congress of the Communist International in Moscow in 1928. On the question of the *raison d'être* of the WPPs, the stand of the Communist International was clarified by Otto Wilhelm Kuusinen who maintained that in the colonial and semi-colonial countries it would be a mistake to encourage the formation of such parties. He said: 'To consider such parties as a substitute for a real communist party would be a serious mistake. We are in bloc with the peasantry, but we will not have anything to do with fusion of various classes.'[35] Criticizing Kuusinen's contention as an example of 'pure and simple professional dogmatism', Tagore, who went to the sixth congress as a representative of the WPP of Bengal, averred that in the colonial and semi-colonial countries the formation of WPPs were of paramount importance because an anti-imperialist front was bound to 'take the organizational form of Workers' and Peasants' Party [WPP] composed of the urban intelligentsia and the petty-bourgeois elements, under the leadership of the proletariat'.[36]

After the sixth congress, Tagore travelled through a number of European countries and when he returned to India in 1934, he found the communists isolated from the national movement. He urged them to eschew their ultra-Left policy and take part in the anti-imperialist national movement. He was, however, totally against the communists' alliance with the INC. And when, in accordance with the resolution of the seventh congress of the Communist International in Moscow in 1935, the communists decided to enter the INC, he broke away from the CPI and formed a new group called the Communist League.

Tagore then launched upon his crusade against almost all the political parties and groups that participated in the united front. He regarded the INC as a bourgeois organization and branded Gandhi as 'the greatest reactionary force in the world'.[37] He also denounced the Congress socialists as betrayers of socialism and declared that the CSP had come into existence as a result of an alliance between the

Congress socialists and the reactionary bourgeoisie.[38] After analysing the class character of different social elements in India, Tagore pointed out that no anti-imperialist revolutionary movement could ever be successful unless it was carried on by the toiling masses under the leadership of the proletariat.[39] He also held that although socialism was the highest goal, during the bourgeois-democratic phase of the revolution in India the proletarian party must put forward a minimum programme on the basis of which the anti-imperialist struggle was to be carried on. This programme should aim at the violent overthrow of British imperialism and the establishment of a provisional revolutionary government and a democratic republic of workers and peasants. And it was on the basis of this programme that Tagore founded the RCPI in 1942. Justifying the formation of the RCPI, Tagore declared that no other Leftist party was capable of achieving a proletarian revolution in India because all the existing parties suffered not only from organizational weakness but also from ideological bankruptcy. The RCPI, he claimed, was the only true Leftist party in the country.

When the war broke out, the RCPI characterized it as an imperialist one and declared that the time was most opportune for the violent overthrow of British rule in India. It rejected the Cripps' proposal and lent its full support to the Quit India Movement.[40]

As the war came to a close, the party believed an Indian revolution to be around the corner; but it felt the revolution did not come off because both the Right reactionaries and the so-called Leftists had betrayed the Indian people and frittered away their revolutionary zeal. Like Forward Bloc and the RSP, the RCPI also held that the transfer of power was the result of a 'political conspiracy hatched by British imperialism and the Indian bourgeoisie'. The partition of the country, it declared, was a betrayal and surrender to British imperialism.[41]

THE BOLSHEVIK PARTY OF INDIA

Like the RCPI, the BPI was also formed by a group of dissident communists who felt that the CPI had failed to champion the cause of the Indian working class. Although it was formally established in 1939, its origin can be traced to the Bengal Labour Party (BLP) organized by N. Dutt Mazumdar in 1933. The BLP adopted a thesis which declared that it represented a 'new front of the toiling classes against the new front of bourgeois constitutionalism' represented by the INC. The twofold task of the party was declared to be the 'emancipation of the nation' and the 'emancipation of the classes'.[42]

Although initially the communists bitterly attacked the new party charging it of 'economism and reformism', by 1936 the BLP became a group inside the CPI.[43] The BLP leaders, however, continued to be highly critical of the communist policy and tactics in regard to a number of crucial questions. They supported Subhas Chandra Bose at the Tripuri session of the INC and castigated the communists for not joining the Forward Bloc and for temporizing with the Right-reactionary leadership of the INC. As the differences with the communists began to grow wider, prominent BLP leaders, such as N. Dutt Mazumdar, Sisir Roy, Ajit Roy and Biswanath Dubey, broke away from the CPI, and formed the BPI in 1939.

When war broke out in Europe, the BPI regarded it as an imperialist war and, like the RCPI, began to campaign for a massive anti-imperialist revolutionary movement against the British. It also declared that as the INC was neither interested in nor capable of leading this struggle, it was to be carried on by the toiling masses of India. After the German attack upon the Soviet Union, the BPI lined up behind the CPI, characterized it as a people's war and advocated unconditional support for British war efforts. When the INC decided to start the Quit India Movement, the BPI went to the extent of demanding that the Quit India Resolution should be withdrawn as a precondition of an early settlement with the British government.[44] In a resolution adopted by its central committee in 1943, it urged all anti-imperialist and anti-fascist forces to rally round British war efforts for the defence of India.[45]

Like all other Leftists, the leaders of the BPI also denounced the transfer of power and partition of the country as an act of treachery on the part of the Indian bourgeoisie.

THE BOLSHEVIK LENINIST PARTY

The Bolshevik Leninist Party was formed in 1941 by a group of Trotskyite revolutionaries who believed that a revolution in India could be brought about not by toeing the line of the Communist International but on the basis of the doctrine of revolutionary radicalism or what is called the theory of 'permanent revolution'.[46] These radical revolutionaries, most prominent of whom were Indra Sen and Ajit Roy, brought out a journal called *New Spark* and in collaboration with the socialist parties of Ceylon and Burma formed the Federation of Bolshevik-Leninist Parties of Burma, Ceylon and India.

Immediately after the formation of the party, it adopted a thesis entitled *The Revolution in India*, which declared that the Indian bourgeoisie, represented by the INC, was a counter-revolutionary force which was neither interested in nor capable of leading a revolutionary mass movement. It also declared that although the character of the impending revolution in India was a bourgeois-democratic one, it could be converted into a proletarian revolutionary movement.[47]

The Bolshevik Leninists' attitude towards other Leftist parties was also equally unfavourable. The Forward Bloc, the CSP and the Radical Democratic Party were nothing but 'defensive coloration of the bourgeoisie before the masses' and as such they were unfit for the task of carrying on the Indian revolution. Similarly, the Bolshevik Leninists held that the CPI, the RCPI and the BPI were also incapable of leading a revolutionary mass movement because both organizationally and ideologically they were either totally bankrupt or servile to the Communist International. Therefore, they could neither represent the toiling masses of India nor could lead them to the path of proletarian revolution. The Bolshevik Leninist Party, it was declared, was the only political organization, which could fulfil this task. The immediate programme of the party was the capture of power, the formation of a revolutionary Constituent Assembly and ultimately the establishment of a workers' and peasants' government under the leadership of the proletariat. It opposed the war throughout as an imperialist war and also characterized the transfer of power as betrayal and treachery of the Indian bourgeoisie.

THE RADICAL DEMOCRATIC PARTY

After his expulsion from the Communist International, M.N. Roy came to India in 1930 and with some of his followers, most notably Tayab Shaikh, Sundar Kabadi, S. Shetty and V.B. Karnik, formed what came to be known as the Roy Group. Soon after his arrival in India when Roy was arrested in connection with the Cawnpore Conspiracy Case, his followers held aloft the banner of Royism and proceeded to organize a Left-nationalist front of radical revolutionaries to espouse the demands of 'the inarticulate masses'.[48] L.P. Sinha wrote:

> The cardinal feature of this new plan was that the masses of the Indian people were not yet politically conscious and that the political issue of national freedom must be made intelligible to them. For this purpose, the Left-wing radicals inside the Congress [INC] should forge themselves into a well-disciplined and functioning party with a scientific programme of national democratic revolution. They should offer the masses a programme of action and lead them in the struggle for partial demands. It was out of this struggle that would grow both a political consciousness of the masses and a mass organization. The Roy Group held that this was the only realistic approach to the situation.[49]

Originally, the Royists lighted upon the idea of organizing a revolutionary party of the working class but soon afterwards gave up this idea and concentrated their attention to the formation of a Left-nationalist front inside the INC. Their efforts found expression in the League of Radical Congressmen, founded under the leadership of Roy in 1937. The league was formed, Roy pointed out, to revitalize and democratize the INC. It was at this time that Roy became a bitter critic of Marxism.

> He started saying that the last word was not said by Marx a century ago; that Marxism was not a body of doctrines but a system or method of studying social facts and phenomena. Philosophically, while still clinging to general creed of materialism, he renamed it as the philosophy of physical realism.[50]

In 1940, when Roy came to realize that it was 'impossible for the revolutionary forces to organize themselves into a political party inside the Congress [INC]', he broke away and formed a separate party called the Radical Democratic Party.[51] After the formation of this party, Roy began to propagate the idea that the impending Indian revolution, which was essentially bourgeois-democratic in character, could be brought about by a multi-class party consisting of the workers, peasants and the petty-bourgeois elements under the leadership of the urban petty-bourgeois radicals. The proletariat alone could not spearhead this revolution because it was not advanced enough to fulfil this revolutionary task.[52] The INC, he maintained, had all the characteristics of such a multi-class party, but it was the reactionary Gandhian leadership which stood in the way of its becoming a revolutionary organization. Roy further pointed out that no other political party in India could fulfil this task. While the Forward Bloc had no ideology worth the name, the CSP had completely surrendered itself to Gandhism. The CPI was also not capable of fulfilling this task because it was based on 'ill-digested' Marxism. Ridiculing the communist idea that a national revolution under the proletarian leadership was imminent in India, Roy contended that the idea of developing the anti-imperialist struggle by sharpening the class struggle was 'sheer humbug' because under the peculiar conditions of India an anti-imperialist revolutionary movement could be waged only on the basis of the 'cohesiveness of social relations and the uniting factors'. In this movement, the proletariat could play its proper role only under the leadership of the petty-bourgeois radicals.[53]

Unlike other Leftist parties, Roy's attitude towards the war was that it was neither an imperialist nor an anti-fascist war and that it could not be regarded as a war between democracy and fascism. While Germany was not an imperialist power, he argued, Britain was also not a democracy in the true sense of the term. Moreover, to think that imperialism could fight its ally fascism was to view the problem from an entirely wrong angle. Describing the war as a war of accident and not of design, Roy averred that it was essentially a conflict between revolutionary and counter-revolutionary forces. The war, he pointed out, would inevitably lead to the defeat of fascism and the consequent strengthening of revolutionary forces all over the world.[54] From this argument, Roy came to the conclusion that India's interest would be best served by collaborating with British war efforts.[55]

Roy's attitude towards the transfer of power was also at variance with that of other Leftist parties. Although he did not like the partition of the country and transfer of power to a particular political party, he, on the whole, accepted the Mountbatten Plan as a *fait accompli*.

NOTES AND REFERENCES (CHAPTER 6)

1 Myron Weiner, *Party Politics in India: The Development of a Multi-Party System* (Princeton, NJ: Princeton University Press, 1957), 118–19.
2 Subhas Chandra Bose, *Selected Speeches of Subhas Chandra Bose* (Delhi: Government of India Publications Division, 1962), 112–13.
3 Ibid., 113.
4 For a detailed account of the genesis of the Forward Bloc, see Subhas Chandra Bose, *The Indian Struggle, 1935–1942*, Vol. II (Calcutta: Netaji Publication Society, 1952). Also see Subhas Chandra Bose, *Crossroads: Collected Works, 1938–1940* (Calcutta: Netaji Research Bureau, 1962), 174–75.
5 Bose, *Crossroads—Collected Works, 1938–1940*, 174–75.
6 *The Congress Socialist* (18 June 1939).
7 Bose, *Crossroads—Collected Works, 1938–1940*, 175.
8 Bose, *Selected Speeches of Subhas Chandra Bose*, 114.
9 Ibid., 115.
10 Ibid.
11 Ibid., 114.
12 Ibid., 116.
13 Ibid. According to Myron Weiner,

> [The Forward Bloc] had no clear ideology as had the other Leftist parties. While Bose talked of Marxism and socialism, he had never clearly spelled out his ideas except as they pertained to the ways and means by which independence was to be attained. The party thus had a programme but it could not be said to have had an ideology, in the sense that it had no general outlook especially for post-independent India.

See Weiner, *Party Politics in India: The Development of a Multi-Party System*, 125.
14 Bose, *The Indian Struggle, 1935–1942*, Vol. II, 89.
15 Bose, *Selected Speeches of Subhas Chandra Bose*, 123.
16 R.C. Majumdar, *History of the Freedom Movement in India*, Vol. III (Calcutta: Firma K.L. Mukhopadhyay, 1963), 606.
17 For Subhas Chandra Bose's subsequent activities leading to the formation of the Indian National Army, see ibid., 700–37.
18 *Programme of the Post-War Revolution: Draft Manifesto of the Forward Bloc* (Bombay: Forward Bloc, 1946), 65.
19 Ashok Ghosh, *A Short History of the All India Forward Bloc* (Calcutta: Bengal Lokmat Printers, 2001), 45.
20 Ibid., 55.
21 *Indian Annual Register* (Calcutta, 1947), 197.
22 For an account of the early terrorist-revolutionary organizations, see the *Sedition Committee Report* (Calcutta: Superintendent Government Printing, 1918).
23 This account of the Hindustan Republic Association was included in a note on 'Terrorism in India' prepared by the Government of India and submitted to the Joint Committee on Constitutional Reforms on 30 November 1933. See Majumdar, *History of the Freedom Movement in India*, Vol. III, 493.
24 For an account of the daring Chittagong Armoury Raid, see Kalpana Dutt, *Chittagong Armoury Raiders: Reminiscences* (Bombay: People's Publishing House, 1945).
25 L.P. Sinha, *Left Wing in India* (Muzaffarpur: New Publishers, 1965), 527.

26 *The Thesis and Platform of Action of the Revolutionary Socialist Party of India: What Revolutionary Socialism Stands For* (Calcutta: RSP, 1946), 7–9.

27 Ibid., 15.

28 For an account of the Subhas Chandra Bose–M.K. Gandhi conflict, see third section, 'The Anti-Imperialist United Front', of Chapter 3, 'Communism in India', of this book.

29 *War Thesis of the RSPI* (Calcutta: RSP, 1940), 21.

30 *Thesis of the RSP on the Russo-German War—Intensify National Struggle: On To Revolutionary Defence of USSR* (Calcutta: RSP, 1941), 15–18.

31 *On National Struggle of August 1942* (Calcutta: RSP, 1942).

32 Sinha, *Left Wing in India*, 552–53.

33 Saumyendranath Tagore, *Historical Development of the Communist Movement in India* (Calcutta: Red Front Press, 1944), 10–11.

34 Ibid.

35 Otto Wilhelm Kuusinen, 'The Revolutionary Movement in the Colonies', *International Press Correspondence*, (4 October 1928).

36 *International Press Correspondence* (30 October 1928).

37 Saumyendranath Tagore, *People's Front or the Front Against the People?* (Calcutta: Ganavani Publishing House, 1940). Also see Saumyendranath Tagore, *United Front or Betrayal?* (Calcutta: Ganavani Publishing House, 1938).

38 For Saumyendranath Tagore's attitude towards the CSP and the CPI, see Saumyendranath Tagore, *Congress Socialism?* (Lucknow: Jagriti Publishing House, 1942) and Saumyendranath Tagore, *Communism and Fetishism* (Calcutta: Provat Sen, 1940).

39 For Saumyendranath Tagore's political ideas, see Saumyendranath Tagore, *Bourgeois-Democratic Revolution and India* (Calcutta: Ganavani Publishing House, 1946) and Saumyendranath Tagore, *Permanent Revolution* (Calcutta: Samar Bose, 1944).

40 Saumyendranath Tagore, *Revolution and Quit India* (Calcutta: Ganavani Publishing House, 1946).

41 For the RCPI's attitude towards independence and partition, see Saumyendranath Tagore, *The Hour Has Struck* (Calcutta: Ganavani Publishing House, 1949).

42 This thesis was published in the first issue of the BPI's organ *New Front* on 1 September 1933, from Calcutta.

43 Sinha, *Left Wing in India*, 268–69. Also see Weiner, *Party Politics in India: The Development of a Multi-Party System*, 123.

44 It may be noted here that N. Dutt Mazumdar did not subscribe to the BPI's policy towards the Second World War and the Quit India Movement. He regarded the war as an imperialist one and supported the Quit India Movement. As a result, he was expelled from the party in 1945.

45 For the BPI's policy towards the Second World War and the Quit India Movement, see *Indian Politics, 1941–1944* (Calcutta: BPI, 1944).

46 For a discussion on the theory of 'permanent revolution', see George Lichtheim, *Marxism: An Historical and Critical Study* (London: Routledge and Kegan Paul, 1961), 122–29.

47 For an account of the Bolshevik Leninist Party's ideology and orientation, see pamphlet *The Revolution in India* (Edinburgh: Tait Memorial Committee, 1942).

48 See S. Shetty's observations in the *Mahratta*, 1 October 1933, as quoted by Sinha, *Left Wing in India*, 265.

49 Sinha, *Left Wing in India*, 265–66.

50 Ibid., 483.

51 *Indian Annual Register* (Calcutta, 1940), 344. Also see M.N. Roy, *Scientific Politics* (Calcutta: Renaissance Publishers, 1942), 148.

52 Roy, *Scientific Politics*, 72–78.

53 Ibid., 112.

54 For a detailed account of the Radical Democratic Party's policy towards the Second World War, see a collection of its resolutions during the war in M.N. Roy, *India and War* (Lucknow: A.P. Singh, 1942).

55 It may be mentioned here that during this period, M.N. Roy was exposed to public odium when it was widely believed that his party received a monthly grant of Rupees 13,000 from the Government of India as a reward for its support to war efforts. See Sinha, *Left Wing in India*, 523.

7 Appraisal

'The evolution of a movement', said Subhas Chandra Bose, 'is analogous to that of a tree. It grows from within and at every stage it throws out new branches, so that there may be ever increasing progress. When no fresh branches sprout forth, the movement may be presumed to be in a process of decay or death'. But, as Bose pointed out, while 'every movement draws its sustenance from the soil from which it springs, it also assimilates nourishment coming from outside—from the atmosphere, environment etc. Internal sustenance and external nourishment are both necessary for a living movement'.[1]

The Leftist movement in India, like all other living movements, also grew from within and drew sustenance from the Indian soil. It emerged out of the complex political web in which India's struggle for freedom was caught at the close of the First World War and became inextricably intertwined with the mainstream of the nationalist movement. Their coalescence not only gave rise to many stresses, strains and cataclysms but also represented an ideological leaven imparting an extraordinary vitality to the national movement. It imparted a new dimension to the freedom movement, gave a new substance to the political task of emancipating the nation from foreign domination and invested the idea of political freedom with a revolutionary socio-economic content.

I

Leftism in India, since the close of the First World War developed along two mainstreams, namely, communism and democratic socialism. While the first was as a projection of the international communist movement controlled at that time by the Communist International, the second corresponded broadly to the tradition of Fabian socialism and represented the most meaningful check to communism in India. Although the character and the course of the movements set in motion by both the ideological systems was conditioned by India's struggle for freedom, during this period communism could hardly identify itself with the ethos of Indian nationalism. As a result, its appeal, which sought to derive potency from the anti-imperialist animus of the people, found lodgement only with a group of sharply oriented indigenous intelligentsia. It was from this group that the communist movement drew its leadership as well as the intermediate layers of cadres while the vast mass of the population remained alienated to the revolutionary tenets of Marxism.

The failure of communism to gain a foothold in India during the nationalist movement can, therefore, largely be attributed to, as Harry J. Benda put it, the close reading of Marxist scriptures, which were actually quite irrelevant to Asian developments at that time.[2] And apart from its isolation from the mainstream of nationalist forces, the factors that contributed to the failure of the communist movement in India were alien loyalty, lack of unified leadership, factionalism and indiscipline and above all, erratic strategy during the entire course of its tortuous career.

Indeed, until the end of the First World War, Marxism in India was one of the least influential intellectual currents that had entered from the West. It would probably have remained in this state if the Bolshevik Revolution had not taken place in Russia in 1917, if a growing section of Indian intellectuals had not become critical of the revolutionary potential of Gandhi and if the rebels among the frustrated Indian émigrés, fired with revolutionary zeal and scattered all over the world, had not tended to look first to Germany and then to Russia for support in India's struggle for freedom. The romantic appeal of the revolutionary ideas of Marx and the reflected glory of the new regime in Russia fired the imagination of this section of Indian intellectuals and erstwhile terrorists who now saw in Gandhi a manifestation of the forces of reaction who had been obstructing the dynamic play of mass struggle by his cult of non-violence. They came to believe that the emancipation of India could be achieved not by the 'weak and watery reformism of Gandhi' but by revolutionary mass struggle against British imperialism and its Indian allies.

Although the appeal of communism came mainly from the Russian Revolution and the regime it brought to power, it is important to bear in mind that by the time Russia emerged as a symbol of resistance to imperialism, India's nascent nationalism had already evolved a set of national ideals which not only 'forestalled the possibility of there being an ideological vacuum' but also precluded the possibility of communism's identification with Indian nationalism.[3] These ideals were characterized by India's traditional social and cultural overtones and as such were somewhat antithetical to the revolutionary creed of Marxism–Leninism. Politically, nationalism in India found expression in, as Carlos Romulo put it: 'A simple and straightforward freedom movement from colonial status, untainted either by the racialist and regionalist appeal of Japanese anti-Western propaganda or by the ideological appeal of communism'.[4]

Thus, although nationalism in India had been linked with anti-imperialism and the demand for political and socio-economic justice, it could not be identified with communism. The leaders of the Indian nationalist movement fought for social and economic reforms as ardently as for freedom from foreign domination, but never subordinated these primary objectives to the ideology of proletarian internationalism. While orthodox leaders, such as Gandhi, subordinated the idea of nationalism as representing the political and economic emancipation of India to less materialistic and more spiritual conceptions of national regeneration, more radical leaders, such as Jawaharlal Nehru, accepted nationalism as an inevitable step to social and economic progress. Of the two distinct varieties of nationalism—the conservative and the reformist—they believed in the latter. They accepted internationalism in the sense of nationalistic universalism—a concept compounded of the political, economic and social liberation of the nation and the universal character of this aspiration.

The dilemma of the Indian communists lay in the fact that they could not rule this nationalistic aspiration out of account in India; neither could they accept it in view of the Marxian theory that nationalism was in essence a bourgeois phenomenon—'an expression of the rivalry over markets among the new entrepreneurial classes of various ethnic groups of nations'. As, according to Marxism, the prime movers of history were not nations but classes, the proletariat of the world were to be united by the bonds of international fraternity. How, then, could the Indian communists fight for nationalism which had its roots in the desire for exclusive domination over economic markets leading to the political separation of the proletariat into national constituents? As the communists were wont to say, cooperation with the national bourgeoisie meant supporting one bourgeois class against another. How, then, were the struggles for national liberation and proletarian internationalism to be reconciled?

This dilemma dates from the second congress of the Communist International in 1920 when Lenin, in his 'Draft Theses on National and Colonial Questions', urged all communist parties to render assistance to the bourgeois-democratic liberation movements. On the question of cooperation with the national movement of the colonial countries, faith in Marxian precepts did not blind Lenin to the potential strength of nationalism in Asia. He realized that in the situation prevailing in India where democratic movement and mass consciousness were still in the process of gestation, the realistic policy for the communists would be to utilize every opportunity to strengthen the anti-imperialist movement carried on by the bourgeois-democratic organizations. Lenin did not hesitate to opt for the same policy to strengthen Kemalist Turkey even while it was crushing the embryonic communist movement in Turkey. This policy, he believed, would weaken the economic foundation of imperialism by depriving the metropolis of markets and investments thus accelerating the process of awakening the colonial countries from feudalism to the stage of bourgeois-democratic revolution. But to the Indian communists, the stages of Indian social, economic and political development remained subjectively incomprehensible and it is little wonder that their objective application of Marxism was characterized by ideological–tactical confusions.

One such confusion related to the communist assessment of 'bourgeois nationalism', 'bourgeois-democratic movement' and 'the nationality question'.

Although the INC was a heterogeneous anti-imperialist national front representing, as it did, different shades of political opinion as well as divergent class interests from the feudal princes to the rack-rented peasants, from the new Indian bourgeoisie to the exploited working class, it may be contended that Indian nationalism was basically free from religious, linguistic, cultural or regional particularism. Leaders, such as Bal Gangadhar Tilak, wanted to combine Hindu revivalism with nationalistic agitation to give Indian nationalism a mass appeal and to provide it with militancy and an aim believed to be more positive than the colonial self-government which was all that the moderate leaders of his time had hoped for. Eventually, however, the alliance of religious revivalism with radical nationalism failed to serve this purpose, because the insistence on religion as the driving force of the national movement retarded the real advance of the movement by alienating wide sections of Muslim opinion from the united struggle of the Indian people against imperialism. But although the combination of religious credo and political struggle did weaken the nationalist movement, it is fairly true to say that at least up to the date of provincial elections in 1937, Indian nationalism was broadly united in character in the sense that nobody till then seriously broached the view that Indians were not a single nation. And it was on this question that the communists demonstrated a regrettable penchant for distorting the character of Indian nationalism.

Although it was pointed out by Stalin that self-determination was a prerogative of the nationalities, not of religious communities, the Indian communists, revolutionary by profession and contemptuous of bourgeois sectarianism, conceded the communal basis of Indian nationalism and hailed the Muslim League as 'the premier political organization of the second largest community' of India. It is interesting to note here that although initially British communists, such as D.N. Pritt, Ben Bradley and R. Palme Dutt, expressed their forthright disapproval of the Muslim League's demand for Pakistan, it was not long before they came round to P.C. Joshi's thesis that the Muslims were a distinct nationality and therefore entitled to separate statehood. The CPI, however, was chary in officially espousing this policy because to do so would be a great blow to the ideological system of Marxism–Leninism. And it was to avoid the embarrassment of repudiating the ideological system of Marxism–Leninism that it was argued that the Indian people were not a single nationality but rather a collection of nationalities, some of them Hindus and some Muslims. It was in conformity with this policy that the CPI adopted a resolution in 1942 declaring India as multinational and classifying as many as 16 Indian nations. Four years later, in 1946, when the Cabinet Mission came to India to negotiate settlement of the Indian political deadlock, the communists put forward their multinational proposal and demanded that as there was no basis for a united India, the country should be divided into a number of states on the model of the Balkans.

Was this opinionated assessment of Indian nationalism conceived out of confusion or tactical compulsions? Perhaps both. For one thing, the Indian communists' failure to comprehend the true character of Indian nationalism came from the false analogy between the historical background and political aspirations of the various diverse elements in India and those in Russia. The analogy was false because the historic nationalities in Russia constituting an ethnographic Tower of Babel: Moldavians and Romanians in the south-west, Poles in the west, Lithuanians, Latvians, Estonians along the Baltic coast, Finns and the Karelians in the north-west and above all, Ukrainians, Georgians, Armenians as well as the whole family of Uralo-Altaic peoples, came into the Tsarist empire not through common aspirations but by force or the threat of it. The situation in India was different. For centuries, the diverse elements of the Indian people, while anxious to preserve their cultural and linguistic distinctiveness, were emotionally determined to forge a strong national unity. It was because of this deep-rooted and broad-based foundation of Indian nationalism that the CPI's demand for the division of the country into 16 separate states found no echo in the millions of Indians.

But it would be an oversimplification to suggest that the CPI's nationality policy resulted from ignorance of the historical perspective of the Indian situation as well as of the unifying bond of the Indian ethos. In fact, that the communist nationality policy was a part of its strategy was indicated by K.M. Ashraf's observation that the question of a separate Muslim state did not arise except in relation to the tactics and strategy of the CPI. Perhaps the communists thought that by weaning away the Muslims from the INC, they would be able to rally the separatist elements in their favour and capture the national movement. Probably they also hoped that if India were divided into a number of sovereign states and if they could capture even one, it would be easy for them to pursue a policy of liberation for the rest.

In the period of its open identification with separatist elements, the CPI was frequently accused of taking pro-Muslim League and anti-national postures. To the faithful, it had been able to explain away this charge by invoking the party's strategy of forging a revolutionary unity among the Muslim groups and eventually among all regional ethnic groups of India. To the less confirmed sympathizers, it sought to defend its policy on the ground that this was consistent with the 'awakening of a distinct nationality to new life and individual national consciousness'. But the rationale of this policy was largely dependent upon the continued INC-League alienation and the absence of a compromise between them. There is, however, little doubt that this policy of driving a wedge in the Indian national unity at a time when the majority of the leaders, the intelligentsia and the common people were desperately hoping for an INC-League rapprochement proved to be a great tactical blunder which contributed heavily to the CPI's political isolation.

Moreover, the CPI could provide few practical guidelines governing its attitude towards Pakistan because the leaders of the Muslim League were not altogether amenable to the idea of an alliance with the communists for the fulfilment of their demand for Pakistan. Tactically, the collaboration with the Muslim League was not to differ radically from the united front with the INC, but the aim was somewhat different. While the primary objective of the earlier front with the INC had been to rally the Left-wing forces that would influence and eventually oust the INC leadership, the communist policy later envisaged the formation of a number of sovereign states so as to capture a stronghold for the purpose of extended action.

II

The mistake of the Indian communists in regard to the nationality policy lay mainly in the fact that in trying to reconcile the compulsion of events at home with the requirements of the international communist movement, they were too accustomed to look to the Soviet Union for inspiration and guidance, too inclined not to detach themselves from their dogmatic position and too little aware of the potentialities of the Indian nationalist movement.

Even Nehru, who saw a 'message of hope to the world' in the changes taking place in Soviet Russia immediately after the Bolshevik Revolution, blamed this for the communists' failing to strike a chord with the commoners in India's national movement.

> I cannot speak with much knowledge of what happened elsewhere, but I know that in India the Communist Party [CPI] is completely divorced from, and is ignorant of the national traditions that fill the minds of the people. It believes that communism necessarily implies a contempt for the past. So far as it is concerned, the history of the world began in November, 1917, and everything that preceded this was preparatory and leading up to it.
>
> Normally speaking, in a country like India with large number of people on the verge of starvation and the economic structure tracking up, communism should have a wide appeal. In a sense there is that vague appeal, but the Communist Party [CPI] cannot take advantage of it because it has cut itself off from the springs of national sentiment and speaks in a language which finds no echo in the hearts of the people. It remains an energetic, but small group, with no real roots.[5]

Thus, lacking the rich practical experience and the flexibility of a Mao Tse-Tung or a Ho Chi Minh, the leaders of the Indian communist movement had been inclined to force reality into the Procrustean bed of Marxism–Leninism and adopted foreign prescriptions, which were ill-suited to Indian conditions.

> The only true communist revolutions which have so far gained power outside Russia's sphere of military domination—those of Yugoslavia, China and North Vietnam—have all been led by men who, thanks to unusual circumstances, had succeeded in emancipating themselves from Russia's leading strings in the actual conduct of their struggles, and who had used this freedom of movement to capture the leadership of a national uprising against invading or colonial powers.[6]

Thus, while in China and Vietnam, the local communist parties could effectively combine the communist and nationalist leitmotifs, in India the communists drew their strength from abroad so much so that most of their policy guidelines had been formulated either in Moscow or in London, with little or no Indian participation. Indeed, one of the major obstacles to the success of communism in India was the fact that its lifeblood depended on frequent transfusions from abroad.

As early as 1919, looking forward to the future character of communist movements in the countries of Asia, Lenin urged the communist leaders of those regions to adapt themselves to the peculiar conditions which did not exist in the European countries and to evolve specific forms of revolutionary struggle against imperialism. But the history of the communist movement in India has been characterized not by the evolution of any specific form of revolutionary struggle but by complete dependence upon foreign guidance. The guidance, indeed, was provided from abroad in such a pervasive manner that in its 40-year-long history, the CPI could hardly evolve its own specific form of struggle and resolve any of its problems *en famille*. And it was this preponderant influence of alien inspiration that deprived the CPI of any special niche within the bloc of fraternal parties.

The CPI's dependence on Moscow was the direct result of two factors—the circumstances leading to the formation of the party and the crisis of leadership that it had faced since the early years of its growth. As the party did not grow spontaneously within India but was formed and nurtured abroad, it could be expected neither to take root in the Indian soil nor to produce a leader who could harness the radical forces arising from the socio-economic and political environment of India and assert the party's independence by projecting its image on to the international movement as a freewheeling entity. It is, indeed, a pity that the CPI, which drew in its ranks scores of brilliant and devoted young men of the country and whose following was only exceeded by the INC, could not produce a charismatic leader who could provide a nationwide revolutionary momentum under his leadership. And in the absence of such a leader, the CPI trod the perilous path of revolution like 'an orphan about whose guardianship nobody seemed certain, though M.N. Roy was the most persistent claimant'.[7]

During the early years of the communist movement, the Indian communists certainly had in Roy, described by Lenin as 'the symbol of revolution in the East', a leader whose extraordinary intellectual gifts, dynamism, experience and above all an overarching personality served as the fount of inspiration and guidance. His rapid and dazzling ascendancy as one of the leaders of the international communist movement also distinguished him as a unique figure among the *dramatis personae* of their time. But his break with the Communist International in 1929 removed from the Indian communist movement a towering figure who was not to be equalled in the years to come.

Roy's expulsion from the Communist International and denigration by his fellow travellers were symptomatic of the intense jealousy, rivalry and factional squabbling not only in the top echelons of the international communist movement but also among the various communist groups in India. In fact, internecine conflict over leadership has remained one of the persistent features of Indian communism throughout the period of this study. The story of the party's formation itself had all the makings of a wrestling bout in which the major contenders for leadership, notably Roy and the members of the Indian Independence Committee in Berlin, applied all tactics of political jiu-jitsu in order to force an outright victory over each other. Many others came from India to join the contest and about the same time the leaders of the CPGB also appeared on the scene to establish, as Roy put it, their 'protectorate' over the Indian communist movement.

Factional squabbling, struggles for leadership and mutual acrimony among the communist leaders not only resulted in disorganization and indiscipline in the party ranks but also created problems for the group leaders working in various parts of the country. When the Indian delegates assembled in Moscow on the occasion of the 10th plenum of the ECCI, there was a general expectation among the communists at home that the party organization would be toned up and there would be a definite orientation of the party's policy towards major national issues. But the proceedings of the 10th plenum, far from holding out any such promise, left the party rank and file in utter confusion. As there was no central party organization at that time in India but only factional groups operating in no fewer than five centres, it became extremely difficult for the group leaders to come to grips with the national issues of the day. And when many of these leaders were arrested, confusion was so great that each group broke up into subgroups claiming direct relation with the Communist International.

Even more indicative of the fragility of the party organization was the complete lack of harmony between the leaders involved in the Meerut Conspiracy Case and the younger recruits who joined the party after the detention of the veteran leaders. Later, this developed into quarrels among the new recruits themselves. Commenting on the squabbles between the 'outright communists and the erstwhile fellow travellers who now felt that they had taken the wrong road in their collaboration with the minions of Moscow', Jawaharlal Nehru, who took a keen interest in the case and served as a member of the Meerut Conspiracy Case Defence Committee, remarked in his *Autobiography* that he and his colleagues had to face great difficulty in dealing with the case owing to intense dissension among the accused leaders themselves.

III

All these factors—the irrelevance of Marxian ideology to Indian nationalism, lack of unified leadership and factional struggle—were responsible for the absence of a uniform and consistent communist policy towards the Indian national movement. That even the monolithic Communist International could not evolve such a policy was due to the fact that

India's national culture, the unique aspirations of her [its] people, the fundamental national ideals and objectives governing the struggle for freedom—all these factors did not enter into the calculations of the

Communist International and the Soviet government. The only consideration which entered into the Comintern [Communist International] and the Soviet calculations with regard to the Indian freedom movement was the actual and potential usefulness of India as a centre of revolt against capitalism and as a base for the further expansion of communism.[8]

As a result, since the inception of the Indian communist movement its attitude towards the nationalist movement oscillated between opposition and cooperation in order to suit the ulterior objectives of international communism.

The history of the communist movement in India from the close of the First World War to independence falls into five distinct periods—each a record of erratic strategy and ideological confusion. The first was the period till the Meerut Conspiracy Case when communism made considerable headway in India. The second was the period of political wilderness when the communists attempted to win over the masses by attacking the nationalist leaders and in the process isolated themselves from the main-stream of the freedom movement. The third was the period of the anti-imperialist united front when the communists identified themselves with the Leftist forces of the country in order to capture the nationalist movement. The fourth was the period when the communists collaborated with British war efforts and as a reward emerged from illegality. And the last was the period of disillusionment between the end of the Second World War and Indian independence.

During the first period, the communists gained considerable influence in the Indian political life, particularly on the labour front. But this was due more to the widespread surge of radical forces in India following the suspension of the Non-Cooperation Movement and genuine popular sympathy for the communists than to the skills of the party leadership. In fact, so great was the popular sympathy for the Meerut prisoners that even the CWC, contrary to its usual practice, set up a central defence committee and made a grant of 1,500 rupees for the defence of the communist leaders. Moreover, INC leaders, such as Motilal Nehru, issued an appeal to the public to contribute liberally to the defence fund of the communist prisoners. Even Gandhi paid a visit to the Meerut prison in the autumn of 1929 to express his sympathy to the communist leaders. It is also noteworthy in this connection that in 1928 when the government introduced in the Central Legislative Assembly the Public Safety Bill, a measure directed against the communists and the foreign agitators, such as Philip Spratt and Ben Bradley, almost all the INC leaders opposed the Bill and ultimately defeated it.

Such a flow of unreserved sympathy for the communists from all shades of nationalist opinion and the Indian press, widespread unrest in every sector of Indian society, the emergence of the Congress Left wing, Jawaharlal Nehru's open predilection for socialist ideas and active participation in the Communist International-sponsored League Against Imperialism, the profound impact of radical ideas on impressionable youth and intellectuals and above all, the awakening of the workers and peasants—all these held out a golden opportunity to the communists to derive a long mileage in their march towards revolutionary goals. But the communists failed to take full advantage of this favourable situation mainly on account of the fact that the CPI was itself a divided house without any articulate leadership. They were also unable to determine the extent to which their policy was compatible with that of the emerging Left within the INC. This, in turn, had resulted from doctrinal confusion and conflicting advice from abroad, which left the party ranks in India groping for their proper place in the nationalist movement. The split in the trade union movement was the direct outcome of this disarray in the party organization and leadership. Thus, although the political atmosphere was sufficiently charged to evoke popular enthusiasm for communist revolutionary methods, the CPI lacked both organizational and ideological articulation which was needed to harness the surging tide of discontent.

During their period in the political wilderness, the emergence of the Congress Left wing under the leadership of Jawaharlal Nehru and Subhas Chandra Bose held out an opportunity to the communists to identify themselves with the radical components of the INC so as to capture the national movement against imperialism. But they not only ignored the Congress Left wing but also openly denounced it as a counter-revolutionary force. They regarded it as 'the most harmful and dangerous obstacle to the victory of the Indian revolution' and declared that their primary task was to expose its 'reformist character'.

This hostile attitude towards the radical forces of the INC stemmed from two factors. In the first place, the disastrous course of events in China where the Communist–Kuomintang alliance ended in a shattering blow to the communist movement, profoundly influenced the Indian communists' attitude towards the INC leadership including its Left wing. In China, the communists tried to capitalize on the gulf between the Right and the Left wings of the Kuomintang and thereby to direct the revolution towards radical socio-economic orientation. This effort resulted in their expulsion from the Kuomintang and the liquidation of many communists. This disastrous outcome of the Communist–Kuomintang alliance in China raised among the Indian communists the inevitable question of whether the class orientation of the INC was the same as that of the Kuomintang. To this question, the Indian communists answered in the affirmative, for they had no doubt that in spite of their radical phrases, the Left elements of the INC could not participate in the communist revolution.

This drawing of a parallel between Indian and Chinese conditions brings us to the second factor: the failure of the Indian communists to comprehend the unique character of the Indian nationalist movement. The fact that there had always been a reluctance within the communist leadership to take a pragmatic approach to the changing conditions of the nationalist movement shows that their tactical guidelines were astonishingly unrealistic. As a result, although radicalism grew apace throughout the turbulent 1920s and 1930s, the communists could neither keep pace with the march of events nor effect a sustained relationship with the Leftist forces inside the nationalist movement. The communist leaders themselves later admitted that it was a mistake to take a Left-sectarian view of the Indian situation and not to parti-cipate in the mass movements organized by the INC and organizations affiliated with it. In the seventh congress of the Communist International, Wang Ming chided the Indian communists for their 'Left-sectarian errors' and pointed out that the CPI had failed to operate as an independent political force because it was too weak and sectarian to lead the masses in their anti-imperialist struggle. He, therefore, urged the Indian communists 'to support, extend and participate in all anti-imperialist mass activities not excluding those which are under national reformist leadership'.

Thus, by the mid-1930s, when the communists decided to emerge from the wilderness and cultivate cooperation with the INC and other progressive forces, the united front could serve little purpose, largely on account of the fact that the new policy was prompted more by the interests of international communism than by those of India's nationalist aspirations. This was evident from the fact that despite slogans of unity, the communists were still equating the class character of the INC with that of the Kuomintang. In fact, they were so accustomed to look at the Indian situation in terms of either Russian or Chinese experience that they were tempted to overlook the innate differences between the INC and the Kuomintang. They forgot that from having been a truly revolutionary organization under Sun Yat Sen, the Kuomintang, after his death in 1924, lost its economic and social purpose and turned into a conservative and reactionary party controlled by the military. Socially, it spearheaded reaction with the slogan of neo-Confucianism, which had no longer any appeal for the people. Economically, it was anchored to a system of bureaucratic capitalism, which led to the concentration of all economic and political power in the hands of a few. Besides, it became ridden with numerous competing factions without any common ideology or a common cause. The dominant factions—the Central Club (CC) (or organization) Clique, the so-called Whampoa Clique and the Political Science Clique—vied with each other for selfish gains without addressing themselves to any clearly defined ideology or programme. It was, therefore, otiose to draw a parallel between this unstable coalition of militarism, reaction and opportunism and the INC, which, its heterogeneous class composition notwithstanding, had a solid party organization, an ideology, a programme and a cause.

Thus, at a time when a united front against imperialism was thought to be of paramount national interest, the communists' ceaseless tirade against the INC, including its Left wing, did more harm than anything else to defeat the very purpose of the united front. It was rightly pointed out by Ming that the Left-sectarian attitude of the Indian communists served as an example of how not to carry on the tactics of an anti-imperialist united front. A popular front of the progressive forces against imperialism could not be brought about on the basis of dubious strategies and superficial attachments, rather it depended for its success on close identification of both ends and means. A combination of mass support and articulate leadership alone could bring success to a revolutionary strategy. And as the Indian communists stood aloof from the masses and their immediate political aspirations, success constantly eluded them.

But despite the failure of the united front, the period definitely provided the communists with some tangible grounds for optimism. Notwithstanding the fact that the CPI was still organizationally illegal, their cooperation with the progressive forces helped them not only to emerge from political quarantine but also to play an increasingly important role in Indian politics. However, this was possible because of the growing political consciousness of the people and an all-round acceleration of political activities in the country. In fact, the period witnessed such a tremendous awakening of the masses that the communists had little difficulty in stepping up their activities and winning a position of considerable strength and influence among the radical elements of the country.

But whatever success the communists thus achieved was thrown away when the Second World War broke out in 1939. As subsequent events showed, the war hit the Indian communists extremely hard and they had to pay dearly for their mistakes and somersaults during the war period. K.M. Panikkar observed:

> Their prestige as a spearhead of nationalism, as a group which was balancing the conservative elements in the National Congress [INC] and as workers among peasants and factory labourers continued to grow till they threw the whole of these assets away by their alliance with the British government after the Soviets entered the war.[9]

In fact, by allying themselves with British imperialism, the Indian communists forfeited their right to identify themselves with the national movement, and it is no wonder that even today this blunder is used as a convenient stick with which to beat the communists.

The international situation in the wake of the Nazi menace provided the Indian communists with a unique opportunity to consolidate their position by joining hands with all the anti-imperialist forces against both British and German imperialism and to ride high on the tide of popular nationalist sentiment. They could have taken advantage of the initial vacillation of the INC leadership in opposing British war policy and rallied the anti-war forces so as to utilize the war crisis for the achievement of national freedom. But the communists failed to seize the opportunity because they were advised by the leaders of the Communist International to continue the united front tactics even at the crucial stage and at the same time to intensify the pressure on the established leadership.

This cautious approach was necessitated by the apprehension of the Communist International that the British might attack the Soviet Union using Iran and India as the springboard of aggression. In the event of such an attack, the subcontinent would become a jumping-off ground of great importance and the renunciation of the anti-imperialist united front policy would only strengthen the hands of the British in its design against the Soviet Union. Apart from this strategic consideration, uncertainty in the international situation might have been another reason for the cautious line urged by the Communist International.

When Germany attacked the Soviet Union in June 1941, the war entered a new phase and alignment of forces both on the international and national fronts underwent a dramatic change. And not surprisingly, the changed scenario created further confusion for the Indian communists. The communists who, since the outbreak of the war, had tried to transform the imperialist war into a war of national liberation, jockeying for leadership within the anti-imperialist liberation movement and trying to undercut the nationalist leadership by feeding on the people's anti-British sentiments, now faced the ordeal of turning round to the same audience and convince it that British imperialism had overnight become a 'prisoner in the people's camp' and that the main enemy of India was no longer Britain but Germany and Japan.

At this most crucial moment of India's struggle for freedom, when all shades of Indian opinion were impatiently looking forward to the end of British rule, the communist decision to collaborate with British war efforts, with or without India's freedom, provoked an avalanche of bitter criticism. Nobody was convinced by the communist argument that the Allies were fighting the scourge of fascism, the defeat of which would pave the way for the next and most decisive phase of the struggle when the people would fight for the overthrow of British domination over India. Why, the people wondered, did the communists have to wait until Russia entered the war on the side of the Allies to come to the conclusion that the interests of the Indian people were bound up with the victory of imperialism over fascism? Even a section of the Indian communists felt that those who supported British war efforts were only 'echoing the imperialist lie'.

Any party in India, which offered unconditional support to British war efforts for the sole purpose of serving Russian interests was bound to risk political ostracism. It is, therefore, no wonder that communists' 'people's war' policy completely isolated them from the nationalist struggle. Indeed, they paid very dearly for letting slip, during the war, the opportunity of identifying themselves with the mainstream of the national movement. Overstreet and Windmiller observed: 'This episode of policy-making in a period of crisis for the CPI demonstrates with exceptional clarity both the international and the domestic influences upon the party's operation and the ultimate superiority of the international influences.'[10] And internationalism among the Indian communists ran invariably towards the Soviet Union.

It was in 1952, at the time of the first general elections, that the communists showed a contrite of spirit and admitted that their wartime alliance with the British government and opposition to the Quit India Movement was a great blunder. It was also this blunder which accounted for their miserable performance in the elections to the Central Legislative Assembly in 1945.

For any revolutionary party, such maladroit policy-making was bound to be an agonizing exercise in political education. No wonder, during the post-war years when events in India began to move rapidly towards the long-awaited culmination in independence, the communists, 'trailing after events rather than anticipating them', pottered about with no clear destination in sight.

IV

As already mentioned, the most meaningful check to communism in India came from democratic socialism as represented by the Congress Left wing. Since the 1930s, 'democratic socialism has developed into India's most influential ideology' mainly because of the fact that it represented a 'bridge between the forward-looking intellectual minority and tradition-bound millions and helped in achieving a dynamic political consensus' for the reconstruction of India.[11]

As a distinct political movement, democratic socialism emerged in India as a 'rationalist revolt' against both Gandhism and communism. The revolt came from those Congressmen who, notwithstanding their adherence to radical and uncompromising views on social, economic and political questions, rejected the mysticism of Gandhi and the dogmatism of the communists. Organizationally their primary allegiance was to the INC and ideologically they were committed to the goals of anti-imperialism, nationalism and socialism. They swore by the ideology of socialism but did not subscribe to everything taught by Marx and Lenin. They believed in the broad principles underlying the new socio-economic structure of Russia but refused to follow blindly everything that was being done by the Soviet communist leaders. They claimed that they were no less Congressmen than other Congressmen and declared that their task was to guide the nationalist movement in the direction of socialism so as to emancipate the masses both from imperialism and the native system of exploitation.

The forces that produced an ideological rethinking of Gandhi's philosophy and techniques of nationalist struggle and eventually gave rise to the formation of a socialist group inside the INC first came to the surface after the suspension of the Non-Cooperation Movement in 1922. The sudden withdrawal of the movement at a time when the entire nation was on the verge of rising in revolt, came as a rude shock to a broad section of radical Congressmen who bitterly resented the religious zeal with which Gandhi sacrificed the end at the altar of the means. They felt that if a stray act of violence by a mob of excited peasants in a remote village was enough to put to an end to the struggle for freedom, then there was something basically wrong with the philosophy and technique of non-violent struggle. Resentment turned into indignation and disillusionment when in May 1933, Gandhi decided to call off the Civil Disobedience Movement and advised Congressmen to carry on the struggle by offering individual *satyagraha*. The Left-wing Congressmen were now convinced that Gandhi's theory of non-violence was 'unsustainable' and based on 'slippery foundations'.

Thus, it was as a reaction against Gandhi's insistence on non-violence as a technique of nationalist struggle and his 'feudal economic outlook' that the CSP was formed in 1934. The party was formed as an organized group within the INC although it had its 'own machinery, discipline and thesis'. The socialists did not form a separate party because they felt that the INC was the only national organization from whose platform they could effectively fight for the realization of their goals. The INC, to them, was not only the prime nationalist organization but also 'the greatest revolutionary force in the country' with a mass base. They recognized that

> no other organization could hope to rival Congress [INC] in building mass support, and if another organization were established it might severely injure the national anti-imperialist movement, a movement which was faced on the one hand with the challenge of British might and on the other with the communalism of the Muslim League.[12]

But despite close organizational links, there were major differences between the INC leadership and the socialists. While the INC became synonymous with Gandhism, the socialists refused to accept the Gandhian technique of non-violence, constitutionalism and reformism. They deplored the fact that Gandhism had become a cloak for vested interests and wanted the INC to represent the toiling masses. To the socialists, freedom meant not only the attainment of political independence but also the emancipation and, above all, the establishment of a socialist state in India.

Apart from these ideological differences, there were many specific issues over which the socialists and the dominant INC leadership held divergent views. One such issue was the question of participation in the 1936–37 elections and the acceptance of office under the new constitution. While the INC leadership decided to take part in the elections and to form government in those provinces where it could win a majority, the socialists condemned the new constitution as a united front of imperialism and the forces of national reaction designed to crush the growing revolt of the masses. Participation in the elections, therefore, would be a 'deflection from the revolutionary path' and the acceptance of office would be a surrender to constitutionalism and reformism. But although the socialists failed to dissuade the Right-wing leadership from participating in the elections, they could somewhat vindicate their position by successfully embodying in the INC election manifesto a programme aiming at the removal of the socio-economic grievances of the masses.

The crucial issue which intensified the disagreement between the socialists and the INC leadership was the question of India's role in the war. While the INC supported the British war efforts in the beginning, the socialists declared that the war was a conflict between the partners of imperialism for the repartition of the world and as such there was no question of India's participation in it—not even in lieu of independence. Independence, they averred, could be achieved not by compromise but by revolutionary mass struggle. And although they had participated in the INC-sponsored Quit India Movement during the war, they advocated methods of their own which were against the avowed principles of the INC. Myron Weiner opined:

> When the Quit India Movement was launched, its leadership soon fell largely into the hands of the socialists, partly because the top Congress [INC] leadership had been incarcerated by the British and partly because the Congressmen who had taken part in the Civil Disobedience Movements of the '20s and '30s were now too old for active participation in a militant movement. Furthermore, while the Congress [INC] leadership reluctantly approved of the civil disobedience programme after the failure of negotiations with the British, the socialists and the non-communist Left enthusiastically welcomed it. The socialists were, therefore, psychologically prepared to lead the struggle and thereby attracted younger militant elements from schools and colleges throughout the country …. With the disruption of the Congress [INC] organization and the arrest of most of the Congress leadership during the war, the socialist-dominated underground paralleled not only British authority, but also the Congress [INC] organization. This meant first of all that the younger newcomers had rejected the efficacy of Gandhism and non-violence, and secondly, that the socialists had developed confidence in their own ability to win mass support.[13]

While all sections of the CSP emphasized their loyalty to the INC during the war, the consequence of the Quit India Movement and the creation of an underground organization which virtually operated outside the INC structure was the development of a new group of socialists whose feeling of loyalty to the parent INC was not as strong as that of the older socialists who had joined the CSP in the 1930s.[14]

With the close of the war when Indian leaders of all shades returned to public life, the socialists and the INC leadership again found themselves at loggerheads. The issue now was the manner in which the freedom movement was to be carried on. The INC leadership sincerely believed that the Labour government was willing to transfer power and as such they were prepared to negotiate with the British Cabinet Mission. But the socialists refused to believe that the Cabinet Mission was really ready to concede independence to India.[15] According to them, the question before the country 'was not whether to accept the so called Constituent Assembly scheme sponsored by British imperialism, but how to utilize the new forces to drive the British out of India'.[16] They believed that it was only by revolutionary mass action that independence could be achieved. But in spite of the socialists' opposition, the CWC decided to participate in the Constituent Assembly.

Thus, although the socialists did not succeed in transforming the INC into a revolutionary mass organization, their influence over the dominant leadership was of great significance. In fact, the socialists could organize themselves as an effective opposition bloc inside the INC because of the latter's unique tolerance for divergent points of view. Weiner observed:

> Such organized groups were a characteristic feature of Congress [INC]. Not only were the socialists, the communists, Marxist Leftists and others allowed to organize their own parties within the party, with their own programme, leadership, party conventions etc. But they were given complete freedom of expression and permitted even to have their spokesmen participate as office bearers of the Congress [INC].[17]

In this connection, it is interesting to note that it was Gandhi, more than anybody else, who wanted the socialists to form a 'second line of leadership' inside the INC. In 1946, he went to the extent of recommending Narendra Deva and Jayaprakash Narayan for the INC presidency. Commenting on Gandhi's relationship with the socialists, J.B. Kripalani wrote:

> Gandhiji had great affection for the young leaders of the socialist party of India [CSP] and in many subtle and psychological ways he affected their views and their opinions about the essentials of his basic principles and philosophy of life and the many schemes of reconstruction which he placed before the country.[18]

It is against this background that it is possible to explain why the relationship between the socialists and the communists was far from cordial. Although the socialists claimed that their ideology was based on the scientific socialism of Marx, the communists refused to accept this contention. They argued that a party which was organizationally affiliated with the INC and whose leaders were under the spell of Gandhi could not be expected to be faithful to a revolutionary creed. The socialism as propagated by the CSP was therefore false and its leaders were nothing but 'social fascists'. The socialists, however, defended their position by declaring that as true Marxists their aim was the establishment of socialism in India; but argued that as the existing stage of Indian struggle was passing through the bourgeois-democratic revolution, it would be suicidal for the socialists to isolate themselves from the nationalist movement represented by the INC. They felt that no true socialist in India would refuse to take part in the nationalist movement simply on the ground that it was being conducted by the INC. It was the duty of the socialists to make every effort to give the movement a socialist direction because in the peculiar condition of India it was possible for every socialist to work within the INC and combine nationalism with socialism.

Such declarations notwithstanding, the Congress socialists found it difficult to give Marxism an Indian character and therefore to formulate an ideology and a programme which were distinct from those of the INC and the CPI. This difficulty had its root in the fact that although the CSP was made up of two major ideological streams—Marxism and democratic socialism—its leaders could never have shaken off the influence of Gandhism. And in their effort to reconcile these two ideological streams and to remain equidistant both from the INC and the communists, the socialists had to make frequent shifts in their posture as a result of which they were always in a dilemma as to their proper place in the Indian political development.

V

The communists and the Congress socialists were not the only exponents of Leftist ideologies during the nationalist movement. In the 1930s, many other Left-wing splinter groups sprang up in various parts of the country, particularly in Bengal, and brought new shades of Leftism on the Indian political scene. Weiner commented:

> In popular writing in the West these parties would probably be called Trotskyite, but in the strict technical sense of being supporters of Trotsky and/or the Fourth International [the wing of the Communist International consisting of the Trotskyites] that term cannot accurately be used here.[19]

The antecedents of these Left-wing groups were to be found in the revolutionary and terrorist organizations that shook the country during the early years of the twentieth century. After the Russian Revolution, although these revolutionaries were imbued with Marxist ideas, most of them decided to participate in the national struggle as members of the INC. They recognized the revolutionary significance of Gandhi's tremendous influence over the Indian masses but did not accept his principle of non-violence. Until the outbreak of the Second World War, most of these groups remained inside the INC but at the same time ceaselessly strove to convert the nationalist struggle from that of a small elite to a revolutionary mass movement. In the words of Weiner: 'There was thus a nationalist movement operating parallel to

Congress [INC] which was prepared to use violence … a movement which broadly accepted the leadership of Gandhi and Congress Party [INC], but which was prepared to use its own methods.'[20]

But compared to the two major Leftist parties—the CPI and the CSP, the role of these splinter groups in the nationalist movement was not of much significance. This was mainly because they were composed of either dissident Congressmen or disgruntled communists and as such they were concerned more with ideological hair-splitting than with constructive revolutionary activities. In fact, on most crucial ideological issues there was hardly any disagreement between these groups. All of them claimed to be Marxists and rejected the principles of parliamentary democracy, constitutionalism and non-violence, they all stood for anti-imperialism and self-determination, they believed that it was only through revolutionary and violent mass movement that fundamental socio-economic transformation could be brought about in India and the working class was viewed by all of them as the vanguard of such a revolution. On specific issues, they advocated nationalization of industry, confiscation of land without compensation, land to the tillers, confiscation of foreign capital and the establishment of a socialist state in India.

In spite of such a wide range of agreement on major ideological and specific issues, however, these groups functioned as separate political organizations because of the fact that almost all of them owed their origin to and evolved around individual personalities. The allegiance and loyalty of the rank and file of these parties were, therefore, to their respective leaders rather than to any distinct ideology. However, these Left-wing groups were not just 'elusive factions', because each of them had a history, a tradition, a leadership and organization and a programme. And in their effort to project their image into the national movement, they clashed not only with the INC leadership but also with the Congress socialists and the communists.

VI

What was the role of the Leftist parties in India's struggle for freedom? To answer this question, we must bring into focus the factors that contributed to the success of the liberation movement by which we mean not only the achievement of political independence but also the development of socio-economic ideas, institutions and values which could absorb and assimilate various important elements from the rest of the world and create a new India on its own historical foundations. Viewed from this angle and from what has been said in the foregoing pages, it will be seen that the Leftist parties did not play a decisive role in India's liberation movement. The Leftists sought to overthrow British rule in India by violent revolution and to transform the Indian society root and branch as the Bolshevik Revolution had done in Russia. But unlike the Russian Revolution which was responsible for one of the most drastic overhauls of a social order of which history has record, the transformation that took place in India neither upset the foundations of society nor challenged the fundamentals of Indian national ethos. It was a transformation which sought to assimilate the social purposes, the political conceptions and the economic organizations of the West while retaining the long-cherished values of Indian life and society. This revolutionary change was not accompanied by violent convulsions and disorders and neither did it succumb to the phenomenon of dictatorship.

For over a century, India had not only shared the liberal democratic experience of the West but had also assimilated it into the mainstream of its own historical traditions. The strength and viability of the Indian national movement lay in the fact that all through the years of its struggle for freedom, India had been able to develop the values of liberalism and build up a massive democratic structure. In sharp contrast to China where liberalism and democracy had long ceased to exist, in India the nationalist movement had developed along the growth of liberal tradition and democratic institutions. The failure of the Leftist parties to achieve the twofold goal of violent revolution and establishment of socialism was almost inevitable because the Leftists failed to make due allowance for the spirit and temper of Indian nationalism. Another striking factor that contributed to their failure was the fact that the Leftist movement had always been imperfectly unified. The movement contained in it radical, ultra-Left revolutionaries as well as those whose ideological orientations were essentially moderate and gradualist. And as their respective attitudes had their roots in dogma, their relationships with each other had always remained uncertain. As a result, the movement as a whole could not be responsive to the demands of the national movement. The strength of the Leftist movement lay in its militant zeal and uncompromising devotion to dogma and curiously, it was from the latter that stemmed its primary weakness, its inflexibility and inadaptability.

NOTES AND REFERENCES (CHAPTER 7)

1   Subhas Chandra Bose, *The Indian Struggle, 1920–1934*, Vol. I (Calcutta: Netaji Publication Society, 1948), 395.
2   Harry J. Benda, 'Communism in Southeast Asia', *The Yale Review*, Vol. 45, No. 3 (New Haven, CT: 1956, March), 417–29.
3   Jayantanuja Bandopadhyaya, *Indian Nationalism Versus International Communism* (Calcutta: Firma K.L. Mukhopadhyay, 1966), 315.
4   Carlos P. Romulo, 'The Crucial Battle for Asia', *New York Times* (11 September 1949), 13.
5   Jawaharlal Nehru, *The Discovery of India* (London: Meridian Books, 1956), 516–17.
6   Richard Lowenthal, 'The Points of the Compass', in *Political Change in Underdeveloped Countries: Nationalism and Communism*, ed. John H. Kautsky (New York, NY: John Wiley and Sons, 1962), 344.
7   K.M. Panikkar, *The Foundations of New India* (London: George Allen and Unwin, 1963), 201.
8   Bandopadhyaya, *Indian Nationalism Versus International Communism*, 317. For the objectives behind the oscillations of communist policy, see ibid., 325.
9   Panikkar, *The Foundations of New India*, 206.
10 Gene D. Overstreet and Marshall Windmiller, *Communism in India* (Bombay: Perennial Press, 1960), 198.
11 Sibnarayan Ray, 'Socialism in India', in *Studies in Indian Democracy*, eds. S.P. Aiyar and R. Srinivasan (Bombay: Allied Publishers, 1965), 47–48.
12 Myron Weiner, *Party Politics in India: The Development of a Multi-Party System* (Princeton, NJ: Princeton University Press, 1957), 46.
13 Ibid., 47–48.
14 Ibid.
15 See Jayaprakash Narayan's statement as reported in the *Amrita Bazar Patrika* (Calcutta, 23 April 1946).
16 *The Hindu* (Madras, 8 July 1946).
17 Weiner, *Party Politics in India: The Development of a Multi-Party System*, 46–47.
18 J.B. Kripalani, 'The Merger', *Vigil* (14 October 1952).
19 Weiner, *Party Politics in India: The Development of a Multi-Party System*, 117.
20 Ibid., 118.

SELECT BIBLIOGRAPHY

BOOKS

Abraham, N.T., R.S. Sabris, A.N. Desai, and K.U. Mada. *A Text Book of Economic History.* Bombay: A.R. Sheth and Company, 1964.

Adhikari, G.M. *Pakistan and National Unity.* Bombay: People's Publishing House, 1942.

———. *From Peace Front to People's War.* Bombay: People's Publishing House, 1944.

———. *The Imperialist Alternative: Churchill–Cripps Conspiracy for a Communal Award.* Bombay: People's Publishing House, 1944.

———. *Food for All.* Bombay: People's Publishing House, 1945.

———. *Resurgent India at the Crossroads.* Bombay: People's Publishing House, 1946.

Aggarwala, R.N. *National Movement and Constitutional Development of India.* Delhi: Metropolitan Book, 1956.

Ahmad, Muzaffar. *The Communist Party of India: Years of Formation, 1921–1933.* Calcutta: National Book Agency, 1959.

———. *The Communist Party of India and Its Formation Abroad.* Calcutta: National Book Agency, 1962.

Aiyar, S.P., and R. Srinivasan., eds. *Studies in Indian Democracy.* Bombay: Allied Publishers, 1965.

Ambedkar, B.R. *What Congress and Gandhi Have Done to the Untouchables.* Bombay: Thacker and Company, 1945.

———. *Gandhi and Gandhism.* Jullundar: Bheem Patrika Publications, 1970.

Andrews, C.F. and Mookerjee, Girija. *The Rise and Growth of the Congress in India.* London: George Allen and Unwin, 1938.

Arnot, R. Page. *How Britain Rules India.* London: CPGB, 1929.

Azad, Abul Kalam. *India Wins Freedom.* Delhi: Orient Longman, 1959.

Bakhale, R.R., ed. *The Directory of Trade Unions.* Bombay: AITUC, 1925.

Ball, William MacMohan. *Nationalism and Communism in East Asia.* Melbourne: Melbourne University Press, 1956.

Bandopadhyaya, Jayantanuja. *Indian Nationalism Versus International Communism.* Calcutta: Firma K.L. Mukhopadhyay, 1966.

Basak, V. *Some Urgent Problems of the Labour Movement in India.* London: Modern Books, 1932.

Batliwala, Soli. *Facts Versus Forgery: Traitorous Role Played by the Communist Party Exposed.* Bombay: National Youth Publications, 1946.

Beloff, Max. *The Foreign Policy of Soviet Russia, 1929–1941.* London: Oxford University Press, 1952.

Bhargava, G.S. *Leaders of the Left.* Bombay: Meherally Book Club, 1951.

Bhattacharya, G.P. *M.N. Roy and Radical Humanism.* Bombay: J.B.H. Wadia, 1961.

Borkenau, Franz. *The Communist International.* London: Faber and Faber, 1938.

Bose, Subhas Chandra. *The Indian Struggle, 1920–1934,* Vol. I. Calcutta: Netaji Publication Society, 1948.

———. *The Indian Struggle, 1935–1942,* Vol. II. Calcutta: Netaji Publication Society, 1952.

———. *Crossroads—Collected Works, 1938–1940.* Calcutta: Netaji Research Bureau, 1962.

———. *Selected Speeches of Subhas Chandra Bose* (with a biographical introduction by S.A. Ayer). Delhi: Government of India Publications Division, 1962.

Bradley, B.F. *Trade Unionism in India.* London: Modern Books, 1932.

Bright, J.S., ed. *Important Speeches—A Collection of Speeches by Jawaharlal Nehru from 1922–1945.* Lahore: Indian Printing Works, 1945.

————. *Before and After Independence: A Collection of the Most Important and Soul-Stirring Speeches by Jawaharlal Nehru, 1922–1950*. New Delhi: Indian Printing Works, 1952.

Brimmel, J.H. *Communism in Southeast Asia*. London: Oxford University Press, 1959.

Brockway, Fenner. *Inside the Left: Thirty Years of Platform, Press, Prison and Parliament*. London: George Allen and Unwin, 1942.

Brown, Giles Tyler. *The Hindu Conspiracy and the Neutrality of the United States: 1914–1917*. California: University of California-Berkeley Press, 1941.

Buch, M.A. *The Rise and Growth of Indian Militant Nationalism*. Baroda: Atmaram, 1940.

Carr, E.H. *The Bolshevik Revolution, 1917–1923*. London: Macmillan, 1950.

Chakravarty, D. and C. Bhattacharyya. *Congress in Evolution: A Collection of Congress Resolutions from 1885 to 1934 and Other Important Documents*. Calcutta: The Book Company 1935.

Chakraberty, Chandra. *New India*. Calcutta: Vijoyakrishna Brothers, 1951.

Chirol, Sir Valentine. *Indian Unrest*. London: Macmillan, 1910.

————. *India Old and New*. London: Macmillan, 1921.

Coatman, J. *Years of Destiny: India 1926–1932*. London: Jonathan Cape 1932.

Cole, G.D.H. *British Trade Unionism Today*. London: Gollancz, 1939.

Coupland, Sir Reginald. *The Constitutional Problem in India*, Vols. I–III. Oxford: Oxford University Press, 1945.

Cumming, Sir John. *Political India, 1832–1932—A Cooperative Survey of a Century*. London: Oxford University Press, 1932.

Dange, S.A. *Gandhi Versus Lenin*. Bombay: Liberty Literature, 1921.

————. *On the Indian Trade Union Movement: Reports to a Convention of Communist Party Members Working in the Trade Union Movement, Calcutta, May 20–22, 1952*. Bombay: CPI 1952.

Das, R.K. *Labour Movement in India*. Berlin: Walter de Gruyter and Company, 1923.

Degras, Jane. *Soviet Documents on Foreign Policy: 1917–1941*, Vols. I–III. London: Oxford University Press, 1951–53.

————. *The Communist International Documents, 1919–1943*, Vols. I–II. London: Oxford University Press, 1956.

Desai, A.R. *Social Background of Indian Nationalism*. London: Oxford University Press, 1948.

Dhawan, G.N. *The Political Philosophy of Mahatma Gandhi*. Bombay: Popular Books Depot, 1946.

Druhe, David N. *Soviet Russia and Indian Communism*. New York, NY: Bookman Associates 1959.

Dutt, Clemens. *Conspiracy Against the King*. London: National Meerut Prisoners' Defence Committee, 1930.

Dutt, Kalpana. *Chittagong Armoury Raiders: Reminiscences*. Bombay: People's Publishing House, 1945.

Dutt, R. Palme. *Modern India*. London: CPGB, 1927.

————. *India Today*. Bombay: People's Publishing House, 1949.

————. *India Today and Tomorrow*. Delhi: People's Publishing House, 1955.

————. *World Politics, 1918–1936*. Patna: Adhar Prakashan, 1961.

————. *Problems of Contemporary History*. London: Lawrence and Wishart, 1963.

Edwardes, Michael. *The Last Years of British India*. London: Cassell and Company, 1963.

Elwin, Verrier. *Truth About India: Can We Get It?* London: George Allen and Unwin, 1932.

Footman, David, ed. *International Communism*. London: Chatto and Windus, 1960.

Foster, William Z. *History of the Three Internationals: The World Socialist and Communist Movements from 1848 to the Present*. New York, NY: International Publishers, 1955.

Gandhi, M.K. *An Autobiography or The Story of My Experiment With Truth*. Ahmedabad: Navajivan Publishing House, 1945.

————. *Hind Swaraj or Indian Home Rule*. Ahmedabad: Navajivan Publishing House, 1946.

————. *Gandhiji's Correspondence with the Government: 1942–1944*. Ahmedabad: Navajivan Publishing House, 1957.

————. *Gandhiji's Correspondence with the Government: 1944–1947*. Ahmedabad: Navajivan Publishing House, 1959.

Gandhi, M.K. and Joshi, P.C. *Correspondence Between Mahatma Gandhi and P.C. Joshi*. Bombay: People's Publishing House, 1945.

Ghosh, Ajoy. *Bhagat Singh and His Comrades*. Bombay: People's Publishing House, 1946.

Ghosh, Ashok. *A Short History of the All India Forward Bloc*. Calcutta: Bengal Lokmat Printers, 2001.

Ghosh, Aurobindo. *Bankim–Tilak–Dayananda* (Bengali). Calcutta: Arya Publishing House, 1947.

Ghosh, Gopal. *Indian Trade Union Movement*. Calcutta: T.U. Publications, 1961.

Giri, V.V. *Labour Problems in Indian Industry*. Bombay: Asia Publishing House, 1959.

Glading, Percy. *India Under British Terror*. Bristol: Burleigh, 1931.

Goel, Sitaram. *Netaji and the CPI*. Calcutta: Society for Defence of Freedom in Asia, 1955.

Har Dayal, Lala. *Forty-four Months in Germany and Turkey, February 1915 to October 1918: A Record of Personal Impressions*. London: P.S. King and Son, 1920.

Hindi, A.K. *M.N. Roy—The Man Who Looked Ahead*. Ahmedabad: Modern Publishing House, 1938.

Hutchinson, L. *Conspiracy at Meerut*. London: George Allen and Unwin, 1935.

Jones, John Price and Hollister, Paul Merrick. *The German Secret Service in America*. Boston: Small, Maynard and Company, 1918.

Joshi, N.M. *Trade Union Movement in India*. Bombay: Longmans, Green and Company, 1927.

Joshi, P.C. *The Indian Communist Party: Its Policy and Work in the War of Liberation*. London: CPGB, 1942.

———. *Congress and Communists*. Bombay: People's Publishing House, 1944.

———. *They Must Meet Again*. Bombay: People's Publishing House, 1944.

———. *Communist Reply to Congress Working Committee's Charges*. Bombay: People's Publishing House 1945.

———. *For the Final Bid for Power: The Communist Plan Explained*. Bombay: People's Publishing House 1946.

Karnik, V.B. *Indian Trade Unions: A Survey*. Bombay: Labour Education Service, 1960.

Kautsky, John H. *Moscow and the Communist Party of India*. New York, NY: John Wiley and Sons and the MIT Press, 1956.

———, ed. *Political Change in Underdeveloped Countries: Nationalism and Communism*. New York, NY: John Wiley and Sons, 1962.

Kaye, Sir Cecil. *Communism in India, 1920–1924*. Delhi: Government of India Press, 1926.

Kendall, Patricia. *India and the British: A Quest for Truth*. London: Charles Scribner's Sons, 1931.

Kennedy, Malcom D. *A Short History of Communism in Asia*. London: Weidenfeld and Nicolson, 1957.

Ker, James Campbell. *Political Trouble in India: 1907–1917*. Calcutta: Superintendent Government Printing, 1917.

Kerzhentsev, P. *Angliiskii Imperializm* (Russian). Moscow: Izdatel'stvo Vsersossiiskogo Tsentral'nogo Ispolnitel'nogo Komiteta Sovetov R.K., K.I.K. Deputatov, 1919.

Krishnan, N.K. *Forgery Versus Facts: Communist Party Exposes the Fifth Column*. Bombay: People's Publishing House, 1943.

———. *National Unity for the Defence of the Motherland*. Bombay: People's Publishing House, 1943.

Lakhanpal, P.L. *History of the Congress Socialist Party*. Lahore: National Publishers and Stationers, 1946.

Laski, Harold. 'Preface'. In *Conspiracy at Meerut*, L. Hutchinson. London: George Allen and Unwin, 1935.

Lenin, V.I. *Left-Wing Communism: An Infantile Disorder*. Moscow: ECCI, 1920.

———. *Imperialism: The Highest Stage of Capitalism*. New York, NY: International Publishers, 1939.

———. *Selected Works*, Vols. I–II. Moscow: Foreign Languages Publishing House, 1947.

———. *The National Liberation Movement in the East*. Moscow: Foreign Languages Publishing House, 1957.

———. *Collected Works*, Vols. I–XXXXV. Moscow: Progress Publishers, 1963–1970.

———. *Alliance of the Working Class and the Peasantry*. Moscow: Progress Publishers, 1965.

———. *Questions of National Policy and Proletarian Internationalism*. Moscow: Progress Publishers, 1970.

Lichtheim, George. *Marxism: An Historical and Critical Study*. London: Routledge and Kegan Paul, 1961.

Limaye, Madhu. *The CPI: Facts and Fiction*. Hyderabad: Chetana Prakashan, 1951.

Majumdar, J.K., ed. *Indian Speeches and Documents on British Rule: 1821–1918*. Calcutta: Longmans, Green and Company, 1937.

Majumdar, R.C. *History of the Freedom Movement in India*, Vols. I–III. Calcutta: Firma K.L. Mukhopadhyay, 1963.

Majumdar, R.C., H.C. Ray Chaudhuri and K.K. Datta. *An Advanced History of India*. London: Macmillan, 1950.

Majumder, Subodh Chandra. *Philosophy of Congress Leftism*. Calcutta: Bharati Press, 1946.

Marx, Karl. *Articles on India*. Bombay: People's Publishing House, 1943.

Marx, Karl and Engels, Friedrich. *Selected Works*, Vols. I–II. Moscow: Foreign Languages Publishing House, 1955.

———. *Selected Correspondence*. Moscow: Foreign Languages Publishing House, 1965.

Marx, Karl and Engels, Friedrich. *On Colonialism*. Moscow, Progress Publishers: 1968.

Masani, M.R. *The Communist Party of India—A Short History*. London: Derek Verschoyle, 1954.

Mazumdar, Amvika Charan. *Indian National Evolution—A Brief Survey of the Origin and Progress of the Indian National Congress and the Growth of Indian Nationalism*. Madras: G.A. Natesan and Company, 1917.

Meherally, Yusuf. *Leaders of India*, Vols. I–II. Bombay: Padma Publications, 1942.

———, ed. *Acharya Narendra Deva, Socialism and the National Revolution*. Bombay: Padma Publications, 1946.

———. ed. *Jayaprakash Narayan, Towards Struggle*. Bombay: Padma Publications, 1946.

———. *The Price of Liberty*. Bombay: National Information and Publications, 1948.

Menon, V. P. *Transfer of Power in India*. Calcutta: Orient Longman, 1957.

Ming, Wang. *The Revolutionary Movement in the Colonial Countries*. New York, NY: Workers Library Publishers, 1935.

Mitra, B. and P. Chakravarty, ed. *Rebel India*. Calcutta: Orient Book Company, 1946.

Montagu, E.S. *An Indian Diary*. London: William Heinemann, 1930.

Moraes, Frank. *Jawaharlal Nehru—A Biography*. Bombay: Macmillan, 1956.

Mukherjee, Dhan Gopal. *Disillusioned India*. New York, NY: E.P. Dutton, 1930.

Mukherjee, Haridas and Uma Mukherjee. *The Growth of Nationalism in India (1857–1905)*. Calcutta: Presidency Library, 1957.

———. *Sri Aurobindo's Political Thought, 1893–1908*. Calcutta: Firma K.L. Mukhopadhyay, 1958.

———. *Sri Aurobindo and the New Thought in Indian Politics*. Calcutta: Firma K.L. Mukhopadhyay, 1964.

Mukhopadhay, Prabhat Kumar. *Bharate Jatiya Andolan* (Bengali). Calcutta: Granthan, 1960.

Mukhtar, Ahmad. *Trade Unionism and Labour Disputes in India*. Bombay: Longmans, Green and Company, 1935.

Murphy, J.T. *New Horizons*. London: John Lane at the Bodley Head, 1941.

Nanda, B.R. *The Nehrus: Motilal and Jawaharlal*. London: George Allen and Unwin, 1962.

Narayan, Jayaprakash. *Why Socialism?* Benaras: CSP, 1936.

———. *Socialist Unity and Congress Socialist Party*. Bombay: CSP, 1941.

Nariman, K.F. *Whither Congress? Spiritual Idealism or Political Realism: Some Random Thoughts on the Poona Conference and After*. Bombay: D.R. Dewoolkar, 1933.

Natesan, G.A., ed. *Congress Presidential Addresses, 1885–1934*, Vols. I–II. Madras: G.A. Natesan and Company, 1934.

Nehru, Jawaharlal. *Soviet Russia*. Bombay: Chetana, 1929.

———. *India and the World*. London: George Allen and Unwin, 1936.

———. *Recent Essays and Writings on the Future of India, Communalism and Other Subjects*. Allahabad: Kitabistan, 1937.

———. *Eighteen Months in India: 1936–1937*. Allahabad: Kitabistan, 1938.

———. *The Unity of India—Collected Writings, 1937–1940*. New York, NY: John Day Company, 1942.

———. *Nehru on Gandhi*. New York, NY: John Day Company, 1948.

———. *The Discovery of India*. London: Meridian Books, 1956.

———. *An Autobiography*. Bombay: Allied Publishers, 1962.

———. *India's Freedom*. London: George Allen and Unwin, 1965.

Nollau, Gunther. *International Communism and World Revolution: History and Methods*. London: Hollis and Carter, 1961.

Overstreet, Gene D. and Marshall Windmiller. *Communism in India*. Bombay: Perennial Press, 1960.

Panikkar, K.M. *Asia and Western Dominance*. London: George Allen and Unwin, 1953.

———. *The Foundations of New India*. London: George Allen and Unwin, 1963.

Park, Richard L. and Irene Tinker, ed. *Leadership and Political Institutions in India*. Madras: Oxford University Press, 1960.

Payne, Robert. *The Revolt of Asia*. New York, NY: John Day Company, 1947.

Petrie, Sir David. *Communism in India, 1924–1927*. Calcutta: Government of India Press, 1927.

Pole, D. Graham. *India in Transition*. London: Hogarth Press, 1932.

Pradhan, R.G. *India's Struggle for Swaraj*. Madras: G.A. Natesan and Company, 1930.

Pratap, Mahendra. *My Life Story of Fifty-five Years*. Dehradun: World Federation, 1947.

Punekar, S.D. *Trade Unionism in India*. Bombay: New Book Company, 1948.

Purcell, A.A. and J. Hallsworth. *Report on Labour Conditions in India*. London: Trade Union Congress General Council, 1928.

Qureshi, I.H. *The Muslim Community of the Indo-Pakistan Subcontinent: 610–1947*. The Hague: Mouton and Company, 1962.

Raghuvanshi, V.P.S. *Indian Nationalist Movement and Thought*. Agra: L.N. Agarwal, 1951.

Rai, Lala Lajpat. *The Political Future of India*. New York, NY: B.W. Huebsch 1919.

Raj Kumar, N.V. *Indian Political Parties*. New Delhi: AICC, 1948.

Ranadive, B.T. *Working Class and National Defence*. Bombay: People's Publishing House, 1943.

———. *Jobs for All*. Bombay: People's Publishing House, 1945.

Ranga, N.G. *The Modern Indian Peasant*. Madras: Kisan Publications, 1936.

———. *Kisans and Communists*. Bombay: Pratibha Publishers, 1949.

Rao, B. Shiva. *The Industrial Worker in India*. London: George Allen and Unwin, 1939.

Ray, P.C. *Life and Times of C.R. Das*. London: Oxford University Press, 1927.

Roy, M.N. *La India: su Pasado, su Presente y su Porvenir* (Spanish). Mexico, 1918.

———. *India in Transition*. Geneva: J.B. Target, 1922.

———. *What Do We Want*. Geneva: J.B. Target, 1922.

———. *Political Letters*. Zurich: The Vanguard Bookshop, 1924.

———. *The Aftermath of Non-Cooperation: Indian Nationalism and Labour Politics*. London: CPGB, 1926.

———. *The Future of Indian Politics*. London: R. Bishop, 1926.

———. *Our Differences*. Calcutta: Saraswati Library, 1938.

———. *India and War*. Lucknow: A.P. Singh, 1942.

———. *Scientific Politics*. Calcutta: Renaissance Publishers, 1942.

———. *Indian Labour and Post-War Reconstruction*. Lucknow: A.P. Singh, 1943.

———. *Letters From Jail*. Dehradun: The Indian Renaissance Association, 1943.

———. *The Future of Socialism*. Calcutta: Renaissance Publishers, 1943.

———. *Revolution and Counter-Revolution in China*. Calcutta: Renaissance Publishers, 1946.

———. *Memoirs*, Bombay: Allied Publishers, 1964.

Roy, M.N. and Evelyn Roy. *One Year of Non-Cooperation: From Ahmedabad to Gaya*. Calcutta: CPI, 1923.

Ruikar, R.S. *Netaji's Politics and Ideology*. Nagpur: Forward Bloc, 1948.

Saklatvala, Sapurji and Gandhi, M.K. *Is India Different? The Class Struggle in India: Correspondence on the Indian Labour Movement and Modern Conditions*. London: CPGB, 1927.

Sardesai, S.G. *People's Way to Food*. Bombay: People's Publishing House, 1943.

Sarkar, B.K. *Naya Banglar Godapattan* (Bengali), Vol. I. Calcutta: Chuckervertty, Chatterjee and Company, 1932.

Schuman, Frederick L. *International Politics: The Western State System and the World Community*. New York, NY: McGraw-Hill, 1958.

Sharma, J.S. *Indian National Congress: A Descriptive Bibliography of India's Struggle for Freedom*. Delhi: S. Chand and Company, 1959.

Singh, Randhir. *The Ghadr Heroes*. Bombay: People's Publishing House, 1945.

Singh, V.B., ed. *Economic History of India, 1857–1956*. Bombay: Allied Publishers, 1965.

Sinha, L.P. *Left Wing in India*. Muzaffarpur: New Publishers, 1965.

Sitaramayya, Pattabhi. *The History of the Indian National Congress*, Vols. I–II. Bombay: Padma Publications, 1946–47.

Spratt, Philip. *Blowing Up India: Reminiscences and Reflections of a Former Comintern Emissary*. Calcutta: Prachi Prakashan, 1955.

Stalin, Joseph. *Problems of Leninism*. Moscow: Foreign Languages Publishing House, 1947.

Tagore, Saumyendranath. *United Front or Betrayal?* Calcutta: Ganavani Publishing House, 1938.

———. *Communism and Fetishism*. Calcutta: Provat Sen, 1940.

———. *People's Front or the Front Against the People?* Calcutta: Ganavani Publishing House, 1940.

———. *Congress Socialism?* Lucknow: Jagriti Publishing House, 1942.

Tagore, Saumyendranath. *Historical Development of the Communist Movement in India*. Calcutta: Red Front Press, 1944.

————. *Permanent Revolution*. Calcutta: Samar Bose, 1944.

————. *Bourgeois-Democratic Revolution and India*. Calcutta: Ganavani Publishing House, 1946.

————. *Revolution and Quit India*. Calcutta: Ganavani Publishing House, 1946.

————. *The Hour Has Struck*. Calcutta: Ganavani Publishing House, 1949.

Tendulkar, D.G. *Mahatma: Life of Mohandas Karamchand Gandhi*, Vols. I–VIII. Bombay: Vithalbhai K. Jhaveri, 1951.

Tse-Tung, Mao. *Selected Works*, Vols. I–III. Peking: Foreign Language Press, 1965.

Usmani, Shaukat. *Peshawar to Moscow*. Benaras: Swarajya Publishing House, 1927.

————. *I Met Stalin Twice*. Bombay: K. Kurian, 1953.

Wadia, P.A. and K.T. Merchant. *Our Economic Problem*. Bombay: New Book Company, 1950.

Weiner, Myron. *Party Politics in India: The Development of a Multi-Party System*. Princeton, New Jersey: Princeton University Press, 1957.

William, Z. Foster. *History of the Three Internationals: The World Socialist and Communist Movements from 1848 to the Present*. New York, NY: International Publishers, 1955.

Williams, L.F. Rushbrook. *India in the Years 1917–1918*. Calcutta: Superintendent Government Printing, 1919.

————. *India in 1924–1925*. Calcutta: Government of India Central Publication Branch 1925.

————. *What About India?* London: Thomas Nelson and Sons, 1938.

Williamson, Sir Horace. *India and Communism*. Simla: Government of India Press, 1935.

Yagnik, Indulal. *Life of Ramchoddas Bhavan Lotvala*. Bombay: The Writers' Emporium, 1952.

Zacharias, H.C.E. *Renascent India: From Rammohan Roy to Mohandas Gandhi*, London: George Allen and Unwin, 1933.

Zaheer, Sajjad. *A Case for Congress-League Unity*. Bombay: People's Publishing House, 1944.

DOCUMENTS

All India Congress Socialist Party: Report of the First Conference. Bombay: CSP, 1934.

Cawnpore Conspiracy Case: *King Emperor Versus Nalina Bhushan Das Gupta, Muhammad Shaukat Usmani, Muzaffar Ahmad, and Shripat Amrit Dange, in the High Court of Judicature at Allahabad, Criminal Side*. Allahabad: Superintendent Government Printing, 1924.

Communist Papers, Documents Selected from Those Obtained on the Arrest of the Communist Leaders on the 14th and 21st October, 1925, Parliamentary Publications, 1926, Vol. XXIII. London: His Majesty's Stationery Office, 1926.

Declaration of Independence—Communist Party Resolution for the Constituent Assembly. Bombay: People's Publishing House, 1946.

Fifth Congress of the Communist International: Abridged Report of Meetings Held at Moscow June 17th to July 8th, 1924. London: CPGB, 1924.

For the Final Assault: Task of the Indian People in the Present Phase of Indian Revolution. Bombay: People's Publishing House, 1946.

From the Fourth to the Fifth World Congress: Report of the Executive Committee of the Communist International. London: CPGB, 1924.

ILO Studies and Reports Series A, No. 41: Industrial Labour in India, London: P.S. King and Son, 1938.

Indian Communist Party Documents, 1930–1956. Bombay: Democratic Research Service, 1957.

Meerut District Court, *Meerut Communist Conspiracy Case: Magistrate's Order of Committal to Trial*. Meerut: Saraswati Press, 1929.

Meerut Sessions Court, *Judgement delivered by R.L. Yorke, Esq., I.C.S., Additional Sessions Judge, Meerut, on 16th January, 1933, in the Meerut Communist Conspiracy Case. Sessions Trial No. 2 of 1930. King Emperor Versus P. Spratt and Others*, Vols. I–II. Simla: Government of India Press, 1932 -1933.

Meerut Sessions Court, *Proceedings of the Meerut Communist Conspiracy Case*, Vols. I–II. Meerut: Saraswati Press, 1929.

Mountbatten Award and After: Political Resolution of the Central Committee of the CPI. Bombay: People's Publishing House, 1947.

On National Struggle of August 1942. Calcutta: RSP, 1942.

Programme of the Post-War Revolution: Draft Manifesto of the Forward Bloc. Bombay: Forward Bloc, 1946.

Report of the Indian Tariff Board, Cotton Textile Industry Enquiry Committee, Vol. I. Calcutta: Government of India Central Publication Branch, 1927.

Resolutions and Theses of the Fourth Congress of the Communist International. London: CPGB, 1922.

Sedition Committee Report, 1918. Calcutta: Superintendent Government Printing, 1918.

Seventh World Congress of the Communist International: Resolutions and Decisions. Moscow: Communist International, 1935.

Terrorism in India, 1917–1936, Intelligence Bureau reports. Simla: Government of India Press, 1937.

The Communist International Between the Fifth and the Sixth World Congresses, 1924–1928. London: CPGB, 1928.

The Faizpur Thesis of the Congress Socialist Party, Resolutions adopted by the party at its third annual conference at Faizpur on December 23, 24 and 25, 1936. Minoo Masani Papers, National Archives of India, Delhi.

The Revolutionary Movement in the Colonies: Theses on the Revolutionary Movement in the Colonies and Semi-Colonies, Sixth World Congress of the Communist International, 1928. London: Modern Books, 1929.

The Second Congress of the Communist International as Reported and Interpreted by the Official Newspapers of Soviet Russia: Petrograd–Moscow, July 19–August7, 1920. Washington, DC: United States Department of State, Government Publishing Office, 1920.

The Second Congress of the Communist International: Proceedings of Petrograd Session of July 17th and Moscow Sessions of July 19th–August 7th, 1920. Moscow: Communist International, 1920.

The Struggle Against Imperialist War and the Tasks of the Communists—Resolution of the Sixth World Congress of the Communist International, July–August 1928. New York, NY: Workers Library Publishers, 1934.

The Thesis and Platform of Action of the Revolutionary Socialist Party of India: What Revolutionary Socialism Stands For. Calcutta: RSP, 1946

Thesis of the RSP on the Russo–German War—Intensify National Struggle: On To Revolutionary Defence of USSR. Calcutta: RSP, 1941.

Thesis of the Workers' and Peasants' Party of India, Resolutions adopted by the first All India Workers' and Peasants' Party Conference in Calcutta on 21st to 24th December, 1928. London: *Labour Monthly*, Vol. II, No. 3, March 1929.

War Thesis of the RSPI. Calcutta: RSP, 1940.

JOURNALS AND NEWSPAPERS

Amrita Bazar Patrika, 1917–47, Calcutta.

Indian Annual Register, 1919–46, Calcutta.

International Press Correspondence, 1921–38. Also known as *Inprecor*, this organ of the Communist International was published first from Vienna and Berlin and later from London.

Labour Monthly, 1922–47, London (Organ of CPGB).

Masses of India, 1925–26, Paris. It was an organ of the CPI founded and edited by M.N. Roy, which was published from various places in Europe.

National Front, 1938–39, Bombay (Organ of CPI).

People's Age, 1945–47, Bombay (Organ of CPI).

People's War, 1942–45, Bombay (Organ of CPI).

The Congress Socialist, 1935–45, Bombay (Organ of CSP).

The Hindu, 1915–47, Madras.

The New Age, 1953–59, Delhi.
The Socialist, 1924, Bombay.
The Vanguard of Indian Independence, 1922–28. M.N. Roy published this newspaper from various places in Europe, such as Berlin, Zurich and Annecy. Its name was also changed to *Advance Guard* on October 1922 to circumvent police interception.
World News and Views, 1938–41, London.

INDEX